# Lecture Notes in Computer Science     14737

## Founding Editors

Gerhard Goos
Juris Hartmanis

## Editorial Board Members

The series Lecture Notes in Computer Science (LNCS), including its subseries Lecture Notes in Artificial Intelligence (LNAI) and Lecture Notes in Bioinformatics (LNBI), has established itself as a medium for the publication of new developments in computer science and information technology research, teaching, and education.

LNCS enjoys close cooperation with the computer science R & D community, the series counts many renowned academics among its volume editors and paper authors, and collaborates with prestigious societies. Its mission is to serve this international community by providing an invaluable service, mainly focused on the publication of conference and workshop proceedings and postproceedings. LNCS commenced publication in 1973.

June Wei · George Margetis

Editors

# Human-Centered Design, Operation and Evaluation of Mobile Communications

5th International Conference, MOBILE 2024
Held as Part of the 26th HCI International Conference, HCII 2024
Washington, DC, USA, June 29 – July 4, 2024
Proccedings, Part I

 Springer

*Editors*
June Wei
University of West Florida
Pensacola, FL, USA

George Margetis
Foundation for Research
and Technology – Hellas (FORTH)
Heraklion, Crete, Greece

ISSN 0302-9743                          ISSN 1611-3349  (electronic)
Lecture Notes in Computer Science
ISBN 978-3-031-60457-7          ISBN 978-3-031-60458-4  (eBook)
https://doi.org/10.1007/978-3-031-60458-4

This Springer imprint is published by the registered company Springer Nature Switzerland AG
The registered company address is: Gewerbestrasse 11, 6330 Cham, Switzerland

If disposing of this product, please recycle the paper.

# Foreword

This year we celebrate 40 years since the establishment of the HCI International (HCII) Conference, which has been a hub for presenting groundbreaking research and novel ideas and collaboration for people from all over the world.

The HCII conference was founded in 1984 by Prof. Gavriel Salvendy (Purdue University, USA, Tsinghua University, P.R. China, and University of Central Florida, USA) and the first event of the series, "1st USA-Japan Conference on Human-Computer Interaction", was held in Honolulu, Hawaii, USA, 18–20 August. Since then, HCI International is held jointly with several Thematic Areas and Affiliated Conferences, with each one under the auspices of a distinguished international Program Board and under one management and one registration. Twenty-six HCI International Conferences have been organized so far (every two years until 2013, and annually thereafter).

Over the years, this conference has served as a platform for scholars, researchers, industry experts and students to exchange ideas, connect, and address challenges in the ever-evolving HCI field. Throughout these 40 years, the conference has evolved itself, adapting to new technologies and emerging trends, while staying committed to its core mission of advancing knowledge and driving change.

As we celebrate this milestone anniversary, we reflect on the contributions of its founding members and appreciate the commitment of its current and past Affiliated Conference Program Board Chairs and members. We are also thankful to all past conference attendees who have shaped this community into what it is today.

The 26th International Conference on Human-Computer Interaction, HCI International 2024 (HCII 2024), was held as a 'hybrid' event at the Washington Hilton Hotel, Washington, DC, USA, during 29 June – 4 July 2024. It incorporated the 21 thematic areas and affiliated conferences listed below.

A total of 5108 individuals from academia, research institutes, industry, and government agencies from 85 countries submitted contributions, and 1271 papers and 309 posters were included in the volumes of the proceedings that were published just before the start of the conference, these are listed below. The contributions thoroughly cover the entire field of human-computer interaction, addressing major advances in knowledge and effective use of computers in a variety of application areas. These papers provide academics, researchers, engineers, scientists, practitioners and students with state-of-the-art information on the most recent advances in HCI.

The HCI International (HCII) conference also offers the option of presenting 'Late Breaking Work', and this applies both for papers and posters, with corresponding volumes of proceedings that will be published after the conference. Full papers will be included in the 'HCII 2024 - Late Breaking Papers' volumes of the proceedings to be published in the Springer LNCS series, while 'Poster Extended Abstracts' will be included as short research papers in the 'HCII 2024 - Late Breaking Posters' volumes to be published in the Springer CCIS series.

I would like to thank the Program Board Chairs and the members of the Program Boards of all thematic areas and affiliated conferences for their contribution towards the high scientific quality and overall success of the HCI International 2024 conference. Their manifold support in terms of paper reviewing (single-blind review process, with a minimum of two reviews per submission), session organization and their willingness to act as goodwill ambassadors for the conference is most highly appreciated.

This conference would not have been possible without the continuous and unwavering support and advice of Gavriel Salvendy, founder, General Chair Emeritus, and Scientific Advisor. For his outstanding efforts, I would like to express my sincere appreciation to Abbas Moallem, Communications Chair and Editor of HCI International News.

July 2024                                                        Constantine Stephanidis

# HCI International 2024 Thematic Areas
# and Affiliated Conferences

- HCI: Human-Computer Interaction Thematic Area
- HIMI: Human Interface and the Management of Information Thematic Area
- EPCE: 21st International Conference on Engineering Psychology and Cognitive Ergonomics
- AC: 18th International Conference on Augmented Cognition
- UAHCI: 18th International Conference on Universal Access in Human-Computer Interaction
- CCD: 16th International Conference on Cross-Cultural Design
- SCSM: 16th International Conference on Social Computing and Social Media
- VAMR: 16th International Conference on Virtual, Augmented and Mixed Reality
- DHM: 15th International Conference on Digital Human Modeling & Applications in Health, Safety, Ergonomics & Risk Management
- DUXU: 13th International Conference on Design, User Experience and Usability
- C&C: 12th International Conference on Culture and Computing
- DAPI: 12th International Conference on Distributed, Ambient and Pervasive Interactions
- HCIBGO: 11th International Conference on HCI in Business, Government and Organizations
- LCT: 11th International Conference on Learning and Collaboration Technologies
- ITAP: 10th International Conference on Human Aspects of IT for the Aged Population
- AIS: 6th International Conference on Adaptive Instructional Systems
- HCI-CPT: 6th International Conference on HCI for Cybersecurity, Privacy and Trust
- HCI-Games: 6th International Conference on HCI in Games
- MobiTAS: 6th International Conference on HCI in Mobility, Transport and Automotive Systems
- AI-HCI: 5th International Conference on Artificial Intelligence in HCI
- MOBILE: 5th International Conference on Human-Centered Design, Operation and Evaluation of Mobile Communications

# List of Conference Proceedings Volumes Appearing Before the Conference

1. LNCS 14684, Human-Computer Interaction: Part I, edited by Masaaki Kurosu and Ayako Hashizume
2. LNCS 14685, Human-Computer Interaction: Part II, edited by Masaaki Kurosu and Ayako Hashizume
3. LNCS 14686, Human-Computer Interaction: Part III, edited by Masaaki Kurosu and Ayako Hashizume
4. LNCS 14687, Human-Computer Interaction: Part IV, edited by Masaaki Kurosu and Ayako Hashizume
5. LNCS 14688, Human-Computer Interaction: Part V, edited by Masaaki Kurosu and Ayako Hashizume
6. LNCS 14689, Human Interface and the Management of Information: Part I, edited by Hirohiko Mori and Yumi Asahi
7. LNCS 14690, Human Interface and the Management of Information: Part II, edited by Hirohiko Mori and Yumi Asahi
8. LNCS 14691, Human Interface and the Management of Information: Part III, edited by Hirohiko Mori and Yumi Asahi
9. LNAI 14692, Engineering Psychology and Cognitive Ergonomics: Part I, edited by Don Harris and Wen-Chin Li
10. LNAI 14693, Engineering Psychology and Cognitive Ergonomics: Part II, edited by Don Harris and Wen-Chin Li
11. LNAI 14694, Augmented Cognition, Part I, edited by Dylan D. Schmorrow and Cali M. Fidopiastis
12. LNAI 14695, Augmented Cognition, Part II, edited by Dylan D. Schmorrow and Cali M. Fidopiastis
13. LNCS 14696, Universal Access in Human-Computer Interaction: Part I, edited by Margherita Antona and Constantine Stephanidis
14. LNCS 14697, Universal Access in Human-Computer Interaction: Part II, edited by Margherita Antona and Constantine Stephanidis
15. LNCS 14698, Universal Access in Human-Computer Interaction: Part III, edited by Margherita Antona and Constantine Stephanidis
16. LNCS 14699, Cross-Cultural Design: Part I, edited by Pei-Luen Patrick Rau
17. LNCS 14700, Cross-Cultural Design: Part II, edited by Pei-Luen Patrick Rau
18. LNCS 14701, Cross-Cultural Design: Part III, edited by Pei-Luen Patrick Rau
19. LNCS 14702, Cross-Cultural Design: Part IV, edited by Pei-Luen Patrick Rau
20. LNCS 14703, Social Computing and Social Media: Part I, edited by Adela Coman and Simona Vasilache
21. LNCS 14704, Social Computing and Social Media: Part II, edited by Adela Coman and Simona Vasilache
22. LNCS 14705, Social Computing and Social Media: Part III, edited by Adela Coman and Simona Vasilache

**https://2024.hci.international/proceedings**

# Preface

With the rapid technological advances of mobile communications, mobile applications are not only changing people's living style but also changing operation, management, and innovation in organizations, industries, and governments in a new way, which further impacts the economy, society, and culture all over the world. Human-computer interaction plays an important role in this transition.

The 5th International Conference on Human-Centered Design, Operation and Evaluation of Mobile Communications (MOBILE 2024), an affiliated conference of the HCI International conference, addressed the design, operation, evaluation, and adoption of mobile technologies and applications for consumers, industries, organizations, and governments. The purpose of this conference is to provide a platform for researchers and practitioners from academia, industry, and government to discuss challenging ideas, novel research contributions, and the current theory and practice of related mobile communications research topics and applications.

The papers accepted for publication this year offer a comprehensive overview of the prevalent themes and subjects in the field of mobile communications. In particular, in the domain of mobile user experience and interaction design the accepted papers explore a diverse range of topics related to user requirements, design research and evaluation across a wide variety of contexts, and delve into preferences and behavior analysis for different target groups. Motivated by the proliferation of smartphones and mobile devices and their potential to revolutionize healthcare, promote healthier lifestyles, and improve overall well-being, a considerable number of submissions have explored the role of intuitive interfaces, personalized experiences, and seamless integration of sensors and wearables to empower users' health and support behavior change. Furthermore, exploring the limitless possibilities of Augmented Reality and mobile technologies, submissions showcased how we can reshape our interactions with the world around us, offering insights into a future of boundless innovation and progress. Finally, articles in this volume introduce examples of mobile applications, detailing their design and overall user experience. Emphasis is placed on application domains where mobile apps have made significant strides, including education, commerce, marketing, but also privacy, and security. We invite readers to delve into this collection of papers, which offers valuable insights and state-of-the-art methods, procedures, and applications to researchers, designers, developers, or simply anyone interested in the transformative potential of mobile technologies toward technology for a better world.

Two volumes of the HCII 2024 proceedings are dedicated to this year's edition of the MOBILE conference. The first focuses on topics related to Mobile Health and Wellbeing, Mobile Applications, Serious Games, and Advanced interfaces, while the second focuses on topics related to Mobile Commerce, Marketing and Retail, Mobile Security, Privacy and Safety, and Mobile User Experience and Design.

The papers of this volume were accepted for publication after a minimum of two single-blind reviews from the members of the MOBILE Program Board or, in some cases, from members of the Program Boards of other affiliated conferences. We would like to thank all of them for their invaluable contribution, support, and efforts.

July 2024                                                                                          June Wei
                                                                                              George Margetis

# 5th International Conference on Human-Centered Design, Operation and Evaluation of Mobile Communications (MOBILE 2024)

Program Board Chairs: **June Wei,** *University of West Florida, USA* and **George Margetis**, *Foundation for Research and Technology – Hellas (FORTH), Greece*

- Annalena Aicher, *Ulm University, Germany*
- Morad Benyoucef, *University of Ottawa, Canada*
- Krishna Chandramouli, *Queen Mary University of London, UK*
- Giuseppe Desolda, *University of Bari Aldo Moro, Italy*
- Dimitris Drossos, *Athens University of Economics and Business, Greece*
- Stefano Federici, *University of Perugia, Italy*
- Shangui Hu, *Ningbo University of Finance & Economics, P.R. China*
- Khutso Lebea, *University of Johannesburg, South Africa*
- Guoxin Li, *Harbin Institute of Technology, P.R. China*
- Joao Magalhaes, *Universidade Nova de Lisboa, Portugal*
- Thamer Horbylon Nascimento, *Instituto Federal Goiano, Brazil*
- Wilson Nwankwo, *Delta State University of Science and Technology, Ozoro, Nigeria*
- Cemalettin Ozturk, *Munster Technological University, Ireland*
- Renato Pereira, *Iscte Business School, Portugal*
- Elisa Prati, *University of Modena and Reggio Emilia, Italy*
- Xiu Quan Qiao, *Beijing University of Posts and Telecommunications, P.R. China*
- Gavriel Salvendy, *University of Central Florida, USA*
- Ingo Siegert, *University Magdeburg, Germany*
- Fabrizzio Soares, *Universidade Federal de Goiás, Brazil*
- Sheng Tan, *Trinity University, USA*
- Chloe Thong, *UCSI University, Malaysia*
- Elias Tragos, *University College Dublin, Ireland*
- Shuiqing Yang, *Hejiang University of Finance and Economics, P.R. China*
- Peiyan Zhou, *Jilin University, P.R. China*

The full list with the Program Board Chairs and the members of the Program Boards of all thematic areas and affiliated conferences of HCII 2024 is available online at:

**http://www.hci.international/board-members-2024.php**

# HCI International 2025 Conference

The 27th International Conference on Human-Computer Interaction, HCI International 2025, will be held jointly with the affiliated conferences at the Swedish Exhibition & Congress Centre and Gothia Towers Hotel, Gothenburg, Sweden, June 22–27, 2025. It will cover a broad spectrum of themes related to Human-Computer Interaction, including theoretical issues, methods, tools, processes, and case studies in HCI design, as well as novel interaction techniques, interfaces, and applications. The proceedings will be published by Springer. More information will become available on the conference website: https://2025.hci.international/.

General Chair
Prof. Constantine Stephanidis
University of Crete and ICS-FORTH
Heraklion, Crete, Greece
Email: general_chair@2025.hci.international

**https://2025.hci.international/**

# Contents – Part I

## Mobile Applications, Serious Games and Advanced Interfaces

# Contents – Part II

# Mobile Health and Wellbeing

# Promoting Nutrition Literacy and Food Neophilia of Middle School Children Through a Serious Hybrid Game

Sofia da Costa[1] , Ana Patrícia Oliveira[2](✉) , Nelson Zagalo[2] ,
and Elisabete Pinto[1,3]

[1] Institute of Public Health, EPIUnit, University of Porto, Porto, Portugal
ecbpinto@ucp.pt

[2] DigiMedia, Department of Communication and Art, University of Aveiro, Aveiro, Portugal
{apoliveira,nzagalo}@ua.pt

[3] CBQF - Centro de Biotecnologia E Química Fina - Laboratório Associado, Escola Superior de
Biotecnologia, Universidade Católica Portuguesa, Porto, Portugal

**Abstract.** This paper aims to assess the impact of a serious hybrid game on nutrition literacy and the promotion of food neophilia and, consequently, the diversification of children's food choices from 10 to 12 years old. FlavourGame is a serious hybrid game that combines a digital component (based on a mobile application, which helps players during the game, acting as an assistant that guides the game's tasks) with a board game. Real foods with their flavors, aromas, and textures were introduced as props to the players during the game. Nutrition messages were also included in the initial cutscene (mobile application) and in the Curiosity's Cards about food and nutrition.

The intervention group involved two different groups of children, in total 19 participants, from 10 to 12 years old, tested the FlavourGame. Sociodemographic information, eating habits, and food neophobia data were collected. A 12-question nutrition quiz was also administered at the beginning and at the end of the game session to evaluate the game's impact on nutrition knowledge. A control intervention involving 26 children (6–12 years old) was conducted.

The results suggested that Flavourgame could be used as a strategy to address and overcome children's fear or aversion to new foods and encourage them to try a variety of foods. Regarding nutrition knowledge acquisition, FlavourGame did not show a great performance, but if children continue playing (as expected in a game) the contact with nutrition facts and messages will persist, and, certainly, the knowledge acquisition will improve.

**Keywords:** Serious Game · Hybrid Game · Nutrition Literacy · Neophilia ·
Neophobia · Middle School Children

## 1 Introduction

Children's food choices play a significant role in their health and well-being, and it is crucial to identify the factors that shape their preferences [1]. One key factor is familiarity with the food. Children are more likely to enjoy and consume foods they are familiar with, and their early interactions with food influence what they like and how much they eat. Studies suggest that the more varied and earlier the exposure to different foods, the healthier a child's diet tends to be [2].

However, children may also exhibit neophobia, a fear of new foods [3]. This fear may seem counterproductive, but it is a protective mechanism, as new foods may contain harmful substances that could lead to sickness or death [4]. Neophobia can hinder healthy eating habits as it leads to less diverse diets and avoidance of certain types of food, such as fruits, vegetables, or animal products. Children with high levels of neophobia tend to be less adventurous in trying new foods, which may lead to nutrient deficiencies and poor health outcomes [3].

To promote healthy habits among children, gamification has been identified as an effective method [5]. Using tools such as social networks, mobile devices, and games can impart knowledge and encourage adherence to healthy behaviors [6]. According to the literature, gamification positively influences dietary behavior and nutritional knowledge, so Game-based interventions could be beneficial in promoting healthy habits [7–10]. Moreover, serious games in health have been seen as exciting tools to motivate players for healthy behaviors [11] with the intent of being engagement devices for socio-cultural change concerning a diversity of themes [12], including lifestyles [13]. However, to the best of our knowledge, anyone previous study aimed to assess the impact of gamification in the decrease of food neophobia.

Peer influence also significantly shapes children's and adolescents' food preferences and eating behaviors. During late childhood and pre-adolescence, peers play a more important role in children's lives, influencing their social and emotional development and potentially shaping their future trajectories [14]. Adolescents' relationships with their peers and close friends can impact decision-making and consumer behavior, including food choices [15]. Being part of a peer group is a key factor in defining social relationships, which can affect adolescents' food preferences and eating behaviors. As friends become a more important source of information about what is acceptable, peer influence on food choice becomes increasingly relevant during this stage of development [16]. Understanding how peer influence affects adolescents' food choices can help develop interventions that promote healthy eating habits and prevent unhealthy behaviors [17]. While children or adolescents playing games, particularly board games, they interact each other, they express their opinions and can influence the perceptions and behaviors of the others.

## 2 Objective of the Paper

To assess the impact of a serious hybrid game on nutrition literacy and the promotion of food neophilia and, consequently, the diversification of children's food choices from 10 to 12 years old.

## 3 Methods

In order to access the effect of a new hybrid game on nutrition knowledge and in the readiness to try new foods, a quasi-experimental study was designed, considering two convenience samples: in one group the nutritional concepts and food tasting context happened during the game playing in a classroom (intervention group); in the other group, nutrition concepts were conveyed through a Power Point presentation in a classroom setting, and the food tasting occurred at the end of the presentation.

For the nutrition knowledge assessment, a quiz was created. The assessment of the willingness to try new foods was made based on the perception of the researchers of accompanied the experiment.

### 3.1  FlavourGame: Short Description of the Game

FlavourGame is a serious hybrid game that combines a digital component, based on a mobile application, with a board game [18]. The game objective is to support the autonomy and motivation of children from 10 to 12 years old regarding healthy food choices. In fact, real foods with their flavors, aromas, and textures (fruits, vegetables, cereals, and nuts) are introduced as props to the players during the game, creating a whole new sensorial experience (Fig. 1).

**Fig. 1.**  Children tasting food earned during the game and interacting with the tablet application.

FlavourGame is a collaborative game where children have to work together to reach the end. During the game, information about healthy eating is conveyed through the narrative and cards with curiosities about food and nutrition. In the game there are also moments when players taste real food. The aim of the game is to explore the territories of a fantastic world. Each player (maximum 3) chooses a character (an archer, a warrior, and a wizard). These characters have different powers to deal with the challenges that arise. The territories are hexagons that represent places such as a Farm, a Mine, Hunting, and Fishing or three battle cards with monsters that threaten these territories. During the game, the players earn various rewards, but also face setbacks that they have to manage collaboratively. In this way, players explore various concepts such as energy, locations, monsters, storage, the market and tastings with real foods (Fig. 2).

**Fig. 2.** Various details of the FlavourGame: game box, pieces, cards, territory hexagons, mobile application (tablet), and storage and market boards.

Being a hybrid game, FlavourGame's interface promotes analog interaction around the game elements, and digital interaction in a tablet application, which orients the players' moves, acting as an assistant that guides the game's tasks with appealing design and illustration.

Regarding the nutrition component of the game, a group of nutritionists was responsible for choosing foods to include in the game, which included the identification of foods to promote among adolescents, the selection of suitable foods to integrate into the game, and the scientific and cultural support of foods selected for use in challenges integrated into the game. Fruits, vegetables, legumes, and nuts were included. Besides

**Fig. 3.** Example of a Curiosity's Card about food and nutrition.

that, it was also responsible for including scientific support for the nutrition messages in the game. These messages were included in the initial cutscene and in Curiosity's Cards (Fig. 3), which the participants randomly picked to read aloud during the game.

## 3.2 Intervention

The intervention group involved two different groups of children: seven children aged 10–12 years who attended an after-school care center (December 2022) and another group of 12 children, from a public school, who visited the University of Aveiro and also had the opportunity to play the game (February 2023). Informed consent for all children was obtained from their legal tutors.

Both interventions (a three-hour game session) took place in a classroom setting, with six participants each time and two researchers present. One researcher focused on introducing and playing the game with the children, observing their engagement and acceptance. The other researcher, a nutritionist, assessed how participants engage with nutritional concepts and their willingness to try new foods, including those mentioned by children as ones they dislike.

In order to characterize the participants, sociodemographic information was collected, including gender, parents' education level, health history, and extracurricular activities. Eating habits were assessed using an 11-question survey developed by the Portuguese General Directorate of Health [19]. This questionnaire categorized eating habits into three levels: level 1 - high adherence to healthy eating habits (score $\geq$ 18 points), level 2 - moderate adherence (score between 8–17 points), and level 3 - low adherence (score $\leq$ 7 points). Food neophobia was evaluated using the Food Neophobia Test Tool (FNTT), a validated instrument of 10 items designed to measure food neophobia in children aged 9–13. For each question, children could choose between one and seven, making the final sum fall between 10 and 70, with a higher score indicating less food neophobia.

A 12-question nutrition quiz was also administered at the beginning and end of the game session to evaluate the game's impact on nutrition knowledge. The quiz was filled out individually. Both researchers who conducted the game observed the participants' intention to try new foods.

## 3.3 Control Group

A control intervention involved a convenience sample of 26 children, aged 6 to 12 years old, who were students at a private school, during the Christmas break on December 2022. The intervention lasted approximately 1 h and 30 min and consisted of a PowerPoint presentation that included all the messages conveyed by the FlavourGame, namely on Curiosity's Cards. The participants in this group also had the opportunity to taste the foods present in the game. In this session, only one researcher was present in the classroom, with the help of a teaching assistant. The perception about the acceptability of new foods was obtained by this researcher (the same nutritionist who participated in the game sessions).

The same quiz applied in the intervention group was also applied at the beginning and at the end of the intervention. Unlike the intervention group, in the control group, there were more children in the same room, making it challenging to ensure that the children completed their quiz without seeing their partners' answers.

## 4  Results

### 4.1  Characterization of Children in Intervention Group

In terms of their dietary patterns, participants in the intervention displayed a high adherence to the Mediterranean diet, as evidenced by the questionnaire results. Specifically, 8 (42.1%) participants demonstrated a high adherence level, while 11 (57.9%) showed moderate adherence. It is worth mentioning that a majority of the parents had attained a higher education degree, with 15 mothers and 14 fathers falling into this category. Moreover, over half of the participants (14 individuals) engaged in physical exercise as an after-school hobby at least twice a week. It is important to note that none of the participants reported any medical conditions or food allergies.

When assessing food neophobia using the Food Neophobic Test Tool, two children in the intervention group displayed high levels of neophobia, scoring a total of 40 on the FNTT. Additionally, eight participants scored above 40, four scored above 50, and four scored above 60.

### 4.2  Effect of the Intervention in Nutrition Knowledge

In Table 1 was displayed the proportions of correct answers for both quiz applications, in the intervention and control group. Regarding nutrition knowledge acquisition, the control group exhibited greater knowledge acquisition.

**Table 1.** Nutrition knowledge before and after intervention, in the intervention and control group

| | Intervention group | | Control group | |
|---|---|---|---|---|
| | Beginning (% corrected answers) | End (% corrected answers) | Beginning (% corrected answers) | End (% corrected answers) |
| A healthy diet involves a wide variety of foods | 100.0 | 100.0 | 100.0 | 100.0 |
| Non-whole grain cereals should form the basis of a healthy diet | 85.0 | 40.0 | 92.3 | 95.8 |
| Legumes should be consumed every day | 90.0 | 75.0 | 96.2 | 95.8 |
| Red meat should be the most consumed animal protein daily | 80.0 | 30.0 | 100.0 | 95.8 |
| Soft drinks can be consumed every day in a healthy diet | 100.0 | 100.0 | 96.2 | 100 |

(*continued*)

**Table 1.** (*continued*)

| | Intervention group | | Control group | |
|---|---|---|---|---|
| | Beginning (% corrected answers) | End (% corrected answers) | Beginning (% corrected answers) | End (% corrected answers) |
| The exterior colour of the egg is related to that of the hen | 57.9 | 45.0 | 11.5 | 100 |
| Beef is the most consumed meat worldwide | 10.5 | 20.0 | 7.7 | 100 |
| Sardines have a higher percentage of fat during the months of the Popular Saints festivities | 57.9 | 30.0 | 73.1 | 87.5 |
| Water is one of the main components of fruit | 95.0 | 90.0 | 80.8 | 91.7 |
| Tomato is a vegetable | 47.4 | 55.0 | 50.0 | 75.0 |
| Lupin beans in their natural state are not toxic to humans | 33.3 | 50.0 | 84.6 | 95.8 |
| Vitamin B is responsible for the colour variation of sweet potatoes | 50.0 | 45.0 | 26.9 | 100.0 |
| Total | 67.3 | 56.7 | 68.3 | 94.8 |

## 4.3 Effect of the Intervention in the Willingness to Test New Foods

During the game session (intervention group) or at the end of presentation (control group) different foods were making available for tasting. Not all food was familiar for all children and some of them mentioned never tried them or even dislike. In the game session, trying different foods was part of the game mechanics, so children wanted to continue playing, challenging themselves to taste these foods. Notably, the intervention group demonstrated a greater willingness to try unfamiliar foods, indicating a higher level of openness and receptiveness.

In the control group, the same foods were making available, but if children did not taste them nothing happens. As a result, only a small number of children showed interest in trying the foods.

## 5 Discussion

In Portugal, the prevalence of obesity and pre-obesity among adolescents (10–17 years old) is 8.7% and 23.6%, respectively [2]. These figures can be partially attributed to the population's low adherence to the Portuguese dietary guidelines, which recommend that approximately 50% of daily food consumption should consist of fruits, vegetables, and legumes. [2]. The World Health Organization (WHO) advises a daily consumption of at least 400 g of fruits and vegetables, a target that three-quarters of Portuguese teenagers fail to meet [3]. Notably, food items such as sweets, cakes, and biscuits are consumed almost daily (93.1% of days), despite not being part of the New Portuguese Food Wheel [3]. Furthermore, Portuguese teenagers exhibit the highest prevalence of soft drink and fruit nectar consumption in the country (42%) [2]. Moreover, there is a suboptimal intake of legumes (<2%) compared to the recommended levels [2].

In response to these challenges, the FlavourGame project focuses on engaging children and teenagers in discussions and understanding around their food choices [1]. It adopts a user-centered design approach that empowers children by giving them a voice and space to express their perspectives [1]. The game also promotes the exploration of real foods as a means to combat food neophobia, a significant influence on children's eating habits and future dietary quality [4]. Additionally, the project aims to highlight the importance of selecting local and seasonal products [1]. Ultimately, the game seeks to modify participants' food consumption patterns by increasing their intake of fruits, vegetables, cereals, legumes, and nuts. This includes the tasting of various foods such as chia seed crackers, lupine, grapes, cherry tomatoes, corn crackers, rice crackers, raspberries, cucumbers, purple cabbage, dried coconut, dried pears, carrots, sweet potato chips, spelled cereal, and peanuts.

As indicated in the results, the control group exhibited a higher level of nutrition information acquisition compared to the intervention group. This disparity in knowledge can be attributed to several factors. Firstly, the inclusion of a private school in the control group suggests that nutrition education may be more comprehensive in such institutions compared to public schools. Furthermore, although we were unable to evaluate it, the children in the control group might come from families with a higher socioeconomic status, which could contribute to their greater nutritional knowledge [20]. Additionally, the individual administration of questionnaires was possible in the intervention group, but the same could not be assured in the control group, since a big number of students were in the same place and shared some information. Moreover, in the intervention group, the focus of the intervention was primarily on the game itself (ludic component) rather than conveying specific nutritional messages. Lastly, unlike the control group, not all game cards in the intervention group were read by the participants due to the game's rules, potentially impacting knowledge acquisition.

The intervention group demonstrated a greater openness and willingness to try unfamiliar foods. These findings indicate a strong inclination within the group to explore new food options. Although the questionnaires were anonymous, making it impossible to match specific answers to individual participants, it was observed that two individuals initially showed resistance to trying new foods, and two participants scored below 40 points on the FNTT. However, as the game progressed, they actively participated and tried almost all of the foods. Notably, one participant mentioned a dislike for fruits but still tried all the presented fruits and discovered a liking for some of them. Fruits appeared to face less resistance when it came to trying new foods. Additionally, the literature suggests that children's preferred foods often have lower nutritional value, with high ratings given to fatty and sugary foods and lower ratings given to vegetables

[21]. This pattern was observed in both groups, with greater resistance to trying vegetables compared to other foods. However, the initial resistance was notably lower in the control group. This can be attributed to group dynamics and the influence of peer pressure within the game context. The tasting of foods played a crucial role in the game's success, which likely motivated participants to be more open to trying new foods [22]. Interestingly, the students were so enthusiastic that they continued eating even after it was no longer required by the game, eagerly consuming leftover food from tastings and eagerly anticipating new food opportunities. Conversely, the control group did not have a specific incentive to taste the foods. Additionally, the larger number of students in the control group and the simultaneous tasting of all foods may have mitigated the impact of peer pressure [14].

The study offers several advantages. Firstly, it employs a hybrid game that specifically targets the issue of food neophobia, aiming to address and combat this common challenge. By combining elements of both traditional and digital gaming, the study provides an innovative approach to engage participants in overcoming their fear of trying new foods. Additionally, using culturally appropriate food and game elements, including trivia and interactive components, ensures that the game is engaging and relevant for the specific age group of the participants. This tailored approach enhances their interest and involvement, leading to more effective intervention in promoting healthier eating habits.

It is important to recognize that nutrition education is often conducted through traditional interventions, which primarily focus on increasing knowledge and awareness about healthy eating habits. These interventions typically involve classroom-based instruction, presentations, and dissemination of informational materials. While these approaches are valuable in enhancing individuals' understanding of nutrition principles, they may not always effectively translate into behavior change. One of the limitations of traditional nutrition education interventions is their reliance on the assumption that knowledge alone will drive behavior modification. However, numerous factors influence food choices and dietary behaviors, extending beyond mere knowledge acquisition. Personal preferences, cultural influences, socioeconomic factors, food accessibility, and individual beliefs all play significant roles in shaping eating habits. Furthermore, it is crucial to consider the social and environmental contexts in which individuals make food choices. Peer influence, family dynamics, and community settings all contribute to shaping dietary behaviors [23]. Therefore, interventions that engage these social networks and create supportive environments are more likely to result in sustained behavior change. Gamification has emerged as a potential tool for enhancing nutrition education and behavior change. This technology provides interactive and personalized experiences that can increase engagement, motivation, and self-efficacy in adopting healthier eating habits [8].

One limitation worth highlighting is the potential bias in the sample selection, as convenience sampling was utilized. Additionally, due to the COVID19 pandemic, alternative sampling methods could not be used. Furthermore, it should be noted that the intervention and control groups had slightly different characteristics, especially in age gaps. Another limitation to consider is the potential influence of the conditions under which the questionnaire was administered in the control group, which could have affected the observed results.

**Acknowledgments.** The authors would like to acknowledge POCI-FEDER and FCT for funding this Project, under the Grant Agreement No. POCI-01–0145-FEDER-031024.

**Disclosure of Interests.** The authors have no competing interests to declare that are relevant to the content of this article.

# References

1. Domel, S.B., Thompson, W.O., Davis, H.C., Baranowski, T., Leonard, S.B., Baranowski, J.: Psychosocial predictors of fruit and vegetable consumption among elementary school children. Health Educ. Res. **11**, 299–308 (1996). https://doi.org/10.1093/her/11.3.299
2. Birch, L.L., Marlin, D.W.: I don't like it; I never tried it: effects of exposure on two-year-old children's food preferences. Appetite **3**, 353–360 (1982). https://doi.org/10.1016/s0195-6663(82)80053-6
3. Cooke, L.: The importance of exposure for healthy eating in childhood: a review. J. Hum. Nutr. Diet. **20**, 294–301 (2007). https://doi.org/10.1111/j.1365-277X.2007.00804.x
4. Rozin, P.: The selection of foods by rats, humans, and other animals. Adv. Study Behav. **6**, 21–76 (1976). https://doi.org/10.1016/s0065-3454(08)60081-9
5. Kostenius, C., Hallberg, J., Lindqvist, A.-K.: Gamification of health education. Health Educ. **118**, 354–368 (2018). https://doi.org/10.1108/he-10-2017-0055
6. Rohde, A., Duensing, A., Dawczynski, C., Godemann, J., Lorkowski, S., Brombach, C.: An app to improve eating habits of adolescents and young adults (challenge to go): systematic development of a theory-based and target group–adapted mobile app intervention. JMIR mHealth uHealth. **7**(8), e11575 (2019). https://doi.org/10.2196/11575
7. Suleiman-Martos, N., et al.: Gamification for the improvement of diet, nutritional habits, and body composition in children and adolescents: a systematic review and meta-analysis. Nutrients. **13**, 2478 (2021). https://doi.org/10.3390/nu13072478
8. Lamas, S., Rebelo, S., da Costa, S., Sousa, H., Zagalo, N., Pinto, E.: The influence of serious games in the promotion of healthy diet and physical activity health: a systematic review. Nutrients **15**, 1399 (2023). https://doi.org/10.3390/nu15061399
9. Yoshida-Montezuma, Y., Ahmed, M., Ezezika, O.: Does gamification improve fruit and vegetable intake in adolescents? A systematic review. Nutr. Health **26**, 347–366 (2020). https://doi.org/10.1177/0260106020936143
10. dos Santos, T.T., et al.: Gamification as a health education strategy of adolescents at school: Protocol for a systematic review and meta-analysis. PLOS ONE **18**(11), e0294894 (2023). https://doi.org/10.1371/journal.pone.0294894
11. Saadatfard, O., Årsand, E.: Serious Games in Healthcare. Faktaark (Nasjonalt senter for e-helseforskning). 11 (2016). https://ehealthresearch.no/files/documents/Faktaark/Fact-sheet-2016-11-Serious-Games-in-Healthcare.pdf
12. Klimmt, C.: Serious Games and Social Change: Why They (Should) Work. In: Ritterfeld, U., Cody, M., & Vorderer, P. (Eds.). Serious Games: Mechanisms and Effects (1st ed.). Routledge (2009). https://doi.org/10.4324/9780203891650
13. Holzmann, S.L., et al.: Short-term effects of the serious game "fit, food, fun" on nutritional knowledge: a pilot study among children and adolescents. Nutrients **11**, 2031 (2019). https://doi.org/10.3390/nu11092031
14. Dykas, M.J., Ziv, Y., Cassidy, J.: Attachment and peer relations in adolescence. Attach. Hum. Dev. **10**, 123–141 (2008). https://doi.org/10.1080/14616730802113679

15. Gorrese, A., Ruggieri, R.: Peer attachment: a meta-analytic review of gender and age differences and associations with parent attachment. J. Youth Adolesc. **41**, 650–672 (2012). https://doi.org/10.1007/s10964-012-9759-6

16. Hendy, H.M., Williams, K.E., Camise, T.S.: "Kids choice" school lunch program increases children's fruit and vegetable acceptance. Appetite **45**, 250–263 (2005). https://doi.org/10.1016/j.appet.2005.07.006

17. Ragelienė, T., Grønhøj, A.: The influence of peers' and siblings' on children's and adolescents' healthy eating behavior. A systematic literature review. Appetite **148**, 104592 (2020). https://doi.org/10.1016/j.appet.2020.104592

18. Oliveira, A.P., Sousa, M., Vairinhos, M., Zagalo, N.: Towards a new hybrid game model: designing tangible experiences. In: 2020 IEEE 8th International Conference on Serious Games and Applications for Health, SeGAH 2020 (2020). https://doi.org/10.1109/SeGAH49190.2020.9201838

19. Gregório, M.J., Teixeira, D., Monteiro, R., Mendes de Sousa, S., Irving, S., Graça, P.: Aconselhamento breve para a alimentação saudável nos cuidados de saúde primários: modelo de intervenção e ferramentas. Programa Nacional para a Promoção da Alimentação Saudável, Ministério da Saúde, Direção-Geral da Saúde (2020). https://www.dgs.pt/documentos-e-publicacoes/dgs-lanca-manual-sobre-alimentacao-saudavel-nos-cuidados-de-saude-primarios-pdf.aspx

20. Spronk, I., Kullen, C., Burdon, C., O'Connor, H.: Relationship between nutrition knowledge and dietary intake. Br. J. Nutr. **111**, 1713–1726 (2014). https://doi.org/10.1017/S0007114514000087

21. Cooke, L.J., Wardle, J.: Age and gender differences in children's food preferences. Br. J. Nutr. **93**, 741–746 (2005). https://doi.org/10.1079/bjn20051389

22. Kappen, D.L., Orji, R.: Gamified and persuasive systems as behavior change agents for health and wellness. XRDS: crossroads. ACM Mag. Students **24**, 52–55 (2017). https://doi.org/10.1145/3123750

23. Gómez-García, G., Marín-Marín, J.A., Romero-Rodríguez, J.-M., Ramos Navas-Parejo, M., Rodríguez Jiménez, C.: Effect of the flipped classroom and gamification Methods in the development of a didactic unit on healthy habits and Diet in primary education. Nutrients **12**, 2210 (2020). https://doi.org/10.3390/nu12082210

# Exploring the Factors Influencing the Adoption of Wrist-Worn Wearable Devices for Well-Being Monitoring Among End Users

Francesco Di Paolo[✉], Michele Di Dalmazi, Marco Mandolfo, and Debora Bettiga

Department of Management, Economics, and Industrial Engineering, Politecnico di Milano, Milan, Italy
francesco.dipaolo@polimi.it

**Abstract.** In monitoring individual health, wearable technologies, especially wrist-worn wearable devices, play a crucial role by actively collecting and displaying fundamental wellness-related data such as steps, calories, skin temperature, heart rate, and sleep patterns. Promoting their widespread acceptance is key for improving overall well-being, benefiting both individuals and society. Employing the Technology Acceptance Model (TAM), the Model of PC Utilization (MPCU), and the Innovation Diffusion Theory (IDT), this paper introduces a novel research model that identifies functional determinants (perceived usefulness, perceived value), social determinants (brand name, social image, perceived prestige), and privacy-related factors (health information sensitivity, perceived privacy risk) influencing the adoption of wrist-worn wearable devices. The study utilizes a survey on end users for data collection, and Structural Equation Modeling is employed to analyze significant factors affecting adoption. The findings reveal that functional aspects significantly impact adoption, particularly when supported by social elements. Privacy considerations emerge as a crucial factor influencing adoption. This research contributes to the field by expanding the spectrum of factors influencing the adoption of wrist-worn wearable devices beyond mere functionality and offers managerial and societal implications.

**Keywords:** wearable technology · wearable device · TAM · MPCU · IDT · SEM

## 1 Introduction

The notion of pervasive health, as outlined by Ruotsalainen et al. (2012), is underpinned by a self-controlled well-being data system, with Wearable Technology (WT) emerging as a key facilitator for its monitoring (Ometov et al., 2021). WT serves as a conduit for individuals to cultivate health-conscious lifestyles, thereby potentially alleviating burdens on healthcare systems. Wrist-worn Wearable Devices (WWD) embody user-friendly attributes such as convenient form factors, readable displays, and customizable features through apps and interconnected devices (Johnson & Picard, 2020, p. 8). The industry has seen substantial growth, with 492.1 million units shipped in 2022 (Jay et al., 2023), indicating a maturation beyond its nascent stages, with wrist-worn gadgets poised

© The Author(s), under exclusive license to Springer Nature Switzerland AG 2024
J. Wei and G. Margetis (Eds.): HCII 2024, LNCS 14737, pp. 14–30, 2024.
https://doi.org/10.1007/978-3-031-60458-4_2

for mainstream adoption. Smartwatches, akin to smartphones, have achieved widespread diffusion, representing the initial wave of smart wearable technology (Jung et al., 2016). WWDs, adept at processing user data for wellness benefits, enjoy significant market penetration, as evidenced by their widespread adoption (Chouk & Mani, 2022). Positioned as quasi-medical devices, wearable technologies are hailed as potent alternatives for continuous health monitoring, potentially driving down healthcare expenditures (Huarng et al., 2022, p. 5), thereby influencing broader societal dynamics (Roman and Conlee, 2015). Consequently, there is a pressing need for updated insights into the adoption patterns of these devices (Nascimento et al., 2018).

Recent comprehensive reviews (Niknejad et al., 2020) underscore the adaptable nature of Wearable Devices (WDs), which can serve diverse purposes across various sectors including healthcare, fitness, education, fashion, job management, safety, gaming, sports, and beyond. The versatility of Wearable Technology (WT) stems from its unique attributes: wearability, functionality, ease of use, design, and price. Consequently, a range of acceptance models has emerged in the literature (Siepmann & Kowalczuk, 2021; Lee & Lee, 2018), each focusing on specific sectors, target demographics, and device types, albeit offering fragmented insights into WT acceptance at a broader scale. The study by Yang et al. (2016) stands out as a notable endeavor in this realm, exploring the determinants of perceived value of WDs among early adopters. Moreover, as technology matures, individual needs evolve beyond basic functionalities, leading to considerations of hedonic value in personal technologies, including wrist-worn smart devices (Dholakia, 2014), thereby influencing affective and experiential aspects of consumption. Social factors, which encapsulate the internalization of subjective cultural norms from reference groups (Smith & Colgate, 2007; Thompson et al., 1991), emerge as pivotal in WD adoption. According to the Value Theory model proposed by Sheth et al. (1991), purchase intention is shaped by the social and functional values associated with a product. While functional drivers of use have been extensively studied, the literature has largely overlooked the intertwined influence of social components, particularly concerning pervasive well-being monitoring (Niknejad et al., 2020). Our research posits that functional drivers of use significantly impact intention to use when complemented by social elements, warranting attention in the adoption of WWDs. In our investigation, social influence is anticipated to play a significant explanatory role. Additionally, given the nature of these devices designed to gather personal data, privacy concerns should be carefully weighed in adoption assessments.

Based on the aforementioned considerations, the current study endeavors to construct a comprehensive model of Wearable Wrist Devices (WWDs) adoption for pervasive individual well-being monitoring, transcending functional aspects to incorporate social drivers of choice and privacy concerns. Employing the Partial Least Squares Structural Equation Modeling (PLS-SEM) technique, we scrutinized data gathered from 311 Italian respondents, aligning our investigation with prior research on end users' behavioral intentions (Tani et al., 2022).

Our study makes an original contribution to the literature on business and technological change by introducing an elaborate model for individuals' adoption of WWDs for well-being monitoring. This endeavor enhances existing frameworks, notably the Technology Acceptance Model (TAM) (Davis, 1989), the Model of PC Utilization (MPCU)

(Thompson et al., 1991), and the Innovation Diffusion Theory (IDT) (Moore & Benbasat, 1991), which inadequately address the drivers of adoption concerning hedonic-oriented technologies like WWDs (van der Heijden, 2004). The investigation delves into functional drivers (perceived usefulness, perceived value), social drivers (brand name, social image, perceived prestige), and privacy-related factors (health information sensitivity, perceived privacy risk). By elucidating the drivers of WWDs adoption, our work furnishes marketers with valuable insights into the elements consumers contemplate when making choices, thereby aiding product managers in refining product design strategies. Moreover, our study assists marketing managers in crafting tailored communication strategies, both during the launch phase of a new device and thereafter, to propel individuals along the adoption trajectory, thereby expanding the customer base. From a policymaker standpoint, our work furnishes guidance on promoting the widespread adoption of well-being monitoring devices, thereby facilitating illness prevention through health-conscious habits and bolstering the efficacy of healthcare systems.

The paper is structured as follows. Section 1 introduces the theory backing the research framework, while Sect. 2 highlights the conceptual model and hypotheses supporting it. Section 3 details the methodology behind the collection and the analysis of the data used to pursue the objective of the research. Section 4 presents the results of the study, while session 5 discusses the main findings. Section 6 presents managerial and social implications. Section 7 concludes the work by exploring the study limitations and providing suggestions for future research.

## 2  Literature Review and Conceptual Model

As posited by Choi & Kim (2016), the characterization of Wrist-Worn Devices (WWDs) as fashionable commodities underscores the necessity to account for intrinsic non-utilitarian motivations driving their adoption. Consequently, we have adopted the Technology Acceptance Model (TAM) (Davis, 1989) to encompass factors related to utilitarian and functional value. In contrast, the Model of PC Utilization (MPCU) (Thompson et al., 1991) and the Innovation Diffusion Theory (IDT) as adapted by Moore & Benbasat (1991) have been integrated into the conceptual framework to enrich it with social factors, particularly non-utilitarian ones. This theoretical framework aligns with prior research endeavors that have investigated the adoption of wearable technologies by synthesizing diverse adoption models (Adapa et al., 2018; Al-Emran et al., 2021). Notably, none of these studies have amalgamated TAM, MPCU, and IDT adoption models within the realm of wrist-worn wearable devices until now.

The Technology Acceptance Model (TAM) (Davis, 1989) stands as a cornerstone in wearable device adoption research, widely utilized in studies exploring this domain (Buenaflor & Kim, 2013; Lee & Lee, 2018; Spagnolli et al., 2014). Recognized as the predominant framework for assessing individual adoption of new technologies, TAM accounts for perceived usefulness, perceived ease of use, and intention to use, offering insights into both beliefs and attitudes towards technology adoption (Kalantari & Rauschnabel, 2018). While TAM provides a robust foundation, it primarily focuses on functional aspects, potentially limiting its ability to encompass the full spectrum of factors influencing adoption, especially for hedonic-oriented technologies (van der Heijden,

2004). In contrast to functional values, which center on perceived utility derived from a technology's functional or utilitarian performance, social factors encapsulate an individual's integration of subjective cultural norms and interpersonal agreements within specific social contexts (Thompson et al., 1991). To comprehensively explore the social dimension, our study adopts a dual analytical perspective integrating key elements from both the Model of Personal Computer Utilization (MPCU) and the Innovation Diffusion Theory (IDT). The MPCU, as conceptualized by Thompson et al. (1991), extends beyond the functional perspective inherent in TAM by highlighting the significant positive impact of social factors on personal computer utilization. By leveraging the MPCU framework, our study aims to capture individual-level factors influencing the adoption of Wrist-Worn Devices (WWDs), with a specific focus on social elements (Taherdoost, 2018). Through the MPCU lens, we delve into cognitive and psychological processes shaping perceptions and intentions related to WWD adoption. On the other hand, IDT, a well-established theoretical framework, elucidates the spread and adoption of innovations within social systems. Building upon the Diffusion of Innovation Theory by Rogers and Everett (1983), Moore and Benbasat (1991) extend the social dimension in adoption decisions, defining social image as the extent to which innovation usage enhances one's social status or image within a social system (Moore & Benbasat, 1991, p. 195). By incorporating IDT principles, our study contextualizes adoption decisions within broader social frameworks, acknowledging the influence of social dynamics on WWD adoption behaviors.

In our analysis, we delve deeper into the impact of social image on the intention to use Wrist-Worn Devices (WWDs) by incorporating brand name as an additional antecedent in our research model. The congruency between brand name and the self-image projected by WWDs to users is significant (Blazquez et al., 2020). Credible and exclusive brands are sought after not only for their functional utilities but also for the social recognition, status, and positive self-image they bestow upon users (Kapferer, 1997; Vigneron and Johnson, 2004). Furthermore, given the key feature of Wearable Devices (WDs) – the collection of personal data – perceived privacy risk must also be considered. Consequently, health information sensitivity, which integrates the theme of privacy, warrants exploration. While the impact of these constructs has been addressed within the medical research community (H. Li et al., 2016), their managerial implications remain to be fully explored. The integration of the Model of Personal Computer Utilization (MPCU), Innovation Diffusion Theory (IDT), and the Technology Acceptance Model (TAM) in our study provides a robust theoretical foundation. These frameworks offer complementary attributes that collectively capture both individual-level and social-level factors influencing the adoption of wearable devices. Moreover, the inclusion of privacy-related factors ensures a comprehensive assessment of the adoption drivers of WWDs.

In the subsequent sections, we will expound upon each construct and its relationship with other constructs, thereby enriching our understanding of the complexities underlying WWD adoption. This comprehensive analysis aims to provide valuable insights for both academia and industry, facilitating informed decision-making and strategy formulation in the domain of wearable technology adoption.

## 2.1  Intention to Use (IU)

Intention to use encompasses the likelihood that an individual intends to use a particular technology, both presently and in the future, as well as the degree to which individuals endorse the usage of that technology (Davis, 1989; Hsu & Lin, 2015). Perceived value and perceived usefulness are pivotal in predicting intention to use. Yang and colleagues (2016) highlight perceived value as a significant precursor to technology adoption across various domains. Conversely, literature suggests that perceived usefulness ranks among the most influential predictors of intention to use wearable technology (WT) (Dehghani et al., 2018). Building on previous research, Bettiga et al. (2020) posit that the impact of perceived usefulness on intention to use has evolved into a well-established relationship within technology acceptance models.

## 2.2  Perceived Usefulness (PU)

Perceived usefulness, originally defined as "the degree to which a person believes that using a particular system would enhance his or her job performance" (Davis, 1989, p. 320), extends its relevance to the context of technology acceptance. Here, it denotes individuals' inclination to use a technology based on their perception of its ability to facilitate their activities (Davis, 1989; Shin, 2007).

In the realm of wearable device adoption research, numerous studies have highlighted perceived usefulness as a critical factor within their models (Chuah et al., 2016; Lee & Lee, 2018; Nasir & Yurder, 2015; Yang et al., 2016). When applied to Wrist-Worn Devices (WWDs) for pervasive well-being, perceived usefulness pertains to the extent to which users believe the device can aid them in achieving personal goals aimed at enhancing their healthy lifestyle. It encapsulates the utilitarian and functional value individuals perceive when considering the adoption of such technology. Following:

**H1.** Perceived usefulness is positively related to the intention to use.

## 2.3  Perceived Value (PV)

Perceived value is conceived as the balance between the effort individuals invest in using technology and the perceived benefits derived from it (Sirdeshmukh et al., 2002). It represents the overall evaluation of a product's utility by weighing the benefits against the sacrifices (Yang et al., 2016). While perceived value is considered a utilitarian factor, it was not originally included in the Technology Acceptance Model (TAM) (Davis, 1989). However, it has been incorporated as an influential factor in adapted versions of the TAM (Venkatesh & Bala, 2008; Venkatesh & Davis, 2000). In the context of Wrist-Worn Devices (WWDs), perceived value serves as an intrinsic factor that influences both the adoption and continued usage of wearable devices (Yang et al., 2016; Hong et al., 2017). It encapsulates users' assessments of the benefits they expect to gain from using the device in comparison to the effort and sacrifices required. Grounding on this:

**H2.** Perceived value is positively related to the intention to use.

## 2.4 Perceived Prestige (PP)

Perceived prestige (PP) denotes the extent to which individuals within a community hold a favorable perception of a particular item, potentially influencing the reputation of the individual associated with it (Cornwell & Coote, 2005). While this construct has not traditionally been explored in the context of Wrist-Worn Devices (WWDs) adoption within marketing and managerial literature, its inclusion in the model enriches our understanding of outward factors. Perceived prestige offers an avenue for enhancing self-esteem through mechanisms of self-identification (Cornwell & Coote, 2005), particularly relevant within the framework of self-categorization within social groups (Abrams, 2001). Its inclusion aligns with the spectrum of WWDs under study, especially considering mainstream middle-range WWDs, where perceived prestige does not necessarily correlate directly with high-priced products (Truong et al., 2009). Incorporating perceived prestige into the model broadens our comprehension of the multifaceted factors influencing WWDs adoption, shedding light on the social dynamics and self-perception intricacies that contribute to individuals' adoption decisions in this context. Hence:

H3. Perceived prestige in using WWD positively influences social image.

## 2.5 Social Image (SI)

Social image (SI) encompasses the utility derived from a product's capacity to enhance one's social identity (Moore & Benbasat, 1991; Sweeney & Soutar, 2001). This concept extends to the impact on self-esteem and self-efficacy, influenced by the beliefs and perceptions of peers and others. Wearable devices (WDs) are posited to affect the social self by projecting characteristics such as tech-savviness, athleticism, and health-consciousness. From a social perspective, WDs may enhance peer recognition when users share health- or fitness-related accomplishments via social media platforms. Moreover, Wrist-Worn Devices (WWDs) are designed to be fashionable accessories, akin to traditional watches. Consequently, wearing such devices becomes integrated into individuals' daily routines and habits. The perceived consistency of these devices and associated services with one's existing behavioral patterns significantly shapes individuals' perceptions (Choi & Kim, 2016, p. 780). In essence, the adoption of WWDs is intertwined with the enhancement of social image, as these devices not only convey specific lifestyle choices but also serve as fashion statements that align with users' aesthetic preferences and daily routines. Thus, the social image associated with WWDs influences how users perceive themselves and are perceived by others within their social milieu. Therefore:

H4a. Social image is positively related to perceived usefulness.

H4b. Social image is positively related to perceived value.

## 2.6 Brand Name (BN)

Brand name (BN) denotes the significance individuals attribute to a brand when making a purchase (Brucks et al., 2000; Lau & Lee, 1999). This construct holds social implications as it serves as a social signal, fulfilling individuals' needs for uniqueness and social reputation (Belén del Río et al., 2001; Lannon & Cooper, 1983). In the context of

Wrist-Worn Devices (WWDs), the inclusion of brand name is pertinent as it enables the examination of how brand-related factors, such as perceived quality, trust, familiarity, recognition, and perceived value, impact the adoption of these devices. Brand name is closely associated with social status and image, as consumers often select well-known and prestigious brands to signify their social standing or desired identity to others. The brand name becomes emblematic, communicating specific social attributes and aspirations. Moreover, brand name can be influenced by social norms and the desire for social acceptance. Individuals may choose a WWD from a particular brand because their social circle or influential individuals endorse or recommend it. This perspective provides valuable insights into the role of brand name in shaping consumers' attitudes and behaviors regarding the intention to use WWDs. By considering brand name within the adoption framework, we gain a deeper understanding of how social dynamics and brand perceptions influence individuals' adoption decisions in the context of wearable technology.

**H5.** Brand name is positively related to perceived value.

### 2.7   Perceived Privacy Risk (PPR)

Perceived risk encompasses the sensation of uncertainty regarding the unforeseen consequences of using a product or service (Featherman & Pavlou, 2003). Within this framework, perceived privacy risk emerges as a dimension of perceived risk, defined as the potential loss of control over personal information without individuals' consent (Featherman & Pavlou, 2003). Given the dual nature of wearable devices – offering distinct benefits in enhancing healthcare efficiency while also presenting heightened privacy risks – individuals' decisions to adopt Wrist-Worn Devices (WWDs) entail a critical privacy assessment. This process involves users navigating the balance between perceived benefits and potential privacy risks, leading to a significant deliberation regarding the trade-off between anticipated advantages and privacy concerns (H. Li et al., 2016). Therefore, perceived privacy risk assumes crucial importance in studying the adoption of wearable devices. When users perceive a high privacy risk associated with using a wearable device, the perceived value it offers may diminish as users become hesitant to share personal information. This hesitancy can limit the device's ability to provide tailored experiences, thereby impacting users' willingness to adopt WWDs. Consequently, understanding and addressing perceived privacy risks is essential for fostering user trust and facilitating widespread adoption of wearable technology, particularly in the context of healthcare applications.

**H6.** Perceived privacy risk is negatively related to perceived value.

### 2.8   Health Information Sensitivity (HIS)

It is widely acknowledged that the extensive collection of personal health-related data profoundly influences users' perceptions of Wrist-Worn Devices (WWDs) from a privacy risk standpoint (Dinev et al., 2013; Malhotra et al., 2004; Milne & Gordon, 1993). Health information sensitivity refers to the degree of discomfort an individual may experience when disclosing personal health data to third parties – such as companies providing WWDs in our case (Dinev et al., 2013; Malhotra et al., 2004). Perceived privacy concerns escalate as apprehensions about the misuse of sensitive data arise (Li, 2014). This hypothesis has been tested in the context of Web 2.0 by Dinev et al. (2013) and in the realm of medical wearable devices by Li and colleagues (2016), focusing on privacy calculus. Seeking to validate this relationship at a more generalized level of usage specificity – specifically pertaining to pervasive wellbeing monitoring – and with a business-oriented perspective, we hypothesize that (Fig. 1):

**H7.** Health information sensitivity positively influences perceived privacy risk in using WWD for pervasive well-being monitoring.

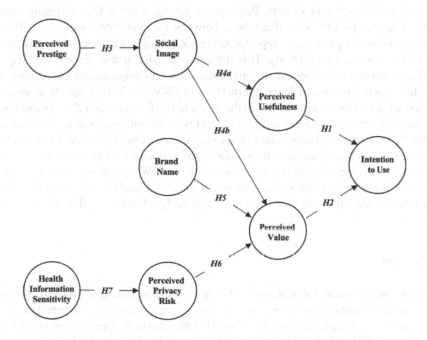

**Fig. 1.** Conceptual model and related hypotheses

# 3 Methodology

To test the proposed model, we gathered data through an online survey on final consumers. The questionnaire was composed of three main sections. In the first section, a descriptive overview including some pictures of the most popular WDs was introduced. In the second one, descriptive data related to respondents' demographics and prior experience with WDs were gathered. Finally, the third section included all the constructs involved in the conceptual model. All the proposed items have been adapted from previous literature. The list of tested constructs included intention to use (4 items) (Davis et al., 1989; Hsu and Lin, 2015), perceived value (3 items) (Sirdeshmukh et al., 2002), perceived usefulness (4 items) (Davis, 1989; Shin, 2007), social image (3 items) (Moore and

Benbasat, 1991; Sweeney and Soutar, 2001), brand name (4 items) (Brucks et al., 2000; Lau and Lee, 1999), perceived prestige (3 items) (Cornwell and Coote, 2005), perceived privacy risk (3 items) (Li, 2014), health information sensitivity (3 items) (Dinev et al., 2013). All the items were measured with Likert scales (from 1 = strongly disagree/never to 7 = strongly agree/always).

The study was conducted from January 2022 to March 2022, with participants recruited from the database of an experimental facility affiliated with a prominent Italian university. Participants were invited to complete a voluntary self-reported questionnaire. The study specifically targeted the most aware and responsive segment of the Wearable Technology (WT) industry in Italy. Participants belonged to the Gen Z demographic in Italy, characterized by individuals born between the mid-1990s and early 2010s. Notably, 86% of the participants reported using wearables to monitor at least one personal wellness-related aspect daily. This statistic is consistent with trends observed in other European countries. Despite this high awareness and usage among Gen Z respondents, the penetration rate of Wrist-Worn Devices (WWDs) in Italy stands at around 25%, indicating room for growth within the market. The focus on Gen Z users and non-users was deliberate, driven not only by their current significance within the industry but also by their projected importance in the global market by 2025. Gen Z is expected to represent a significant segment for products and services, both in the mid-term and long-term future. Therefore, exploring the antecedents of WWD intention to use for pervasive well-being among Gen Z users and non-users is essential for enhancing the value of the industry and addressing the evolving needs and preferences of this demographic cohort.

# 4  Results

The questionnaire was distributed among 331 Italian respondents aged 18 to 30, encompassing both wearable device owners and non-owners. From this distribution, 271 responses were collected. Respondents primarily belonged to the Gen Z segment, with an average age of slightly below 24 years old ($M_{age}$ = 23.59; SD = 1.68). Males comprised 53.1% of the respondents, while women accounted for the remaining 46.9%. Notably, 39.11% of respondents reported never owning a wearable device. The data collected were analyzed using Partial Least Squares – Structural Equation Modeling (PLS-SEM). PLS-SEM is a multivariate data analysis method that serves as a valid alternative to standard structural equation modeling, particularly suitable for exploratory research. It allows for the examination of relationships between a set of independent variables and multiple dependent variables. PLS-SEM enables researchers to explore complex relationships and make predictions based on the data collected. The estimations and data manipulations for this study were conducted using SmartPLS3, a widely used software tool for PLS-SEM analysis. Through this analytical approach, the study aims to elucidate the factors influencing the intention to use Wrist-Worn Devices (WWDs) for pervasive well-being monitoring among the Gen Z demographic in Italy.

Since the number of respondents was more than 10 times the largest number of structural paths directed to a latent construct, the sample size has been defined as satisfactory (Barclay et al., 1995). The number of iterations to find convergence was 6, suggesting the goodness of the model (Wong, 2013). We first examined the reliability and validity measures for the model constructs. Cronbach's alpha higher than 0.7 means high reliability and consistency of the questionnaire dimensions (Peterson, 1994). All the factors of the model respected this threshold, as summarized in Table 1. Additional indicators have been reported to consolidate the validity of our model, as shown in Table 1. The outcomes of the confirmatory factor analysis reveal that factor loadings were greater than 0.70, eventually explaining a high convergent validity (Appendix B). Composite reliability (CR) values were greater than 0.80, thus above the suggested threshold (Hundleby & Nunnally, 1968), which is an excellent consistency indicator. The average variance extracted (AVE) was greater than 0.50, ultimately demonstrating a strong capacity to explain variability (Chin, 1998).

**Table 1.** Reliability and validity analysis

| Construct | Composite Reliability | Average Variance Extracted (AVE) | Cronbach's Alpha |
| --- | --- | --- | --- |
| Brand Name | 0.732 | 0.529 | 0.714 |
| Health Information Sensitivity | 0.746 | 0.654 | 0.735 |
| Intention to Use | 0.876 | 0.728 | 0.875 |
| Perceived Prestige | 0.826 | 0.723 | 0.809 |
| Perceived Privacy Risk | 0.878 | 0.792 | 0.869 |
| Perceived Usefulness | 0.856 | 0.674 | 0.840 |
| Perceived Value | 0.845 | 0.763 | 0.845 |
| Social Image | 0.861 | 0.777 | 0.857 |

The measurement model exhibited a good fit, with a Standardized Root Mean Square Residual (SRMR) of 0.07. According to Hu & Bentler (1999), models with SRMR values below 0.08 are considered valid and free from misspecifications, aligning with our findings. Additionally, the model did not present critical collinearity issues among the measured constructs, as indicated by Variance Inflation Factor (VIF) coefficients below 5 (Hair et al., 2019). After model validation, the relationships among the constructs were tested through bootstrapping with 5,000 samples (Hair et al., 2019). Cross-validated redundancy values (Q2) for Intention to Use, Perceived Privacy Risk, Perceived Usefulness, Perceived Value, and Social Image were all above zero, indicating adequate reconstruction of observed values and predictive relevance (Henseler & Fassott, 2010). The structural model results, as shown in Table 2, confirm our hypotheses, with correlation coefficients supporting the proposed relationships. R Square and R Square Adjusted values (Table 4) were found to be adequate, as per Falk & Miller (1992). Specifically, Chin (1998) suggests thresholds of 0.19 for weak variance explanation, 0.33 for moderate, and 0.67 for substantial. In our model, the variance of the dependent variable (i.e., intention to use) is substantially explained, indicating a satisfying outcome. The proposed model demonstrates high predictive power regarding the adoption of Wrist-Worn Devices (WWDs), with an R square value of 0.689 for intention to use. This underscores the significance of social factors and privacy-related elements in WWD adoption, surpassing the influence of functional aspects.

**Table 2.** Model path analysis

| Construct | R Square | R Square Adjusted |
|---|---|---|
| Intention to Use | 0.682 | 0.679 |
| Perceived Privacy Risk | 0.553 | 0.551 |
| Perceived Usefulness | 0.138 | 0.135 |
| Perceived Value | 0.198 | 0.189 |
| Social Image | 0.267 | 0.264 |

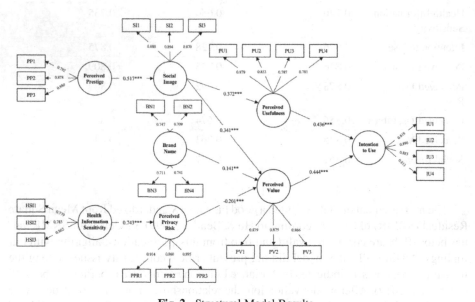

**Fig. 2.** Structural Model Results

As shown in Fig. 2, all the hypotheses proposed are supported. Results show that perceived prestige strongly influences social image. Perceived privacy risk is significantly affected by health information sensitivity, but its absolute impact on perceived value is anyway lower than social image. Perceived value is influenced by brand name. Social image has a direct influence on perceived usefulness. As expected, perceived usefulness and perceived value equally influence the intention to use when preceded by social factors. The resulting structural model is shown in Fig. 2.

# 5 Discussion

The paper contributes significantly to the discourse surrounding the benefits of wearable technologies for healthcare and well-being monitoring, particularly in terms of enhancing individual adoption of such devices. Through the development and testing of an enriched model, the study offers insights into the adoption of Wrist-Worn Devices (WWDs) for well-being monitoring, integrating both functional and social drivers of choice along with privacy factors. By leveraging established theories of adoption such as TAM (Davis, 1989), MPCU (Thompson et al., 1991), and IDT (Moore & Benbasat, 1991), the model provides a comprehensive framework for understanding the drivers of WWDs' use. The findings reveal that functional drivers exert a direct influence on the intention to use wearable devices when complemented by social and privacy-related factors. Perceived usefulness emerges as a robust determinant of intention to use WWDs, consistent with prior research (Chuah et al., 2016; Lee & Lee, 2018; Nasir & Yurder, 2015; Yang et al., 2016). This underscores the perception among individuals, including young demographics, that wearables serve as valuable tools for enhancing health and well-being. From a theoretical standpoint, despite critiques of TAM, the model demonstrates its validity in predicting technology adoption among individuals. The significance of perceived value on intention to use underscores the evaluation process individuals undertake when considering the adoption of WWDs, weighing the effort and time required to learn the technology against the perceived benefits it offers. This finding aligns with prior literature that identifies perceived value as a critical driver of technology adoption and continued usage (Yang et al., 2016).

The findings of the study underscore the significant influence of social factors on perceived usefulness and perceived value, highlighting the importance of affective elements in shaping individuals' interest in WWDs. Specifically, the results confirm that social image plays a pivotal role in influencing both perceived value and perceived usefulness, aligning with the hypothesis (H4) that wearable devices serve as symbols of status, tech-savviness, or fashionability (Choi & Kim, 2016). Moreover, the findings elucidate that social image is positively influenced by perceived prestige, which fosters self-identification within a community (Cornwell & Coote, 2005). Consequently, wearing WWDs may enhance self-esteem through affiliation with peer groups sharing similar needs. This insight is valuable for driving WWDs adoption, as it facilitates their acceptance within reference groups and accelerates their transition from niche products for innovators to mainstream items for a broader population. From both managerial and societal perspectives, this shift holds promise for disease prevention and self-monitoring, underscoring the broader benefits of WWDs adoption. Furthermore, the study reveals that brand name exerts a direct positive influence on perceived value, supporting hypothesis H5 and reaffirming previous findings (Brucks et al., 2000; Lau & Lee, 1999) in the domain of wearable technologies. This emphasizes the significance of social signaling in adoption processes and underscores the importance of brand recognition and reputation in shaping consumers' perceptions of WWDs.

Above social drivers, privacy risk emerges as a relevant inhibitor, confirming our H6, and showing a negative impact on the perceived value of the product. As wearable devices do collect data on daily user activities, the risk of data leakage is relevant. Perceived privacy risk is led by health information sensitivity, which is the degree of discomfort the individuals feel in revealing personal data to third parties. Thus, we confirm that the fear of personal data misusing is a relevant inhibitor in the field of WWDs. (Li, 2014).

## 6 Managerial Implications

The study underscores the importance of understanding the factors driving the intention to use smart wrist-worn wearable devices (WWDs), particularly in the context of fostering a health-conscious lifestyle. By elucidating the influential role of perceived value, perceived usefulness, and social components, the research provides valuable insights for companies operating in the wearable technology (WT) industry. Targeting the Gen Z segment, which represents a responsive and profitable market for WWD providers in Italy and Europe, holds significant potential for accelerating the adoption of WWDs and promoting health-conscious behaviors among individuals.

From a societal perspective, the widespread adoption of WWDs has the potential to yield substantial benefits, including easing pressure on healthcare systems, reducing long-term costs, and enhancing overall quality of life (Chianella, 2021). By fostering disease prevention and control and promoting personal safety, WWDs contribute to the well-being of individuals and the sustainability of healthcare systems, especially in the face of potential future pandemics like COVID-19 (Cohen et al., 2008). To effectively target Gen Z consumers, practitioners should employ marketing strategies that focus on enhancing social values and fostering community engagement around the adoption and use of WWDs. Stimulating peer-to-peer relationships and community building can be instrumental in driving adoption rates and cultivating a sense of belonging among users. Furthermore, practitioners can leverage elements that directly impact perceived usefulness and value, such as social image, brand name, and perceived privacy risk, to differentiate their offerings and attract diverse consumer segments. Strategies may include enhancing product aesthetics, partnering with the fashion industry, and implementing gamification techniques to incentivize usage and promote fitness goals. However, it is imperative to address privacy and security concerns associated with WWDs. Effective communication strategies should emphasize the benefits of WWDs while ensuring user privacy and implementing robust security measures. Close-ended data management systems can help mitigate privacy risks and enable companies to leverage collected data for targeted advertising, promotions, and retention strategies.

Innovative approaches, such as mood detection through physiological signals monitoring, present opportunities for the development of new technological ecosystems and personalized experiences for users. By integrating artificial intelligence, machine learning, and wearable technologies, companies can enhance user engagement and deliver tailored services that cater to individual preferences and needs.

## 7 Limitations and Future Research Avenues

From a theoretical perspective, our model contributes to the existing literature on the intention to use personal technology. Specifically, we have reexamined the Technology Acceptance Model (TAM) within the context of wearable devices designed for pervasive wellbeing. Drawing from other adoption frameworks such as the Model of PC

Utilization (MPCU) and the Innovation Diffusion Theory (IDT), we have expanded the scope of our analysis. Our model has been empirically tested on Generation Z, a demographic known for its openness to such technologies and potential for future growth. However, exploring adoption drivers across diverse demographics could yield valuable insights for promoting the use of Wearable Well-being Devices (WWDs) among a broader audience. Additionally, researchers might explore how societal and experiential values manifest as a technology becomes ingrained in collective consciousness, as evidenced by the mainstream integration of WWDs. This investigation could extend to other technological domains, examining whether hedonistic considerations influence adoption beyond merely fashionable items to include purely functional ones. Such inquiries carry sociological implications alongside business and marketing ramifications, potentially revealing disparities across industries, segments, and nations. Furthermore, we advocate for ongoing research into the sustained utilization of WWDs, as this would extend the applicability of our model across temporal dimensions. While our current focus lies in fostering awareness of WWDs for health-conscious living, continuous adoption can reinforce these benefits over time. Thus, our study represents an initial endeavor to elucidate how WWDs may effectively enhance both individual and societal health.

**Disclosure of Interests.** The authors have no competing interests to declare that are relevant to the content of this article.

# References

Abrams, D.: Social Identity, psychology of. In: International Encyclopedia of the Social & Behavioral Sciences, pp. 14306–14309 (2001). Elsevier. https://doi.org/10.1016/B0-08-043076-7/01728-9

Adapa, A., Nah, F.F.H., Hall, R.H., Siau, K., Smith, S.N.: Factors influencing the adoption of smart wearable devices. Int. J. Hum.-Comput. Interact. **34**(5), 399–409 (2018). https://doi.org/10.1080/10447318.2017.1357902

Al-Emran, M., Granić, A., Al-Sharafi, M.A., Ameen, N., Sarrab, M.: Examining the roles of students' beliefs and security concerns for using smartwatches in higher education. J. Enterp. Inf. Manag. **34**(4), 1229–1251 (2021). https://doi.org/10.1108/JEIM-02-2020-0052

Barclay, D., Thompson, R., dan Higgins, C.: The Partial Least Squares (PLS) approach to causal modeling: personal computer adoption and use an illustration. Technol. Stud. **2**, 285–309 (1995)

Belén del Río, A., Vázquez, R., Iglesias, V.: The role of the brand name in obtaining differential advantages. J. Prod. Brand. Manag. **10**(7), 452–465 (2001). https://doi.org/10.1108/EUM0000000006242

Bettiga, D., Lamberti, L., Lettieri, E.: Individuals' adoption of smart technologies for preventive health care: a structural equation modeling approach. Health Care Manag. Sci. **23**(2), 203–214 (2020). https://doi.org/10.1007/s10729-019-09468-2

Brucks, M., Zeithaml, V.A., Naylor, G.: Price and brand name as indicators of quality dimensions for consumer durables. J. Acad. Mark. Sci. **28**(3), 359–374 (2000). https://doi.org/10.1177/0092070300283005

Buenaflor, C., Kim, H.-C.: Six human factors to acceptability of wearable computers. Int. J. Multimedia Ubiquit. Eng. **8**(3), 103–114 (2013)

Chianella, R., Mandolfo, M., Lolatto, R., Pillan, M.: Designing for self-awareness: evidence-based explorations of multimodal stress-tracking wearables. In: Kurosu, M. (ed.) Human-Computer Interaction. Interaction Techniques and Novel Applications. LNCS, vol. 12763, pp. 357–371. Springer, Cham (2021). https://doi.org/10.1007/978-3-030-78465-2_27

Choi, J., Kim, S.: Is the smartwatch an IT product or a fashion product? A study on factors affecting the intention to use smartwatches. Comput. Hum. Behav. **63**, 777–786 (2016). https://doi.org/10.1016/j.chb.2016.06.007

Chouk, I., Mani, Z.: Does the learning ability of smart products lead to user resistance? J. Eng. Tech. Manage. **66**, 101706 (2022). https://doi.org/10.1016/j.jengtecman.2022.101706

Chuah, S.H.-W., Rauschnabel, P.A., Krey, N., Nguyen, B., Ramayah, T., Lade, S.: Wearable technologies: the role of usefulness and visibility in smartwatch adoption. Comput. Hum. Behav. **65**, 276–284 (2016). https://doi.org/10.1016/j.chb.2016.07.047

Cohen, J.T., Neumann, P.J., Weinstein, M.C.: Does preventive care save money? Health economics and the presidential candidates. N. Engl. J. Med. **358**(7), 661–663 (2008). https://doi.org/10.1056/NEJMp0708558

Cornwell, T.B., Coote, L.V.: Corporate sponsorship of a cause: the role of identification in purchase intent. J. Bus. Res. **58**(3 SPEC. ISS.), 268–276 (2005). https://doi.org/10.1016/S0148-2963(03)00135-8

Davis, F.D.: Perceived usefulness, perceived ease of use, and user acceptance of information technology. MIS Q. Manag. Inf. Syst. **13**(3), 319–339 (1989). https://doi.org/10.2307/249008

Dehghani, M., Kim, K.J., Dangelico, R.M.: Will smartwatches last? Factors contributing to intention to keep using smart wearable technology. Telematics Inform. **35**(2), 480–490 (2018). https://doi.org/10.1016/j.tele.2018.01.007

Dholakia, U.M.: Three senses of desire in consumer research. SSRN Electron. J. (2014). https://doi.org/10.2139/ssrn.2420250

Dinev, T., Xu, H., Smith, J.H., Hart, P.: Information privacy and correlates: an empirical attempt to bridge and distinguish privacy-related concepts. Eur. J. Inf. Syst. **22**(3), 295–316 (2013). https://doi.org/10.1057/ejis.2012.23

Falk, R.F., Miller, N.B.: A Primer for Soft Modeling. University of Akron Press (1992)

Featherman, M.S., Pavlou, P.A.: Predicting e-services adoption: a perceived risk facets perspective. Int. J. Hum. Comput. Stud. **59**(4), 451–474 (2003). https://doi.org/10.1016/S1071-5819(03)00111-3

Hair, J.F., Risher, J.J., Sarstedt, M., Ringle, C.M.: When to use and how to report the results of PLS-SEM. Eur. Bus. Rev. **31**(1), 2–24 (2019). https://doi.org/10.1108/EBR-11-2018-0203

Henseler, J., Fassott, G.: Testing moderating effects in PLS path models: an illustration of available procedures. In: Esposito Vinzi, V., Chin, W., Henseler, J., Wang, H. (eds.) Handbook of Partial Least Squares, pp. 713–735. Springer, Heidelberg (2010). https://doi.org/10.1007/978-3-540-32827-8_31

Hsu, C.-L., Lin, J.C.-C.: What drives purchase intention for paid mobile apps? – An expectation confirmation model with perceived value. Electron. Commer. Res. Appl. **14**(1), 46–57 (2015). https://doi.org/10.1016/j.elerap.2014.11.003

Hu, L., Bentler, P.M.: Cutoff criteria for fit indexes in covariance structure analysis: conventional criteria versus new alternatives. Struct. Equ. Model. **6**(1), 1–55 (1999). https://doi.org/10.1080/10705519909540118

Huarng, K.H., Yu, T.H.K., Lee, C.F.: Adoption model of healthcare wearable devices. Technol. Forecast. Soc. Change **174** (2022). https://doi.org/10.1016/j.techfore.2021.121286

Hundleby, J.D., Nunnally, J.: Psychometric theory. Am. Educ. Res. J. **5**(3), 431 (1968). https://doi.org/10.2307/1161962

Johnson, K.T., Picard, R.W.: Advancing neuroscience through wearable devices. Neuron **108**(1), 8–12 (2020). https://doi.org/10.1016/j.neuron.2020.09.030

Jung, Y., Kim, S., Choi, B.: Consumer valuation of the wearables: the case of smartwatches. Comput. Hum. Behav. **63**, 899–905 (2016). https://doi.org/10.1016/j.chb.2016.06.040

Kalantari, M., Rauschnabel, P.: Exploring the early adopters of augmented reality smart glasses: the case of Microsoft HoloLens. In: Jung, T., tom Dieck, M.C. (eds.) Augmented Reality and

Virtual Reality. PI, pp. 229–245. Springer, Cham (2018). https://doi.org/10.1007/978-3-319-64027-3_16

Lannon, J., Cooper, P.: Humanistic advertising. Int. J. Advert. **2**(3), 195–213 (1983). https://doi.org/10.1080/02650487.1983.11104974

Lau, G.T., Lee, S.H.: Consumers' trust in a brand and the link to brand loyalty. J. Mark.-Focus. Manag. **4**(4), 341–370 (1999). https://doi.org/10.1023/A:1009886520142

Lee, S.Y., Lee, K.: Factors that influence an individual's intention to adopt a wearable healthcare device: the case of a wearable fitness tracker. Technol. Forecast. Soc. Chang. **129**, 154–163 (2018). https://doi.org/10.1016/j.techfore.2018.01.002

Li, H., Wu, J., Gao, Y., Shi, Y.: Examining individuals' adoption of healthcare wearable devices: an empirical study from privacy calculus perspective. Int. J. Med. Inform. **88**, 8–17 (2016). https://doi.org/10.1016/j.ijmedinf.2015.12.010

Li, Y.: The impact of disposition to privacy, website reputation and website familiarity on information privacy concerns. Decis. Support. Syst. **57**, 343–354 (2014). https://doi.org/10.1016/j.dss.2013.09.018

Malhotra, N.K., Kim, S.S., Agarwal, J.: Internet users' information privacy concerns (IUIPC): the construct, the scale, and a causal model. Inf. Syst. Res. **15**(4), 336–355 (2004). https://doi.org/10.1287/isre.1040.0032

Milne, G.R., Gordon, M.E.: Direct mail privacy-efficiency trade-offs within an implied social contract framework. J. Public Policy Mark. **12**(2), 206–215 (1993). https://doi.org/10.1177/074391569101200206

Moore, G.C., Benbasat, I.: Development of an instrument to measure the perceptions of adopting an information technology innovation. Inf. Syst. Res. **2**(3), 192–222 (1991). https://doi.org/10.1287/isre.2.3.192

Nascimento, B., Oliveira, T., Tam, C.: Wearable technology: what explains continuance intention in smartwatches? J. Retail. Consum. Serv. **43**, 157–169 (2018). https://doi.org/10.1016/j.jretconser.2018.03.017

Nasir, S., Yurder, Y.: Consumers' and physicians' perceptions about high tech wearable health products. Procedia Soc. Behav. Sci. **195**, 1261–1267 (2015). https://doi.org/10.1016/j.sbspro.2015.06.279

Niknejad, N., Ismail, W.B., Mardani, A., Liao, H., Ghani, I.: A comprehensive overview of smart wearables: the state of the art literature, recent advances, and future challenges. Eng. Appl. Artif. Intell. **90** (2020). https://doi.org/10.1016/j.engappai.2020.103529

Ometov, A., et al.: A survey on wearable technology: history, state-of-the-art and current challenges. Comput. Netw. **193** (2021). https://doi.org/10.1016/j.comnet.2021.108074

Pancar, T., Ozkan Yildirim, S.: Exploring factors affecting consumers' adoption of wearable devices to track health data. Univ. Access Inf. Soc. **22**(2), 331–349 (2023). https://doi.org/10.1007/s10209-021-00848-6

Peterson, R.A.: A meta-analysis of Cronbach's coefficient alpha. J. Consum. Res. **21**(2), 381 (1994). https://doi.org/10.1086/209405

Ruotsalainen, P.S., Blobel, B.G., Seppälä, A.V., Sorvari, H.O., Nykänen, P.A.: A conceptual framework and principles for trusted pervasive health. J. Med. Internet Res. **14**(2), 3–14 (2012). https://doi.org/10.2196/jmir.1972

Sheth, J.N., Newman, B.I., Gross, B.L.: Why we buy what we buy: a theory of consumption values, vol. 22 (1991)

Shin, D.-H.: User acceptance of mobile Internet: implication for convergence technologies. Interact. Comput. **19**(4), 472–483 (2007). https://doi.org/10.1016/j.intcom.2007.04.001

Siepmann, C., Kowalczuk, P.: Understanding continued smartwatch usage: the role of emotional as well as health and fitness factors (2021). https://doi.org/10.1007/s12525-021-00458-3/Published

Sirdeshmukh, D., Singh, J., Sabol, B.: Consumer trust, value, and loyalty in relational exchanges. J. Mark. **66**(1), 15–37 (2002). https://doi.org/10.1509/jmkg.66.1.15.18449

Smith, J.B., Colgate, M.: Customer value creation: a practical framework. J. Market. Theory Pract. **15**(1), 7–23 (2007). https://doi.org/10.2753/MTP1069-6679150101

Spagnolli, A., Guardigli, E., Orso, V., Varotto, A., Gamberini, L.: Measuring user acceptance of wearable symbiotic devices: validation study across application scenarios. In: Jacucci, G., Gamberini, L., Freeman, J., Spagnolli, A. (eds.) Symbiotic Interaction. LNCS, vol. 8820, pp. 87–98. Springer, Cham (2014). https://doi.org/10.1007/978-3-319-13500-7_7

Sweeney, J.C., Soutar, G.N.: Consumer perceived value: the development of a multiple item scale. J. Retail. **77**(2), 203–220 (2001). https://doi.org/10.1016/S0022-4359(01)00041-0

Taherdoost, H.: A review of technology acceptance and adoption models and theories. Procedia Manufact. **22**, 960–967 (2018). https://doi.org/10.1016/j.promfg.2018.03.137

Tani, M., Troise, C., O'Driscoll, A.: Business model innovation in mobile apps market: exploring the new subscription plans with a behavioral reasoning perspective. J. Eng. Tech. Manage. **63**, 101674 (2022). https://doi.org/10.1016/j.jengtecman.2022.101674

Thompson, R.L., Higgins, C.A., Howell, J.M.: Personal computing: toward a conceptual model of utilization utilization of personal computers personal computing: toward a conceptual model of utilization. MIS Q. **15**(1) (1991)

Truong, Y., McColl, R., Kitchen, P.J.: New luxury brand positioning and the emergence of Masstige brands. J. Brand Manag. **16**(5–6), 375–382 (2009). https://doi.org/10.1057/bm.2009.1

van der Heijden: User acceptance of hedonic information systems. MIS Q. **28**(4), 695 (2004). https://doi.org/10.2307/25148660

Venkatesh, V., Bala, H.: Technology acceptance model 3 and a research agenda on interventions. Decis. Sci. **39**(2), 273–315 (2008). https://doi.org/10.1111/j.1540-5915.2008.00192.x

Venkatesh, V., Davis, F.D.: A theoretical extension of the technology acceptance model: four longitudinal field studies **46**(2) (2000). https://about.jstor.org/terms

Wong, K.K.K.: Partial least squares structural equation modeling (PLS-SEM) techniques using SmartPLS. Market. Bull. **24**, 1–32 (2013)

Chin, W.W.: Commentary: issues and opinion on structural equation modeling. MIS Q. **22**, 7–16 (1998)

Yang, H., Yu, J., Zo, H., Choi, M.: User acceptance of wearable devices: an extended perspective of perceived value. Telematics Inform. **33**(2), 256–269 (2016). https://doi.org/10.1016/j.tele.2015.08.007

# Engagement of Electronic Word-of-Mouth on M-Health Platforms

Meiling Hong(✉), Xu Huang, and Zhenfeng Ge

Ningbo University of Finance and Econom Ics, Ningbo, Zhejiang, China
hongmeiling@nbufe.edu.cn

**Abstract.** The demand for online health consultations has exploded since the COVID-19 pandemic. Hence, electronic word-of-mouth is essential to obtaining information and reducing uncertainty for potential customers on mobile health platform. Based on an internet-based survey of 552 people from Zhejiang Province, China, this study investigated the influencing factors of electronic word-of-mouth on mobile health applications. The research model and related hypotheses were verified by linear regression models. We found that electronic word-of-mouth was influenced by electronic health literacy, perceived usefulness, the preference for positive comments, and the preference for physicians with advanced titles. Perceived usefulness partly mediated the relationship between electronic health literacy and electronic word-of-mouth. Furthermore, the preference for consulting physicians with more advanced titles and backgrounds positively moderated the relationship between electronic health literacy and electronic word-of-mouth. The empirical results offer insights on whether and how mobile health service platforms could serve patients better in the digital era.

**Keywords:** Mobile health · Electronic health literacy · Electronic word-of-mouth

## 1 Introduction

The COVID-19 pandemic boosted the rapid growth of mobile health consultation demand by forcing people to accelerate digital space access [1], which led to a greater focus on mobile healthcare in recent years. Many patients use mobile consultations to obtain preliminary health knowledge before going to an offline medical treatment or to obtain additional medical information. Additionally, mobile health consultation platforms encourage customers to share opinions via recommendations, ratings, and reviews across diverse service categories, which leads to the engagement of electronic word-of-mouth (eWOM). Previous survey shows that eWOM plays an important role in decision-making [2, 3]. Considering the high information asymmetry in the healthcare service industry, potential customers need to check reviews and comments on mobile healthcare service platforms to know other people's opinions about the services [4, 5].

However, there are two research gaps in the mobile health eWOM literature. First, most studies focus on how eWOM influences customers' decision-making but do not

J. Wei and G. Margetis (Eds.): HCII 2024, LNCS 14737, pp. 31–44, 2024.
https://doi.org/10.1007/978-3-031-60458-4_3

reveal whether users create eWOM or not. Second, most empirical studies only use online healthcare platforms as sample boundaries and ignore the regional differences in the development of the digital economy. To address these research gaps, we used detailed data collected from the most digitally developed area in China, Zhejiang Province, to investigate why people create eWOM. We analyzed the influencing factors of electronic word-of-mouth engagement on mobile health platform including the demographic variables, electronic health (e-health) literacy, perceived usefulness, positive comments preference, and high title doctor preference. It is hope that empirical results can provide insights on whether and how mobile health service platforms could serve patients better in the digital era.

## 2   Conceptual Model and Hypotheses

### 2.1   Conceptual Model

Combined with the previous studies and research on eWOM, this study aims to test the eWOM model based on electronic health (e-health) literacy, perceived usefulness, positive comments preference, and high title doctor preference (Fig. 1 below).

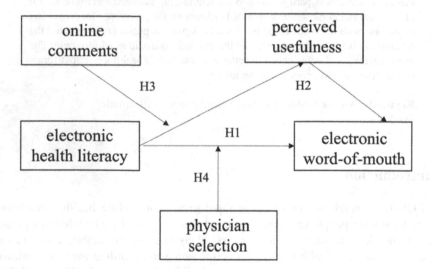

**Fig. 1.** Moderated mediation model of electronic health literacy, perceived usefulness, and electronic word-of-mouth

### 2.2   Hypotheses

**Electronic Health Literacy, Perceived Usefulness, and Electronic Word of Mouth.**  Health literacy is the set of competencies required for individuals to identify health information needs, identify possible information sources, and use them to retrieve relevant information, assess the quality of information, and apply it to specific situations [6, 7]. With the development of information technology, health literacy has undergone dynamic development, and a series of similar concepts have been derived. For example, media health literacy, digital health literacy, and e-health literacy are similar concepts, among which e-health literacy and its related research provide rich content and results. The e-health literacy focuses on the application of digital technology in health, which refers to the ability to use digital technology to search, select, evaluate, and apply online health information to then interact with physicians or service providers online [6, 7]. Accordingly, the e-Health Literacy Scale (eHEALS) is the first e-health literacy assessment tool that measures individuals' self-perceived skills in seeking and applying online health knowledge. Those with high e-Health literacy can actively choose to read and trust highly accurate reviews with high content quality and have higher satisfaction with post-decision healthcare. Groups with higher e-health literacy are therefore more likely to use the Internet and social media to access and share health information. Conversely, when individuals lack e-health literacy, they are more likely to obtain health information from social networking sites but are unable to effectively discern the accuracy of the information, have a lower sense of perceived usefulness after using online consultation services, and are less likely to generate word-of-mouth recommendations.

Word-of-mouth (WOM) is defined as a channel for communicating information about a product or service [8], which usually includes positive reviews and publicity. With the explosive growth of the internet, e-commerce has gradually become a tactical highlight concerning businesses and consumers, and the interest in the phenomenon of WOM has been redefined as eWOM [9, 10], which are available to a multitude of individuals and organizations through the web [11, 12]. This information is sometimes perceived as a more trustworthy source than general advertising [13]. On the one hand, word-of-mouth engagement means taking responsibility, because the information delivered through word-of-mouth is directed to people with whom one has strong social ties, such as relatives, friends, or colleagues, and is highly likely to promote purchase behavior.

On the other hand, people with lower education background fail to accurately describe discomfort symptoms or assess the effectiveness of the physician's medical advice. Therefore, customers need to evaluate the service through some marginal information and are more inclined to provide an evaluation [14]. For example, patients will be grateful for the effort and patience of the doctor and will leave positive comments on the service platform to express gratitude to the doctor or share their experience with the service. As a result, when customers have a positive experience using the service and are satisfied in terms of functional or emotional values, such as a timely response to a health consultation, they are more likely to engage in eWOM by leaving detailed and positive comments on the platform and recommending them to a wider group of people [13, 15, 16]. Therefore, hypotheses 1 and 2 are proposed:

H1: e-Health literacy positively impacts eWOM engagement toward mobile health services.
H2: e-Health literacy positively impacts eWOM engagement toward mobile health services indirectly through perceived usefulness.

**The Moderating Effect of Online Comments Preference.** Medical and health consultations are highly specialized, and it can be challenging for customers to make decisions. One effective way to find out whether a mobile health consultation is useful is to check the previous customer reviews. However, for potential consumers, the huge number of reviews can be overwhelming [17]. They need to filter "useful" reviews based on specific criteria to find essential information which leads to purchase decisions [18]. At the same time, most mobile health platforms provide filter functions, such as prioritizing the display of high-rated customer comments. Reviewing positive comments only makes potential customers develop similar attitudes or expectations, which in turn triggers users' use or purchase behavior. Specifically, strongly positive ratings can positively influence sales growth [19]. However, positive comments screening preferences cannot guarantee consultation quality and satisfaction. On the one hand, when viewing high-rated reviews or reviews with positive affective tendencies, potential customers have higher expectations about the value of the service they are about to receive [20]. Therefore, after receiving the service, if it does not reach the expectation as that shown in the positive reviews, customers will regret their decision and not even mention that enhancing perceived usefulness. On the other hand, customers will also mitigate review homogeneity by intentionally providing lower reviews. Once they find that there are many positive comments on a platform, they will leave lower ratings [21]. Therefore, hypothesis 3 is proposed:

H3: The positive relationship between e-health literacy and perceived usefulness is negatively moderated by online comments preferences, such that the positive relationship is weaker (i.e., less positive) when the preference for looking up positive reviews is higher.

The moderating effect of preference for physicians. Physicians' titles and qualifications are evaluated by the government according to the physician's professional abilities. Potential customers assume that if the physician is theoretically proficient and has had a great deal of experience, they would have a high title [3]. Physicians' titles endorse the physician's reputation and play a crucial role in the patient's selection of their physician [22]. Therefore, mobile health consultation platforms display physicians' titles and personal profiles. As far as the current situation is concerned, the content of the personal profile varies. For some physicians, there are few words about their working experience and expertise areas. While others have detailed profiles, introducing education experience (even disclosing supervisors during graduate school), publications and current research work, and so forth. Because of the uneven disclosure of physicians' profiles on the same platform, this study only chose the title as a reflection of the physician's reputation. At present, among China's health professional and technical personnel title evaluation system, the titles of medical categories at all levels are medical nurse, physician, attending (supervising) physician, deputy chief physician, and chief physician. The chief physician is considered to have higher professional competence and richer experience in hospital work [23], and more skills in communicating with patients and providing clear medical solutions during their years of work, which has a significant promotion effect on users' online behaviors (e.g., consultation and evaluation) [24]. Therefore, users are more likely to engage in proactive messaging behaviors and generate eWOM when they have high-title physician screening preferences. Therefore, hypothesis is proposed:

H4: The relationship between e-Health literacy and eWOM is positively moderated by physician selection preference, such that the positive relationship is stronger (i.e., more positive) when users prefer to select physicians with higher titles.

## 3   Data and Method

### 3.1   Data Collection

The data collection work of this study was conducted from July 2021 to December 2021. All sample data was collected via the online platform Credamo, which is widely accepted for data collection at home and abroad [25] for its accuracy in sampling and quality control. For this research, we distributed 800 questionnaires and received 652 valid questionnaires; 100 were used in the pilot test, and 552 were used in the formal test.

To reflect the respondents' mobile health services, use, we used the following methods. First, questionnaires were sent via mobile phones, while excluding the samples of questionnaires with answers completed on a PC to ensure that respondents had the basis and habit of using mobile services. Second, before starting the questionnaire, respondents were asked whether they had used mobile health services, and those who only answered "yes" would continue with the follow-up questions. Third, considering the influence of geographic location on digital skills and health literacy [26], we collected data from Zhejiang Province, the most digitally developed region in China. Since the end of 2017, Zhejiang Province has given priority to developing digital economy and accelerated its pace of using digital tools to boost industrial upgrading. According to the White Paper on Zhejiang's Digital Economy Development (2022), the value added by the digital economy of the province reached 3.57 trillion-yuan last year, notching 48.6 percent of its Gross Domestic Product (GDP).

### 3.2   Measurement Tools and Pre-Test

The survey is based on previously validated scales. The specific scale items, as well as relevant references, are listed in Table 1. All variables were evaluated using a 5-point Likert scale, with 1 indicating "*strongly disagree*" and 5 indicating "*strongly agree.*" To avoid the influence of other control variables, genders, ages, incomes, education, and occupations were chosen as covariates in this study.

The scales we used had originally been developed in English. We translated them into Chinese while publishing the questionnaires, to make the questionnaires fit the context of China and the Chinese language style. Therefore, to guarantee the reliability of the scales, we conducted pilot studies with 100 valid questionnaires. As shown in Table 2, the reliability of all variables was above 0.6, which means the scales are trustworthy.

The validity of the scales is presented in Table 3. Most KMO values are over 0.6, indicating that all items can perform factor analysis

Furthermore, we conducted a factor analysis to test the validity of scale structure. According to the results shown in Table 4, there are five factors consistent with the original settings.

**Table 1.** Variable indicators

| Variables | Numbers | Items | References |
|---|---|---|---|
| Electronic health literacy | EH1 | I know how to find helpful health resources on the Internet | Norman & Skinner, 2006 [6] |
| | EH2 | I know how to use the Internet to answer my health questions | |
| | EH3 | I know what health resources are available on the Internet | |
| | EH4 | I know where to find helpful health resources on the Internet | |
| | EH5 | I know how to use the health information I find on the Internet to help me | |
| | EH6 | I have the skills I need to evaluate the health resources I find on the Internet | |
| | EH7 | I can tell high quality from low quality health resources on the Internet | |
| | EH8 | I feel confident in using information from the Internet to make health decisions | |
| Perceived usefulness | PU1 | The mobile internet-based health service platform is useful for searching and obtaining the information I need | Yoon, 2009 [29]; Bhattacherjee & Premkumar, 2004 [30] |
| | PU2 | The mobile internet-based health service platform enhances my effectiveness in obtaining healthcare services | |
| | PU3 | The mobile internet-based health service platform enables me to get healthcare services faster | |

*(continued)*

**Table 1.** (*continued*)

| Variables | Numbers | Items | References |
|---|---|---|---|
| | PU4 | Using mobile internet-based health service platform will improve my performance | |
| | PU5 | Using mobile internet-based health service platform will increase my productivity during health service process | |
| Electronic word-of-mouth | eWOM1 | I am willing to recommend MIHS to others | Kim, et al., 2001 [31];Singh, 1990 [32] |
| | eWOM2 | I will tell the other person that MIHS is very good | |
| | eWOM3 | I am willing to tell other people about the good aspects of MIHS | |
| | eWOM4 | I have told my friends and relatives about my good experience of using MIHS | |
| | eWOM5 | I will mention how good the service of MIHS is to others quite frequently | |
| | eWOM6 | I am proud to tell others that I use the MIHS service | |
| Online comments | OC1 | I prefer to read online comments that are positive | Yang et al., 2015 [8] |
| | OC2 | I prefer to read comments by customers who highly rated the service | |
| | OC3 | I prefer to read online comments before making purchase decision | |
| Physician selection | PS1 | I prefer to choose physicians who work at a reputable hospital | Yang et al., 2019 [28] |

(*continued*)

**Table 1.** (*continued*)

| Variables | Numbers | Items | References |
|---|---|---|---|
| | PS2 | I prefer to choose physicians with high titles | |
| | PS3 | I prefer to choose physicians who are experienced | |

MIHS: patient-oriented Mobile Internet-based Health Service

**Table 2.** Reliability analysis of pilot test

| Items | Cronbach's Alpha | N |
|---|---|---|
| Electronic health literacy | 0.845 | 8 |
| Perceived usefulness | 0.690 | 4 |
| Electronic word-of-mouth | 0.818 | 6 |
| Online comments | 0.832 | 3 |
| Physician selection | 0.684 | 3 |

**Table 3.** KMO and Bartlett's test

| Item | KMO coefficient | Significance of Bartlett's test |
|---|---|---|
| Electronic health literacy | 0.847 | 0.000 |
| Perceived usefulness | 0.706 | 0.000 |
| Electronic word-of-mouth | 0.832 | 0.000 |
| Online comments | 0.607 | 0.000 |

# 4   Results

## 4.1   Demographic Statistics Analysis

Among 552 survey participants, 64.4% of them were female and 35.6% were male. There were more female participants in the mobile health service survey. One of the reasons is that digital labor is showing a gendered division in urban China [27]. Women are more likely to utilize mobile health platforms for their family's health consultations. Moreover, over 68% of respondents were under 30 and most of the participants were well-educated. Additionally, 47% of the participants' monthly incomes were between 3001–7000 RMB.

**Table 4.** Rotated component matrix

|  | Component | | | | |
|---|---|---|---|---|---|
|  | 1 | 2 | 3 | 4 | 5 |
| EH1 | 0.697 | | | | |
| EH2 | 0.679 | | | | |
| EH3 | 0.705 | | | | |
| EH5 | 0.636 | | | | |
| EH6 | 0.686 | | | | |
| EH4 | 0.74 | | | | |
| EH7 | 0.693 | | | | |
| EH8 | 0.641 | | | | |
| WOM1 | | 0.699 | | | |
| WOM2 | | 0.729 | | | |
| WOM3 | | 0.736 | | | |
| WOM4 | | 0.533 | | | |
| WOM5 | | 0.691 | | | |
| WOM6 | | 0.744 | | | |
| PU1 | | | 0.492 | | |
| PU2 | | | 0.694 | | |
| PU3 | | | 0.629 | | |
| PU4 | | | 0.592 | | |
| PS1 | | | | 0.809 | |
| PS2 | | | | 0.665 | |
| PS3 | | | | 0.82 | |
| OC1 | | | | | 0.708 |
| OC2 | | | | | 0.943 |
| OC3 | | | | | 0.93 |

## 4.2 Main Effect and the Mediating Effect

As shown in Table 5, the significance of model 1 was less than 0.05 and reached the significance level. According to the regression results, the significance level of eWOM was less than 0.05. In model 2, both e-health literacy and perceived usefulness had a significant and positive influence on eWOM. Comparing model 2 with model 1, the coefficients of e-health literacy changed from 0.657 to 0.359. The decrease of the coefficient testified that perceived usefulness had a partial mediating effect on the relationship between e-health literacy and eWOM. Hypotheses 1 and 2 were supported.

**Table 5.** Regression of electronic health literacy, perceived usefulness, and electronic word-of-mouth

| Models | Unstandardized coefficients | | Standardized coefficients | t | sig |
|---|---|---|---|---|---|
| | B | Standard error | Beta | | |
| Model 1 | | | | | |
| (Constant) | 1.376 | 0.145 | | 9.511 | 0.000 |
| Electronic health literacy | 0.657 | 0.037 | 0.613 | 17.684 | 0.000 |
| R | | | 0.613 | | |
| R Square | | | 0.376 | | |
| Adjusted R Square | | | 0.374 | | |
| Std. Error of the Estimate | | | 0.561 | | |
| F | | | 312.738 | | |
| P | | | 0.000 | | |
| **Model 2** | | | | | |
| (Constant) | 0.193 | 0.168 | | 1.148 | 0.251 |
| Electronic health literacy | 0.359 | 0.043 | 0.335 | 8.391 | 0.000 |
| Perceived usefulness | 0.565 | 0.051 | 0.444 | 11.133 | 0.000 |
| R | | | 0.704 | | |
| R Square | | | 0.496 | | |
| Adjusted R Square | | | 0.494 | | |
| Std. Error of the Estimate | | | 0.505 | | |
| F | | | 255.314 | | |
| P | | | 0.000 | | |

## 4.3 Moderating Effect

According to the result, review screening preference showed no negative moderating effect on the relationship between e-health literacy and perceived usefulness. As can be seen from Table 6, in model 3, e-health literacy showed an independent significant effect on perceived usefulness (t = -18.259, p = 0.000 < 0.05). However, the interactive variable of term between e-health literacy and review screening showed an insignificant effect on perceived usefulness (t = 0.053, p = 0.957 > 0.05). Hypothesis 3, the negative moderating effect of online comments was not supported.

**Table 6.** Moderating effect of online comments

|  | Model 3 | Model 4 | Model 5 |
|---|---|---|---|
| Constant | 4.116** | 4.116** | 4.116** |
|  | (−215.449) | (−215.243) | (−214.657) |
| Electronic health literacy | 0.527** | 0.527** | 0.527** |
|  | (−18.259) | (−18.209) | (−18.181) |
| Review screening |  | −0.002 | −0.002 |
|  |  | (−0.060) | (−0.063) |
| Electronic health literacy*Online Comments |  |  | 0.003 |
|  |  |  | (−0.053) |
| $R$ Square | 0.391 | 0.391 | 0.391 |
| Adj. $R$ Square | 0.39 | 0.388 | 0.387 |
| $F$ | $F(1,520) = 333.407, p = 0.000$ | $F(2,519) = 166.386, p = 0.000$ | $F(3,518) = 110.712, p = 0.000$ |
| $\Delta R$ Square | 0.391 | 0 | 0 |
| $\Delta F$ | $F(1,520) = 333.407, p = 0.000$ | $F(1,519) = 0.004, p = 0.953$ | $F(1,518) = 0.003, p = 0.957$ |

Dependent Variable: Perceived usefulness.
* $p < 0.05$ ** $p < 0.01$ t statistics in parentheses

According to the result, physician selection showed a positive moderating effect. As shown in Table 7, the moderating effect test was divided into three models. Model 6 only included the independent variable, e-health literacy. Model 7 added the moderating variable, physician selection to model 6, and model 8 added the interaction term (e-health literacy*physician selection) to model 7. For model 6, the purpose was to investigate the effect of the independent variable (e-health literacy) on the dependent variable (eWOM) when the interference of the moderating variable (physician selection) was not considered. As can be seen from Table 7, e-health literacy had a significant relationship with eWOM (t = 17.684, p = 0.000 < 0.05). The interactive variable of e-health literacy and physician selection showed a significant effect on eWOM (t = 2.416, p = 0.016 < 0.05). Hypothesis 4, the relationship between e-Health literacy and eWOM is positively moderated by physician selection preference is supported.

**Table 7.** Moderating effect of physician selection (n = 522)

| | Model 6 | Model 7 | Model 8 |
|---|---|---|---|
| Constant | 3.897** (158.490) | 3.897** (160.519) | 3.878** (153.006) |
| Electronic health literacy | 0.657** (17.684) | 0.614** (15.959) | 0.612** (15.983) |
| Physician selection | | 0.169** (3.795) | 0.181** (4.058) |
| Electronic health literacy*Physician selection | | | 0.163* (2.416) |
| R Square | 0.376 | 0.392 | 0.399 |
| Adj. R Square | 0.374 | 0.39 | 0.396 |
| F | $F_{(1,520)} = 312.738, p = 0.000$ | $F_{(2,519)} = 167.599, p = 0.000$ | $F_{(3,518)} = 114.721, p = 0.000$ |
| $\Delta$R Square | 0.376 | 0.017 | 0.007 |
| $\Delta$F | $F_{(1,520)} = 312.738, p = 0.000$ | $F_{(1,519)} = 14.401, p = 0.000$ | $F_{(1,518)} = 5.839, p = 0.016$ |

Dependent Variable: eWOM.
* $p < 0.05$ ** $p < 0.01$ t statistics in parentheses

## 5   Discussion and Conclusion

Overall, this study is the first to consider the regional variance on the digital economy level while examining eWOM engagement in the post-COVID-19 period. Based on an internet-based survey of 552 users from one of the most advanced regions of the digital economy of China, Zhejiang Province, we investigated the main factors of eWOM in m-health consultation services. We found that eWOM engagement was influenced by e-health literacy, perceived usefulness, and a preference for doctors with more advanced titles. The perceived usefulness partly mediated the relationship between e-health literacy and eWOM. The preference for consulting doctors with more advanced titles positively moderated the relationship between e-health literacy and eWOM. This research provides theoretical insights into whether and how m-health service platforms could facilitate indicators of eWOM engagement in an online health consultation context.

In future studies, we suggest multiple measurements of e-health literacy. There is a gap between real e-health literacy and self-reported level. Therefore, some experimental tools and methods can be used to bridge the measurement gap in the future. Meanwhile, we can conduct more detailed and targeted research based on various healthcare needs and special groups, such as the generation mechanism of eWOM in the context of traditional Chinese medicine consultation services in Asia.

**Acknowledgement.** This research was supported by the following funding: Yongjiang Social Science Young Talent Grant (2022), Chinese National Funding of Social Sciences (No. 23BJY134), and the Philosophy and Social Science Research Base Project of Ningbo (No. JD6–013).

# References

1. Barnes, S.J.: Information management research and practice in the post-covid-19 world. Int. J. Inf. Manage. **55**, 102175 (2020)
2. Smith, A., Anderson, M.: Online shopping and e-commerce. Pew Research Center (2016)
3. Liu, X., Guo, X., Wu, H., Wu, T.: The impact of individual and organizational reputation on physicians' appointments online. Int. J. Electron. Commer. **20**(4), 551–577 (2016). https://doi.org/10.1080/10864415.2016.1171977
4. Gupta, P., Harris, J.: How E-Wom recommendations influence product consideration and quality of choice: a motivation to process information perspective. J. Bus. Res. **63**(9–10), 1041–1049 (2010)
5. Lee, E., Han, S.: Determinants of adoption of mobile health services. Online Inf. Rev. **39**(4), 556–573 (2015). https://doi.org/10.1108/OIR-01-2015-0007
6. Norman, C.D., Skinner, H.A.: Eheals: The Ehealth Literacy Scale. J. Med. Internet Res. **8**(4), e507 (2006)
7. Neter, E., Brainin, E.: Ehealth literacy: extending the digital divide to the realm of health information. J. Med. Internet Res. **14**(1), e1619 (2012)
8. Yang, L., Cheng, Q., Tong, S.: 8 - Empirical study of Ewom's influence on consumers' purchase decisions. In: Yang, H., Morgan, S.L., Wang, Y., (eds.) The Strategies of China's Firms. Chandos Publishing, pp. 123–135 (2015)
9. Fu, J.-R., Ju, P.-H., Hsu, C.-W.: Understanding why consumers engage in electronic word-of-mouth communication: perspectives from theory of planned behavior and justice theory. Electron. Commer. Res. Appl. **14**(6), 616–630 (2015). https://doi.org/10.1016/j.elerap.2015.09.003
10. Hollebeek, L.D., Glynn, M.S., Brodie, R.J.: Consumer brand engagement in social media: conceptualization, scale development and validation. J. Interact. Mark. **28**(2), 149–165 (2014)
11. Chu, S.-C., Lien, C.-H., Cao, Y.: Electronic word-of-mouth (Ewom) on Wechat: examining the influence of sense of belonging, need for self-enhancement, and consumer engagement on Chinese Travellers' Ewom. Int. J. Advert. **38**(1), 26–49 (2019). https://doi.org/10.1080/02650487.2018.1470917
12. Filieri, R.: What makes online reviews helpful? A diagnosticity-adoption framework to explain informational and normative influences in E-Wom. J. Bus. Res. **68**(6), 1261–1270 (2015)
13. Nieto, J., Hernández-Maestro, R.M., Muñoz-Gallego, P.A.: Marketing decisions, customer reviews, and business performance: the use of the toprural website by Spanish rural lodging establishments. Tour. Manage. **45**, 115–123 (2014). https://doi.org/10.1016/j.tourman.2014.03.009
14. Dorfman, R.G., Purnell, C., Qiu, C., Ellis, M.F., Basu, C.B., Kim, J.: Happy and unhappy patients: a quantitative analysis of online plastic surgeon reviews for breast augmentation. Plast. Reconstr. Surg. **141**(5), 663e–e673 (2018)
15. Lam, D., So, A.: Do happy tourists spread more word-of-mouth? The mediating role of life satisfaction. Ann. Tour. Res. **43**, 646–650 (2013)
16. Wang, Y., Fesenmaier, D.R.: Towards understanding members' general participation in and active contribution to an online travel community. Tour. Manage. **25**(6), 709–722 (2004)
17. Jones, Q., Ravid, G., Rafaeli, S.: Information overload and the message dynamics of online interaction spaces: a theoretical model and empirical exploration. Inf. Syst. Res. **15**(2), 194–210 (2004)
18. Mudambi, S.M., Schuff, D.: Research note: what makes a helpful online review? A study of customer reviews on amazon. Com. MIS Q. **34**, 185–200 (2010)
19. Clemons, E.K., Gao, G.G., Hitt, L.M.: When online reviews meet hyperdifferentiation: a study of the craft beer industry. J. Manag. Inf. Syst. **23**(2), 149–171 (2006)

20. Wang, H., Du, R., Shen, W., Qiu, L., Fan, W.: Product reviews: a benefit, a burden, or a trifle? How seller reputation affects the role of product reviews. How Seller Reputation Affects the Role of Product Reviews (June 23, 2021) Forthcoming in MIS Quarterly (2021)
21. Yan, M., Tan, H., Jia, L., Akram, U.: The antecedents of poor doctor-patient relationship in mobile consultation: a perspective from computer-mediated communication. Int. J. Environ. Res. Public Health 17(7), 2579 (2020)
22. Greif, D.N., Shah, H.A., Luxenburg, D., Hodgens, B.H., Epstein, A.L., Kaplan, L.D., et al.: Word of mouth and online reviews are more influential than social media for patients when selecting a sports medicine physician. Arthroscopy Sports Med. Rehabil. 4(3), e1185–e1191 (2022). https://doi.org/10.1016/j.asmr.2022.04.022
23. Zhang, X., Liu, S., Deng, Z., Chen, X.: Knowledge sharing motivations in online health communities: a comparative study of health professionals and normal users. Comput. Hum. Behav. 75, 797–810 (2017). https://doi.org/10.1016/j.chb.2017.06.028
24. Chen, S., Guo, X., Wu, T., Ju, X.: Exploring the online doctor-patient interaction on patient satisfaction based on text mining and empirical analysis. Inf. Process. Manage. 57(5), 102253 (2020). https://doi.org/10.1016/j.ipm.2020.102253
25. Gai, P.J., Puntoni, S.: Language and consumer dishonesty: a self-diagnosticity theory. J. Consum. Res. 48(2), 333–351 (2021)
26. Mahmoodi, H., Moradzadeh, R., Iranpour, A.: Gender-based inequalities in health literacy among an iranian kurd population: results of a community research square (2020). https://doi.org/10.21203/rs.3.rs-60909/v1
27. Peng, Y.: Gendered division of digital labor in parenting: a qualitative study in Urban China. Sex Roles 86(5), 283–304 (2022). https://doi.org/10.1007/s11199-021-01267-w
28. Yang, Y., Zhang, X., Lee, P.K.C.: Improving the effectiveness of online healthcare platforms: an empirical study with multi-period patient-doctor consultation data. Int. J. Prod. Econ. 207, 70–80 (2019). https://doi.org/10.1016/j.ijpe.2018.11.009
29. Yoon, C.: The effects of national culture values on consumer acceptance of e-commerce: online shoppers in china. Inf. Manage. 46(5), 294–301 (2009). https://doi.org/10.1016/j.im.2009.06.001
30. Bhattacherjee, A., Premkumar, G.: Understanding changes in belief and attitude toward information technology usage: a theoretical model and longitudinal test. MIS Q. 28(2), 229–254 (2004). https://doi.org/10.2307/25148634
31. Kim, W.G., Han, J.S., Lee, E.: Effects of relationship marketing on repeat purchase and word of mouth. J. Hospitality Tourism Res. 25(3), 272–288 (2001). https://doi.org/10.1177/109634800102500303
32. Singh, J.: Voice, exit, and negative word-of-mouth behaviors: an investigation across three service categories. J. Acad. Mark. Sci. 18(1), 1–15 (1990). https://doi.org/10.1007/BF02729758

# Design Mobile Exergames to Large-Scalely Promote Adolescent Physical Activity Based on Interval Training Theory

Pufeng Hua, Chengyi Li, Xing Sun, and Shiguang Ni(✉)

Tsinghua Shenzhen International Graduate School, Tsinghua University, Shenzhen, China
{hpf21,lichengy}@mails.tsinghua.edu.cn,
{sunxking,ni.shiguang}@sz.tsinghua.edu.cn

**Abstract.** Exercise games have shown significant potential in promoting physical activities, especially in encouraging the youth demographic to engage in sports. Despite this, research on promoting adolescent exercise through game science remains limited. This study, grounded in scientific exercise theory - interval training, designed and developed an exercise game tailored for adolescents. The game was deployed on the widely-used WeChat Mini Program platform, utilizing smartphone cameras to enable direct game control through physical movements. The effectiveness of this game was tested and evaluated through both online and offline methods. The offline tests primarily recorded participants' heart rate data and physical activity perception scales, while the online tests collected data on user visit times, gameplay duration, and scores. The results indicate that the game provides a moderate-intensity exercise effect, similar to traditional training methods, but with enhanced enjoyment and a sense of achievement. These findings offer robust support for promoting youth physical activities through game science, demonstrating the considerable potential of exercise games in health promotion.

**Keywords:** Exergames · Interval Training · Mini Program · Adolescents

## 1 Introduction

According to the World Health Organization's *World health statistics 2022* [1], there has been a continued increase in global life expectancy and healthy life expectancy. Despite the alarming COVID-19 death toll, which has reached 6.2 million globally, non-communicable diseases are now emerging as the predominant causes of mortality. In an era where more individuals are avoiding or surviving infectious diseases, leading to prolonged lifespans, non-communicable diseases have emerged as the primary health risk factor. This situation is exacerbated by high incidences of obesity, hypertension, and anemia across various age groups, underscoring the gravity of the current health challenges.

J. Wei and G. Margetis (Eds.): HCII 2024, LNCS 14737, pp. 45–58, 2024.
https://doi.org/10.1007/978-3-031-60458-4_4

Moreover, research indicates a worrying trend of declining physical activity and health levels among children and adolescents over recent decades. A reduction in physical exercise activities is closely associated with heightened risks of obesity, hypertension, and other high-risk baseline diseases [2]. Regular physical activity is proven to significantly mitigate the risks associated with cardiovascular diseases and certain types of cancer [3]. Nevertheless, the modality of physical activity for adolescents warrants special consideration. The unique physiological characteristics of adolescents mean that exercise programs designed for adults may not be suitable for this demographic. Additionally, adolescents often find traditional training methodologies unengaging and monotonous.

Therefore, the aim of this study is to design and develop a sports video game tailored for the adolescent demographic, deployed on a more convenient mobile app platform. When evaluating the effectiveness of the game, it is expected to achieve a moderate to high level of physical activity, comparable to traditional training. The game is designed to be controllable and engaging, offering greater sustainability compared to conventional training methods.

## 2   Related Work

### 2.1   Interval Training

Exercise is defined as a physical activity that involves planned, structured, and repetitive bodily movements aimed at improving health in one or more body parts; it's essentially a means to strengthen the body through sports. Exercise primarily falls into two categories: aerobic and anaerobic. Studies have shown that endurance training is generally associated with aerobic activities and anti-fatigue exercises, while anaerobic exercise relates to muscle growth and strength enhancement [4].

The current mainstream strategy for healthful exercising is Interval Training theory, a series of high-intensity workouts interspersed with rest or light activity periods. Key strategies within interval training include Fartlek Training, Sprint Interval Training (SIT) [20], High-Intensity Interval Training (HIIT) [21], Small-Sided Games (SSG) [19], and the Vigorous Intermittent Lifestyle Physical Activity (VILPA) approach introduced in 2021 [5].

Recent studies have highlighted the efficacy of interval exercises as an effective physical training method in improving the physical health and fitness levels of adolescents. Research by Sabia et al. indicates that a combination of continuous aerobic and intermittent anaerobic exercises [6], along with nutritional guidance, can significantly improve the weight, body composition, lipid levels, and aerobic capacity of obese adolescents. This suggests that interval training, coupled with proper nutritional advice, plays a vital role in adolescent weight management and physical improvement.

Furthermore, research by Bento et al. has discovered that High-Intensity Interval Training (HIIT) implemented in school settings significantly enhances the physical health and activity levels of adolescents [7]. Due to its efficiency and ease of implementation, this form of training is considered an effective option for adolescent physical exercise. However, studies also indicate that adolescents tend to have lower adherence to sustained physical training compared to adults, implying that motivational methods more appealing to adolescents may be needed.

## 2.2  Exergames

In recent years, gamified exercise programs have emerged as an innovative method to promote physical activity, particularly gaining traction in the realm of youth sports. Traditional physical training methods may lack appeal for the younger generation, while gamified approaches, blending entertainment and interactivity, have shown potential in encouraging youth participation in sports activities.

Research by Schwarz et al. underscores the importance of design features like clear interfaces, reward systems, multiplayer modes, social interaction, challenges with personalized difficulty levels, self-monitoring, and diverse customization options in enhancing youth engagement in mobile health and sports activities [8].

A study by Farrow et al. explored the effects of Virtual Reality exercise gaming (VR-exergaming) on enhancing performance and enjoyment in High-Intensity Interval Training (HIIT) [9]. The findings revealed that VR-exergaming significantly increased the enjoyment of the exercise compared to standard gym equipment. This suggests the potential of Virtual Reality technology in boosting adolescent interest in high-intensity physical activities.

Additionally, a systematic review and meta-analysis conducted by Mazéas et al. investigated the effectiveness of gamified interventions on physical activity [11]. The study indicated that gamified interventions had a small to moderate overall effect in increasing physical activity behavior, demonstrating good applicability across diverse user groups, including adolescents and patients with chronic illnesses.

Gamified approaches, offering engaging, interactive, and technology-driven experiences, have significant advantages in increasing youth participation in physical activities. These methods not only enhance the enjoyment of exercise but also show good adaptability and universality among various user groups. However, there are some challenges: the gamified programs in the studies lack guidance from scientific training theories, and they require computers or wearable devices (e.g. VR) for assistance, which can raise the barrier to exercise. Additionally, long-term use of devices like VR can cause discomfort [10], potentially decreasing long-term enthusiasm for physical activity.

## 3  Method

### 3.1  Design and Development of the Exergame

This study aims to develop a functional game specifically designed for the adolescent demographic to motivate and promote physical activity. Following the functional game software engineering framework proposed by Carlier et al. [13], the design of this game focuses on answering three core questions: Why personalize the game? Which parameters are suitable for personalization? And how to implement personalization? To effectively address these questions, we have divided the game's design and development tasks among three key stakeholders: domain experts, game developers, and software engineers. Each role focuses on different aspects of the game design, collaborating together to achieve the final objective. Here are the three key aspects of its implementation:

**Domain Experts: Interval Training Guidance Based.** In designing a game aimed at increasing the participation of adolescents in physical activities, we closely integrated the theory of Interval Training with the constraints of the actual gaming environment. This study meticulously considers the exercise intensity requirements of interval training (as seen in Table 1), to ensure that adolescents can achieve scientifically sound exercise effects through the game [22].

**Table 1.** Heart Rate Training Zone Guide

| Intensity Zone | Heart Rate | Exercise Duration | Training Benefits |
|---|---|---|---|
| Maximum | 90–100% (171–190 bpm) | Less than 5 min | Increases maximum sprint speed, feels very taxing on breathing and muscles Suitable for very fit individuals and those with a competitive training background |
| Hard | 80–90% (152–171 bpm) | 2–10 min | Increases maximum performance capacity, feels muscle fatigue and breathing difficulty Suitable for people with strong physical adaptability and short-term exercise |
| Moderate | 70–80% (133–152 bpm) | 10–40 min | Helps improve aerobic fitness level, feels light muscle load, easy breathing Suitable for general public, moderately long exercises |
| Easy | 60–70% (114–133 bpm) | 40–80 min | Helps with basic endurance and recovery, feels comfortable, easy breathing Low muscle load, suitable for long-duration and frequently repeated short exercises |
| Very Easy | 50–60% (104–114 bpm) | 20–40 min | Helps improve overall health and metabolism, feels very relaxed Suitable for beginners or basic recovery training |

To effectively implement the recommended high-intensity training intervals, we carefully selected movements that significantly affect the body's center of gravity, such as jumping and squatting. These movements are designed to rapidly increase heart rate in a short period, achieving the desired effect of interval training. Furthermore, we paid special attention to the fact that when adolescent users wish to exercise through video games, they often do so in limited indoor spaces. Therefore, we consciously chose exercises that do not require extensive movement or large-scale bodily actions, ensuring the safety of adolescent players in smaller spaces and making the game easily adaptable to various environments.

Additionally, to enable adolescents to reach higher heart rates and obtain effective exercise in the game, we designed a progressively escalating difficulty curve for the levels. This design not only mobilizes the enthusiasm of adolescent users for exercise but also ensures a gradual increase in heart rate, adhering to scientific exercise principles. Through this approach, our game not only increases its fun aspect but also achieves the goal of health promotion, allowing adolescents to enjoy effective physical exercise while engaging in the game.

**Game Designers: Integrating MDA Theory for Casual Game Design.** In the design of this game, we employed the MDA (Mechanics, Dynamics, Aesthetics) framework [16], a classic approach that integrates game design, analysis, and technical research. The MDA theory emphasizes understanding how games generate enjoyment and engagement from the user experience perspective. In this study, we focused specifically on the casual fun experience type of games, as our goal was to create a short, efficient exercise game that could be accepted and enjoyed by most adolescents.

To achieve this objective, our design efforts concentrated on the following aspects:

1. **Thorough Research into Adolescents' Preferred Casual Game Types:** We conducted extensive research to understand the gameplay styles and visual aesthetics that might appeal to the adolescent demographic. This step helped us identify the most attractive game types, ensuring the game's broad appeal.
2. **Simple and Intuitive Rules and Scoring Mechanisms:** To ensure the game was easy to understand and engage with, we designed simple and intuitive rules and scoring methods. This approach made the game accessible to adolescent players of varying skill levels while maintaining its challenge and enjoyment.
3. **Short and Casual Game:** Considering the psychological burden of long-duration physical exercise on users, each game session is designed to last no more than two minutes. This approach is light-hearted and fun, also helping to control the tendency of game addiction among adolescents [14].
4. **Strong Feedback of Joy in Victory and Satisfaction:** We placed special emphasis on the feeling of victory and achievement within the game, enhancing players' sense of satisfaction and accomplishment through visual and sound effects. This not only increased the game's appeal but also encouraged adolescents to continuously participate in the physical activities within the game.

By combining the MDA theory and focusing on the casual experience [15], our design aims to create a game environment that not only promotes effective physical exercise among adolescents but is also fun and engaging.

**Software Engineers: Mobile Gaming Based on Phaser.** In this study, to broaden the reach of our exercise game to a wider audience of mobile and mini-program users, we chose Phaser 3.0 as our game development framework. Phaser 3.0 is a powerful and flexible open-source framework for HTML5 game development. It not only supports cross-platform compatibility, ensuring smooth gameplay on a variety of mobile devices and browsers, but also offers a wealth of features and flexibility, enabling us to create engaging game interfaces and animation effects. Additionally, the active developer community and abundant resources of Phaser provide strong support for our game development, facilitating rapid iterations and updates. This ensures that our game can adapt to rapidly changing technological and market demands, maintaining its appeal and effectiveness over the long term.

## 3.2  System Design

In the game design developed for this study, we adopted a simple yet effective input-feedback model, as illustrated in Fig. 1. This model focuses on enhancing the interactivity between the player's actions and the game system, thus ensuring an intuitive gaming experience with high engagement.

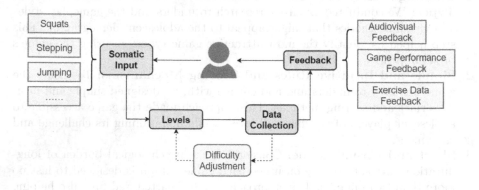

**Fig. 1.** System Design

Firstly, at the input end, we particularly emphasized the application of gesture-based interaction technology. This means that physical movements of the player, such as stepping, jumping, or swinging, are directly translated into input signals within the game. This design allows players to interact with the game world in a natural and intuitive manner, enhancing their sense of immersion and experience.

These input signals are then captured by the game levels and used to influence characters or the environment within the game. For example, a player's jump might enable the game character to leap over obstacles or gain rewards.

In this way, the game transforms the player's real-world actions into meaningful interactions within the game world, thereby increasing the game's fun and engagement factor.

Once the player's inputs are received by the game system, the system immediately processes this data and generates corresponding feedback. This feedback is primarily presented in the form of audio-visual effects. For instance, when a player successfully dodges an obstacle or hits a target, the game reinforces the player's sense of achievement and satisfaction through instant sound effects and visual cues. This rapid and intuitive feedback mechanism is crucial for sparking and maintaining the player's interest and motivation.

In terms of platform selection, this study has chosen WeChat Mini Programs as the primary development platform, a decision primarily based on the widespread use and ease of use of WeChat in China. WeChat, being a nearly universally used social media application, offers its Mini Program feature as a gateway to a vast potential user base. The user-friendliness and convenience of the WeChat Mini Program platform also provide a seamless gaming experience. Users can access and play games directly within WeChat without the need to download and install a separate app. By choosing WeChat Mini Programs, we are able to more easily reach a broader audience, which is crucial for the future promotion and popularization of our game.

We have adopted the VKSession.detectFace open-source model from the WeChat platform as our solution for mobile camera-based posture recognition technology. This model was selected for its comprehensive advantages in terms of recognition accuracy, performance consumption, and device compatibility. The VKSession.detectFace model not only accurately identifies player movements but also maintains low performance consumption while being compatible with a wide range of devices. This is vital for ensuring smooth gameplay on various types of mobile devices. Through this technological choice, our game effectively captures and responds to player movements, providing an engaging and effective exercise experience.

### 3.3 System Implementation

We have developed a collection of exercise mini-games, comprising four main sports games: *Fighter War, Puppy Dash, Jumping Knife,* and *Rhythmic Jump* (as shown in Fig. 2 and Table 2). Users can freely choose any game from the interface according to their preferences and start playing. The game design follows the aforementioned design guidelines, with the main aspects as follows:

1. **Simple and Understandable Rules:** Users can grasp the gameplay within seconds of starting a game, without the need for detailed instructions.
2. **Easy Control:** The games are controlled directly through users' physical movements, typically involving simple actions like jumping or dodging, and do not require the camera to capture the entire body. In some games, smooth gameplay is possible even if only the user's head is within the camera's range.

3. **Guided Physical Activity:** Through reasonably challenging game levels, users are guided to undertake varying intensities of physical activity, motivating them to gradually improve their physical abilities and fitness levels.
4. **Engaging Feedback:** Users can earn points within the game, with every scoring action receiving immediate feedback. This incentivizes users to aim for higher scores, fostering their enthusiasm to participate.

**Table 2.** 4 Exergames

| Name | Exercise | Introduction |
|------|----------|--------------|
| Fighter War | step & move | Control: Step to shoot, move to dodge Shoot bullets to eliminate enemy fighters |
| Puppy Dash | step & jump | Control: Step to run, jump to dodge Dodge obstacles and run farther |
| Jumping Knife | jump | Control: Jump to launch a knife Launch more knives onto the stakes |
| Rhythmic Jump | move & jump | Control: Move and jump Jump to the rhythm and guess the blocks |

## 4    System Testing and Evaluation

### 4.1    Methodology

The experiment was divided into offline and online parts, as illustrated in Fig. 3. In the offline experiment, we recruited 17 participants to test the games. Before the experiment, a maximum heart rate assessment was conducted, and during the experiment, heart rate measurements were taken using the Polar H10 heart rate Sensor. Following adequate rest, participants first engaged in 90 s of traditional physical training (jumping jacks) with continuous heart rate monitoring at one-second intervals.The HR data was represented as a percentage of HRmax and HRreserve, calculating the average HR for each training session. The percentages of HRmax and HRreserve were computed using the formula 1 and 2 [17]. After completing this, they filled out the Physical Activity Enjoyment Scale (PACES) [18]. At the same time the next day, they played a chosen exercise game, with continuous heart rate monitoring throughout. After gameplay, they completed the PACES again, along with the Exergame Enjoyment Questionnaire (EEQ) [12] and an optional open-ended question about their gaming and exercise experience.

$$\%HRmax = \frac{HR_{mean}}{HR_{max}} \times 100\% \tag{1}$$

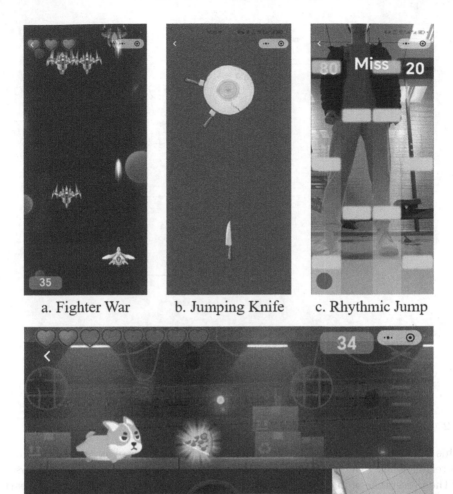

a. Fighter War     b. Jumping Knife     c. Rhythmic Jump

d. Puppy Dash

**Fig. 2.** 4 Exergames

$$\%HRreserve = \frac{HR_{mean} - HR_{rest}}{HR_{max} - HR_{rest}} \times 100\% \qquad (2)$$

For the online part of the experiment, the games were released via the WeChat Mini Program platform. We recorded online users' visit times, game types, playing durations, and scores. From September 1, 2023, to December 31, 2023, there were a total of 169,116 visits and play sessions. Excluding sessions less than 15 s, which were deemed to have no exercise effect, we were left with 118,312 play sessions data.

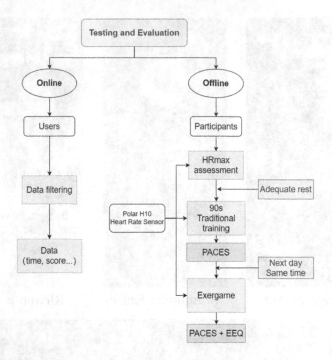

**Fig. 3.** Testing and Evaluation

## 4.2   Results

This study utilized IBM SPSS Statistics 27 for the analysis of experimental data. In terms of heart rate monitoring evaluation, we conducted comparative analyses of the percentage of maximum heart rate (%HRmax) and the percentage of heart rate reserve (%HRreserve). According to the experimental results, there were no significant differences between these indicators in the exercise game group and the 90-second traditional training group ($p > 0.05$), as shown in Table 3. This indicates that the exercise game we developed is similar in training effect to traditional 90-second exercise methods. Additionally, the evaluation results of the PACES and the EEQ show that there were significant differences in physical sensations between participating in traditional training and the exercise game ($p < 0.01$), as shown in Table 4, suggesting that the physical sensations after exercising through the game were better than those after direct traditional training. In the EEQ, users rated the game highly in terms of fun and controllability, further indicating the game's overall appeal and user satisfaction with game control.

The online data, as shown in Table 5, reveals that each game garnered a substantial number of visits and play sessions during the four-month test period, with a significant correlation between exercise duration and scores ($p < 0.01$). This further proves a positive relationship between the physical activity in the game and the rewards received.

In summary, this study demonstrates that game-based physical exercise not only yields effects similar to traditional training but also has significant advantages in enhancing users' enjoyment of exercise and physical sensations.

**Table 3.** Heart Rate Evaluation

| Variables | Training type | Mean ± SD | p |
|---|---|---|---|
| HRmean | Traditional Training Exergame | 122.71 ± 7.24 <br> 119.35 ± 7.50 | 0.194 |
| %HRmax | Traditional Training Exergame | 64.10 ± 3.89 <br> 62.36 ± 4.18 | 0.218 |
| %HRreserve | Traditional Training Exergame | 46.78 ± 5.56 <br> 44.28 ± 5.00 | 0.176 |

**Table 4.** Measurement

| Measurement | Mean ± SD |
|---|---|
| PACES score (Traditional Training): measured on 1–7-point Likert-scale | 52.00 ± 8.65 |
| PACES score (Exergame): measured on 1–7-point Likert-scale | 90.70 ± 12.51 |
| EEQ score (Exergame): measured on 1–5-point Likert-scale | 76.71 ± 3.89 |

**Table 5.** Online Statistics (Sep. 1, 2023–Dec. 31, 2023)

| Exergames | Online Play Sessions |
|---|---|
| Fighter War | 44,273 |
| Puppy Dash | 40,075 |
| Jumping Knife | 17,507 |
| Rhythmic Jump | 12,851 |

# 5   Discussion

The results of this study demonstrate that the collection of exercise mini-games designed for adolescents, based on interval training guidance, can achieve effects similar to traditional training and are more appealing to the youth demographic. The gaming environment effectively mitigates the fatigue and monotony associated with exercise, while accomplishing game tasks provides users with a significant sense of achievement. Additionally, the application's deployment on the widely used and user-friendly WeChat Mini Program platform enhances the game's universality and accessibility, making it easier for a broader group of adolescents to participate in the exercise activities within the game.

However, there are certain limitations in the experimental exploration of this study. The online data collection couldn't completely eliminate the possibility of participant cheating, the sample size for the offline experiment was relatively limited, and there was a lack of long-term follow-up studies on training adherence. Future research should expand the participant scale of the offline experiment and conduct more in-depth studies on long-term training behaviors to strengthen the persuasiveness of the experimental conclusions. Additionally, the online experiment should fully leverage the large user base and introduce more data dimensions, such as exploring different adolescent groups' reactions to exercise games, and the extent of control and impact on physical activity.

## 6    Conclusion

This study designed and developed a set of adolescent exercise games based on scientific training theories, deployed on the widely used and easy-to-operate WeChat Mini Program platform. The results from both online and offline experiments indicate that this set of games provides moderate-intensity physical training while also incorporating the fun aspects of gaming. These outcomes encourage us to continue exploring and developing more efficient and enjoyable exercise games to promote physical activity and health among adolescents.

**Acknowledgments.** This study was funded by Shenzhen R & D sustainable development funding (KCXFZ20230731093600002), Guangdong Digital Mental Health and Intelligent Generation Laboratory (Grant No. 2023WSYS010), the Shenzhen Key Research Base of Humanities and Social Sciences (Grant No. 202003), and Shenzhen Education Science "14th Five-Year Plan" 2023 major policy research project (Grant No. zdzc23013).

## References

1. World Health Organization. World health statistics 2022: monitoring health for the SDGs, sustainable development goals. World Health Organization (2022)
2. Kraus, W.E., et al.: Physical activity, all-cause and cardiovascular mortality, and cardiovascular disease. Med. Sci. Sports Exerc. **51**(6), 1270 (2019). NIH Public Access
3. Gill, J.M.R.: Linking volume and intensity of physical activity to mortality. Nat. Med. **26**(9), 1332–1334 (2020). Nature Publishing Group US New York
4. Baar, K.: Training for endurance and strength: lessons from cell signaling. Med. Sci. Sports Exerc. **38**(11), 1939–1944 (2006). LWW

5. Stamatakis, E., Huang, B.H., Maher, C., et al.: Untapping the health enhancing potential of vigorous intermittent lifestyle physical activity (VILPA): rationale, scoping review, and a 4-pillar research framework. Sports Med. **51**(1), 1–10 (2021). Springer

6. Sabia, R., Santos, J.E., Ribeiro, R.P.: Effect of continuous Aerobic vs. Intermittent Anaerobic Exercise associated with nutritional orientation on weight reduction in obese adolescents. Revista Brasileira de Medicina do Esporte **10**(5), 349–355 (2004). https://doi.org/10.1590/S1517-86922004000500002

7. da Silva Bento, A.F.P., Páez, L.C., Raimundo, A.: High-intensity interval training in the school context: physical fitness, physical activity, and potential for educational outcomes. J. Teach. Phys. Educ. **40**(4) (2021). https://doi.org/10.1123/jtpe. 2020-0187

8. Schwarz, A., Winkens, L., de Vet, E., Ossendrijver, D., Bouwsema, K., Simons, M.: Design features associated with engagement in mobile health physical activity interventions among youth: systematic review of qualitative and quantitative studies. J. Med. Internet Res. **11**, e40898 (2022). https://doi.org/10.2196/40898

9. Farrow, M., Lutteroth, C., Rouse, P., Bilzon, J.: Virtual-reality exergaming improves performance during high-intensity interval training. Eur. J. Sport Sci. **19**, 719–727 (2018). https://doi.org/10.1080/17461391.2018.1542459

10. Lu, Y., Xue, Y., Ni, S.: SeekingHeart: a biofeedback-based VR game for mindfulness practice. In: 2023 IEEE 11th International Conference on Serious Games and Applications for Health (SeGAH), pp. 1–8. IEEE (2023)

11. Mazéas, A., Duclos, M., Pereira, B., Chalabaev, A.: Evaluating the effectiveness of gamification on physical activity: systematic review and meta-analysis of randomized controlled trials. J. Med. Internet Res. **24**, e26779 (2022). https://doi.org/10. 2196/26779

12. Fitzgerald, A., Huang, S., Sposato, K., Wang, D., Claypool, M., Agu, E.: The exergame enjoyment questionnaire (EEQ): an instrument for measuring exergame enjoyment (2020)

13. Carlier, S., Naessens, V., De Backere, F., de Turck, F.: A software engineering framework for reusable design of personalized serious games for health: development study. JMIR Serious Games **11**, e40054 (2022). https://doi.org/10.2196/ 40054

14. Lin, L., Ding, R., Ni, S.: How does parents' psychological distress relate to adolescents' problematic gaming? The roles of parent-adolescent relationship and adolescents' emotion regulation. J. Behav. Addictions **12**(4), 953–963 (2023). Akadémiai Kiadó Budapest

15. Duarte, L.C.S., Battaiola, A.L.: Distinctive features and game design. Entertainment Comput. **21**, 83–93 (2017). Elsevier

16. Hunicke, R., Marc, L., Zubek, R.: A formal approach to game design and game research. GDC, San Jose (2004)

17. Dellal, A., Chamari, K., Pintus, A., Girard, O., Cotte, T., Keller, D.: Heart rate responses during small-sided games and short intermittent running training in elite soccer players: a comparative study. J. Strength Conditioning Res. **22**(5), 1449–1457 (2008). LWW

18. Kendzierski, D., DeCarlo, K.J.: Physical activity enjoyment scale: two validation studies. J. Sport Exerc. Psychol. **13**(1), 50–64 (1991)

19. Selmi, O., Ouergui, I., Levitt, D.E., Nikolaidis, P.T., Knechtle, B., Bouassida, A.: Small-sided games are more enjoyable than high-intensity interval training of similar exercise intensity in soccer. Open Access J. Sports Med. **11**, 77–84 (2020). Taylor & Francis

20. Hardcastle, S.J., Ray, H., Beale, L., Hagger, M.S.: Why sprint interval training is inappropriate for a largely sedentary population. Front. Psychol. **5**, 1505 (2014). Frontiers Media SA
21. Cooper, S.B., Dring, K.J., Nevill, M.E.: High-intensity intermittent exercise: effect on young people's cardiometabolic health and cognition. Curr. Sports Med. Rep. **15**(4), 245–251 (2016). LWW
22. Bendiksen, M., et al.: Heart rate response and fitness effects of various types of physical education for 8-to 9-year-old schoolchildren. Eur. J. Sport Sci. **14**(8), 861–869 (2014). Taylor & Francis

# Unlocking the Potential of mHealth for Smoking Cessation: An Expert Viewpoint

Arian Kashefi[1]([⊠])[iD], Kyana Bosschaerts[2][iD], Stephen Murphy[1][iD],
Sofie Van Hoecke[2][iD], Mariek Vanden Abeele[1][iD], Lieven De Marez[1][iD],
Femke Ongenae[2][iD], and Peter Conradie[1][iD]

[1] MICT, Ghent University-imec, Miriam Makebaplein 1, 9000 Gent, Belgium
Arian.Kashefi@UGent.be
[2] IDLab, Ghent University-imec, Technologiepark 126, 9050 Gent, Belgium
Kyana.Bosschaerts@UGent.be

**Abstract.** Smoking remains a critical global health issue, with significant mortality and economic costs. Traditional cessation methods, though effective, face challenges in accessibility and scalability, highlighting the potential of mobile health (mHealth) applications. However, many existing mHealth apps for smoking cessation underperform when compared to established methods, theorised to be caused by the high attrition rates due to their low levels of personalization and a general lack of proven theoretical underpinning for feature selection. This study aims to enhance smoking cessation mHealth app design by incorporating expert insights from the field.

Engaging with licensed smoking cessation experts in Flanders, Belgium, we conducted in-depth interviews to gather their views on essential app features and design principles. The experts emphasized the need for features regarding personalization, goal-setting, and user-friendly interfaces among others. Their recommendations aligned with established behaviour change theories such as Self-Determination Theory, Goal-Setting Theory, and Human-Computer Interaction principles such as Nielsen's Usability Heuristics, underscoring the importance of a multidisciplinary approach in mHealth app development.

Our findings present a list of categorised design requirements critical for developing effective and engaging smoking cessation apps. By integrating expert knowledge and behavioural theory, this research offers a foundation for developing more effective, user-centric mHealth solutions, advancing the fight against the global smoking epidemic. This study helps close the gap between the current shortcomings of mHealth application and their potential to provide accessible and cost-effective healthcare to broad audiences around the globe.

**Keyword:** Smoking Cessation · Behaviour Change · mHealth · Expert Opinion · Digital Interventions · HCI

## 1 Introduction

Smoking tobacco remains a major global public health crisis, recognized as a leading cause of preventable deaths worldwide. It accounts for nearly 8 million deaths annually, due to a range of tobacco-related illnesses including cancer, heart disease, lung diseases,

J. Wei and G. Margetis (Eds.): HCII 2024, LNCS 14737, pp. 59–79, 2024.
https://doi.org/10.1007/978-3-031-60458-4_5

diabetes, and chronic obstructive pulmonary disease, among others [1]. Despite continuous efforts to reduce tobacco consumption, a recent WHO report [2] reveals that even though there has been a global decrease in tobacco use, the pace of reduction is significantly slower than anticipated. Consequently, it is projected that the global goals for reducing tobacco use prevalence by 2025 will not be achieved. This alarming trend underscores the urgent need for increased efforts to curb tobacco use worldwide, especially as the absence of interventions will increase the annual death toll in the coming decades due to the delayed nature of the health effects attributed to smoking [1]. The risks associated with smoking go even beyond direct health issues for the smoker, also afflicting secondary effects on those around them by way of second-hand smoke exposure. Non-smokers, including children and adults, who are regularly exposed to second-hand smoke, are also at an increased risk of developing cancer, respiratory and cardiovascular diseases with studies estimating that exposure to second-hand smoke results in approximately 1.3 million deaths of non-smokers each year [1, 3].

Furthermore, the consequences associated with smoking extend to significant healthcare costs. The treatment of diseases caused by tobacco use places an enormous financial burden of around \$422 billion on healthcare systems around the world [4]. Additional economic impacts beyond direct medical expenses, such as productivity losses due to illness and premature death, should also be taken into account, affecting not only public health budgets but also broader economic stability. All this signifies the global negative ramifications of tobacco use which extends beyond smokers to harm bystanders and society at large, both financially and medically.

This battle against smoking has long relied on traditional cessation methods, which, despite their relatively high effectiveness, exhibit significant pragmatic shortcomings in addressing the global smoking epidemic [5]. While the efficacy of conventional methods such as nicotine replacement therapy, counselling, and pharmacological treatments is a crucial aspect, a pragmatic evaluation of interventions within a healthcare system must also consider factors such as accessibility and cost-effectiveness to ensure broad reach and sustainability in a healthcare setting [6]. One-on-one counselling with smoking cessation specialists for example requires a large body of trained professionals, which requires substantial investment from the healthcare sector and is very time-intensive for smokers, increasing the barrier to entry [7]. Pharmacological treatments also face availability challenges, such as shortages or even being taken off the market, as is the case with Chantix or Champix® (Varenicline) during the past 3 years [8].

Accessibility also remains a key issue, as many smokers might lack easy access to cessation specialists or clinics, especially in rural or underprivileged areas [9]. The cost of treatments, both for individuals and healthcare systems, can be prohibitive, restricting the reach of these methods to more affluent populations. Moreover, the scalability of face-to-face interventions is limited; they cannot be easily expanded to meet the needs of a large number of smokers worldwide [10]. Therefore, given the pressing need for large-scale intervention to help the remaining 1.3 billion smokers worldwide, innovative solutions are essential [2]. Here, the global proliferation of smartphones presents a unique opportunity to tackle this issue. With more than half of the world's population reportedly owning smartphones [11], leveraging this technology to promote smoking cessation can provide widespread access to necessary healthcare interventions at a relatively low cost. This is where mobile health (mHealth) applications can play a significant role. Aiming to leverage the ubiquity of smartphones, these digital interventions can provide personalized support, track progress, and deliver evidence-based techniques directly to users' smartphones to address major health concerns, such as smoking cessation, on a grand scale [12].

However, the path towards implementing mHealth solutions is not without its challenges. While mHealth applications offer advantages in reach and cost-effectiveness, a rush to deployment without thorough research and understanding could lead to ineffective solutions. It is crucial to recognize that the design and functionality of these apps can significantly impact public health outcomes [12, 13]. Poorly designed mHealth interventions might not only fail to assist users in quitting smoking but could also turn users against all mHealth and possibly prevent future cessation attempts [14]. As we explore the prevalence and design flaws of mHealth apps in our literature review, it becomes evident that despite their potential, the effectiveness of these tools is frequently compromised by inadequate design decisions [14]. This study seeks to rectify these deficiencies by concentrating on refining the design of mHealth apps for smoking cessation through the integration of expert insights. The necessity of our research stems from the observation that personalized approaches to health behaviour change are significantly more effective than generic ones [15]. However, current mHealth smoking cessation applications tend to be generic, lacking in personalization and effectiveness, and are not designed for long-term use [16]. We believe that incorporating more expert insights from smoking cessation specialists, whose successful smoking cessation rates are among the best of current methods [15], can address these issues by ensuring that the apps are tailored to meet the individual needs of users, thereby enhancing their effectiveness and encouraging sustained use.

## 2 Literature Review

### 2.1 Rising Popularity of mHealth Applications

Mobile health applications, commonly known as mHealth applications, have seen a significant surge in popularity as a promising tool in combating the global smoking crisis [17]. Reports suggest that the number of mHealth apps on major platforms surpassed the 325,000 mark back in 2018 [18] and downloads growing by 65% globally in 2020 [19]. This popularity aligns with the tendency of many smokers across various countries to attempt quitting without the use of any traditional cessation methods, opting instead for 'cold turkey' or self-help approaches, such as using booklets, videos and mostly apps [20, 21]. However, these methods exhibit significantly lower long-term cessation rates, around 2% to 5%, when compared to established methods involving behavioural therapy by trained professionals and pharmacological treatments with success rates of around 10 to 15% [15, 22]. Nevertheless, tailoring to pre-existing preferences is easier than altering them, as per behaviour change literature [23]. Therefore, the inherent alignment of mHealth applications with quitting preferences demonstrates its potential to complement popular methods and enhance their current lacklustre engagement and low success rates in smoking cessation.

The popularity of mHealth apps in the realm of smoking cessation can be attributed to several key advantages that address the limitations of traditional cessation methods. By leveraging the ubiquity of smartphones, these apps provide on-the-go support for smokers seeking to quit, making them more accessible than traditional methods that often require physical presence in healthcare settings. This accessibility eliminates practical obstacles to quitting smoking, such as the availability of specialists or the difficulty of commuting, which could otherwise hinder a cessation attempt. This is also particularly crucial in areas with limited healthcare infrastructure or where access to specialized smoking cessation services is constrained [24]. mHealth apps also offer unmatched convenience, allowing users to engage with smoking cessation tools at their own pace and in private settings, which is essential for those who may have busy schedules or prefer privacy in their quitting journey [25]. This enhanced sense of privacy may speak to a group of smokers trying to quit, but who may feel ashamed to be confronted on the subject by others [26]. This ease of use and flexibility in engagement are key factors in maintaining user adherence to smoking cessation programs. In terms of cost, mHealth apps present a more affordable alternative to traditional methods due to the scaling laws. Once developed, mHealth applications can be distributed easily across a large population and as the number of users increases, the cost per intervention decreases, providing immediate support and personalized feedback based on user data, at a fraction of the cost of conventional treatments, making them a cost-effective option for a wider range of users [27]. The personalization offered by mHealth apps is another significant advantage [28]. These apps can be tailored to fit individual preferences and needs, providing a customized approach to smoking cessation. This level of personalization could directly cater to the user's unique smoking habits and motivational triggers, potentially increasing the effectiveness of the cessation effort further [16].

All these features paint the picture of an ideal solution to the smoking cessation problem, however, despite numerous potential advantages, mHealth apps have faced criticism for lacking scientific rigour, high attrition rates and generally not living up to their theoretical potential, leading to concerns regarding their overall efficacy. Studies attribute this to an absence of evidence-based practices and behaviour change theories, which are crucial for successful smoking cessation strategies [29, 30]. This issue seems particularly prevalent because a considerable number of these apps are developed by commercial companies with profit-driven motives, often resulting in them neglecting the incorporation of scientific theory utilised by experts in traditional smoking cessation [22]. Furthermore, most existing smoking cessation mHealth apps adopt a generic, one-size-fits-all approach, offering no personalization beyond basic customization and simplistic metrics, like the count of cigarettes avoided or financial savings, which provide little meaningful value tailored to the users' unique characteristics or behaviours [16, 28]. As a result, there is a considerable gap between the potential of mHealth apps and their actual impact on smoking cessation, highlighting the need for more scientifically grounded app designs.

Consequently, the critical need for integration of theory in the development of mHealth apps cannot be overstated. Many scholars have called for a more fundamental incorporation of evidence-based behaviour change techniques and validated health interventions into mHealth app design [29–31]. Various studies also have shown that mHealth apps incorporating behaviour change techniques are more likely to be effective and lead to positive health outcomes [32, 33]. These results are however not replicated in smoking cessation applications and may not apply to the same extent. Thus, we propose that the same scientific rigour should be applied to the design of smoking cessation applications to potentially achieve these improved outcomes. Additionally, we will discuss how this approach could be enhanced even further by applying human-computer interaction (HCI) principles to the application interfaces. Such a holistic approach should ensure that users receive and perceive the evidence-based information provided within smoking cessation apps as intended by the intervention designers, eliciting the desired health outcomes [34].

## 2.2 Bridging Behaviour Change Theory and HCI

To address the shortcomings of current mHealth apps, an interdisciplinary approach that combines insights from behaviour change experts with principles of HCI, such as Nielsen's usability heuristics, is required [35]. Such a holistic approach makes intuitive sense and researchers have already pointed out the importance of combining HCI and behavioural research to increase the effectiveness of all types of mHealth apps, however, the two disciplines seem to stay separated to date [34]. With HCI literature focussing more on the design process of mHealth applications and their user interface [36] and behavioural research focusing on the contents of these applications and their health outcomes [33]. While both disciplines have their own merits, we posit that truly well-rounded interventions are created through the combination of the two. The integration of these disciplines therefore seems vital in creating apps that not only provide the right intervention strategies based on behaviour change theory but are also engaging and user-friendly through the incorporation of HCI insights. This involves understanding the nuances of smokers' behaviour, motivation, and challenges faced during the cessation process, and reflecting these insights in the design of the app interfaces [36].

The development process of effective smoking cessation apps should thus follow a pathway that integrates both the theoretical underpinnings of smoking cessation and practical aspects of app usability. This goes beyond simply tracking smoking behaviour or financial savings, by also providing continuous support, motivation, and personalized feedback to the user. Such a user-centred design approach ensures that the intervention resonates with the target audience, theoretically leading to higher engagement. In doing so, the role of HCI principles becomes critical in ensuring that the app's functionality aligns with user expectations and usability standards [13, 37].

From a behaviour change perspective, two prevalent theories seem highly applicable to our context, Self-Determination Theory (SDT) [38] and Goal-Setting Theory (GST) [39]. Firstly, SDT posits that satisfying basic psychological needs—autonomy, competence, and relatedness—fuels motivation for various favourable behaviour patterns and consequently promotes sustained health behaviour change [38]. In the realm of smoking cessation, this suggests that apps should empower users, offering them control over their quitting journey to increase autonomy, providing feedback that enhances their sense of competence, and fostering a sense of connection with supportive communities or resources to enhance relatedness. Self-determination theory has been repeatedly applied across various health behaviours including smoking cessation and has proven useful in predicting long-term abstinence [40]. Similarly, GST underscores the importance of setting specific, challenging yet attainable goals to motivate behaviour change [39]. According to the theory, clear and well-defined goals lead to higher levels of performance compared to vague or easy objectives. Applied to smoking cessation apps, this translates into enabling users to set personalized quitting goals such as specific quit dates and track their progress towards these objectives. Additionally, incorporating milestones within the app can help break down the overall goal into smaller, manageable tasks, providing users with a sense of achievement as they progress towards their larger quitting objectives [41]. Feedback mechanisms play a crucial role in this theory, as timely and constructive feedback helps users evaluate their progress towards their goals. Moreover, integrating social support features, such as community forums or the ability to share goals and achievements with friends or family, can enhance the relatedness aspect of SDT while complementing GST [42].

On the HCI front, Nielsen's Usability Heuristics [35], although not a rigid set of guidelines, offer an accessible framework for making smoking cessation apps more engaging and user-friendly [43]. When viewed through the lens of SDT and GST, it also presents an opportunity to seamlessly embed the concepts of behaviour change into the application's interface. The principles of 'visibility of system status', 'error prevention', and 'user control and freedom' directly support SDT's need for competence by ensuring users feel capable and in control of their interactions with the app. These heuristics help build users' confidence in navigating the app and making informed decisions about their smoking cessation journey, thereby enhancing their sense of efficacy and motivation [44]. Similarly, the heuristics 'match between the system and the real world', along with 'recognition rather than recall', align with SDT's need for autonomy. These principles ensure that the app speaks the users' language and integrates seamlessly into their daily lives, empowering them to engage with the app on their terms. This autonomy is crucial for fostering intrinsic motivation, which is a key driver in sustained behaviour change and goal achievement [45]. The 'flexibility and efficiency of use' heuristic resonates with both SDT and GST by allowing users to personalize their experience and set achievable, meaningful goals. This personalization acknowledges each user's unique quitting paths and supports their autonomy and competence, making goal attainment more feasible and motivating [28, 42]. Moreover, 'aesthetics and minimalist design', alongside 'consistent standards', contribute to a streamlined user experience that minimizes distractions and frustrations. This environment supports users in focusing on their goals, thereby aiding in the clarity and specificity required by GST for effective behaviour change [43]. Overall, Nielsen's Heuristics provide a solid foundation for developing mHealth app interfaces that cater to the psychological needs outlined in SDT while also facilitating the clear, challenging, and attainable goal-setting essential for motivating behaviour change.

As we move forward in attempting to enhance the design and functionality of mHealth apps for smoking cessation, it is clear that a multidisciplinary approach is beneficial. The remainder of this paper aims to bridge the existing gap in mHealth app development by providing designers with concrete requirements based on the above-mentioned theories and HCI principles. The findings from this research, while focussed on smoking cessation mHealth apps, could potentially be applied to the development of mHealth applications targeting different health behaviours. This is due to the underlying logic that behaviour change, user engagement, and app effectiveness transcend the specific context of smoking cessation [46]. Although each health behaviour presents its unique challenges, the strategies and frameworks identified for encouraging smoking cessation can serve as a blueprint for addressing other health-related behaviours, demonstrating the universal applicability of these learnings across the mHealth spectrum [47], similar to the general applicability of SDT to various health behaviours [40].

## 3 Methodology

### 3.1 Expert Selection and Data Collection

In the present study, smoking cessation specialists were chosen as key informants as their theoretical knowledge and practical user experience position them as invaluable contributors to our research goal. They provide a dual perspective, combining an understanding of the scientific principles underlying behaviour change with insights into the real-world needs and challenges of users.

Between January and April 2023, we conducted interviews with 11 established smoking cessation practitioners active in Flanders, Belgium, all registered in the national VRGT[1] database. The deliberate choice to only include practitioners from this database stems from the understanding that the expertise and methodologies in smoking cessation vary significantly by location [48]. In some regions such as Belgium, the path to becoming a certified smoking cessation specialist is through comprehensive and centralized education curricula, a policy that, while potentially limiting the pool of practitioners, ensures a high standard of care quality [49]. This approach contrasts with practices in other areas, like the UK, where practitioners may achieve certification through more accessible means, such as online courses [50]. While this increases the number of certified practitioners, concerns arise regarding the consistency and depth of such training. Specifically, in Belgium, where our sample is based, prospective smoking cessation specialists undergo a comprehensive year-long training program coordinated by multiple universities. This training focuses on both practical knowledge necessary for supporting individuals through their quitting journey and an in-depth understanding of various behaviour change theories such as Self-Determination Theory, Cognitive Behavioural Therapy, and the Transtheoretical Model [49].

The recruitment process for these experts began with outreach via Tabakstop, Belgium's national tobacco cessation organization, and VRGT, the Flemish authority responsible for training smoking cessation specialists. This was followed by contacting professionals listed in the VRGT database. Out of the 52 experts initially approached, 11 were selected to participate in our study. Theoretical considerations were the main factor determining the number of interviews conducted, although pragmatic aspects also played a role. Research in qualitative studies indicates that most new data typically emerge between the 7th and 12th interviews [51]. Additional selection criteria

---

[1] Abbreviation for 'Vlaamse Vereniging voor Respiratoire Gezondheidszorg en Tuberculosebestrijding' (Flemish Association for Respiratory Healthcare and Tuberculosis Control).

included factors such as current activity status, the extent of patient treatment, experience, and availability. The final selection of experts can be consulted in the appendix on OSF (https://osf.io/gfb3p), which includes prominent figures like the CEO of a leading behaviour change company and both the former and current coordinator of a major smoking cessation agency in Belgium. Every expert involved had at least more than one full year of experience in the smoking cessation field, with the most experienced individual having over 20 years of expertise.

### 3.2 Interview Guide and Data Analysis

In this study, we opted for an iterative approach regarding participant selection, development and modification of interview topic guides, and the processes of data collection and analysis. The interview topic guide underwent three revisions throughout the study and was finalized by the fourth interview. Its semi-structured format, however, allowed for flexibility during all interviews, meaning that strict adherence to the questions was not enforced to ensure a natural flow of conversation and ideas [52]. In these interviews, roughly half of the time was spent discussing the practitioners' current smoking cessation methods to understand the present landscape of smoking cessation efforts. The other half delved into technology-related queries, focusing particularly on experts' views about how and if technology should be integrated into behaviour change initiatives, specifically in smoking cessation. Insights on designing effective mHealth applications were drawn from the responses to these discussions, incorporating experts' existing practices and their ideas for future technological tools.

The initial transcription of the interviews was performed using the OpenAI Whisper transcription model [53]. For data analysis, we used the specialized qualitative data analysis software, NVivo 14 [54]. These transcripts were comprehensively compared to the original interview recordings to verify content accuracy and correct any grammatical inaccuracies resulting from the automated transcription process. Subsequently, thematic analysis of the texts was performed as outlined by Braun & Clark [55]. The first author actively read all transcriptions to be familiarized with the data, annotate sections of importance, summarize thoughts, and make a first attempt at recognizing patterns. Following this, every interview was coded in its entirety using open codes, labelling relevant excerpts. Next, the entire dataset was reviewed again to refine these codes and identify specific requirements. After identifying an initial set of requirements, a second comprehensive dataset review was conducted to both fine-tune and assess the universality and significance of the requirements by verifying their prevalence across the complete dataset. This resulted in an initial set of 54 requirements. It is worth noting that not all requirements were explicitly stated by the experts but are interpreted as such by the authors, therefore the quotes included in the appendix serve as justification for this interpretation. Open codes were labelled as requirements when their contents were deemed applicable to either the design or development process of mHealth smoking cessation applications.

In the next step, this list was refined further by conducting a thorough review, checking for identical or redundant requirements, the removal of which resulted in a final count of 50 distinct requirements, each assigned a priority of implementation value of Low (L), Medium (M) or High (H) based on the number of experts advocating for each requirement and its respective importance. Each requirement is also complemented with quotes from the experts, justifying its selection. These requirements were then reviewed again by the second author—a computer scientist with extensive app development experience—and validated for relevance, and subsequently analysed for their implementation feasibility and rated. Here, we define implementation feasibility as the amount of time required to implement the features or requirements in an app. Each implementation feasibility rating is also briefly justified in the appendix on OSF (https://osf.io/gfb3p). Lastly, all remaining requirements were reviewed again and grouped into broader categories or 'themes' encompassing experts' concerns and desired features. This led to the requirements structure presented in Table 1.

## 4  Findings and Discussion

The following 10 categories capture essential features deemed crucial for effective smoking cessation mHealth apps. These requirements range from highly specific features, an SOS button designed to offer tips for relapse prevention during cravings, to more overarching strategies, embedding behaviour change theories within the app's framework. Given the breadth and depth of insights contained within Table 1., a detailed exploration of every requirement would extend beyond the scope of this study. To maintain conciseness, we will focus on discussing the overarching categories derived from these requirements. This discussion aims to elaborate upon the key functionalities and features identified by experts as integral for the development of more effective smoking cessation apps. Further, we will discuss the significance of these categories, connecting them to the previously mentioned theoretical frameworks of Self-Determination Theory, Goal-Setting Theory, and Nielsen's Usability Heuristics.

**Table 1.** Categorised requirements for effective smoking cessation mHealth apps.

| Category | Requirement | Priority | Feasibility | Expert |
|---|---|---|---|---|
| User Interface and User Experience | | | | |
| UIX1 | **Progress Overview:** Provide users an accurate overview of their progress in smoking cessation | H | H | 1–7 |
| UIX2 | **User-Friendly Design:** Minimize front-end complexity, accommodating users with varying levels of technological proficiency | H | M | 1, 2, 6, 9, 10 |
| UIX3 | **Broad Accessibility:** Broadly accessible, catering to a wide audience, including those not yet ready to quit smoking | M | H | 1, 2, 8 |
| UIX4 | **Simple Language:** Straightforward and non-commanding language, avoiding jargon and complex explanations | H | H | 1 |

*(continued)*

**Table 1.** (*continued*)

| Category | Requirement | Priority | Feasibility | Expert |
|---|---|---|---|---|
| UIX5 | **Short Questionnaires:** Avoid lengthy questionnaires | M | H | 1 |
| UIX6 | **Interactive App:** Interactive, avoiding repetitive loops | M | M | 9 |
| UIX7 | **Non-Overwhelming Interface:** Maintain a user-friendly interface, avoiding overwhelming content or features | M | M | 3, 11 |
| UIX8 & T1 | **Ad-Free Experience:** Advertisement-free, supported by appropriate funding to ensure a free user experience | L | H | 4, 6 |
| Goal Setting | | | | |
| GS1 | **Goal Setting:** Enable users to establish specific goals and track their progress | H | H | 1, 4–6 |
| GS2 | **Rewards System:** Reward users upon achieving goals | H | H | 1, 4–6, 10 |
| GS3 & SS1 | **Achievement Sharing:** Enable users to share their accomplishments with others | M | H | 1, 6 |
| GS4 & SS2 | **Social Circle Notification:** Enable users to inform their social circle about their smoking cessation efforts | M | M | 5, 6 |
| Personalization | | | | |
| P1 | **Smoking Profile Creation:** Generate personalized smoking profiles for each user, identifying the function of smoking | H | H | 1, 3, 5, 8 |
| P2 | **Personalized Messages:** Tailor responses to users to enhance personalization | M | L | 1 |
| P3 | **Customization Options:** Adapt to each user's preferences like information presentation style and preferred distraction techniques | H | L | 1, 2, 4–11 |
| P4 | **Behaviour-Based Personalization:** Personalize content based on user behaviour | H | M | 3, 11 |

(*continued*)

**Table 1.** (*continued*)

| Category | Requirement | Priority | Feasibility | Expert |
|---|---|---|---|---|
| P5 | **Survey Response Utilization:** Use survey outcomes to influence awareness and motivation | H | L | 3, 5, 6, 8 |
| P6 & CI1 | **Information Diversity:** Offer a diverse range of information, allowing customization based on user preferences | M | L | 3, 10 |
| P7 & TP1 | **Relapse vs. Misstep:** Distinguish relapse and minor setbacks and respond appropriately | H | M | 3–5, 8 |
| P8 & UIX9 | **Disabling Features:** Allow certain non-essential features to be disabled | H | H | 3–5, 11 |
| P9 & BC1 | **Implementation Intentions:** Allow users to set implementation intentions to facilitate smoking cessation | L | M | 5 |
| Behaviour Change | | | | |
| BC2 | **SOS Button:** An SOS button, offering a range of practical tips for challenging situations, including relapse prevention and mental wellness tips | M | H | 1, 3, 5, 6, 8, 9, 11 |
| BC3 | **Avoiding Craving Provocation:** Avoid triggering smoking thoughts in users, especially when they are disengaged | H | H | 3 |
| BC4 | **Alternative Strategies:** Propose accessible and practical alternative coping strategies to users | M | H | 3, 10, 11 |
| BC5 | **Quitting Preparation:** Prepare users adequately for their quitting journey before cessation | M | M | 8 |
| BC6 | **Behaviour Change Theory:** Integrate principles of behaviour change theory | H | H | 8 |
| BC7 | **Tool Provision:** Provide comprehensive information about other smoking cessation resources | M | L | 8 |
| BC8 & TP2 | **Craving Prediction:** Predict craving episodes and offer pre-emptive advice to avert relapses | H | L | 9, 10 |

(*continued*)

**Table 1.** (*continued*)

| Category | Requirement | Priority | Feasibility | Expert |
|---|---|---|---|---|
| BC9 & ESI1 | **Coach/Companion Role:** Emulate the role of a real-life coach by acting as a supportive coach or companion to the user | M | L | 9, 10 |
| Expert Support and Integration | | | | |
| ESI2 | **Professional Contact:** Provide the option to seek professional assistance | M | H | 1, 6, 8 |
| ESI3 | **Professional Tool Functionality:** Serve as a comprehensive back-end tool for professionals, akin to a centralized medical record | L | L | 2, 3 |
| ESI4 | **Specialist Integration:** Ingrain specialists to facilitate quick assistance | M | M | 2–4, 6, 10 |
| Motivation and Engagement | | | | |
| ME1 | **Engagement Strategy:** Actively engage users from and maintain their engagement over time | M | M | 1, 2, 5, 8 |
| ME2 | **Motivation Enhancement:** Assess and enhance user motivation continuously | H | M | 4–6, 8, 9, 11 |
| Cat. | Requirement | Priority | Feasibility | Expert |
| Content and Information | | | | |
| CI2 | **Concise Information:** Convey information succinctly, offering clear, additional resources where necessary | M | L | 1, 3 |
| CI3 | **Health Benefits Info:** Inform users about the *immediate* health benefits of quitting smoking, steering clear of long-term effects like cancer | M | H | 1, 4, 5, 8, 11 |
| CI4 | **Risk Awareness:** Educate users about the risks associated with smoking | M | H | 1, 9 |
| CI5 | **Accurate Information:** Deliver accurate, current information in collaboration with a trusted partner, ensuring all content is evidence-based | H | L | 2–4, 6 |
| CI6 | **Quitting Benefits:** Highlight all benefits of quitting smoking, health and financial gains alike | M | H | 3, 8 |

(*continued*)

**Table 1.** (*continued*)

| Category | Requirement | Priority | Feasibility | Expert |
|---|---|---|---|---|
| CI7 | **Visual Database:** Include a visual database and practical examples | H | H | 3, 9 |
| CI8 & ME3 | **Educational Quizzes:** Engage users with smoking-related quizzes, using their responses to initiate conversations and correct misconceptions | L | M | 9 |
| CI9 & SS3 | **Shareable Content:** Provide content sharing options with family and friends | L | H | 3 |
| CI10 & TP3 | **Timely Information Delivery:** Provide relevant information at the right time for optimal impact | M | L | 3, 9 |
| CI11 & T2 | **Easy Adjustability:** Provide an adaptability backend, terms of content and OS updates | M | H | 1, 2, 10 |
| Technical | | | | |
| T3 | **Edge Case Management:** Effectively manage unusual usage scenarios, such as prolonged use | L | H | 1 |
| T4 | **Constant Availability:** Guarantee 24/7 availability, support and ensure long-term funding | H | L | 2, 10, 11 |
| Tracking and Prediction | | | | |
| TP4 | **Behaviour Tracking:** Track and inform users about their smoking patterns | H | H | 1, 3, 4, 9, 10 |
| TP5 | **Quitting Status:** Determine users' smoking cessation status to prevent unnecessary notifications | L | M | 3 |
| Social Interaction and Support | | | | |
| SS4 | **Testimonials Incorporation:** Incorporate experiences from (ex)smokers | L | H | 1 |
| SS5 | **Support Network Creation:** Connect quitters to foster a support network | L | L | 5, 6 |

**User Interface and User Experience.** The User Interface (UI) and User Experience (UX) category underscores the necessity of creating apps that are intuitive, accessible, and engaging for all users, regardless of their technological proficiency or stage in the quitting process (UIX3). Experts for example advocated for the use of simple language (UIX4), avoidance of lengthy questionnaires (UIX5) which frustrate users to the point of quitting using apps in their initialisation stage and simplified and non-overwhelming interfaces which present information in a manageable manner (UIX7). These features ensure that users find the app approachable and easy to navigate, enhancing their overall experience and likelihood of sustained use. Additionally, features such as a progress overview of the users' smoking cessation journey (UIX1) with the inclusion of interactive elements (UIX6) further consolidated the need for sound UI and UX design among experts. The alignment with Nielsen's Principles, particularly usability and aesthetic and minimalist design, is evident here, emphasizing the importance of user-centred design in promoting effective interaction with the app [43].

**Behaviour Change.** Experts also explicitly called for the direct integration of behaviour change theories into the app design in their applied form of behaviour change techniques (BC6). An example of this is an SOS button offering users a range of practical tips for challenging situations, including relapse prevention and mental wellness tips (BC2). Further, the importance of being able to set and execute implementation intentions [56], the behavioural equivalent of if-this-then-that rules was highlighted, signifying experts' commitment to evidence-based strategies (BC1). These features are designed not only to provide immediate support in moments of crisis but also to educate and empower users with strategies for long-term behaviour modification (BC4, BC7). This aligns with both CBT and SDT by offering practical tools for coping and autonomy in decision-making during the difficult smoking cessation process [7, 57].

**Goal Setting.** Continuing and extending the behaviour change category in a more specific manner is the goal-setting theme. Incorporating directly taps into the previously mentioned and similarly named behaviour change theory, GST, which posits that specific and challenging goals enhance motivation and performance [39]. By enabling users to set personalized goals and track their progress (GS1) [58], the app not only fosters a sense of achievement (GS2) but also aligns with the psychological need for competence as outlined in SDT, enhancing intrinsic motivation towards cessation [45]. To achieve this effect, however, the app interface must facilitate an effortless user experience in both setting these specific goals and wherever possible automatically tracking progress towards them, offloading the effort away from users [35]. Additionally, sharing these goals and their achievement should be rewarded both within the app and by facilitating the sharing of these achievements to encourage social support (GS3).

**Social Interaction and Support.** Enabling social interaction and support features addresses the need for relatedness, a key component of SDT, by leveraging the power of community and shared experiences [44]. This can be achieved by leveraging the testimonials of ex-smokers sharing their struggles, bringing current users trying to quit some solace and invoking feelings of camaraderie (SS4). Features such as achievement sharing (SS1) and support network creation (SS5) not only provide motivation and encouragement but also foster a sense of belonging and accountability, which are crucial for sustained behaviour change [59]. Native incorporation of these social elements in the app can remove barriers and facilitate the creation of such interactions much faster.

**Personalization.** Personalization features aim to cater to the individual's unique quitting journey, preferences, and behaviours. The development of personalized smoking profiles (P1) for example is a key aspect of this category. By analysing users' smoking habits, triggers, and past cessation attempts (P3, P4), the app can generate a nuanced profile that reflects the specific challenges and needs of each individual. This approach should go beyond generic advice, offering tailored recommendations and strategies that are more likely to resonate with the user (P2) [28]. Also, by adjusting to each user's informational needs and offering customized content (P6), the app addresses the SDT component of autonomy by offering choice and empowering users to tailor their experience [57]. This personalization should extend to adapting intervention strategies based on specific user behaviour (P4), reinforcing the app's role as a supportive tool that adjusts to each individual's specific needs, increasing their trust in the app [60], by increasing autonomy in steering the intervention. The principle is applicable from an HCI perspective, ensuring user control and freedom in using the interface [43].

**Content and Information.** This category of requirements is foundational in providing users with the knowledge and resources necessary to make informed decisions about their health. By offering concise (CI2) and specific information on the health benefits of quitting (CI3), risks of smoking (CI4), and alternative coping strategies to smoking, the app should serve as an educational platform that supports rational and informed approaches to behaviour change, delivering sufficient requested information in easily digestible interfaces [61]. Additionally, the provision of a visual database (CI7) and shareable content (CI9) enhances understanding and encourages engagement with the app, underlining the role of clear and accessible information in supporting cessation.

**Expert Support and Integration.** Perhaps somewhat unsurprisingly, the experts recommended facilitating access to professional help (ESI2) and integrating cessation experts into the app to bring an additional layer of support and credibility (ESI4). This not only provides users with access to expert advice but also reinforces the app's reliability and the validity of the information and strategies provided. It underscores the importance of integrating professional insights and source credibility cues into digital health interventions to enhance user trust and subsequent outcomes [62].

**Tracking and Prediction.** Features focused on tracking smoking behaviour (TP4) and predicting potential relapse moments (TP1) embody the personalized and proactive approach necessary for effective cessation support. These predictive capabilities allow the app to offer just-in-time and tailored interventions (TP3) [63], potentially increasing the user's self-awareness and ability to cope with cravings (TP2) by detecting potential craving-evoking contexts. This proactive stance on tracking and prediction highlights the importance of adaptive interventions in behaviour change efforts to build on top of the personalization and offers users unique and personal insights on their behaviour.

**Technical and Miscellaneous.** Ensuring technical robustness and constant availability addresses (T4) the practical aspects of app design that impact user engagement and retention. Features like easy adjustability (T2) and ad-free experience (T1) reflect an understanding of the technical and aesthetic factors that contribute to a positive user experience, aligning with Nielsen's usability heuristics such as user control and freedom, and error prevention [35]. They also highlight the minimum functionality and reliability that the app must provide to its users to gain their trust and potentially engage them long-term, necessary for difficult processes such as smoking cessation [64].

**Motivation and Engagement.** Lastly, motivation and engagement are pivotal in sustaining user interest and participation over the long term, both in the literature [45] and confirmed by the experts. This encompasses strategies to not only capture but also maintain user involvement through continuous motivation enhancement (ME2). This is achieved by actively engaging users from the beginning (ME1), ensuring that the app experience is interactive and rewards users for their progress and achievements. Such features directly resonate with SDT, specifically addressing the psychological need for competence by acknowledging progress, and for relatedness by fostering a sense of community and connection [42]. Furthermore, these motivational elements are crucial for habit formation, a key aspect of sustained behaviour change [65]. The motivational aspects of the app, when coupled with interactive elements (ME3), also adhere to Nielsen's principles, particularly 'user control and freedom', and 'engagement'. By offering users a sense of control over their cessation journey and continuous feedback on their progress, these features enhance the overall user experience, making the process of quitting smoking more manageable and less daunting [66].

In summary, the discussed categories each tackle a vital part of the user's journey towards quitting smoking. By integrating these varied but linked features, smoking cessation apps should aim to create a supportive, impactful, and appealing environment tailored to users' needs and preferences. Merging these aspects with behavioural change theories like SDT and GST, alongside Nielsen's HCI principles, emphasizes the value of a holistic, theory-informed, and user-focused approach in the development process to achieve effective and engaging mHealth applications.

## 5   Limitations and Future Research

While this study provides insights into the design of mHealth apps for smoking cessation, it's important to acknowledge the inherent limitations shaped by its qualitative nature and geographical focus. Recruiting experts through the VRGT database, while ensuring a high level of expertise, might have led to selection bias, potentially overlooking dissimilar perspectives from experts in different countries. It is for example feasible that certain features may be effective in industrialised countries but not in other regions due to differences in cultural norms, healthcare systems, and rates of technology adoption.

Furthermore, the inductive thematic analysis approach [55] employed in this study heavily relies on subjective interpretations, both from experts and researchers. Therefore, the presented requirements, their justification and implementation feasibility were shaped by their experiences and knowledge [52]. The qualitative nature of the study also limits the ability to quantify the impact of suggested design elements on cessation success. While the study identified key features and design elements, it did not empirically test these in a real-world mHealth application. Thus, the effectiveness of these recommendations remains theoretical until applied and evaluated in practical settings [33]. Future research should focus on implementing the identified features in a working mHealth app and providing quantitative evidence of their effectiveness in aiding smoking cessation. Such studies should observe user interaction with mHealth apps over an extended period to offer insights into long-term engagement and efficacy, addressing the sustainability of behaviour change. Putting the focus entirely on the user side could also be beneficial, in the same way that the present study has done with expert feedback. Direct user feedback and usability studies can be pivotal in refining app design, ensuring the app's practicality and effectiveness from the user's perspective [13, 47].

Future studies might also benefit from including a wider range of experts, such as app developers, HCI researchers, and ex-smokers who have successfully quit smoking through mHealth apps, to provide a more holistic view of effective app design [34, 36]. This could be done cross-culturally to include both users and experts from different geographical locations to understand the universal applicability of the findings and to incorporate diverse cultural perspectives in mHealth design. Finally, the rapid evolution of technology, such as the introduction of LLMs and novel multi-modal user interfaces, seemingly outpace the current findings, and while this offers new opportunities for behaviour change applications, it also necessitates continuous updates to the current recommendations based on the latest technological advancements [67].

# 6 Conclusion

In this study, we aimed to address the shortcomings of existing smoking cessation mHealth apps by integrating smoking cessation specialists' insights with behaviour change theories and HCI principles. We present a series of refined design requirements aimed at overcoming the current limitations of generic, one-size-fits-all solutions that lack deep personalization and fail to engage users effectively over the long term. Our findings reveal a significant alignment between theoretical frameworks and practical design considerations, highlighting the potential for creating more effective, user-centred smoking cessation apps. The study underscores the critical role of multidisciplinary approaches in mHealth development, demonstrating how expert-driven design can lead to apps that are not only engaging and user-friendly but also grounded in evidence-based strategies for supporting successful smoking cessation efforts.

**Acknowledgments.** This study was funded by The Research Foundation – Flanders (grant number G0D5322N) (FWO) project IMPERIO.

**Disclosure of Interests.** The authors have no competing interests to declare that are relevant to the content of this article.

# References

1. Reitsma, M.B., et al.: Spatial, temporal, and demographic patterns in prevalence of smoking tobacco use and attributable disease burden in 204 countries and territories, 1990–2019: a systematic analysis from the Global Burden of Disease Study 2019. Lancet **397**, 2337–2360 (2021). https://doi.org/10.1016/S0140-6736(21)01169-7
2. WHO: WHO global report on trends in prevalence of tobacco use 2000–2030. World Health Organization, Geneva (2024)
3. Murray, C.J.L., et al.: Global burden of 87 risk factors in 204 countries and territories, 1990–2019: a systematic analysis for the global burden of disease study 2019. Lancet **396**, 1223–1249 (2020). https://doi.org/10.1016/S0140-6736(20)30752-2

4. Goodchild, M., Nargis, N., d'Espaignet, E.T.: Global economic cost of smoking-attributable diseases. Tob. Control. **27**, 58–64 (2018). https://doi.org/10.1136/tobaccocontrol-2016-053305
5. Taylor, G.M.J., Dalili, M.N., Semwal, M., Civljak, M., Sheikh, A., Car, J.: Internet-based interventions for smoking cessation. Cochrane Database Syst. Rev. (2017). https://doi.org/10.1002/14651858.CD007078.pub5
6. Castelnuovo, G., Pietrabissa, G., Cattivelli, R., Manzoni, G.M., Molinari, E.: Not only clinical efficacy in psychological treatments: clinical psychology must promote cost-benefit, cost-effectiveness, and cost-utility analysis. Front. Psychol. **7** (2016)
7. Wagner, B., Horn, A.B., Maercker, A.: Internet-based versus face-to-face cognitive-behavioral intervention for depression: a randomized controlled non-inferiority trial. J. Affect. Disord. **152–154**, 113–121 (2014). https://doi.org/10.1016/j.jad.2013.06.032
8. FDA: Pfizer Expands Voluntary Nationwide Recall to include All Lots of CHANTIX® (Varenicline) Tablets Due to N-Nitroso Varenicline Content. https://www.fda.gov/safety/rec alls-market-withdrawals-safety-alerts/pfizer-expands-voluntary-nationwide-recall-include-all-lots-chantixr-varenicline-tablets-due-n. Accessed 18 Jan 2024
9. Murray, R.L., Bauld, L., Hackshaw, L.E., McNeill, A.: Improving access to smoking cessation services for disadvantaged groups: a systematic review. J. Public Health **31**, 258–277 (2009). https://doi.org/10.1093/pubmed/fdp008
10. Al-Worafi, Y.M.: Smoking cessation in developing countries: challenges and recommendations. In: Al-Worafi, Y.M. (ed.) Handbook of Medical and Health Sciences in Developing Countries : Education, Practice, and Research, pp. 1–20. Springer, Cham (2023). https://doi.org/10.1007/978-3-030-74786-2_316-1
11. Olson, J.A.: Smartphone addiction is increasing across the world: a meta-analysis of 24 countries. Comput. Hum. Behav. **129**, 107138 (2022). https://doi.org/10.1016/j.chb.2021.107138
12. Messner, E.-M., Probst, T., O'Rourke, T., Stoyanov, S., Baumeister, H.: MHealth applications: potentials, limitations, current quality and future directions. In: Baumeister, H., Montag, C. (eds.) Digital Phenotyping and Mobile Sensing. SNPBE, pp. 235–248. Springer, Cham (2019). https://doi.org/10.1007/978-3-030-31620-4_15
13. Farao, J., Malila, B., Conrad, N., Mutsvangwa, T., Rangaka, M.X., Douglas, T.S.: A user-centred design framework for mHealth. PLoS ONE **15**, e0237910 (2020). https://doi.org/10.1371/journal.pone.0237910
14. Jakob, R., et al.: Factors influencing adherence to mHealth apps for prevention or management of noncommunicable diseases: systematic review. J. Med. Internet Res. **24**, e35371 (2022). https://doi.org/10.2196/35371
15. West, R., et al.: Health-care interventions to promote and assist tobacco cessation: a review of efficacy, effectiveness and affordability for use in national guideline development. Addiction **110**, 1388–1403 (2015). https://doi.org/10.1111/add.12998
16. Rivera-Romero, O., Gabarron, E., Ropero, J., Denecke, K.: Designing personalised mHealth solutions: an overview. J. Biomed. Inform. **146**, 104500 (2023). https://doi.org/10.1016/j.jbi.2023.104500
17. Ghorai, K., Akter, S., Khatun, F., Ray, P.: MHealth for smoking cessation programs: a systematic review. J. Personalized Med. **4**, 412–423 (2014). https://doi.org/10.3390/jpm4030412
18. Nouri, R., Niakan Kalhori, S.R., Ghazisaeedi, M., Marchand, G., Yasini, M.: Criteria for assessing the quality of mHealth apps: a systematic review. J. Am. Med. Inform. Assoc. **25**, 1089–1098 (2018). https://doi.org/10.1093/jamia/ocy050
19. Tarricone, R., Petracca, F., Ciani, O., Cucciniello, M.: Distinguishing features in the assessment of mHealth apps. Expert Rev. Pharmacoecon. Outcomes Res. **21**, 521–526 (2021). https://doi.org/10.1080/14737167.2021.1891883

20. Papadakis, S., et al.: Quitting behaviours and cessation methods used in eight European countries in 2018: findings from the EUREST-PLUS ITC Europe surveys. Eur. J. Public Health **30**, iii26–iii33 (2020). https://doi.org/10.1093/eurpub/ckaa082
21. Fiers, S., Braekman, E.: Preventiebarometer: Tabak. Sciensano (2022). https://doi.org/10.25608/CS3T-FY57
22. Seo, S., Cho, S.-I., Yoon, W., Lee, C.M.: Classification of smoking cessation apps: quality review and content analysis. JMIR mHealth uHealth **10**, e17268 (2022). https://doi.org/10.2196/17268
23. Borland, R.: Understanding Hard to Maintain Behaviour Change: A Dual Process Approach. Wiley (2014)
24. McCool, J., Dobson, R., Whittaker, R., Paton, C.: Mobile Health (mHealth) in low- and middle-income countries. Annu. Rev. Public Health **43**, 525–539 (2022). https://doi.org/10.1146/annurev-publhealth-052620-093850
25. Saldivar, M.M.: Enrique: Opportunities and Obstacles in the Adoption of mHealth. mHealth. HIMSS Publishing (2012)
26. Brownlow, L.: A review of mHealth gambling apps in Australia. JGI. (2021). https://doi.org/10.4309/jgi.2021.47.1
27. Iribarren, S.J., Cato, K., Falzon, L., Stone, P.W.: What is the economic evidence for mHealth? A systematic review of economic evaluations of mHealth solutions. PLoS ONE **12**, e0170581 (2017). https://doi.org/10.1371/journal.pone.0170581
28. Gosetto, L., Ehrler, F., Falquet, G.: Personalization dimensions for mHealth to improve behavior change: a scoping review. In: Värri, A., et al. (eds.) Studies in Health Technology and Informatics. IOS Press (2020). https://doi.org/10.3233/SHTI200698
29. Walsh, J.C., Groarke, J.M.: Integrating behavioral science with mobile (mHealth) technology to optimize health behavior change interventions. Eur. Psychol. **24**, 38–48 (2019). https://doi.org/10.1027/1016-9040/a000351
30. Istepanian, R.S.H., AlAnzi, T.: Mobile health (m-Health): evidence-based progress or scientific retrogression. In: Feng, D.D. (ed.) Biomedical Information Technology, 2nd edn., pp. 717–733. Academic Press (2020). https://doi.org/10.1016/B978-0-12-816034-3.00022-5
31. Ammenwerth, E., Rigby, M.: Evidence-Based Health Informatics: Promoting Safety and Efficiency Through Scientific Methods and Ethical Policy. IOS Press (2016)
32. Salwen-Deremer, J.K., Khan, A.S., Martin, S.S., Holloway, B.M., Coughlin, J.W.: Incorporating health behavior theory into mHealth: an examination of weight loss, dietary, and physical activity interventions. J. Technol. Behav. Sci. **5**, 51–60 (2020). https://doi.org/10.1007/s41347-019-00118-6
33. Dugas, M., Gao, G. (Gordon), Agarwal, R.: Unpacking mHealth interventions: a systematic review of behavior change techniques used in randomized controlled trials assessing mHealth effectiveness. Digit. Health **6**, 2055207620905411 (2020). https://doi.org/10.1177/2055207620905411
34. Poole, E.S.: HCI and mobile health interventions: how human–computer interaction can contribute to successful mobile health interventions. Transl. Behav. Med. **3**, 402–405 (2013). https://doi.org/10.1007/s13142-013-0214-3
35. Nielsen, J.: Usability inspection methods. In: Conference Companion on Human Factors in Computing Systems - CHI 1994, pp. 413–414. ACM Press, Boston, Massachusetts, United States (1994). https://doi.org/10.1145/259963.260531
36. Noorbergen, T.J., Adam, M.T.P., Teubner, T., Collins, C.E.: Using co-design in mobile health system development: a qualitative study with experts in co-design and mobile health system development. JMIR mHealth uHealth **9**, e27896 (2021). https://doi.org/10.2196/27896
37. Williams, L., Hayes, G.R., Guo, Y., Rahmani, A., Dutt, N.: HCI and mHealth wearable tech: a multidisciplinary research challenge. In: Extended Abstracts of the 2020 CHI Conference

on Human Factors in Computing Systems, pp. 1–7. Association for Computing Machinery, New York, NY, USA (2020). https://doi.org/10.1145/3334480.3375223

38. Deci, E.L., Ryan, R.M.: Self-determination theory. In: Wright, J.D. (ed.) International Encyclopedia of the Social & Behavioral Sciences, 2nd edn., pp. 486–491. Elsevier, Oxford (2015). https://doi.org/10.1016/B978-0-08-097086-8.26036-4

39. Latham, E.A.L., Gary, P.: Goal setting theory: the current state. In: New Developments in Goal Setting and Task Performance. Routledge (2012)

40. Ng, J.Y.Y., et al.: Self-determination theory applied to health contexts: a meta-analysis. Perspect. Psychol. Sci. **7**, 325–340 (2012). https://doi.org/10.1177/1745691612447309

41. Locke, E.A., Latham, G.P.: Goal setting theory. In: Motivation: Theory and Research. Routledge (1994)

42. Sullivan, G.S., Strode, J.P.: Motivation through goal setting: a self-determined perspective. Strategies **23**, 18–23 (2010). https://doi.org/10.1080/08924562.2010.10590899

43. Nurhudatiana, A., Seo, J.Y.: An mHealth application redesign based on Nielsen's usability heuristics: a case study of Halodoc. In: Proceedings of the 2020 The 6th International Conference on E-Business and Applications, pp. 85–89. Association for Computing Machinery, New York, NY, USA (2020). https://doi.org/10.1145/3387263.3387267

44. Fu, H.N.C., Wyman, J.F., Peden-McAlpine, C.J., Draucker, C.B., Schleyer, T., Adam, T.J.: App design features important for diabetes self-management as determined by the self-determination theory on motivation: content analysis of survey responses from adults requiring insulin therapy. JMIR Diab. **8**, e38592 (2023). https://doi.org/10.2196/38592

45. Ryan, R.M., Deci, E.L.: Intrinsic and extrinsic motivation from a self-determination theory perspective: definitions, theory, practices, and future directions. Contemp. Educ. Psychol. **61**, 101860 (2020). https://doi.org/10.1016/j.cedpsych.2020.101860

46. Kwasnicka, D., Dombrowski, S.U., White, M., Sniehotta, F.: Theoretical explanations for maintenance of behaviour change: a systematic review of behaviour theories. Health Psychol. Rev. **10**, 277–296 (2016). https://doi.org/10.1080/17437199.2016.1151372

47. Hilliard, M.E., Hahn, A., Ridge, A.K., Eakin, M.N., Riekert, K.A.: User preferences and design recommendations for an mHealth app to promote cystic fibrosis self-management. JMIR mHealth uHealth **2**, e3599 (2014). https://doi.org/10.2196/mhealth.3599

48. Sheffer, C.E., et al.: Increasing the quality and availability of evidence-based treatment for tobacco dependence through unified certification of tobacco treatment specialists. J. Smok. Cessat. **11**, 229–235 (2016). https://doi.org/10.1017/jsc.2014.30

49. VRGT: Programma | Rookstop. https://rookstop.vrgt.be/vorming-opleiding/hoe-word-ik-tabakoloog/programma. Accessed 29 Oct 2023

50. NCSCT: NCSCT e-learning. https://elearning.ncsct.co.uk/england. Accessed 29 Oct 2023

51. Guest, G., Bunce, A., Johnson, L.: How many interviews are enough? An experiment with data saturation and variability. Field Methods **18**, 59–82 (2006). https://doi.org/10.1177/1525822X05279903

52. Flick, U.: The SAGE Handbook of Qualitative Data Collection. SAGE (2017)

53. Radford, A., Kim, J.W., Xu, T., Brockman, G., Mcleavey, C., Sutskever, I.: Robust speech recognition via large-scale weak supervision. In: Proceedings of the 40th International Conference on Machine Learning, pp. 28492–28518. PMLR (2022)

54. Lumivero: NVivo (2023)

55. Braun, V., Clarke, V.: Thematic analysis. In: APA Handbook of Research Methods in Psychology. Research Designs: Quantitative, Qualitative, Neuropsychological, and Biological, vol. 2, pp. 57–71. American Psychological Association, Washington, DC, US (2012). https://doi.org/10.1037/13620-004

56. Conner, M.: Long-term effects of implementation intentions on prevention of smoking uptake among adolescents: a cluster randomized controlled trial. Health Psychol. **29**, 529–538 (2010). https://doi.org/10.1037/a0020317

57. Williams, G.C., et al.: Testing a self-determination theory intervention for motivating tobacco cessation: supporting autonomy and competence in a clinical trial. Health Psychol. **25**, 91–101 (2006). https://doi.org/10.1037/0278-6133.25.1.91
58. Harkin, B., et al.: Does monitoring goal progress promote goal attainment? A meta-analysis of the experimental evidence. Psychol. Bull. **142**, 198–229 (2016). https://doi.org/10.1037/bul0000025
59. Choi, J., Noh, G.-Y., Park, D.-J.: Smoking cessation apps for smartphones: content analysis with the self-determination theory. J. Med. Internet Res. **16**, e3061 (2014). https://doi.org/10.2196/jmir.3061
60. Seitz, L., Bekmeier-Feuerhahn, S., Gohil, K.: Can we trust a chatbot like a physician? A qualitative study on understanding the emergence of trust toward diagnostic chatbots. Int. J. Hum. Comput. Stud. **165**, 102848 (2022). https://doi.org/10.1016/j.ijhcs.2022.102848
61. Hardeman, W., Houghton, J., Lane, K., Jones, A., Naughton, F.: A systematic review of just-in-time adaptive interventions (JITAIs) to promote physical activity. Int. J. Behav. Nutr. Phys. Act. **16**, 31 (2019). https://doi.org/10.1186/s12966-019-0792-7
62. Liu, Y., Yan, W., Hu, B., Li, Z., Lai, Y.L.: Effects of personalization and source expertise on users' health beliefs and usage intention toward health chatbots: Evidence from an online experiment. Digit. Health **8**, 20552076221129720 (2022). https://doi.org/10.1177/20552076221129718
63. Wang, L., Miller, L.C.: Just-in-the-moment adaptive interventions (JITAI): a meta-analytical review. Health Commun. **35**, 1531–1544 (2020). https://doi.org/10.1080/10410236.2019.1652388
64. Ozawa, S., Sripad, P.: How do you measure trust in the health system? A systematic review of the literature. Soc Sci Med **91**, 10–14 (2013). https://doi.org/10.1016/j.socscimed.2013.05.005
65. Pinder, C., Vermeulen, J., Cowan, B.R., Beale, R.: Digital behaviour change interventions to break and form habits. ACM Trans. Comput.-Hum. Interact. **25**, 15:1–15:66 (2018). https://doi.org/10.1145/3196830
66. Gonzalez-Holland, E., Whitmer, D., Moralez, L., Mouloua, M.: Examination of the use of Nielsen's 10 usability heuristics & outlooks for the future. Proc. Hum. Fact. Ergon. Soc. Ann. Meet. **61**, 1472–1475 (2017). https://doi.org/10.1177/1541931213601853
67. Meskó, B.: The impact of multimodal large language models on health Care's future. J. Med. Internet Res. **25**, e52865 (2023). https://doi.org/10.2196/52865

# Mental Health Mobile Applications: Opportunities and Challenges

Erin Li[1(✉)] and Sean Li[2]

[1] Cherry Hill High School East, 1750 Kresson Road, Cherry Hill, NJ 08003, USA
`erinxinranli@gmail.com`
[2] University of California, Berkeley, 130 Hilgard Way, Berkeley, CA 94709, USA
`seanhli@berkeley.edu`

**Abstract.** The prevalence of mental health issues throughout the world is alarmingly high, and it has only increased because of the COVID-19 pandemic. Despite this truth, there continues to be a large gap between the demand for mental healthcare and the actual provision of such services. However, the rapidly expanding digital world offers a solution to this discrepancy: AI-driven mental health mobile applications. With the development of these apps, millions of patients are benefiting from the availability and affordability of many services, including but not limited to mood trackers, accurate diagnoses, assessment tools, frequent reminders, useful resources, and community building opportunities. Nevertheless, AI-driven mobile apps have their disadvantages. For instance, these apps have raised concerns regarding low patient engagement, lack of privacy and security, little evidence to support effectiveness, as well as inability to mimic human emotions. To assess the uses of mental health mobile applications, we analyzed 15 different apps, of which 5 involved AI. Through this analysis, we aim to discover patterns and inadequacies in the approaches and focuses of mental health apps. This way, we will be able to explain the opportunities and challenges of mental health apps while simultaneously offering suggestions that will help fill the mental health care gap.

**Keywords:** Mental Health · Stress · Mobile App · Artificial Intelligence

## 1 Introduction

Mental illnesses, such as depression, bipolar disorder, post-traumatic stress disorder (PTSD), schizophrenia, eating disorders, etc., can severely disrupt an individual's behavior, emotions, and thoughts [1]. Various factors can contribute to the development of a mental illness, such as genetics, inequality, abuse, violence, disability, poverty, and more [1]. Globally, 1 in 8 people have a mental illness [1] and, in America, 1 in 5 adults have a mental illness [2]. In the US in 2021, more females than males suffered from any mental illness; more young adults (18–25) suffered from mental illnesses than adults (26–49) and older adults (50 and older), and the prevalence of a mental illness was highest among adults of more than one race, second highest among American Indian/Alaskan Native adults, third highest among white people [2].

© The Author(s), under exclusive license to Springer Nature Switzerland AG 2024
J. Wei and G. Margetis (Eds.): HCII 2024, LNCS 14737, pp. 80–89, 2024.
https://doi.org/10.1007/978-3-031-60458-4_6

The COVID-19 pandemic, which led to a great deal of unemployment, poverty, social isolation, inactivity, decreased support, and more, severely increased the prevalence of mental health issues [3]. However, there remains a huge gap between the need for quality support for people suffering mental illnesses and the actual provision of such support [1]. In the US, more than half of all adults (56%) with a mental health issue do not receive treatment. Additionally, around 25% of all American adults with a mental disorder who need treatment do not receive it [4]. Various factors prevent individuals from receiving the necessary treatment: lack of psychiatrists and/or mental health professionals, limited or no insurance, no access to different treatment services, a shortage of money to cover medical expenses, and a dissociation between primary care and behavioral health services [4].

The employment of AI-driven mental health applications to address these factors may prove to be critical in ensuring increased access to better mental health services [5]. As the digital world continues to grow and develop, an increasing number of people are gaining access to mobile phones, thus presenting a distinctive possibility for using online health applications to improve individuals' behavioral and mental health [5].

In this paper, we assess the uses of 15 mental health mobile applications (including 5 AI-driven mobile apps) to identify patterns and inadequacies in the approaches and focuses of mental health apps. The opportunities and challenges of mental health apps and suggestions that will help fill the mental health care gap are discussed.

## 2  Background

### 2.1  Mental Health Mobile Applications

Mental health mobile applications are defined as "mobile technology applications that offer clinical and non-clinical methods of offering mental health support" [8]. In a 2015 survey by the World Health Organization, it was revealed that 29% of 15,000 mobile health applications prioritized mental health [9]. Additionally, according to a study, in 2016, the number of mental health applications increased by 57%, demonstrating the expanding interest and use of apps to supplement and improve health care [7]. As of 2019, there were more than 10,000 mental health applications available for people to use [6]. And, because of the pandemic and the quarantine that it induced, there has also been a significant increase in the prevalence of mental health apps to help patients cope with behavioral and/or mental illnesses [8].

According to the National Institute of Mental Health (NIMH) as well as other health organizations, mental health mobile applications have proven to be adaptable and practical methods of reducing the discrepancy between the demand for mental health services and the provision of it [9]. Mental health applications primarily focus on education or information provision on mental health, treatments or coping methods, mood tracking or assessment tools, and support groups [6]. In addition, they can help improve various mental health issues, such as stress, anxiety, depression, sleep, eating disorders, and trauma [10], and they address many different stages of health care provision, including diagnosis, crisis support, prevention, primary treatment, post-treatment management, and more [9]. To provide these services, mental health apps generally adopt five management approaches: cognitive improvement, community support, data collection, self-assessment, and behavior tracking [9].

### 2.2  AI-Driven Mental Health Mobile Applications

Many mental health mobile apps that have high ratings from many users are utilizing artificial intelligence to achieve their goals, demonstrating the potential for AI to benefit mental health services [12]. AI-driven mental health apps have the potential to support mental health through the collection of data, assessment of risk factors, personalization of user interfaces, and provision of support and treatment [12]. By employing AI in mental health apps, it will be possible to engage in conversations with users, track patients' moods and symptoms, make assessments regarding risk factors, and provide suggestions for potential treatment [12]. AI-driven mental health apps may also be able to prevent mental health illnesses among patients by tailoring to individuals and each of their unique experiences in life [11]. Furthermore, through the collection of data from various sources, AI has the capability of diagnosing mental illnesses in patients better than human doctors and therapists can [15]. AI can review patients' conversations, medical records, physical activity, and social media presence to track their moods, symptoms, and behavioral patterns to assess whether they have a mental illness and, if so, what kind of treatment would be best fit for them [15]. As shown, AI offers a new and unique approach to offering mental health care through mobile apps to patients.

This paper aims to analyze the existing research regarding AI-driven mental health mobile applications as well as to assess the opportunities and challenges of designing and developing such apps. Through this review we hope to answer the following research questions (RQs):

- RQ1: What are some mental health mobile applications that are currently out there and how many of them utilize AI?
- RQ2: What are the opportunities and challenges offered by AI-driven mental health mobile applications?

## 3  Identifying Mental Health Mobile Applications

Using the search query "mental health mobile apps," we used ChatGPT to generate 30 names of mobile applications used to address mental health for people of all ages and backgrounds. After generating the 30 apps, we read through their descriptions on the App Store and eliminated 15 of them on the basis that they were too specific (i.e., they targeted only young children and/or adolescents rather than catering to the general population regardless of age). The remaining 15 mobile applications were selected for this review and were assigned reference codes ranging from A1 to A15 (as seen in Table 1) to make it easier to analyze their different capabilities, goals, and approaches (as seen in Tables 2, 3, and 4).

**Table 1.** Names and Reference Codes of the 15 Studied Mobile Applications.

| App Reference Code | App Name |
| --- | --- |
| A1 | BetterHelp |
| A2 | Breathe2Relax |
| A3 | Calm |
| A4 | Daylio |
| A5 | Happify |
| A6 | Headspace |
| **A7** | **MindDoc** |
| **A8** | **Replika** |
| A9 | Sanvello |
| A10 | Smiling Mind |
| A11 | SuperBetter |
| A12 | Talkspace |
| **A13** | **Woebot** |
| **A14** | **Wysa** |
| **A15** | **Youper** |

Next, we analyzed the AI capabilities of the mobile applications. As can be seen, 5 of the 15 apps in the Table 1 were AI-driven, including MindDoc, Replika, Woebot, Wysa and Youper (highlighted in Bold font). Most of the AI-driven apps (80%) used AI chatbots, but one of them (MindDoc) primarily used assessment tools to determine symptoms and patterns of mental illnesses in patients. Figures 1, 2, 3, 4 and 5 show the screenshots of the five AI-driven mental health apps.

All the selected mobile applications addressed mental illnesses; however, most of them differed in the mental health issues that they primarily targeted (Table 2). The most popular target mental health issue among the apps was anxiety, with all 15 of the apps addressing this issue. Closely following anxiety were depression and stress, with 13 of the mobile applications addressing both mental illnesses. Of all the target mental health issues, sleep had the lowest popularity, as only 6 apps addressed it. Additionally, many applications (about 53.3%) also addressed other mental health issues, such as social relationship problems, productivity, concentration, eating disorders, addiction, and more.

**Table 2.** Target Mental Health Issues

| Target Mental Health Issue | App Reference Codes | Total |
|---|---|---|
| Anxiety | A1, A2, A3, A4, A5, A6, **A7, A8**, A9, A10, A11, A12, **A13, A14, A15** | 15 |
| Depression | A1, A2, A3, A4, A5, A6, **A7**, A9, A11, A12, **A13, A14, A15** | 13 |
| Stress | A2, A3, A4, A5, A6, **A8**, A9, A10, A11, A12, **A13, A14, A15** | 13 |
| Sleep | A3, A4, A6, A9, A10, **A14** | 6 |
| Others | A1, A4, A6, A7, A8, A12, **A13, A14** | 8 |

In Table 3, we analyzed the different management approaches employed by mental health applications. There was a large variety of management approaches, including AI chatbots, assessment tools, meditation, mood tracking, physical exercise, and therapy, but meditation was the most popular approach, with 6 of the 15 apps employing it to help users cope with mental health issues. On top of all these management approaches, 7 out of the 15 apps employed various other techniques, such as breathing exercises, gratitude diaries, science-based activities and games, music, and visualizations.

**Table 3.** Management Approaches

| Management Approach | App Reference Codes | Total |
|---|---|---|
| AI Chatbot | **A8, A13, A15** | 3 |
| Assessment Tools | **A7**, A9 | 2 |
| Meditation | A3, A5, A6, A9, A10, **A14** | 6 |
| Mood Tracking | A4, A9, A10 | 3 |
| Physical Exercise | A4, A6, A10 | 3 |
| Therapy | A1, A9, A12, **A14** | 4 |
| Others | A2, A3, A4, A5, A6, A11, **A14** | 7 |

## 4  Discussion

Though there are many potential benefits to mental health mobile applications, the use of such apps also has various disadvantages, including but not limited to concerns regarding the protection of users' private information, the lack of evidence to support that such approaches work, as well as the inability of these apps to ensure continuous participation from users [13]. Most user privacy and security concerns arise from the fact that many

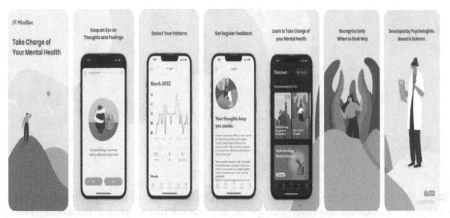

**Fig. 1.** MindDoc: Your Companion: "Log your mental health and mood in real-time. Get insights and summaries on your symptoms, behaviors, and general emotional well-being to help you recognize patterns and find the best resources for you. Discover our library of courses and exercises to help you on your journey toward emotional well-being" [9].

**Fig. 2.** Replika – Virtual AI Companion: "Create your own unique chatbot AI companion, help it develop its personality, talk about your feelings or anything that's on your mind, have fun, calm anxiety and grow together. You also get to decide if you want Replika to be your friend, romantic partner or mentor. Replika can help you understand your thoughts and feelings, track your mood, learn coping skills, calm anxiety and work toward goals like positive thinking, stress management, socializing and finding love. Improve your mental well-being with Replika" [10].

mental health mobile apps either do not have a privacy policy or, if they do have one, do not sufficiently convey how the data collected from users will be used [14]. For example, a study has shown that fewer than half of the mobile applications focused on depression provide privacy policies for their users to read and accept before utilizing the app [14].

Designing effective and impactful health mobile applications needs to overcome a couple of obstacles [9]. First, since apps do not provide face-to-face human interaction, they need to come up with new and innovative ways of frequently engaging users. For instance, they may consider utilizing reminders, games, and community interactions [9].

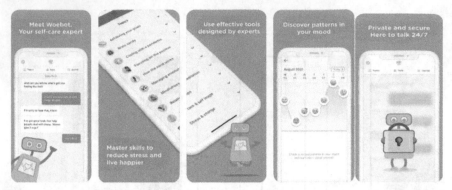

**Fig. 3.** Woebot: Your Self-Care Expert: "Think and talk through situations with a chatbot using step-by-step guidance and proven therapeutic frameworks like Cognitive Behavioral Therapy (CBT), Master skills to reduce stress and live happier through 100+ evidence-based stories from the clinical team. Help inform research to develop new mental health resources and treatments" [15].

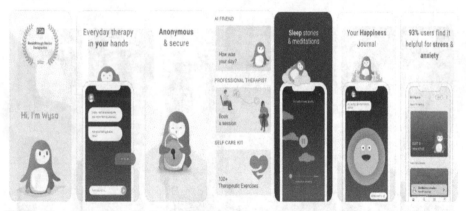

**Fig. 4.** Wysa: Mental Health Support: "Think and talk through situations with a chatbot using step-by-step guidance and proven therapeutic frameworks like Cognitive Behavioral Therapy (CBT), Master skills to reduce stress and live happier through 100+ evidence-based stories from the clinical team. Help inform research to develop new mental health resources and treatments" [16].

Secondly, to benefit the specific target group of these apps–patients with mental illnesses who likely have some degree of cognitive impairment—it is important to make the user interface simple, engaging, and easy to navigate [9]. Thirdly, because users may suffer from multiple mental health issues simultaneously, it would be beneficial for these apps to adopt a transdiagnostic approach, allowing them to identify the symptoms, patterns, and necessary treatments for patients with more than one mental illness [9]. Lastly, a crucial aspect of the road to recovery from mental illness is patients' ability to self-assess. Thus, apps should provide opportunities for users to think about their own emotions and actions in order to increase their self-awareness [9].

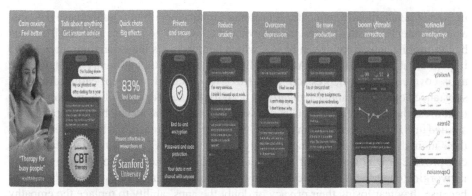

**Fig. 5.** Youper – CBT Therapy Chatbot: "Manage stress, cope with anxiety, and improve mental health. Stop negative thinking, rumination, and toxic self-talk. Deal with stressful situations and find solutions for life challenges. Feel more motivated and achieve your goals. Build self-esteem and foster stronger relationships" [17].

Furthermore, though AI-driven mental health mobile applications offer a unique and promising method of supplying mental health care, there are still some reservations that we must consider [15]. For instance, despite AI and its increasing complexity, it is still incapable of mimicking human emotions such as trust and empathy, which are key aspects of human interactions when it comes to therapy and the treatment of various mental illnesses [15]. Though mental health mobile apps are becoming increasingly more complex and capable, they are still unable to replace human interactions and diagnoses. Nevertheless, apps can act as a useful supplement to therapy through reminders, community building, mood trackers, and more [14].

This study has limitations. First, because we used ChatGPT to generate the list of mental health mobile apps, the list was certainly not comprehensive and did not cover any of the newly developed apps since September 2021, which was the date of the last knowledge update for ChatGPT. Additionally, due to the nature and extent of this paper, we were only able to cover a very limited number of mobile applications that certainly do not represent the entire pool of tens of thousands of mental health apps. Furthermore, when determining our inclusion/exclusion criteria, we decided to exclude any apps that focused exclusively or primarily on the mental health of teens and/or children. Instead, we focused only on apps that addressed mental health for people of all groups, which presents another limitation to this review. The reason for this exclusion was that we wanted our study on general mobile health apps for people of all ages, not simply a specific age group. Despite these limitations, this paper is still significant because it draws attention to the prevalence of mental health apps as well as their potential uses.

## 5 Conclusion and Future Research

In this paper, we analyzed the uses of 15 mental health mobile applications, and discussed the opportunities and challenges of mental health apps and suggestions that will help fill the mental health care gap. With the increasing demand for mental health care, AI in mental health mobile applications presents a unique opportunity to increase patients' access to mental health services. In our review, we saw that 5 out of the selected 15 mental health mobile apps were driven by AI, which demonstrates the expanding interest and implementation of this field. Additionally, we saw that, though many mental health apps covered anxiety, depression, and stress, few focused on sleep, eating disorders, substance abuse, and trauma, indicating a need for the development of more mobile apps to address these different mental health issues. Almost all the mental health apps that we studied utilized different combinations of management approaches to help patients battle their mental illnesses. In this increasingly digital world, AI-driven mental health apps can provide crucial assessment tools, mood trackers, personalization techniques, and networking opportunities. However, many patients remain uncertain of using these apps because they fear losing their privacy or doubt the apps' ability to replace the empathy that accompanies face-to-face human interactions. Thus, in order to take full advantage of the opportunities presented by AI in mental health apps, there is still a great deal of research to be done to address the concerns of patients and healthcare providers alike.

Going forward, we are looking to improve on this review by increasing the sample of mental health mobile applications in order to provide a more comprehensive assessment of the types of apps currently available and the ones that have yet to be developed. Furthermore, the opinions of users are a key aspect of this research, so we are looking to conduct our own survey to discover how patients perceive the usefulness of these apps. This way, we can determine the changes that still have to be made for AI-driven mental health apps to be accepted by the general population. We believe that incorporating AI into mental health mobile apps will greatly benefit people suffering from mental illnesses by providing them with affordable and accessible healthcare resources. Thus, it is certainly worth the time and investment to do more research on this field to offer new and innovative ways of combating mental health issues.

# References

1. Ahmed, A., et al.: A review of mobile chatbot apps for anxiety and depression and their self-care features. Comput. Methods Programs Biomed. Update **1**, 100012 (2021)
2. American Psychiatric Association Homepage. https://www.psychiatry.org/news-room/apa-blogs/mental-health-apps-evidence-not-so-plentiful. Accessed 14 Sept 2023
3. App Store. Better Help–Therapy. https://apps.apple.com/us/app/betterhelp-therapy/id9952 52384. Accessed 12 Feb 2024
4. App Store. Breathe2Relax. https://apps.apple.com/us/app/breathe2relax/id425720246. Accessed 12 Feb 2024
5. App Store. Calm. https://apps.apple.com/us/app/calm/id571800810. Accessed 12 Feb 2024
6. App Store. Daylio Journal – Daily Diary. https://apps.apple.com/us/app/daylio-journal-daily-diary/id1194023242. Accessed 12 Feb 2024
7. App Store. Happify: for Stress & Worry. https://apps.apple.com/us/app/happify-for-stress-worry/id730601963. Accessed 12 Feb 2024
8. App Store. Headspace: Sleep & Meditation. https://apps.apple.com/us/app/headspace-sleep-meditation/id493145008. Accessed 12 Feb 2024
9. App Store. MindDoc: Your Companion. https://apps.apple.com/us/app/minddoc-your-companion/id1052216403. Accessed 12 Feb 2024

10. App Store. Replika-Virtual AI Companion. https://apps.apple.com/us/app/replika-virtual-ai-companion/id1158555867. Accessed 12 Feb 2024
11. App Store. Sanvello: Anxiety & Depression. https://apps.apple.com/us/app/sanvello-anxiety-depression/id922968861. Accessed 12 Feb 2024
12. App Store. Smiling Mind: Meditation App. https://apps.apple.com/us/app/smiling-mind-meditation-app/id560442518. Accessed 12 Feb 2024
13. App Store. Super Better: Mental Health. https://apps.apple.com/us/app/superbetter-mental-health/id536634968. Accessed 12 Feb 2024
14. App Store. Talkspace Therapy and Support. https://apps.apple.com/us/app/talkspace-therapy-and-support/id661829386. Accessed 12 Feb 2024
15. App Store. Woebot: The Mental Health Ally. https://apps.apple.com/us/app/woebot-the-mental-health-ally/id1305375832. Accessed 12 Feb 2024
16. App Store. Wysa: Mental Health Support. https://apps.apple.com/us/app/wysa-mental-health-support/id1166585565. Accessed 12 Feb 2024
17. App Store. Youper – CBT Therapy Bot. https://apps.apple.com/us/app/youper-cbt-therapy-chatbot/id1060691513. Accessed 12 Feb 2024
18. Chandrashekar, P.: Do mental health mobile apps work: evidence and recommendations for designing high-efficacy mental health mobile apps. Mhealth **4**, 6 (2018)
19. ChatGPT 9/2/23: search query – uses of mental health apps
20. Götzl, C., et al.: Artificial intelligence-informed mobile mental health apps for young people: a mixed-methods approach on users' and stakeholders' perspectives. Child Adolesc. Psychiatry Ment. Health **16**(1), 1–19 (2022)
21. Harvard Health Homepage. https://www.health.harvard.edu/blog/is-a-mobile-app-as-good-as-a-therapist-202202072683. Accessed 14 Sept 2023
22. KFF Hompage. https://www.kff.org/mental-health/issue-brief/rise-in-use-of-mental-health-apps-raises-new-policy-issues. Accessed 14 Sept 2023
23. Milne-Ives, M., Selby, E., Inkster, B., Lam, C., Meinert, E.: Artificial intelligence and machine learning in mobile apps for mental health: a scoping review. PLOS Digit. Health **1**(8), e0000079 (2022)
24. Minerva, F., Giubilini, A.: Is AI the future of mental healthcare? Topoi Int. Rev. Philos. **42**(3), 1–9 (2023). Advance Online Publication, https://doi.org/10.1007/s11245-023-09932-3
25. Moreno, C., et al.: How mental health care should change as a consequence of the COVID-19 pandemic. Lancet Psychiatry **7**(9), 813–824 (2020)
26. NIMH Homepage, 14 September 2023. https://www.nimh.nih.gov/health/statistics/mental-illness
27. O'Loughlin, K., Neary, M., Adkins, E.C., Schueller, S.M.: Reviewing the data security and privacy policies of mobile apps for depression. Internet Interv. **15**, 110–115 (2019)
28. Reinert, M., Fritze, D., Nguyen, T.: The state of mental health in America 2022 (2021)
29. Torous, J., Wisniewski, H., Liu, G., Keshavan, M.: Mental health mobile phone app usage, concerns, and benefits among psychiatric outpatients: comparative survey study. JMIR Mental Health **5**(4), e11715 (2018)
30. WHO Homepage. https://www.who.int/news-room/fact-sheets/detail/mental-disorders. Accessed 14 Sept 2023

# Design and Evaluation of an Intelligent Rehabilitation System for Children with Asthma

Lanyu Liu and Gangqiang Zheng(⊠)

Wuhan University of Technology, Wuhan, People's Republic of China
zhenggq@whut.cn

**Abstract.** Establish a demand index system for children's asthma product service systems to provide theoretical basis and guidance for the design of children's asthma machines, ensure that the design practice plan meets the basic needs of target users and improve the user experience. The Affinity Diagram (KJ) method was used to screen and organize the needs of target users, and the functional requirements of 26 children's asthma product service systems were obtained through literature research, user interviews, etc., and the Analytical Hierarchy Process was used to conduct forward and reverse analysis of the obtained functional requirements. In accordance with the questionnaire, the comprehensive weight values are derived, and subsequently, a consistency test is conducted to ascertain the design elements of the product. Combining research conclusions and design practice, a children's asthma machine product system was designed from the aspects of intelligent software, interesting shape, comfortable use, and visual screen. The system design of children's asthma products obtained by combining KJ method and AHP method in product design and conducting fuzzy comprehensive evaluation analysis is practical. Through qualitative and quantitative analysis, the real needs of users can be accurately captured, and strategies for applying new theories to solve problems can be summarized more intuitively and effectively.

**Keywords:** Health · Covid-19 · Asthmatic children · User centered design · Rehabilitation system · Creative product design

## 1 Introduction

With the development of big data, the Internet and artificial intelligence, the traditional medical model is transforming into intelligent, data-based and systematic. On the one hand, the development of digital medical care has proposed new design directions for the update of medical products; on the other hand, the effective Asthma is one of the most common chronic diseases in the world, affecting approximately 300 million people worldwide. According to the World Health Organization, the number of Asthma is a complex respiratory disease. Its pathogenesis involves the interaction between the human immune system and the diseased respiratory tract [1]. After triggering, the patient's organs will become inflamed and narrowed, resulting in difficulty breathing [2]. Research on asthma prevention and treatment has confirmed that asthma is a chronic airway inflammatory disease, and symptoms during an asthma attack include wheezing, shortness of

J. Wei and G. Margetis (Eds.): HCII 2024, LNCS 14737, pp. 90–103, 2024.
https://doi.org/10.1007/978-3-031-60458-4_7

breath, chest tightness and other symptoms [3]. Among them, the triggers of asthma attacks include many factors, which are roughly divided into genetics, environmental factors, food irritation and specific allergens. Asthma patients will increase to 400 million by 2025. Asthma has become a global public health problem [4]. Bronchial asthma has become an internationally recognized child health-related disease with the highest prevalence and health care expenditure. The DALYs rate of asthma shows a U-shaped characteristic at the age level, with a peak DALYs rate between 5 and 9 years old [5]. Children as Susceptible groups need early treatment, and children with asthma require continuous health management and treatment, which places a heavy burden on patients' families and society. At present, the health management of childhood asthma is still in the exploratory stage. The behaviors of stakeholders such as asthmatic children, medical staff, and parents of patients are relatively independent [6]. The correlation between medical treatment, home care and other services is weak, and the medical treatment process is relatively complex. Medical units in various regions Problems such as uneven ability to deal with childhood asthma are not conducive to the healthy management of childhood asthma. Hospital treatment and home care are both important links in the health management of children with asthma. Improving the health management experience of children with asthma will help the asthma medical service system operate well. At present, some scholars have conducted innovative designs on children's asthma-related products and asthma medical systems through human-machine experiments and analysis of asthma medical service processes. Comprehensive literature research found that current children's asthma rehabilitation products are mostly focused on optimizing appearance and color matching, lack accurate classification and organization of children's needs and systematic design of intelligent medical systems and asthma products.

Therefore, this article starts from the perspective of children, uses affinity diagram method and analytic hierarchy process to optimize the design of existing products and service systems, and provides a new idea for the design of rehabilitation product systems for asthmatic children with the purpose of improving user experience satisfaction. It helps children's asthma self-management and improves user experience, has certain practical significance for the research on children's asthma rehabilitation products.

## 1.1 Children's Asthma Rehabilitation Products

The nebulizer can precisely filter the medicine through atomization and then give it to the user for inhalation. It is simple to operate and the treatment speed is faster than oral medicine [7]. It is currently the fastest and best feasible method with the smallest side effects. Nebulization treatment at home can reduce children's fear of hospital treatment and avoid cross-infection in the post-epidemic era, which has a positive effect on treatment. Children's household atomizers with high sales on the market are roughly divided into two types: compression atomizers and handheld atomizers. Although handheld nebulizers are small and slender in appearance and suitable for carrying when going out, compression nebulizers are more popular among parents and doctors for long-term home treatment. In terms of appearance, as the first visual point of the product, it plays a leading role in the entire design [8]. Visual perception drives the senses and affects the treatment emotions of children. Most of the compression nebulizers on the market have a square shape and simple color matching, which can easily give children a sense of distance and similarity with hospital products, lack interest [8]. The appearance design of aerosol products for children with asthma should avoid design elements that make children feel disgusted, make family products more friendly, build trust among children, and guide children to interact with the product in the next step [9]. In terms of function, compression nebulizers are more comprehensive than handheld nebulizers, but they are larger in size and are usually treated with matching masks. Children are less fond of them, resulting in a lack of interest in treatment. Strong; The aerosol products for children with asthma can be functionally integrated with games to stimulate children's eager to learn and inquiring behavior, making the treatment process more interesting. In terms of usage process and user feedback, the handheld nebulizer is easier for children to use, but the treatment time of both types of nebulizers is fixed at 10 min. Children are active and have unstable attention. Although they have become accustomed to daily treatment, if they are slightly affected by uncontrollable factors, they will immediately develop a negative attitude, which manifests as looking around, shaking their heads, and even crying. At this time, parents often use various rewards to induce children to persist in treatment and maintain attention.

In 2020, the China Asthma Alliance submitted a work summary report at the World Asthma Day event. Affected by the 2019 new coronavirus epidemic, they have further confirmed the importance of personalized online treatment. In the self-management of asthma patients, the correct use of peak flow meters and accurate asthma diary recording are crucial parts, which can effectively prevent and reduce the number of asthma attacks. However, a 2016 survey found that only 10.1% of patients had ever used peak flow meters, and 65.2% of non-users said that their doctors had never introduced them. Additionally, only 15% of health care professionals can demonstrate the correct use of medical products such as inhalers. Therefore, there is an urgent need to develop individualized treatment plans and establish a barrier-free communication platform to promote and guide the use of asthma medical products. With the update of technology, the combination of asthma monitoring products and home smart medical devices will assist patients in better self-monitoring management. New smart products and information management platforms, including electronic medical records and treatment analysis databases, are well connected and rely on Internet technology to promote doctor-patient communication. The service platform manages and analyzes product equipment and monitoring-related information, communicates the results to hospitals and families in a data-based and visual way. These new smart medical products will gradually develop into the field of home self-management with the update of Internet technology.

Judging from the current products and management platforms, the monitoring model for the huge number of children with asthma is relatively backward. Asthma has not yet developed effective remote monitoring, and it is difficult to quickly achieve scale in a short time. The design of smart medical monitoring products for asthma is gradually deepening. At this stage, product monitoring systems in various countries are being established, but the overall level is insufficient. Among the intelligent medical monitoring products, Future Medical has launched an intelligent diagnosis and treatment management system for respiratory diseases and has gradually improved its development, creating a new monitoring system through full-process management, dynamic monitoring and other functions. Overall, there are some attempts at asthma monitoring medical products, but there are few designs for the entire management system and medical products for children's asthma.

## 1.2 Asthma Rehabilitation System

Asthma management systems were gradually established around the world. In 1994, the World Health Organization and other agencies convened more than 30 experts from 17 countries to formulate a global asthma initiative, the GINA plan. The Global Initiative for Asthma has been dedicated to research on the pathogenesis of asthma over the past two decades and has gained tremendous attention in its ability to effectively control asthma [10]. The World Asthma Day event launched by the World Health Organization promotes knowledge about asthma and strengthens the prevention and treatment of this disease among patients and the public [11]. The first World Asthma Day was held in 1998, and since 2000, Asthma Day events have been held every year [12]. Asthma is a chronic respiratory disease, and long-term, continuous, standardized, and individualized treatment must be adhered to in management [13]. Children's home medical monitoring products can be roughly divided into monitoring, treatment, nursing, rehabilitation, first aid and other management products. There are still many problems in the use of asthma medical products. The China Asthma Alliance made a work summary report on the World Asthma Day event in 2020. Affected by the 2019 new coronavirus epidemic, the importance of individualized online treatment has been more affirmed [14].

With the advancement of informatization transformation, asthma chronic disease management is gradually moving towards informatization. The modern medical consultation model has gradually evolved into a new management model with "equipment + application + service" as the core, including diagnosis, treatment, and follow-up of the full management of asthma, and gradually increased attention to the treatment of severe asthma. An online asthma patient management platform established in Guangzhou, China, also launched an asthma patient database system to establish a closed-loop asthma management model, aiming to gradually improve the level of asthma control in my country. The project will rely on Internet technology to achieve a closed-loop management model that combines in-hospital follow-up with self-management of asthma patients outside the hospital. Internet medical care plays an important role in online disease education, doctor-patient communication, and online treatment guidance, effectively improving patients' treatment compliance and ability to self-manage their diseases. Despite the many benefits brought by Internet medical care, there are still a series of problems in the field of asthma management. A pivotal facet of the self-management of asthma patients involves the accurate utilization of peak flow meters and the meticulous maintenance of asthma diaries. Effectively employing these tools can play a significant role in averting and minimizing the frequency of asthma attacks, thereby constituting a crucial component in objectively assessing the asthma condition. These problems urgently require customized personalized treatment plans and barrier-free communication platforms to promote and guide the use of asthma medical products. Asthma monitoring products are updated with technology, and home smart medical equipment will assist patients in better self-monitoring and management. The new smart products are well connected with the information management platform, including the management of electronic medical records and treatment analysis databases, as well as relying on Internet technology. Promote doctor-patient communication. The service platform manages and analyzes product equipment and monitoring-related information, communicates the results to hospitals and families in a digital and visual way. The process evolution of data and user data are saved in the system data to ensure that all stakeholders understand the treatment progress. New smart medical products will develop towards home self-management with the update of Internet technology.

## 2 Methodology

In the design process, the KJ method, AHP method, and FCE method are combined. The affinity diagram method (KJ) can clearly present the chaotic and disordered demand elements, helping researchers to quickly clarify research ideas and easily solve problems. The KJ method is a qualitative analysis research method used to summarize and classify data. Applying the KJ method to the analysis of user demand elements of the children's asthma rehabilitation system will help simplify and organize the user demand data of the asthma rehabilitation system. The AHP analytic hierarchy process is an analytical research method that combines qualitative and quantitative methods. It uses the method of solving the eigenvectors of the judgment matrix to obtain the priority weight of elements in each layer to the elements in the upper layer. The Analytical Hierarchy Process (AHP) can improve the objectivity of the process of extracting children's needs and formulating design plans. The fuzzy comprehensive evaluation method (FCE) can improve the scientific nature of the design evaluation of children's asthma rehabilitation products and reduce the subjective factors of design evaluators.

### 2.1 KJ Method Analysis Requirements

The KJ method is a method for summarizing and summarizing messy information proposed by Professor Jiro Kawakita of Tokyo Institute of Technology in 1964. Its main content is to analyze different levels according to correlation and sort out the correspondence between information and conditions. Relation [15]. The operation steps of this method are to collect relevant information about unknown issues, make inductive adjustments, and finally organize it into a clear information framework. Applying the KJ method in the user research process can help researchers collect and organize relevant information, form a clear information structure, and efficiently complete the preliminary research work [16]. After searching relevant journals, it was confirmed that product design research completed through the KJ method is accurate and effective.

In order to achieve the purpose of this study, the KJ method was first used to determine the interviewees and interview locations. The interviewees included parents of asthmatic children (40), asthmatic children (10), and medical staff (50); the research location was in central China. Three tertiary hospitals (Tongji Hospital Affiliated to Tongji Medical College of Huazhong University of Science and Technology, Wuhan University People's Hospital, Wuhan Children's Hospital); then interviewed the interviewees and comprehensively collected product functional requirements information through brainstorming; finally, the collected requirements were The information is screened and summarized to form secondary demand indicators, and the secondary indicators are integrated again to obtain first-level demand indicators, and the function list is organized.

## 2.2 Analysis of Functional Requirements Elements

AHP Analytical Hierarchy Process is a method of establishing a hierarchical structure model for issues that require decision-making and conducting systematic analysis. Through questionnaire surveys or interviews, the subjects need to compare their evaluation indicators with each other using the 1–9 scale method [17]. Clearly prioritize decision-making options. The designer then analyzes the functional requirement indicators of the portable oxygen concentrator based on the indicator results, completes the consistency check of the weight values of each indicator based on the analysis results [18].

The children's asthma medical product hierarchy was determined through AHP as 1 target layer, 5 criterion layers and 26 program layers. After the criterion indicators and program indicators are established, the 5 criterion indicators are compared first, and then the 26 program indicators are compared. In order to make the results more objective, 5 designers, 1 mechanical engineer, 10 parents, 26 doctors and 20 nurses conducted pairwise comparisons of each evaluation index to obtain the comprehensive weight of hierarchical functional indexes of the asthma rehabilitation system (Table 1). According to Table 1, The order of importance of the children's asthma rehabilitation system is safety, intelligence, comfort, aesthetics and portability. Users rate the product's smart software, material safety, and interesting styling highly. They also hope product have anti-slip designs, stable assembly, and easy wearing.

After obtaining the weight value, a consistency test is performed. The consistency index can be used as the basis for analysis of data compatibility. The calculation method of the consistency index of the constructed judgment matrix is: At that time, the data can be considered to pass the consistency test; on the contrary, the data cannot pass for consistency testing, the data structure needs to be adjusted before analysis. The data consistency index can be expressed as follows:

$$CI = \frac{\lambda_{max} - n}{n - 1}$$

Among them, $\lambda_{max}$ refers to the maximum eigenvalue in the judgment matrix, refers to the matrix order.

The consistency checks, as per the aforementioned method, is outlined as follows:

$$CR = \frac{CI}{RI} = 0 < 0.1$$

Among them, is the average random value in the consistency index, when it is 1 and 2; when equal to 3, 4, 5, 6, 7, 8, the values of are 0.58, 0.90, 1.12, 1.24, 1.32, 1.41.

After conducting the consistency test, the values of A, B1, B2, B3, B4, and B5 were 0.083, 0.049, 0.014, 0.067, 0.066, and 0.034 respectively. It can be seen that the values of each judgment matrix are less than 0.1, passing the consistency test.

Since there are many elements in the program layer, the top two program layers C11, C12, C21, C25, C32, C34, C41, C42, C51 and C53 of each criterion layer are used as the

**Table 1.** Comprehensive weights of the design elements

| Target hierarchy | Criterion hierarchy | Weights | Object Hierarchy | Weights | Comprehensive Weights |
|---|---|---|---|---|---|
| Improved design of Intelligent rehabilitation system A | Intelligence B1 | 0.264 | Smart software C11 | 0.782 | 0.048 |
| | | | Visual interface C12 | 0.289 | 0.080 |
| | | | Dressing change reminder C13 | 0.084 | 0.020 |
| | | | Mist volume adjustment C14 | 0.179 | 0.048 |
| | | | Allergen testing C15 | 0.087 | 0.020 |
| | | | Respiratory flow detection C16 | 0.097 | 0.023 |
| | | | low noise C17 | 0.059 | 0.017 |
| | Safety B2 | 0.458 | Material safety C21 | 0.446 | 0.189 |
| | | | Anti-slip design C22 | 0.160 | 0.066 |
| | | | Safe operation process C23 | 0.116 | 0.043 |
| | | | High impact strength C24 | 0.087 | 0.040 |
| | | | Good wear resistance C25 | 0.221 | 0.099 |
| | Aesthetics B3 | 0.113 | Simple structure C31 | 0.108 | 0.011 |
| | | | Interesting look C32 | 0.387 | 0.039 |
| | | | Bright colors C33 | 0.168 | 0.013 |
| | | | Mechanism is natural C34 | 0.271 | 0.030 |
| | | | Fun interaction C35 | 0.089 | 0.008 |
| | Comfort B4 | 0.143 | light weight C41 | 0.299 | 0.041 |
| | | | Strong stability C42 | 0.305 | 0.042 |
| | | | Comfortable grip C43 | 0.216 | 0.028 |
| | | | Breathing port fits the face C44 | 0.187 | 0.024 |

*(continued)*

**Table 1.** (*continued*)

| Target hierarchy | Criterion hierarchy | Weights | Object Hierarchy | Weights | Comprehensive Weights |
|---|---|---|---|---|---|
| | Portability B5 | 0.049 | Easy to assemble C51 | 0.321 | 0.018 |
| | | | | 0.226 | 0.007 |
| | | | Easy to carry C52 | 0.417 | 0.023 |
| | | | Easy to disassemble C53 | 0.076 | 0.004 |
| | | | | 0.069 | 0.004 |
| | | | Easy to clean C54 | | |
| | | | Easy to store C55 | | |

main demand indicators of the target users for analysis of design elements. In terms of intelligence, the top needs of users are intelligent software and visual interfaces. Since traditional children's asthma rehabilitation products are relatively lacking in intelligence and lack supporting software to assist rehabilitation treatment, intelligent software and visual interfaces have become urgent needs of users. Therefore, in the design process of the children's asthma rehabilitation system, the supporting APP can be designed to connect children, doctors and parents, and intelligently assist children in asthma rehabilitation treatment. In terms of safety, material safety and wearing comfort are what users are most concerned about. Therefore, when designing products, we should focus on the selection of product materials, and give priority to the use of medical-grade plastic as the main material of the product. When designing the structure, consider the fit between the components and the face to ensure the user's comfort when inhaling. In terms of aesthetics, considering that the user group is children, an interesting appearance design is needed. In terms of comfort, light weight and strong stability are what users need. Modern people's lifestyles are gradually becoming more mobile. Unnecessary components should be reduced in product design, and lightweight materials should be used to reduce the physical exertion of users carrying them in daily life.

## 3   Proposed Concept

The analysis results of the design elements of children's asthma rehabilitation products are combined with design practice to design intelligent medical products. The products are designed with the user's safety and comfort as the main demand points, and at the same time, the appearance is designed to be interesting and in line with children's aesthetics. And design accessibility features for portability. This design first uses the affinity diagram method to analyze user demand points, and then combines the hierarchical analysis method to analyze the importance of design elements, which can more accurately grasp user needs [19]. The analysis results of the design elements of children's asthma machines are combined with design practice to design a product suitable for the rehabilitation of asthmatic children. The design focuses on children's aesthetics and use, with the user's safety and intelligence as the main needs. At the same time, consider the comfort during use, the aesthetics of the product and the portable auxiliary functions. Based on the sorting of design elements and the actual product, a sketch plan is conceived and drawn to form a final plan, which is then initially established and rendered using keyshot software, as shown in Fig. 1. The color scheme of the final renderings is blue as the main color, and the shape is a simple and cute elephant. The elephant's ears are designed as a switch for inhaling medicine, and the elephant's tail is designed as a storage line for easy portability (Fig. 1). Product material selection is an important part of product design, and material safety is the basis of product design. In order to further match the requirements of the standard level, the scheme was designed in depth, taking into account the needs of users and the feasibility of manufacturing. In terms of material selection, medical plastic (PVC) was selected as the material of the outer shell. This material is easy to process and form, and has low manufacturing costs [20]. It is low in temperature and has good physical and mechanical properties, stable biological and mechanical properties, can meet the physiological functions of users and the use needs of different environments, and is convenient for daily household disinfection (high-temperature steam, ultraviolet lamp disinfection, etc.) to meet the daily breathing needs of children. Medication and breathing exercises required (Fig. 2).

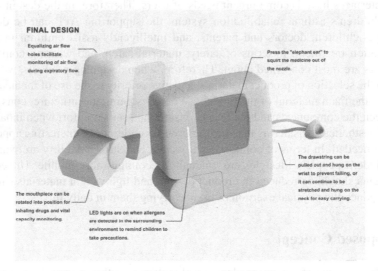

**Fig. 1.** Photograph of the asthma rehabilitation product

With the development of information technology and the use of modern new technologies and new service methods to change the traditional service industry, the current product design field has been expanded, and more and more physical products and service products have been developed together [21]. From products to services, service-oriented technology and product integration are becoming the development trend of various industries. Products are not just user-oriented products, but services. The assistance of app software can make the overall plan implementation process more in-depth, more systematic and more scientific. In alignment with the intelligent demand design for the corresponding intelligent interactive interface, the intelligent software encompasses various

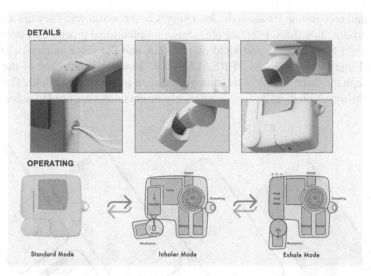

**Fig. 2.**  Detail of the asthma rehabilitation product.

functions, including but not limited to condition record, medication record, medication reminder, community discussion, and doctor-patient communication (Fig. 3).

Condition record: Solve the problem of full online medical monitoring through the jump page of treatment plan, solve the problem of management of personal health files and management of allergen and incidence records through the jump page of health log, solve the problem of obtaining popular science knowledge through the jump page As for the problem of asthma medical knowledge, the problem of choosing doctors and medical institutions during the treatment process can be solved through the jump page recommended by famous doctors.

Medication records: The monitoring page manages a series of products. The page includes screen guidance before use, interactive screens during use and data visualization after use. The monitoring page is used to connect to the peak flow meter product to solve the problem of regular testing. The intelligent data recording to generate an asthma diary can save family members time in data management. Connecting the atomizer to record medication status is conducive to data management of treatment status.

Medication reminder: The page mainly obtains the purchase of medical products, accessories and medicines, solves product use, purchase of series products, and a jump page to ask a doctor to solve problems in product use and purchase.

Community discussion: Provides a communication platform for patients, relieves the psychological pressure of family members during the treatment process, and provides communication and encouragement through uploading pictures, comments and likes.

A software prototype simulates the final interaction between the user and the interface. The prototype can simulate the entire app or just a single interaction. The necessity of prototypes is to discover and solve feasibility problems before the product is formed. It can test out areas where the product needs improvement, let users test them, and continuously iterate on design reasons. High-fidelity prototypes are usually used to test usability and recognition issues in the later stages of the workflow. They are a means of showing product functions, interface elements, and functional processes. Function icon design should be as concise and vivid as possible, and the color and shape should fit the overall interface expression. "BREALEFENT" combines the shape of the product with an elephant shape to reflect the humanistic care in the medical field. The color is aimed at children's medical design, so relatively bright colors are used to reflect interest (Fig. 4).

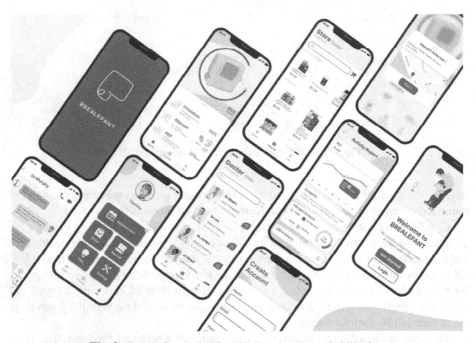

**Fig. 3.** Interaction design for childhood asthma rehabilitation.

Evaluation testing is to compare and improve the design solutions that users expect [22]. Before the product is officially released, it is evaluated whether the set functions of the product meet expectations. Through evaluation and scoring, the usability of the product, interactive functional features, and the value of the product can be tested (Fig. 5). The problems revealed during the testing process allow the product and software design parts to be corrected with a coherent concept and sufficient details. In order to detect the degree of achievement of user demand element goals, Analysis of variance (ANOVA) was selected during the evaluation. 20 experts were invited to be divided into 4 groups. The experts in group one experienced the original children's asthma rehabilitation system. The experts in group two only experienced online asthma rehabilitation services. The experts in group three only experienced asthma rehabilitation products. The experts in group four fully experienced service. The questionnaire adopts a 5-point scale evaluation form. The statistical results show that group 4 has the highest average score of each item. The average values of group 2 and group 3 are both higher than group 1. The significance values are both less than 0.01 (Table 2).

**UI STANDARD**

**Visual Identity**

Logo design uses children's graffiti lines
to outline the shape of the product,
reflecting the theme of the product at
the same time fun and affinity.
The brand name is a combination of
breath and alefant, which is old Spanish
for elephant. The name combines the
theme and inspiration of the product.

BREALEFANT

Color

#e81fff

#0093a4

#595959    #919191    #18d172

Front

Aa

Alibaba Sans

Regular
Medium
**Bold**

**Fig. 4.** UI for childhood asthma rehabilitation.

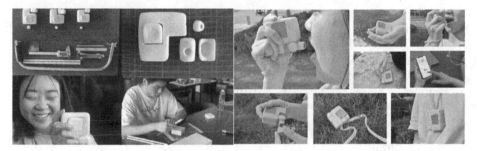

**Fig. 5.** Modeling and evaluation of asthma rehabilitation product.

**Table 2.** Comparison table of four groups of controlled experiments

| Source | Group 1 | Group 2 | Group 3 | Group 4 | F | p-Value |
|---|---|---|---|---|---|---|
| | Mean ± S.D | Mean ± S.D | Mean ± S.D | Mean ± S.D | | |
| Intelligence | 1.52 ± 0.503 | 3.43 ± 0.502 | 3.03 ± 0.526 | 4.78 ± 0.415 | 306.577 | 0.000[**] |
| Safety | 1.14 ± 0.361 | 3.56 ± 0.503 | 2.99 ± 0.620 | 4.69 ± 0.466 | 358.110 | 0.000[**] |
| Aesthetics | 1.44 ± 0.502 | 3.39 ± 0.491 | 3.14 ± 0.607 | 4.66 ± 0.473 | 262.199 | 0.000[**] |
| Comfort | 1.37 ± 0.489 | 3.29 ± 0.453 | 2.99 ± 0.530 | 4.63 ± 0.481 | 702.247 | 0.000[**] |
| Portability | 1.51 ± 0.516 | 3.53 ± 0.514 | 2.93 ± 0.639 | 4.59 ± 0.492 | 230.218 | 0.000[**] |

# 4    Conclusion and Discussion

The rehabilitation treatment of most asthmatic children depends on their families. How
to better empower the families of asthmatic children and encourage children to actively
participate in asthma rehabilitation treatment is the key to the health management of

asthmatic children. The design thinking of this study explores the rehabilitation product service system for asthmatic children, uses a variety of methods to find the pain points and needs of children, and proposes a common product and app service based on intelligence, portability, aesthetics, safety and comfort. Coordination, hospital-family-child collaborative participation model improves the service links of children's asthma rehabilitation by strengthening cooperation and exchanges among hospitals, families, and schools, fully develops and utilizes existing medical resources, and optimizes the medical treatment process.

This paper analyzes the design elements of a child asthma rehabilitation system through AHP and verifies the feasibility of the methodology through design practice and evaluation. The design improves children's experience of using asthma rehabilitation products, enhances children's motivation for treatment, increases the efficiency of out-of-hospital follow-up by healthcare professionals, strengthens the management of children with asthma, and broadens the research perspectives on the design and development of asthma rehabilitation systems for children.

# References

1. Gauthier, M., Ray, A., Wenzel, S.E.: Evolving concepts of asthma. Am. J. Respir. Crit. Care Med. **192**(6), 660–668 (2015)
2. Partridge, M.R., van der Molen, T., Myrseth, S.-E., Busse, W.W.: Attitudes and actions of asthma patients on regular maintenance therapy: the INSPIRE study. BMC Pulm. Med. **6**(1), 1–9 (2006)
3. Alwarith, J., et al.: The role of nutrition in asthma prevention and treatment. Nutr. Rev. **78**(11), 928–938 (2020)
4. Pawankar, R.: Allergic diseases and asthma: a global public health concern and a call to action. World Health Organ. **7**, 1–3 (2014). Ed. BioMed Central, 2014
5. Asher, M.I., García-Marcos, L., Pearce, N.E., Strachan, D.P.: Trends in worldwide asthma prevalence. Eur. Respir. J. **56**(6), 2002094 (2020)
6. Roberts, G., et al.: EAACI guidelines on the effective transition of adolescents and young adults with allergy and asthma. Allergy **75**(11), 2734–2752 (2020)
7. Martin, A.R., Finlay, W.H.: Nebulizers for drug delivery to the lungs. Expert Opin. Drug Deliv. **12**(6), 889–900 (2015)
8. Stein, S.W., Thiel, C.G.: The history of therapeutic aerosols: a chronological review. J. Aerosol Med. Pulm. Drug Deliv. **30**(1), 20–41 (2017)
9. Dolovich, M.B., Dhand, R.: Aerosol drug delivery: developments in device design and clinical use. Lancet **377**(9770), 1032–1045 (2011)
10. Bateman, E.D., et al.: Global strategy for asthma management and prevention: GINA executive summary. Eur. Respir. J. **31**(1), 143–178 (2008)
11. Bousquet, J., Bousquet, P.J., Godard, P., Daures, J.-P.: The public health implications of asthma. Bull. World Health Organ. **83**, 548–554 (2005)
12. Rabe, K.F., et al.: Worldwide severity and control of asthma in children and adults: the global asthma insights and reality surveys. J. Allergy Clin. Immunol. **114**(1), 40–47 (2004)
13. Li, J., et al.: A multicentre study assessing the prevalence of sensitizations in patients with asthma and/or rhinitis in China. Allergy **64**(7), 1083–1092 (2009)
14. Deng, S.-Z., Jalaludin, B.B., Antó, J.M., Hess, J.J., Huang, C.-R.: Climate change, air pollution, and allergic respiratory diseases: a call to action for health professionals. Chin. Med. J. **133**(13), 1552–1560 (2020)

15. Scupin, R.: The KJ method: a technique for analyzing data derived from Japanese ethnology. Hum. Organ. **56**(2), 233–237 (1997)
16. Barnum, C.M.: Usability Testing Essentials: Ready, set... test! Morgan Kaufmann, Burlington (2020)
17. Vaidya, O.S., Kumar, S.: Analytic hierarchy process: an overview of applications. Eur. J. Oper. Res. **169**(1), 1–29 (2006)
18. Wang, G., Gunasekaran, A., Ngai, E.W., Papadopoulos, T.: Big data analytics in logistics and supply chain management: certain investigations for research and applications. Int. J. Prod. Econ. **176**, 98–110 (2016)
19. Margolin, V., Buchanan, R.: The Idea of Design. MIT Press, Cambridge (1995)
20. Rosato, D.V., Rosato, D.V., v Rosato, M.: Plastic Product Material and Process Selection Handbook. Elsevier, Amsterdam (2004)
21. Barrett, M., Davidson, E., Prabhu, J., Vargo, S.L.: Service innovation in the digital age. MIS Q. **39**(1), 135–154 (2015)
22. Rubin, J., Chisnell, D.: Handbook of Usability Testing: How to Plan, Design, and Conduct Effective Tests. Wiley, New York (2008)

# Wearable Wellness: Exploring User Experiences with Fitness Systems on Smartwatches

Fang-Wu Tung[1]([✉]) and Po-Kai Liang[2]

[1] National Tsing Hua University, Hsinchu 300, Taiwan
fwtung@mx.nthu.edu.tw
[2] National University of Science and Technology, Taipei 106, Taiwan

**Abstract.** This study explores the user experience of fitness service systems integrated into smartwatches, with a particular focus on users of running apps. By combining diary studies with chatbot technology and co-creation workshops, the research seeks to comprehend the needs of users within digital fitness products and services through a "designing with users" methodology. Initially, this study undertook an online diary activity facilitated by chatbots, yielding insights into their experiences, pain points, and aspirations. Leveraging these insights, the study developed co-creation toolkits and conducted co-creation workshops. The toolkits, comprising card decks, a co-creation canvas, and scenario images, were pivotal in motivating participants to share their experiences and engage actively in the co-creation process. The methodology of this study, integrating diary studies and co-creation workshops, provides a holistic approach to understanding and improving the user experience of digital fitness products and services. The findings reveal significant differences in requirements between novice and experienced users, offering critical insights for future product development. This research underscores the vital role of user participation and the need for personalized experiences in the design of health service systems, setting a new benchmark for user-centered design in the digital health and fitness domains.

**Keywords:** Wearable Technology · Digital Health Service · User-Centered Design · Smart Product-Service System

## 1 Introduction

The integration of wearable technology into the fitness and health sectors has altered the dynamics of personal wellness management. Devices ranging from basic activity trackers to advanced smartwatches now enable users to monitor their physical activities and overall health, marking a pivotal shift towards empowered self-care and wellness management. This evolution is driven by rapid technological advancements, changing consumer behaviors, and an evolving healthcare environment, heralding a proactive, data-informed approach to personal health. Particularly, wearable fitness devices have catalyzed the "quantified self" movement, empowering individuals to actively manage their health through data analytics [1]. These devices are pivotal in encouraging health behavior changes by leveraging social dynamics and goal-setting mechanisms, thereby exerting a significant impact on public health outcomes [2].

J. Wei and G. Margetis (Eds.): HCII 2024, LNCS 14737, pp. 104–115, 2024.
https://doi.org/10.1007/978-3-031-60458-4_8

The increasing impact of wearable devices on well-being has sparked scholarly interest in examining user requirements for enhancing fitness through technology. Research has identified that users prioritize aspects such as hedonic motivation, functional congruence, and social influence, while also expressing concerns over privacy risks and vulnerability [3]. Further investigations into the motivations for using sports and fitness wearables have emphasized the essential role of user engagement in promoting device adoption [4].

Given the rise in wearable device usage for fitness and well-being, gaining a deep understanding of user experiences and requirements is crucial for advancing well-being and driving industry innovation. Studies by Tikkanen, Heinonen [5] and Lee, Kim [6] have highlighted the vital role of user experience and acceptance in improving the positive well-being outcomes enabled by wearable technologies. Aligning product designs with user needs and expectations is essential for manufacturers to deliver devices that not only offer technological advancements but also resonate deeply with users, thereby enriching their well-being. A comprehension of user requirements is key to driving innovation, guiding product development, and achieving market success. Such foundational insights fundamental in developing wearable technologies that meet user expectations, thereby ensuring beneficial outcomes for users, industry stakeholders, and the wearable technology ecosystem.

As user sophistication grows alongside technological advancements, expectations from wearable devices become increasingly complex. This evolving scenario necessitates a refined approach to wearable device/service design and development, attuned to the shifting desires and motivations of users. Embracing this dynamic allows manufacturers to create products/services that not only satisfy current user demands but also inspire and facilitate a healthier, more active lifestyle. Consequently, this study employs user-centered methodologies to engage users actively in the research process, aiming to uncover their experiences and expectations comprehensively. The methodologies and insights derived from this study offer valuable guidance for researchers and practitioners alike, aiming to navigate the intricate landscape of user-centered design in the fitness wearable domain.

## 2   User-Centered Design: Diary Studies and Co-creation

User-Centered Design (UCD) represents a paradigm shift towards a more user-inclusive approach within design philosophy. It places the user at the heart of the design process, emphasizing the importance of understanding users' needs, behaviors, and contexts. This understanding is achieved through various methods, including user research, persona development, and usability testing, which are essential for ensuring the optimal design and functionality of wearables. The transition from "design for users" to "design with users" marks a evolution in design research and practice, transforming users from passive subjects to active collaborators. This shift focuses on creating products and services that are not just technically sound but also deeply resonate with users' needs and experiences. Co-creation and diary studies further amplify this concept by engaging users not only as subjects of research but as active participants in the creation process.

Co-creation, a collaborative process characterized by active user participation [7], offers an avenue for involving users in the design of sports wearable technology. This approach ensures that the final product meets the specific needs and preferences of the target user [8]. Moreover, involving end-users in the ideation, design, and testing phases fosters a sense of ownership and empowerment, leading to the development of wearables that are both technologically sophisticated and personally meaningful to end-users [9]. These methodologies are instrumental in creating wearables that align closely with the needs and desires of users, providing a practical approach to identifying user requirements for sports wearables.

Active user involvement in the design process and capturing their real-time experiences through diary studies equip researchers and designers with insights into the contextual factors influencing the usage and acceptance of wearables [10]. This approach yields a comprehensive understanding of user needs. Diary studies are effective for capturing user experiences, aiding in the identification of user requirements and detecting patterns and trends in user preferences [11].

Building on the aforementioned points, involving users in design research and practice through co-creation and diary studies facilitate an understanding of user perspectives. This study aims to integrate these two methodologies to explore user experiences and requirements for fitness wearable devices/services comprehensively. The methodology and tools developed for co-creation and diary studies serve as valuable references for researchers in the field.

## 3 Methodology

This research employed running as a case study to explore smartwatch users' requirements for digital fitness services, aiming to investigate the design and development of digital fitness services within wearable devices. Reflecting the paradigm shift in design practice from "designing for users" to "designing with users," this study recognizes users as evolving from passive recipients to active participants and co-creators. This evolution signifies a pivotal change in both design research and practice, emphasizing the importance of user involvement in the creation process.

To achieve this objective, the research methodology is structured into two distinct phases:

**Phase One: Diary Study via Chatbots.** In the initial phase, participants engage in a diary study conducted through chatbots. They are prompted to record their daily experiences with the smartwatch, focusing on usage contexts, challenges encountered, and their expectations. This approach provides an empirical basis for the subsequent development of co-creation tools, ensuring that these tools are grounded in real user experiences and needs.

**Phase Two: Co-creation Workshop.** The second phase involves conducting a co-creation workshop aimed at developing tools that enhance user involvement in the design process. This workshop facilitates a deep understanding of user needs by engaging participants in activities that mirror the co-creation process. Through this collaborative effort, participants contribute to the development of digital fitness services that are not only innovative but also closely aligned with user expectations and requirements.

By integrating diary studies with co-creation workshops, this methodology offers a framework for engaging users directly in the design and development of digital fitness services. This dual-phase approach ensures that the resulting digital fitness service systems are user-centered, addressing the specific needs and preferences of smartwatch users.

## 3.1  Phase One: Diary Study

**Development of Research Tools.** The diary study, a widely used method for exploring user experiences, specifically targeted smartwatch users who frequently engage with digital products. To conduct this study, we chose to utilize chatbots due to their high interactivity and digital capabilities, which offer a modern alternative to traditional paper-based methods. By employing the BotBonnie chatbot platform, we crafted an interactive diary script tailored to capture a wide array of user experiences.

Participants were prompted to share detailed information covering various aspects of their exercise routines. This included their exercise goals, relevant data such as time spent exercising, heart rate, distance covered, feature usage, future fitness plans, levels of fatigue, emotional states, and whether they had an exercise companion. The script utilized a tree structure and a modular design, as illustrated in Fig. 1, enabling the chatbot to offer customized feedback or pose additional inquiries based on the responses from participants.

To enhance the user experience and enrich the collected data, we introduced stickers within the chatbot interface. These stickers were designed to encourage participants to express their thoughts and emotions, making the diary completion process more interactive and engaging. This approach aimed not only to gather comprehensive user data but also to foster a more enjoyable and participatory environment for the study participants.

Utilizing chatbots for diary studies enabled us to modify interactive queries in response to participants' immediate feedback, allowing for a more comprehensive investigation of their actual usage experiences. Participants can fill out the exercise diary on any digital device, aiming to reduce participation barriers and enhance convenience and efficiency. This diary research tool is expected to yield genuine and detailed user data, offering a robust basis for future design and research efforts.

**Fig. 1.** The use of a chatbot platform for diary method

**Participant's Recruitment.** Considering the individual differences in user needs, we recruited and categorized participants according to two crucial dimensions: experience with running and experience with digital fitness services. In line with this strategy, we recruited 11 participants and classified them into four types based on these dimensions: users with both rich digital fitness and running experience, users with digital fitness experience but less running experience, runners with rich running experience but less digital fitness experience, and users who are beginners in both aspects.

This method of segmentation is designed to reveal the specific needs and preferences of different user groups towards digital fitness solutions. It allows for the delivery of personalized and effective digital fitness services to each group, thereby enhancing user experience and fulfilling specific requirements. This technique enhances the focus and utility of the research and offers guidance for the design of inclusive and diverse digital fitness services.

**Data Collection and Analysis.** After completing the diary study, we collected and thoroughly analyzed the feedback provided by participants through the chatbot. After analyzing the data, we identified key categories such as critical touchpoints, pain points, and the features and services used by participants during their exercise routines.

This phase enhanced our initial understanding of digital fitness service usage across diverse user groups and provided essential information based on real-life experiences for subsequent co-creation workshops and tool design. This approach allowed us to gain a deep understanding of the real needs and challenges encountered by users of digital fitness services. The outcomes of the analysis will inform the development of co-creation tools, guaranteeing that they adequately facilitate user involvement in co-creation processes and foster the creation of digital fitness solutions aligned with user requirements. This process emphasizes a user-centered design philosophy, which is guided by users' actual experiences in the development of products and services.

### 3.2 Phase Two: Co-creation Collaboration

**Development of Co-creation Toolkits.** Based on the analysis of the diary study data, we devised a co-creation toolkit comprising personal profile cards, a diverse card set, six types of scenario cards, and a co-creation canvas (see Fig. 2). The card deck is organized into seven categories: feedback, triggers, touchpoints, devices, services, data, and themes, encompassing a total of 96 cards. The co-creation canvas integrates the concept of the user journey, directing participants through the co-creation stages in the pre, during, and post phases of running. The scenario cards graphically depict specific instances before, during, and after running, prompting participants to reflect on their experiences and engage in thorough discussion.

**Participant Recruitment.** For the co-creation workshop of this study, participants were recruited based on two criteria previously applied in diary studies: experience with running and usage of digital fitness services. A total of sixteen participants were enlisted and segmented into four distinct groups according to these criteria.

**Co-creation Workshop.** The co-creation workshop process is organized into ten steps, aiming to guide participants on a journey of exploration and conceptualization from

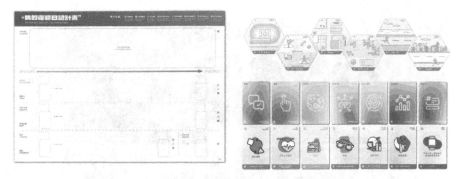

**Fig. 2.** Co-creation Toolkits

various perspectives (see Fig. 3). This journey ultimately leads to the creation of a design solution for a fitness service system. The steps are as follows:

Creating Personal Profile Cards: Participants complete basic information and share their perspectives on wearable devices and exercise attitudes, promoting self-reflection and enhancing team understanding.

Defining Usage Scenarios: Participants select scenario cards that resonate with their running experiences to place on the co-creation canvas, thereby mapping out the different stages of running and deepening the collective understanding of the running experience.

Identifying Touchpoints: This stage is centered on identifying key touchpoints throughout the running experience, aiming to gain an insight into user interactions with digital fitness devices and services, as well as their engagement with the environment.

Highlighting Issues and Pain Points: Through group discussions, participants share their running experiences and identified touchpoints to unearth any issues or inconveniences, thereby identifying opportunities for improvement.

Envisioning Desired Features: After identifying pain points, participants engage in reflection on the functions or services that could address these issues or augment the exercise experience.

Determining Data Requirements for Fitness Services: This step focuses on discussing and deciding the data support essential for implementing the desired features.

Setting Trigger Actions: Participants think about the actions or conditions that would initiate the desired functions or services.

Choosing Feedback Modalities: This step focuses on determining the type and timing of feedback during service usage.

Conceptualizing Device Integration: Participants consider how wearable devices, such as smartwatches, could be integrated with other devices to optimize the user experience.

Sharing and Interviews: Finally, participants share the results and experiences from the co-creation activities and engage in interviews to discuss their perspectives on smart-watch fitness services, providing insights and suggestions for improving the co-creation workshop process.

**Outcomes of the Co-creation Workshop.** In this study, participants were organized according to their "experience with running" and "experience with digital fitness ser-vices" to discern the needs and preferences of diverse user groups regarding digital

**Fig. 3.** Co-Creation workshops

fitness products. Contrary to expectations, the findings indicated minimal variance in the requirements for digital fitness products between experienced and novice runners. On the other hand, categorization based on "experience with digital fitness services" unveiled disparities in functional needs and perceptions among the different groups.

Through the analysis of user journey maps for novice users, distinct insights into their unique requirements for digital fitness service systems were obtained. "Training recommendations" and "immediate feedback" emerged as the primary needs for utilizing digital fitness products. Novice users anticipate receiving personalized training advice prior to exercising. During the exercise, there is a notable demand for "real-time feedback" and "voice-guided training." Additionally, there was a demonstrated interest in "virtual partners" capable of providing companionship and motivation both before and after exercise sessions. Regarding wearable technology such as smartwatches, users particularly value the importance of these devices being lightweight and non-intrusive.

These insights not only uncover the specific needs of novice users for digital fitness products but also highlight their desire for digital services to provide an array of features such as more training suggestions, challenges, feedback, and virtual companionship to boost motivation and enjoyment during exercise. It's clear that users new to smartwatch fitness services are particularly keen on receiving support and companionship during their workouts, showcasing their recognition of the benefits provided by the integrated product-service system.

For experienced users, the journey maps reveal their preferences concerning device specifications, feedback mechanisms, and design preferences. "Training recommendations" and "digital coach" functionalities stand out as critical requirements for these users during their running sessions. Detailed analysis indicates a preference for personalized training suggestions tailored to their pre-exercise fatigue levels. During workouts, they favor voice feedback to decrease the need to check devices frequently, thereby reducing interruptions. Additionally, there is a preference for wearable devices to be designed with ergonomics in mind, prioritizing comfort and usability.

Compared to novice users, experienced individuals exhibit more needs for posture correction, showing a preference for receiving fitness services post-exercise. They lean towards utilizing video demonstrations and digital coach advice for posture adjustment, aiming to enhance the precision and effectiveness of their movements.

Regarding functional needs, a distinction emerges between novice and advanced users. Novice users predominantly seek extensive information feedback and immediate correction during their exercise routines, alongside the support of a virtual partner. In contrast, advanced users prefer to have information aggregated into a summary post-exercise, aiming to minimize distractions during their workouts to maintain focus on the physical activity itself.

Despite these differences in specific preferences, both groups converge on the expectations for device design, expressing a unanimous desire for devices that are lightweight, non-intrusive, and seamlessly integrate into daily life. Furthermore, both novice and advanced users underscore the importance of training recommendations and exercise correction, indicating a shared emphasis on improving exercise efficiency and ensuring safety across all user levels.

## 4  Discussion

The goal of this study is to gain an understanding of users' experiences and requirements for digital fitness services offered through wearable devices. By incorporating diary studies, co-creation workshops, and qualitative interviews, the study seeks to understand the perspectives, opinions, and goals of users engaging with digital fitness product-service systems.

The study identifies a divergence in the functional requirements of digital fitness services between novice and experienced users. Novice users gravitate towards uncomplicated, entry-level advice, highlighting the importance of pre-exercise preparation and receiving correction feedback like pace and breath optimization during running activities. On the other hand, experienced users seek personalization, preferring training plans customized to their fatigue levels and analysis of their running performance, accompanied by post-exercise recommendations for enhancement. When it comes to interactivity and sociability, novice users display an inclination towards virtual companionship and gamification features, which could boost their motivation and participation. In contrast, experienced users prioritize efficiency and concrete results, showing keen interest in data analytics and sophisticated training capabilities.

The findings of this study reveal that individuals' needs and expectations from sports wearables evolve as they continue using these devices, reflecting their changing requirements and experiences. Kim TaeJung and Chiu WeiSheng [12] emphasized the importance of technology readiness in the adoption of sports wearable technology by consumers, highlighting how prolonged usage is crucial for achieving meaningful fitness and health outcomes. Advancements in technology enhance the functionality of these devices and provide users with comprehensive data about their physical activities. This wealth of detailed insights allows users to develop a deeper understanding of their health and fitness, leading to more sophisticated demands from their wearables. Users' requirements vary based on their familiarity and experience with the product-service systems, indicating a movement towards a more personalized and user-centric approach in personal fitness.

Understanding user needs enables developers of digital fitness products and services to create more personalized and feature-rich solutions, tailored to address the specific needs of diverse user groups. This strategy enhances the effective satisfaction of various user requirements over time, thereby fostering innovation and promoting growth in the digital fitness product industry.

**Opportunities and Challenges of Using Chatbots in Diary Studies.** The use of chatbots as a tool for conducting diary studies in this research represents an innovative approach aimed at capturing the authentic experiences of users with digital fitness products or services. By integrating chatbots into diary studies, we introduce a dynamic method for data collection that enables participants to engage in diary-like interactions. This facilitates the real-time capture of both qualitative and quantitative data, potentially offering a more engaging and interactive way for participants to record their daily experiences, behaviors, and reflections. Moreover, this method allows researchers to efficiently gather data on a larger scale and in varied settings.

Participants' feedback on the use of chatbots for diary studies was positive. Many described the process as both enjoyable and engaging, which in turn encouraged deeper reflection on their usage experiences. The social dimension of the diary platform played a crucial role in boosting participants' willingness to engage and their overall level of involvement. The introduction of social and interactive features, such as emoji stickers, not only increased participants' affinity towards the research but also promoted more active engagement and contributions.

Despite the novel opportunities presented by chatbots in diary research, this method also exposed certain limitations, particularly the challenge of conducting in-depth explorations. Finding strategies to unearth deeper insights for more meaningful analysis remains an area for future investigation. The tools used in this study have opened new pathways for conducting user research in the digital age, highlighting areas that require further exploration and improvement. Future research could consider combining traditional and cutting-edge methods to achieve a deeper and more comprehensive understanding of user experiences.

**Co-creation Tools and Workshops.** The integration of co-creation tools and workshops in this study introduces a novel approach to digital fitness product-service design. By leveraging a co-creation toolkit, informed by insights from diary studies, we established an environment conducive to a deep exploration of user experiences, needs, and perspectives. This toolkit, featuring personal profile cards, a diverse set of cards, scenario cards, and a co-creation canvas, provided a structured yet flexible framework for engaging participants effectively.

The workshops were designed to guide participants through a step-by-step process, from creating personal profile cards to engaging in sharing and interviews. This methodical approach ensured a comprehensive exploration of the digital fitness service ecosystem, deepening our understanding of user needs and evaluating the toolkit's practicality and applicability. Participants reported that the workshops facilitated a deeper reflection on their experiences, highlighting challenges and issues encountered with digital fitness products and services. They explored required functionalities, services, and data, including activation methods and feedback mechanisms, providing a platform for participants to consolidate their thoughts and express their preferences regarding device types.

Feedback on the toolkit emphasized its role in promoting logical thinking and ease of expression. The tools were designed to encourage systematic and logical analysis, enabling participants to thoroughly understand challenges and devise viable solutions. Additionally, the toolkit offered a straightforward means for participants to articulate their views and ideas clearly.

However, the co-creation process also revealed challenges in fostering creative and productive dialogue among users. The rich imagination displayed by some participants regarding functional requirements indicated a need for future co-creation tools and workshops to offer more flexibility and creative freedom. This adjustment would allow users to fully express their creativity and incorporate these unique ideas into the product design process. Moreover, translating user insights into actionable design principles and features remains a complex endeavor, necessitating a delicate balance between meeting user desires and ensuring technical feasibility.

The application of co-creation tools and workshops has proven valuable in unlocking deep insights into user needs and preferences. By actively involving a diverse range of users in the design process, we uncovered critical information that conventional research methods might overlook. This user-centric approach holds the promise of enhancing the design of digital fitness services and driving an innovative, responsive product development process. Future research should continue to refine these methodologies, ensuring that digital fitness product-service systems evolve to meet the changing needs and expectations of users.

## 5   Conclusion

In this study, we embarked on a journey to explore the multifaceted experiences, requirements, and perspectives of users engaging with digital fitness products. By adopting a mixed-methods approach that encompassed diary studies, co-creation workshops, and qualitative interviews, we aimed to not only enrich our understanding of user needs but also to assess the potential of this approach in fostering meaningful user involvement and enhancing user studies.

The utilization of chatbots as innovative tools for diary research marked a significant advancement in our methodological toolkit, providing a dynamic platform for instant interaction that spurred participant involvement and reflection. Feedback from participants regarding their experience with chatbots was positive, highlighting the engaging and motivational nature of this approach. Despite its benefits, this method also revealed certain limitations in capturing the full depth of user experiences, pointing to the necessity for further refinement and exploration in future studies.

Furthermore, the execution of co-creation workshops showcased the utility of the specially developed co-creation toolkit in enhancing participants' ability to logically reason and articulate their thoughts. The structured guidance offered by the toolkit empowered participants to methodically dissect and analyze their interactions with the digital fitness product, leading to more insightful discussions and feedback.

In summary, the methodologies employed in this research have opened new avenues for conducting user studies in the digital era, emphasizing the critical role of innovative tool design within the co-creation framework. As we look to the future, there is a clear opportunity to blend traditional research methods with these novel approaches to achieve a richer and more nuanced understanding of user needs and preferences. Through continued exploration and innovation, we aspire to contribute valuable insights to the ongoing development of digital fitness products, with the goal of enhancing user experience and satisfaction. This study lays the groundwork for future research endeavors that will continue to push the boundaries of how we understand and engage with users in the digital fitness domain.

**Acknowledgments.** This material is based upon work supported by the National Science and Technology Council of the Republic of China under grant NSTC 112-2410-H-007-101 -

**Disclosure of Interests.**    The authors have no competing interests to declare that are relevant to the content of this article.

# References

1. Swan, M., Sensor mania! The internet of things, wearable computing, objective metrics, and the quantified Self 2.0. J. Sens. Actuat. Netw. **1**(3), 217–253 (2012)
2. Lunney, A., Cunningham, N.R., Eastin, M.S.: Wearable fitness technology: a structural investigation into acceptance and perceived fitness outcomes. Comput. Hum. Behav. **65**, 114–120 (2016)
3. Gao, Y., Li, H., Luo, Y.: An empirical study of wearable technology acceptance in healthcare. Ind. Manag. Data Syst. **115**(9), 1704–1723 (2015)
4. Asimakopoulos, S., Asimakopoulos, G., Spillers, F.: Motivation and user engagement in fitness tracking: heuristics for mobile healthcare wearables. Informatics. MDPI (2017)
5. Tikkanen, H., Heinonen, K., Ravald, A.: Smart wearable technologies as resources for consumer agency in well-being. J. Interact. Mark. **58**(2–3), 136–150 (2023)
6. Lee, J., et al.: Sustainable wearables: wearable technology for enhancing the quality of human life. Sustainability **8**(5), 466 (2016)
7. Kristensson, P., Matthing, J., Johansson, N.: Key strategies for the successful involvement of customers in the co-creation of new technology-based services. Int. J. Serv. Ind. Manag. **19**(4), 474–491 (2008)
8. Tung, F.-W.: Co-creation with crowdfunding backers for new products and entrepreneurial development: a longitudinal study on design entrepreneurs in Taiwan. Des. J. **25**(5), 768–788 (2022)
9. Tung, F.W., Lai, C.Y.: Development of a co-creation toolkit for designing smart product–service systems: a health device–related case study. In: Marcus, A., Rosenzweig, E., Soares, M.M. (eds.) HCII 2023. LNCS, vol. 14031, pp. 544–554. Springer, Cham (2023). https://doi.org/10.1007/978-3-031-35696-4_40
10. Bartlett, R., Milligan, C.: Diary Method: Research Methods. Bloomsbury Publishing, London (2020)

11. Rapp, A., Cena, F.: Personal informatics for everyday life: how users without prior self-tracking experience engage with personal data. Int. J. Hum Comput Stud. **94**, 1–17 (2016)
12. Kim, T., Chiu, W.: Consumer acceptance of sports wearable technology: the role of technology readiness. Int. J. Sports Mark. Spons. **20**(1), 109–126 (2018)

# Young Consumers' Discontinuance Intention to Use Smartphone Fitness Applications – A Study of Generation Z Consumers in Bangkok

Ping Xu[1] , Bing Zhu[2](✉) , and Thanat Saenghiran[2]

[1] Guangzhou Sport University, Guangdong 510500, USA
[2] Assumption University, Bangkok 10210, Thailand
bingzhu@msme.au.edu

**Abstract.** The rapid development of digital technology has empowered users to engage with fitness applications. While these apps have significantly facilitated user participation in fitness activities, a critical issue is the discontinuation of app usage after a certain period. This study delves into users' discontinuance intention regarding smartphone fitness applications, explicitly focusing on Generation Z consumers in Bangkok. Leveraging the Technology Readiness and Acceptance Model (TRAM), the research aims to uncover the impact of technology readiness on users' perceived usefulness and ease of use, subsequently influencing their discontinuance intention. The objectives of this study include examining the extent to which different dimensions of technology readiness influence users' perceptions of smartphone fitness app usefulness and ease of use. It also investigates the influence of perceived usefulness and ease of use on users' discontinuance intention and explores whether these dimensions mediate the impact of technology readiness on discontinuance intention. The research findings reveal significant relationships and mediation effects that shed light on the factors impacting users' decisions to persist with or abandon fitness applications. Optimism and innovativeness positively affect users' perceptions of usefulness and ease of use, highlighting their role in fostering app adoption. Furthermore, the study underscores the pivotal role of perceived ease of use in reducing discontinuance intention. The implications of these findings for app developers and providers are discussed, emphasizing the importance of user-friendly design and personalization to meet the diverse needs of Generation Z consumers.

**Keywords:** Generation Z · Fitness Applications · Discontinuance Intention

## 1 Introduction

The development of digital information has brought tremendous changes to our lives and, to a large extent, has affected our lifestyle, especially regarding fitness and health [26]. Many people choose fitness to maintain their health and build a muscular physique. Traditionally, people would prefer to exercise in a fitness centre, where they can freely

J. Wei and G. Margetis (Eds.): HCII 2024, LNCS 14737, pp. 116–133, 2024.
https://doi.org/10.1007/978-3-031-60458-4_9

select different equipment to practice, enrol in specific fitness courses or even hire a fitness coach. However, the rapid development of digital technology has made fitness applications accessible to users [24]. This led people to download, use, and terminate it anytime and anywhere. Fitness apps are defined as "programs that use data collected from a smartphone's inbuilt tools, such as the Global Positioning System, accelerometer, microphone, speaker and camera, to measure health and fitness parameters (p. 11) [23, 65]". Smartphone fitness apps have become prevalent because of convenience, especially after the Covid-19 outbreak in 2020 [3]. Fundamentally, smartphone fitness apps provide "exercise instruction, feedback on performance, goal setting, self-monitoring, social support, and contingent rewards" (p. 980) [13, 40], which encourage users to exercise regularly and enhance their involvement in different activities through "training apps, tracking apps and fitness game" (p. 979) [13, 27].

Although fitness apps have extensively promoted users' participation in fitness exercises, a practical problem cannot be ignored: users hardly use fitness applications for a long time [14]. It was found that users tend to stop using fitness apps after using them for a time [13, 14]. For instance, 30% of users stop using fitness trackers after six months [15, 33]. Thus, this phenomenon signifies a low level of commitment to fitness and workout apps [12], which poses challenges to related parties. From a business perspective, if users do not use the application consistently, it is difficult for application developers to solicit user feedback and make further improvements in technology and functionality [11]. Application developers are unlikely to obtain financial benefits from "advertisement, in-app purchases, subscriptions, sponsorships, and other sources" (p. 979) [13, 23]. From the user's viewpoint, the termination of continuous use of fitness apps and related fitness courses will harm the user's development of healthy exercise habits [14]. For these reasons, understanding users' discontinuance behaviour becomes desirable, especially in emerging markets. What are the advantages of grasping users' pain points and letting them continue to use the apps?

The fitness apps segment in Thailand is experiencing significant growth and has a promising outlook. With a growing interest in health and fitness, fitness apps have increased. For instance, the user penetration for fitness apps in Thailand was estimated to reach 5.02% in 2023 [60], indicating that a notable portion of the population already uses fitness apps to support their health and wellness goals. The user penetration is projected to reach 6.71% by 2027 [60]. In addition, in 2023, the revenue in the Health & Wellness Coaching market was projected to reach US$153.10 million, with an expected compound annual growth rate (CAGR 2023-2028) of 10.98% [60]. This data underscores the growing popularity of fitness apps in Thailand and their significant revenue potential in the coming years. In addition, according to the information in Thailand, many fitness apps, including Samsung Health, Fitness & Bodybuilding Pro, Abs – Workout, My FitnessPal and Nike Training Club, Sweat, FitOn Workouts & Fitness Plans, Mi Fitness, Google Fit, etc. are commonly used in Thailand [59]. However, the cost of using certain apps can create a barrier for some users, hindering their ability to continue using them consistently [51].

According to the information in Thailand, many potential fitness app users are currently using an application. Many fitness apps are commonly used in Thailand, such as Samsung Health, Fitness & Bodybuilding Pro, Abs – Workout, My FitnessPal and Nike

Training Club, Sweat, FitOn Workouts & Fitness Plans, Mi Fitness, Google Fit, etc. [59]. Most fitness apps were selected by ease of use, tracking and record system, various features and programs, suggestions from their family or acquaintance, and advertisement. Some people used to have fitness apps because of their reasons. They struggle with inaccurate information and the complexity of fitness apps. In addition, they feel insecure about their privacy and are depressed or stressed. Lastly, some fitness apps have very high costs to use those applications [51].

There are many potential reasons for users to stop using fitness apps. Some users stop using fitness apps after reaching the expected goals, others stop using fitness apps because they fail to meet the predetermined health objectives, and some stop using them because of technology challenges [4]. In short, understanding users' discontinuance behaviour can help app developers and providers deepen their knowledge of user behaviour. While the study addresses essential questions related to users' discontinuance intention in the context of smartphone fitness applications and the role of technology readiness, it's crucial to emphasise the specific research gaps that this study aims to fill:

**The Underexplored Generation Z.** One of the significant research gaps this study addresses is the lack of in-depth understanding of Generation Z's discontinuance intention regarding fitness apps. This generation, born in the mid-1990s to early 2010s, represents a unique demographic that has grown up in a digital age. Their attitudes and behaviours towards fitness apps may differ from those of older generations, so examining their motivations and challenges is essential.

**The Role of Technology Readiness.** As a relatively novel construct, technology readiness is under-researched in the context of fitness apps and discontinuance intention. This research will contribute to bridging this gap by shedding light on how an individual's readiness for technology adoption influences their app usage.

**Practical Implications.** Another research gap that this study seeks to address is the lack of valuable insights and implications for app developers and providers. Understanding users' discontinuance behaviour can help developers create more user-friendly and effective fitness apps, ultimately improving user retention. By identifying the factors influencing discontinuation, this study offers actionable recommendations to enhance the design and features of fitness applications.

These research gaps highlight the unique contributions of the study in unravelling the complexities of Generation Z's discontinuance intention regarding smartphone fitness applications, the role of technology readiness, and the mediating effects of perceived usefulness and ease of use. The study aims to provide valuable insights for researchers and industry professionals by addressing these gaps. In this context, the technology readiness and acceptance model (TRAM) is applied to specifically disclose how technology readiness affects users' perceived usefulness and ease of use, thereby influencing their discontinuance intention of using fitness apps. Notably, this present study tries to address the following objectives:

**Objective One.** To what extent does each dimension of technology readiness affect users' perceived usefulness and ease of use of smartphone fitness apps?

**Objective Two.** To what extent do perceived usefulness and perceived ease of use influence users' discontinuance intention of using smartphone fitness apps?

**Objective Three.** To what extent do perceived usefulness and perceived ease of use mediate the influences of each dimension of technology readiness on users' discontinuance intention of using smartphone fitness apps?

The structure of this present study is as follows: first, a literature review of previous studies and hypothesis development is provided in Sect. 2. The conceptual framework and research design are explained in Sect. 3, followed by research findings in Sect. 4. Discussion and conclusion are available in Sect. 5, and implications are addressed in Sect. 6.

## 2 Literature Review

The technology readiness and technology acceptance model (TRAM) was developed by Lin [35], which integrates technology readiness (TR) into the technology acceptance model (TAM) to understand better individual consumer's adoption behaviour of novel products or technologies [12]. TRAM posits that TR is a critical antecedent of TAM, indicating that individual factors serve as the basis for understanding users' perceptions of new technologies, thereby revealing their intentions to use such technologies [36, 46].

Mainly, TR reflects how individual consumers' attitudes or beliefs would affect the use of up-to-date technology in daily life [45]. The TAM profoundly examines consumers' acceptance of novel technologies [16, 36]. Lin [35] believed that the melding of individual factors (TRI) and system traits (TAM) could not only broaden the practicability of these two models but also further explain individual consumer's acceptance of new technologies in depth [54]. As an emerging model for consumers' technology use, TRAM has been applied in recent studies of health and fitness applications [12], mobile payment applications [47], electronic voting systems [43], AI-based self-service technology [8], mobile shopping [32], and app download and usage [9], etc.

### 2.1 Technology Readiness (TR) Model

The continuous propagation of technology has not only become the main force driving economic and social development. However, it is also widely integrated into our daily lives and closely relates to our social life. Understanding the readiness of consumers to consider using technology-based items has attracted the attention of mainstream academics as their responses to technology vary [30, 44, 45]. For this purpose, the theory of technology readiness (TR) was proposed.

Parasuraman (p. 308) [44] explained that technology readiness is "people's propensity to embrace and use new technologies for accomplishing goals in home life and at work." Interactions between individuals and new technologies simultaneously present different perspectives, such as feelings, perceptions, beliefs, etc., [39]. In this context, TR is also a multidimensional concept that can be categorised into positive and negative TR [31, 44]. Positive TR consists of optimism and innovativeness, viewed as "motivators" facilitating an individual's TR. At the same time, negative TR comprises discomfort and insecurity, representing "inhibitors" that lower an individual's TR (p. 652) [5, 44]. A high score on optimism and innovativeness implies that consumers are optimistic and proactive about new technology products and services because they are open-minded to new things; on the contrary, a high score on discomfort and insecurity reflects those consumers are sceptical and hesitant when using new technology products [37]. Specifically, Parasuraman (p. 311) [44] defined four dimensions in detail:

**Optimism.** Optimism is "a positive view of technology and a belief that offers people increased control, flexibility and efficiency in their lives."

**Innovativeness.** Innovativeness represents "a tendency to be a technology pioneer and thought leader."

**Discomfort.** Discomfort signifies "a perceived lack of control over technology and feeling overwhelmed by it."

**Insecurity.** Insecurity implies "distrust of technology and scepticism about its ability to work properly."

The development of TR has gone through two stages: technology readiness index 1.0 (TRI 1.0) and technology readiness index 2.0 (TRI 2.0). The first version contained 36 items but was deemed insufficient to determine consumers' beliefs towards technologies, and the second version was created with 16 items yet retained the four dimensions of optimism, innovativeness, discomfort, and insecurity. Now, TR has been acknowledged as a stable construct that well reflects trait-like characteristics at an individual level [5], which attempts to investigate consumers' beliefs, attitudes, and decisions towards timely technology-based products and services such as app download and usage intention [9], sport wearable devices [31], among others.

### 2.2 Technology Acceptance Model (TAM)

Based on the theory of reasoned action (TRA) [2, 19], Davis [16] introduced the technology acceptance model (TAM) to explain how a constellation of determinants influences user acceptance of new technology [29, 38]. Traditionally, TAM treats perceived usefulness (PU) and perceived ease of use (PEOU) as the main elements in learning about an individual's intention to use specific technology [16, 28]. Perceived ease of use is the belief that using technology (e.g., fitness apps) will be simple and take little effort. In contrast, perceived usefulness means that individual users believe using technology (e.g., fitness apps) will be helpful in task completion [46].

### 2.3 Discontinuance Intention

Based on Lee [34] stated that user continuance and discontinuance are commonly seen throughout the innovation diffusion process [1]. User continuance and discontinuance manifest different concepts, but this does not affect their simultaneous existence [62]. It is worth noting that while mainstream scholars consistently favour users' continuance behaviour, little is known about user discontinuance to use a particular technology, which in fact, is an inevitable phenomenon when understanding post-adoption behaviour [6,

56]. Discontinuance refers to "the active rejection of a new system after initial adoption" (p. 589) [6, 53]. In this study, discontinuance intention is the user's intention to cease using fitness applications shortly.

From a general perspective, Lin [35] treats TR as one variable that contains four sub-factors (optimism, innovativeness, discomfort, and insecurity) to predict users' acceptance of technology. Being treated as a higher-order construct, TR has been examined its relationship with PEOU and PU, thereby indicating consumer acceptance of new technology by various scholars such as Jin [25], Kim and Chiu [31], Oh [42] and Chiu & Cho [12]. However, Park [46] argued that the four elements of TR, referring to optimism, innovativeness, discomfort, and insecurity, should be tested independently as a single variable. Logically speaking, motivators and inhibitors affect users' behaviour to varying degrees, resulting in different outcomes. Therefore, studying these four dimensions independently makes it possible to portray users' attitudes and reactions toward new technologies in more detail.

Most importantly, prior studies have revealed inconsistent findings when testing the influence of the TR construct on users' acceptance of technology [9, 10, 46]. Thus, in this study, optimism, innovativeness, discomfort, and insecurity will be tested independently to disclose how each dimension affects perceived usefulness and ease of use, thereby influencing users' discontinuance intention to use fitness applications (Fig. 1). With this, the following hypotheses were developed:

**H1a.** *Optimism positively influences perceived usefulness*

**H1b.** *Optimism positively influences perceived ease of use*

**H2a.** *Innovativeness positively influences perceived usefulness*

**H2b.** *Innovativeness positively influences perceived ease of use*

**H3a.** *Discomfort negatively influences perceived usefulness*

**H3b.** *Discomfort negatively influences perceived ease of use*

**H4a.** *Insecurity negatively influences perceived usefulness*

**H4b.** *Insecurity negatively influences perceived ease of use*

**H5.** *Perceived ease of use negatively influences users' discontinuance intention of using fitness applications*

**H6.** *Perceived usefulness negatively influences users' discontinuance intention of using fitness applications*

In addition, Lin [35] proposed that individual differences have an impact on technology readiness on an individual's eventual adoption and acceptance of novelty, which is mediated by technology-related useful attributes such as perceived ease of use (PEOU) and perceived usefulness (PU) For this reason, the following hypotheses were developed:

**H7a.** *The influence of optimism on user discontinuance intention of using smartphone fitness applications is mediated by perceived usefulness*

**H7b.** *The influence of optimism on user discontinuance intention of using smartphone fitness applications is mediated by perceived ease of use*

**H8a.** *The influence of innovativeness on user discontinuance intention of using smartphone fitness applications is mediated by perceived usefulness*

**H8b.** *The influence of innovativeness on user discontinuance intention of using smartphone fitness applications is mediated by perceived ease of use*

**H9a.** *The influence of discomfort on user discontinuance intention of using smartphone fitness applications is mediated by perceived usefulness*

**H9b.** *The influence of discomfort on user discontinuance intention of using smartphone fitness applications is mediated by perceived ease of use.*

**H10a.** *The influence of insecurity on user discontinuance intention of using smartphone fitness applications is mediated by perceived usefulness*

**H10b.** *The influence of insecurity on user discontinuance intention of using smartphone fitness applications is mediated by perceived ease of use*

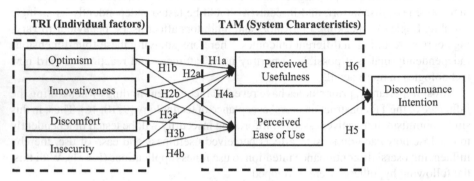

**Fig. 1.** Conceptual framework. Source: Developed by authors based on Chen & Lin et al. [35]

## 3   Research Design

Due to Covid 19, people are encouraged to work from home or study online, which has triggered the download of fitness applications. The scenario is that some people continue using fitness applications to achieve their goals while others discontinue using them. So, what factors might motivate people to continue using it? An online survey was conducted in Bangkok from May to September 2021 to answer this question. Snowball and convenient sampling techniques were used to collect responses from the target participants with experience using fitness applications (such as Keep-Home Workout Trainer, Nike Training Club, Runkeeper, Fitbit, Google Fit, etc.) for at least three months. The minimum sample size was determined by G* Power 3.1 [17]. The result suggested a minimum sample size of 123 that assures the research model a statistical power of 0.9 with a medium effect size of 0.15. Consequently, 300 sets of questionnaires with comprehensive information were returned, valid for data analysis.

The measurement items were assessed on a 5-point Likert scale, as Chen & Lin [9] and Lin [35] proposed. Specifically, the measurement items of technology readiness were adopted from Parasuraman [45], while the items of discontinuance intention were adopted from Turel [62]. The TAMTAM components of perceived usefulness and perceived ease of use were taken from Davis [16].

The statistical analysis used the partial least square structural equation model (PLS-SEM). The PLS-SEM method assesses statistical models constructed to present a causal relationship [21, 55, 64]. The data analysis follows the guidelines of Hair [21], in which the measurement and structural models were evaluated. Also, the bootstrapping technique was applied to test the mediation effect.

## 4 Findings

### 4.1 Respondent Profile

The participants are mainly female (59.3%), whose ages ranged from 18 to 25 years old (61%), with monthly income lower than 20,000 baht (59.7%) and obtained bachelor's degree (91.7%).

### 4.2 Common Method Bias

Harman's one-factor test for common method bias was applied in this present study. No issue or problem has been found since the total variance extracted by one factor is 23.888%, less than the recommended threshold of 50%.

### 4.3 Evaluation of Measurement Model

**Internal Consistency and Convergent Validity.** The results of convergent validity and internal consistency analysis are presented in Table 1. The factor loadings and average variance extracted (AVE) were calculated to assess convergent validity. The factor loading of 0.5 or higher is considered reasonably significant, and an AVE value greater than 0.5 presents adequate convergence [20]. In this study, all loading values are more powerful than 0.5, and all AVE values surpass the threshold value of 0.5; hence, the convergent validity is proven. Next, the evaluation of internal consistency contains Cronbach's alpha, composite reliability, and Dijkstra–Henseler's rho_A [21]. Cronbach's alpha values varied from 0.705 to 0.931, which exceeded the threshold value of 0.7 [41]. As for composite reliability, all values are more significant than a cut-off value of 0.7, as suggested by Hair [21]. Hair [21] articulates that the conservativeness of Cronbach's alpha and liberty of composite reliability give rise to pA, which is viewed as "the most important and consistent measure of internal consistency reliability" (p. 83) [49]. Byrne [7] suggested a threshold value of 0.7. Again, values of Cronbach's alpha, composite reliability, and rho_A outperformed the recommended values; thus, internal consistency is confirmed.

**Discriminant Validity.** Heterotrait-Monotrait (HTMT) Ratio of the Correlation is recommended to assess discriminant validity in PLS-SEM [21, 22, 63]. HTMT is indicated as "the mean value of the item correlations across constructs relative to the (geometric) mean of the average correlations for the items measuring the same construct" (p. 9) [21, 66], and a threshold value of 0.9 is suggested by Henseler [22]. All HTMT values in Table 2 are lower than 0.9, so the study's discriminant validity is verified.

**Table 1.** Construct validity and reliability.

| | Factor Loading | Cronbach's Alpha | rho_A | Composite Reliability | AVE |
|---|---|---|---|---|---|
| Discomfort | | 0.715 | 0.805 | 0.833 | 0.627 |
| DISCOM2 | 0.681 | | | | |
| DISCOM3 | 0.800 | | | | |
| DISCOM4 | 0.881 | | | | |
| Innovativeness | | 0.705 | 0.714 | 0.817 | 0.529 |
| INNOV1 | 0.750 | | | | |
| INNOV2 | 0.733 | | | | |
| INNOV3 | 0.658 | | | | |
| INNOV4 | 0.764 | | | | |
| Insecurity | | 0.759 | 0.802 | 0.838 | 0.565 |
| INS1 | 0.757 | | | | |
| INS2 | 0.700 | | | | |
| INS3 | 0.748 | | | | |
| INS4 | 0.800 | | | | |
| Optimism | | 0.735 | 0.745 | 0.834 | 0.558 |
| OPT1 | 0.657 | | | | |
| OPT2 | 0.746 | | | | |
| OPT3 | 0.814 | | | | |
| OPT4 | 0.763 | | | | |
| Perceived ease of use | | 0.882 | 0.894 | 0.918 | 0.738 |
| PEASE1 | 0.813 | | | | |
| PEASE2 | 0.884 | | | | |
| PEASE3 | 0.868 | | | | |
| PEASE4 | 0.868 | | | | |
| Perceived usefulness | | 0.852 | 0.857 | 0.899 | 0.691 |
| PUSE1 | 0.826 | | | | |
| PUSE2 | 0.834 | | | | |
| PUSE3 | 0.841 | | | | |
| PUSE4 | 0.823 | | | | |

*(continued)*

**Table 1.** (*continued*)

|  | Factor Loading | Cronbach's Alpha | rho_A | Composite Reliability | AVE |
|---|---|---|---|---|---|
| Discontinue intention |  | 0.931 | 0.969 | 0.945 | 0.877 |
| DISINT1 | 0.927 |  |  |  |  |
| DISINT2 | 0.944 |  |  |  |  |
| DISINT3 | 0.938 |  |  |  |  |

**Table 2.** Heterotrait-Monotrait ratio (HTMT).

|  | Discomfort | Discontinue intention | Innovativeness | Insecurity | Optimism | Perceived ease of use | Perceived usefulness |
|---|---|---|---|---|---|---|---|
| Discomfort |  |  |  |  |  |  |  |
| Discontinue intention | 0.359 |  |  |  |  |  |  |
| Innovativeness | 0.280 | 0.117 |  |  |  |  |  |
| Insecurity | 0.762 | 0.385 | 0.104 |  |  |  |  |
| Optimism | 0.284 | 0.141 | 0.571 | 0.238 |  |  |  |
| Perceived ease of use | 0.065 | 0.284 | 0.185 | 0.091 | 0.222 |  |  |
| Perceived usefulness | 0.153 | 0.201 | 0.394 | 0.189 | 0.489 | 0.502 |  |

## 4.4 Evaluation of Structural Equation Model

Hair (p. 11) [21] explained that "coefficient of determination ( $R^2$), the blindfolding-bases cross-validated redundancy measure ($Q^2$), path coefficients" and the assessment of out-of-sample predictive power based on PLSpredict [57] are necessary to evaluate the structural model.

**Collinearity and Path Coefficients.** The significance of the structural model was tested based on the bootstrapping technique, and the results are presented in Table 3. Firstly, the significances were found in the paths from optimism to perceived usefulness (H1a) and to perceived ease of use (H1b), from innovativeness to perceived usefulness (H2a). Nevertheless, perceived ease of use is negatively associated with discontinuance intention (H5), which means that the more consumers perceive fitness applications as easy, the less intention they have to stop using them. Also, the confidence intervals test shows that zero does not exist in these four hypotheses; hence, a significant effect is established. In addition, multicollinearity was tested. Since all variation inflation factor (VIF) values are less than 5 [21], it is confirmed that multicollinearity does not exist in this present study. Moreover, the path analysis was visually illustrated in Fig. 2 by addressing both t-values and p-values.

**Table 3.** Structural model path coefficients.

| | | Path coefficient | T values | P values | 95% Confidence intervals | Results |
|---|---|---|---|---|---|---|
| H1a | OPTI -> PU | 0.304 | 5.060 | *** | [0.186, 0.421] | Accept |
| H1b | OPTI -> PEOU | 0.154 | 2.255 | ** | [0.025, 0.289] | Accept |
| H2a | INNOV -> PU | 0.191 | 3.359 | *** | [0.084, 0.309] | Accept |
| H2b | INNOV -> PEOU | 0.096 | 1.501 | 0.113 | [−0.054, 0.183] | Reject |
| H3a | DISCOM -> PU | −0.050 | 0.627 | 0.531 | [−0.200, 0.121] | Reject |
| H3b | DISCOM- > PEOU | −0.051 | 0.524 | 0.601 | [−0.228, 0.140] | Reject |
| H4a | INSECU -> PU | 0.136 | 1.234 | 0.217 | [−0.180, 0.285] | Reject |
| H4b | INSECU -> PEOU | −0.041 | 0.355 | 0.723 | [−0.254, 0.183] | Reject |
| H5 | PEOU -> DIS_INT | −0.234 | 3.714 | **** | [−0.359, − 0.109] | Accept |
| H6 | PU - > DIS_INT | −0.084 | 1.245 | 0.217 | [−0.225, 0.042] | Reject |

Note (s): *** $p < 0.01$, ** $p < 0.05$

**In-Sample Prediction.** $R^2$ is used to assess the model's explanatory power, indicated as in-sample predictive power [21, 52]. In this present study, the value of $R^2$ for discontinuance intention is 0.173, which means a weak-to-moderate predictive power. The values of $R^2$ for perceived ease of use and perceived usefulness are 0.045 and 0.197, demonstrating weak and weak-to-moderate predictive power. However, the interpretation of $R^2$ should be context-based, and the number of constructs largely influences the results of $R^2$ [21, 48]. Therefore, it is possible that relatively few constructs could result in relatively low $R^2$ in this present study.

Concerning $Q^2$ it is to assess the predictive accuracy of the PLS path model [19, 59] through the blindfolding approach [22] (Hair et al. 2019b). According to the rule of thumb, $Q^2$ values greater than 0, 0.25, and 0.50 reflect "small, medium, and large predictive relevance of the PLS-path model" (p. 12) [21]. The blindfolding results in this study showed that a $Q^2$ value of 0.061 in discontinuance intention presents a strong predictive relevance in the proposed model. Also, $Q^2$ values of 0.024 in perceived ease of use and 0.126 in perceived usefulness depict moderate to large predictive accuracy in the model.

**Table 4.** PLSpredict assessment of manifested variables.

| | PLS-SEM | | LM | PLS-SEM-LIM RMSE |
|---|---|---|---|---|
| | RMSE | $Q^2$_predict | RMSE | |
| DISINT3 | 1.115 | 0.007 | 1.068 | 0.047 |
| DISINT1 | 1.116 | 0.010 | 1.061 | 0.055 |
| DISINT2 | 1.145 | 0.003 | 1.092 | 0.053 |
| PEASE3 | 0.917 | −0.007 | 0.952 | −0.035 |
| PEASE2 | 0.951 | 0.012 | 0.984 | −0.033 |
| PEASE4 | 0.931 | −0.001 | 0.957 | −0.026 |
| PEASE1 | 0.877 | 0.003 | 0.911 | −0.034 |
| PUSE3 | 0.823 | 0.081 | 0.833 | −0.01 |
| PUSE4 | 0.829 | 0.142 | 0.857 | −0.028 |
| PUSE1 | 0.848 | 0.147 | 0.871 | −0.023 |
| PUSE2 | 0.883 | 0.062 | 0.902 | −0.019 |

**Table 5.** Hypothesis testing on mediation effect.

| | Path | Std. Beta | Std. Error | T values | P values | Confidence intervals | Results |
|---|---|---|---|---|---|---|---|
| H7a | OPTI -> PU -> DIS_INT | − 0.026 | 0.023 | 1.177 | 0.239 | [− 0.074, 0.013] | Reject |
| H7b | OPTI -> PEOU -> DIS_INT | − 0.036 | 0.019 | 1.910 | ** | [− 0.078, − 0.005] | Accept |
| H8a | INNOV -> PU -> DIS_INT | − 0.016 | 0.014 | 1.119 | 0.263 | [− 0.048, 0.009] | Reject |
| H8b | INNOV -> PEOU -> DIS_INT | − 0.023 | 0.016 | 1.321 | 0.186 | [− 0.061, 0.005] | Reject |
| H9a | DISCOM -> PU -> DIS_INT | − 0.011 | 0.010 | 0.431 | 0.667 | [− 0.014, 0.028] | Reject |
| H9b | DISCOM -> PEOU -> DIS_INT | 0.012 | 0.024 | 0.484 | 0.628 | [− 0.032, 0.064] | Reject |
| H10a | INSECU -> PU -> DIS_INT | − 0.011 | 0.015 | 0.750 | 0.454 | [− 0.042, 0.023] | Reject |
| H10b | INSECU-> PEOU-> DIS_INT | 0.010 | 0.028 | 0.339 | 0.735 | [− 0.040, 0.069] | Reject |

Note (s): ** $P < 0.05$

**Out-of-Sample Prediction.** PLSpredict, developed by Shmueli [57], is used to "a model's evaluate out-of-sample predictive power" (p. 2324) [58]. Shmueli [57] addressed

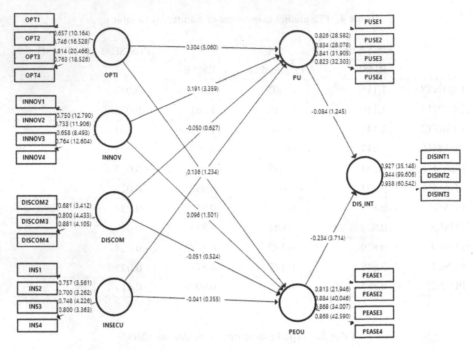

**Fig. 2.** Structural model presenting p-values and path coefficient.

that out-of-sample prediction is suitable to assess "the model on an analysis sample" and to assess "its predictive performance on the data" (p. 12) [21, 57, 66]. As an emerging technique, the usage and interpretation of PLSpredict results still lack a clear guideline [50]; as a result, PLSpredict results in this present study were analysed based on the recommendations of Shmueli [58]. First, ten folds were applied in PLSpredict to examine the predictive performance of endogenous constructs: discontinuance intention, perceived ease of use, and perceived usefulness. Next, as the $Q^2$ predicted value of all indicators was more significant than 0, a further comparison between RMSE and the naïve LM benchmark was conducted. Since most indicators in the PLS-SEM produce more minor prediction errors than the naïve LM benchmark, a medium predictive power in the proposed model is confirmed [58] (Table 4).

## 4.5  Mediation Analysis

The mediation analysis was carried out based on the Bootstrapping technique. The results show that only perceived ease of use (H11b) significantly mediates the influence of optimism on discontinuance intention, and zero does not exist in the 95% boot CI bias corrected. At the same time, the rest of the mediation effects remain insignificant (Table 5).

# 5   Discussion and Conclusion

This study aims to understand users' post-adoption behaviour of a particular technology by studying users' discontinuance intention of using fitness apps based on the technology readiness and acceptance model (TRAM). The results reveal three significant and positive relationships in the path from optimism to perceived usefulness (H1a) and to perceived ease of use (H1b), from innovativeness to perceived usefulness (H2a). In contrast, the perceived ease of use was found to affect discontinuance intention significantly and negatively (H5). Mediation analysis discloses that only perceived use of ease (H7b) substantially mediates the influence of optimism on discontinuance intention.

Firstly, the findings highlight the role of optimism in affecting perceived usefulness and ease of use. Optimism triggered respondents' technology readiness as they were open-minded and actively embraced new technologies. Consequently, this positivity enhances respondents' confidence that using fitness apps is simple and that they do not need to put much effort into dealing with it. Therefore, using fitness apps becomes a helpful mechanism to help users achieve their goals, improving their performance, productivity, and effectiveness in exercising. Besides, as innovativeness positively affects perceived usefulness, it manifests that our respondents present a tendency to be pioneers and thought leaders in using fitness apps because they find them beneficial to their lives. Thus, they do hesitate to use and continue to use it. As perceived ease of use negatively impacts users' discontinuance intention in using fitness apps, it indicates that the better and the more manageable the fitness app's functions are, the stronger the users' desire to continuously use it and the lower the intention to stop using it. Accordingly, fitness apps should be easy to operate and meet different fitness needs simultaneously. Therefore, app developers can create diversified course content according to the needs of other user groups to have varied options.

Moreover, the mediation tests reveal that perceived ease of use fully mediates the relationship between optimism and discontinuous intention of using fitness apps. This underlines the value of the simplicity of fitness apps. Even if users are open and optimistic about fitness apps, if their use is complicated and cannot provide a good user experience, users will not continuously use the apps.

# 6   Implications

## 6.1   Theoretical Implication

This present study was conducted in the scope of the technology readiness and acceptance model (TRAM) in Thailand, in which the up-to-date empirical findings will enrich the existing works of literature. Also, this present study portrays how users in Thailand react to new technology represented by fitness apps and sheds light on motivators (optimism and innovativeness) in stimulating the users' readiness for technology.

## 6.2   Managerial Implications

Several potential strategic solutions exist to encourage consumers' continued usage of smartphone fitness apps. First, it can be stimulated by maintaining user stickiness to strengthen the continuity of users' utilisation of fitness apps. User stickiness is one of the prerequisites for product longevity, and some consumers are unwilling to give up their previous efforts. In this scenario, developers can enhance the user experience to increase consumers' engagement. Second, in response to users' needs for simplicity and diversification of fitness application operations, developers can strengthen the digital intelligent fitness experience, provide professional and rich course content, meet the fitness guidance needs of different groups, and improve efficiency through exercise data monitoring and analysis. Third, app developers and providers can emphasise their apps' positive aspects and benefits when marketing fitness apps to Generation Z users in Thailand. Highlighting the ease of use and potential for simplifying users' fitness routines can attract more optimistic users. This can also enhance users' desirability to continue using the app and reduce the likelihood of discontinuation. Lastly, Fitness apps should offer diversified course content and customization options to meet Generation Z consumers' varied needs and preferences. Moreover, as consumers' expectations and technology readiness evolve, staying updated with emerging trends and incorporating user feedback is essential. Regular updates, bug fixes, and new features can increase consumers' satisfaction and engagement. In conclusion, understanding how optimism, perceived ease of use, and technology readiness influence consumers' discontinuance intention can guide the development of more effective and user-friendly fitness applications. By focusing on simplicity, personalisation, and continuous improvement, developers can enhance users' experiences, increase retention rates, and meet the evolving needs of Generation Z consumers in Thailand's dynamic fitness app market.

## 7  Limitations

Inevitably, this present study has some limitations. Firstly, quantitative results may need to be deeper to reveal user insights; therefore, qualitative, in-depth interviews are recommended for future research. Secondly, this study is limited to user behaviour research, ignoring the focus on application developers or providers. Therefore, future research should consider the business aspect and explore the development of fitness apps from a business perspective to make the research on fitness apps more practical for marketers and fitness app providers.

**Acknowledgements.** This study was funded by the Guangdong Provincial Education Department of China (2021GXJK619).

**Disclosure of Interests.** The authors have no competing interests to declare that are relevant to the content of this article.

## References

1. Abraham, S.C.S., Hayward, G.: Understanding discontinuance: towards a more realistic model of technological innovation and industrial adoption in Britain. Technovation **2**(3), 209–231 (1984)

2. Ajzen, I., Fishbein, M.: Understanding attitude and predicting social behavior. Prentice Hall, Englewood Cliffs, New Jersey (1980)
3. Barbosa, F.H., García-Fernández, J., Pedragosa, V., Cepeda-Carrion, G.: The use of fitness central apps and its relation to customer satisfaction: a UTAUT2 perspective. Int. J. Sports Mark. Spons. 23(5), 966–985 (2021)
4. Bioon Homepage, 8 major trends in digital medical product consumption: 1 in 4 respondents will abandon wearable devices. https://news.bioon.com/article/1c9d660023d1.html. Accessed 29 Nov 2023
5. Blut, M., Wanng, C.: Technology readiness: a meta-analysis of conceptualizations of the construct and its impact on technology usage. J. Acad. Mark. Sci. 1(48), 649–669 (2020)
6. Butcher, L., Tucker, O., Young, J.: Path to discontinuance of pervasive mobile games: the case of Pokémon Go in Australia. Asia Pac. J. Mark. Logist. 33(2), 584–606 (2021)
7. Byrne, M.B.: Structural Equation Modeling with Amos: Basic Concepts, Applications, and Programming. Routledge, New York (2016)
8. Castillo, S.M.J., Bigne, E.: A model of adoption of AR-based self-service technologies: a two country comparison. Int. J. Retail Distrib. Manage. 49(7), 875–898 (2021)
9. Chen, M.F., Lin, N.P.: Incorporation of health consciousness into the technology readiness and acceptance model to predict app download and usage intentions. Internet Res. 28(2), 351–373 (2018)
10. Chen, S., Chen, H., Chen, M.: Determinants of satisfaction and continuance intention towards self-service technologies. Ind. Manag. Data Syst. 109(9), 1248–1263 (2009)
11. Chi, Y.S., Kang, M.Y., Han, K.S., Choi, J.I.: A study on the discontinuance intention on o2o commerce: With a focus on the mediating effects of perceived risk and user resistance. Int. J. U- and E- Service. Sci. Technol. 9(2), 207–218 (2016)
12. Chiu, W.S., Cho, H.: The role of technology readiness in individuals' intention to use health and fitness applications: a comparison between users and non users. Asia Pac. J. Mark. Logist. 33(3), 807–825 (2021)
13. Chiu, W.S., Cho, H., Chi, G.C.: Consumers' continuance intention to use fitness and health apps: an integration of the expectation–confirmation model and investment model. Inf. Technol. People 34(3), 978–998 (2021)
14. Cho, J.: The impact of post-adoption beliefs on the continued use of health apps. Int. J. Med. Inform. 87, 75–83 (2016)
15. Coorevits, L., Coenen, T.: The Rise and Fall of Wearable Fitness Trackers. Academy of Management. Briarcliff Manor, New York (2016)
16. Davis, F.D.: Perceived usefulness, perceived ease of use, and user acceptance of information technology. MIS Q. 13(3), 319–340 (1989)
17. Faul, F., Erdfelder, E., Lang, A.G., Buchner, A.: G*Power 3: a flexible statistical power analysis program for the social, behavioral, and biomedical sciences. Behav. Res. Methods 39, 175–191 (2007)
18. Fishbein, M., Azjen, I.: Belief, attitude, intention, and behaviour: an introduction to theory and research. Philos. Rhetor. 41(4), 842–844 (1977)
19. Geisser, S.: A predictive approach to the random effects model. Biometrika 61(1), 101–107 (1974)
20. Hair, J.F., Black, W.C., Babin, B.J., Anderson, R.E.: Multivariate data analysis, cengage learning. Hampshire, United Kingdom (2019a)
21. Hair, J.F., Risher, J.J., Sarstedt, M., Ringle, C.M.: When to use and how to report the results of PLS-SEM. Eur. Bus. Rev. 30(1), 2–24 (2019)
22. Henseler, J., Ringle, M.C., Sarstedt, M.: A new criterion for assessing discriminant validity in variance-based structural equation modeling. J. Acad. Mark. Sci. 43(1), 115–135 (2015)
23. Higgins, J.P.: Smartphone applications for patients' health and fitness. Am. J. Med. 129(1), 11–19 (2016)

24. Hu, J., He, W.: Examining the impacts of fitness app functionalities. AMCIS 2020 Proceedings, 5. https://aisel.aisnet.org/amcis2020/healthcare_it/healthcare_it/5. Accessed 29 Nov 2023
25. Jin, C.: The perspective of a revised TRAM on social capital building: the case of Facebook usage. Inf. Manage. **50**(4), 162–168 (2013)
26. Jones, P., Ratten, V., Hayduk, T.I.: Sport, fitness, and lifestyle entrepreneurship. Int. Entrep. Manag. J. **16**, 783–793 (2020)
27. Khaghani-Far, I., Nikitina, S., Baez, M., Taran, E.A., Casati, F.: Fitness applications for home-based training. IEEE Pervasive Comput. **15**(4), 56–65 (2016)
28. Kim, J.K., Shin, D.H.: An acceptance model for smart watches: implications for the adoption of future wearable technology. Internet Res. **25**(4), 527–541 (2014)
29. Kim, K.J., Wang, S.: Understanding the acceptance of the internet of things: an integrative theoretical approach. Aslib J. Inf. Manag. **73**(5), 754–771 (2021)
30. Kim, T.J., Chiu, W.S., Chow, F.K.M.: Sport technology consumers: segmenting users of sports wearable devices based on technology readiness. Sport, Bus. Manage. **9**(2), 134–145 (2019)
31. Kim, T.J., Chiu, W.S.: Consumer acceptance of sports wearable technology: the role of technology readiness. Int. J. Sports Mark. Spons. **20**(1), 109–126 (2019)
32. Kumar, A., Mukherjee, A.: Shop while you talk: determinants of purchase intentions through a mobile device. Int. J. Mob. Mark. **8**(1), 23–37 (2013)
33. Ledger, D., McCaffrey, D.: Inside wearables: how the science of human behavior change offers the secret to long-term engagement. Endeavour Partners **200**(93), 1 (2014)
34. Lee, D.O.K., Lee, S., Suh, W., Chang, Y.: Alleviating the impact of SNS fatigue on user discontinuance. Ind. Manag. Data Syst. **122**(1), 292–321 (2021)
35. Lin, C.H., Shih, H.Y., Sher, P.J.: Integrating technology readiness into technology acceptance: the TRAM model. Psychol. Mark. **24**(7), 641–657 (2007)
36. Lin, J.C., Chang, H.: The role of technology readiness in self-service technology acceptance. Managing Serv. Q. Int. J. **21**(4), 424–444 (2011)
37. Louis, L., Chen, C.C.: E-health/m-health adoption and lifestyle improvements: exploring the roles of technology readiness, the expectation confirmation model, and health-related information activities. Telecommunic. Policy **43**(6), 563–575 (2017)
38. McNamara, A.J., Sepasgozar, S.M.E.: Developing a theoretical framework for intelligent contract acceptance. Constr. Innov. **20**(3), 421–445 (2020)
39. Meng, J., Elliott, K.M., Hall, M.C.: Technology readiness index (TRI): assessing cross-cultural validity. J. Int. Consum. Mark. **22**(1), 19–31 (2009)
40. Middelweerd, A., Mollee, J.S., Van Der Wal, C.N., Brug, J., Te Velde, S.J.: Apps to promote physical activity among adults: a review and content analysis. Int. J. Behav. Nutrition Phys. Activity, 11 (2014)
41. Nunnally, J.C., Bernstein, I.H.: Psychometric Theory. McGraw-Hill, New York (1994)
42. Oh, J.C., Yoon, S.J., Chung, N.: The role of technology readiness in consumers' adoption of mobile internet services between South Korea and China. Int. J. Mobile Commun. **12**(3), 229–248 (2014)
43. Omotayo, F.O., Chigbundu, M.C.: Use of information and communication technologies for administration and management of schools in Nigeria. J. Syst. Inf. Technol. **19**(3/4), 183–201 (2017)
44. Parasuraman, A.: Technology readiness index (TRI) a multiple-item scale to measure readiness to embrace new technologies. J. Serv. Res. **2**(4), 307–320 (2000)
45. Parasuraman, A., Colby, L.C.: An updated and streamlined technology readiness index: TRI 2.0. J. Serv. Res. **8**(1), 59–74 (2015)
46. Park, J.S., Ha, S., Jeong, S.W.: Consumer acceptance of self-service technologies in fashion retail stores. J. Fash. Mark. Manag. **25**(2), 371–388 (2021)

47. Rafdinal, W., Senalasari, W.: Predicting the adoption of mobile payment applications during the COVID-19 pandemic. Int. J. Bank Mark. **39**(6), 984–1002 (2021)
48. Raithel, S., Sarstedt, M., Scharf, S., Schwaiger, M.: On the value relevance of customer satisfaction. Multiple drivers and multiple markets. J. Acad. Mark. Sci. **40**(4), 509–525 (2012)
49. Ramayah, T., Cheah, J., Chuah, F., Ting, H., Memon, A.M.: Partial least squares structural equation modeling (pls-sem) using smartpls 3.0: An updated and practical guide to statistical analysis. Malaysia Pearson, Kuala Lumpur (2018)
50. Rasoolimanesh, S.M., Ali, F.: Editorial: Partial least squares (PLS) in hospitality and tourism research. J. Hosp. Tour. Technol. **9**(3), 238–248 (2018)
51. Rich, E., Lewis, S., Miah, A., Lupton, D., Piwek, L.: Digital Health Generation? Young People's Use of 'Healthy Lifestyle' Technologies. University of Bath, Bath (2020)
52. Rigdon, E.E.: Rethinking partial least squares path modeling: in praise of simple methods. Long Range Plan. **45**(5–6), 341–358 (2012)
53. Rogers, E.M.: Diffusion of Innovations. Simon and Schuster, New York (2003)
54. Rojas-Méndez, J.I., Parasuraman, A., Papadopoulos, N.: Demographics, attitudes, and technology readiness: a cross-cultural analysis and model validation. Mark. Intell. Plan. **35**(1), 18–39 (2017)
55. Sarstedt, M., Ringle, C. M., Hair, J. F.: Partial least squares structural equation modeling. In: Handbook of Market Research. Springer, Heideberg (2017)
56. Shen, X.L., Li, Y.J., Sun, Y.: Wearable health information systems intermittent discontinuance: a revised expectation-disconfirmation model. Ind. Manag. Data Syst. **118**(3), 506–523 (2018)
57. Shmueli, G., Ray, S., Velasquez, E.J.M., Chatla, S.B.: The elephant in the room: evaluating the predictive performance of PLS models. J. Bus. Res. **69**(10), 4552–4562 (2016)
58. Shmueli, G., et al.: Predictive model assessmet in PLS-SEM: guidelines for using PLSpredict. Eur. J. Mark. **53**(11), 2322–2347 (2019)
59. Similarweb Homepage, Top Apps Ranking. https://www.similarweb.com/apps/top/google/app-index/th/health-fitness/top-free/. Accessed 29 Nov 2023
60. Statista Homepage, Digital fitness & well-being – Thailand. https://www.statista.com/outlook/hmo/digital-health/digital-fitness-well-being/thailand/. Accessed 29 Nov 2023
61. Stone, M.: Cross-validatory choice and assessment of statistical predictions. J. Roy. Stat. Soc. Ser. B (Methodol.) **36**(2), 111–147 (1974)
62. Turel, O.: Untangling the complex role of guilt in rational decisions to discontinue the use of a hedonic information system. Eur. J. Inf. Syst. **25**(5), 432–447 (2016)
63. Voorhees, M.C., Brady, M.K., Calatone, R., Ramirez, E.: Discriminant validity testing in marketing: an analysis, causes for concern, and proposed remedies. J. Acad. Mark. Sci. **44**(1), 119–134 (2016)
64. Wold, H.O.A.: Soft modeling: The basic design and some extensions. Systems Under Indirect Observations: Part II, 1–54 (1982)
65. Yang, Y., Koenigstorfer, J.: Determinants of fitness app usage and moderating impacts of education-, motivation-, and gamification-related app features on physical activity intentions: cross-sectional survey study. J. Med. Internet Res. **23**(7), e26063 (2021)
66. Zhu, B., Charoennan, W., Embalzado, H.: The influence of perceived risks on millennials' intention to use m-payment for mobile shopping in Bangkok. Int. J. Retail Distrib. Manage. **50**(4), 479–497 (2021)

# Mobile Applications, Serious Games and Advanced Interfaces

# Development of Scenario-Based Approach for Interface Design Aided by Key PSFs and Its Application to Design of New Autonomous Vehicles Monitoring System

Hirotaka Aoki[1]([✉]) [iD], Nozomi Kobayashi[1], Mizuki Fuke[1], and Tomonori Yasui[2]

[1] Tokyo Institute of Technology, Tokyo, Japan
aoki.h.ad@m.titech.ac.jp
[2] Mitsubishi Electric Corporation, Hyogo, Japan

**Abstract.** This paper develops an interface design methodology in which the scenario-based design is aided by predetermined performance shaping factors. The methodology is developed to enables us to create the scenarios, which is the key success components in the designing processes, efficiently and effectively by showing context factors shaping human behavior/performance. We performed a case study where the developed methodology was applied to design a future user-centered interface of autonomous vehicle monitoring and controlling systems. Based on the results and implications obtained from the application, the potential uses of our methodology are discussed.

**Keywords:** Human-Centred Design Technique for New Products Development · Autonomous Vehicles · Improved Scenario-Based Design · Human Machine Interface Design

## 1 Introduction

In the present paper, we develop a human-centred design methodology to create an interface in a new product. In the human-centred design principles, it is critical to specify the context of use and users' requirements to make produced design solutions human-centred (e.g., [1]). The specification of the above-mentioned context and requirements is, however, seems very challenging when the product to be developed is really new. In the current paper, development processes of interface in an autonomous vehicles monitoring system to be implemented in the near future is taken as a case study. This kind of systems are quite new since the level of autonomous vehicles system is still in the infancy in Japan at the time of writing. Thus the reasons of challenges in hu-man-centred design of a new product are explained by using the autonomous vehicles system as a typical example.

As shown in various reports (e.g., [2]), the future society with high-level autonomous vehicles such as those having levels 4 to 5 is clearly anticipated. However, there still remains much uncertainty relating to how autonomous vehicles are implemented in terms of platform technology (e.g., AI, image processing, etc.), social norms (e.g., laws, safety responsibility, etc.), context of use (e.g., human role, allocated tasks, etc.) and so forth. For example, it is unclear the followings: What can be done automatically by the platform technologies of autonomous vehicles (i.e., uncertainty in technological advancement), what kind of socio-technical support can be given when human operators have to inter- vene in a critical incident that cannot be managed automatically (i.e., uncertainty in tasks required to human), etc. Caused by these uncertainties, it is very difficult to determine the details of the con-text of use, users' tasks required, task allocations between human and machine and so forth, which are key success factor of human-centred design.

The paper proposes a design approach adapting to the above-mentioned background issues. The most part of the approach is based on scenario-based design [3, 4]. This is referred to as the technique to elicit effective specifications of interface based on scenarios in which how a human uses and interacts with a specific system are vividly described to capture the essence of inter-action and physical design. By examining the description of the users' and systems' behavior, specifications/features of the systems that should be implemented to realize the behavior can be elicited. This technique, in general, is recognized as a promising and powerful tool for new product designs. The scenario-based design is applicable for a new product design, however, creating successful scenario having appropriate level of details and in which key behaviors/tasks and their contexts are covered requires rich knowledge about interaction design as well as expertise/experiences in practice. In order to eliminate the difficulty in creating scenarios, we propose a series of additional processes where scenarios are created and refined iteratively sup-ported by using a list of PSFs (performance shaping factors). The list of PSFs are, in our processes, used as guidelines/heuristics not only to obtain insight for creating narrative description of a human, but also to keep consistency of envisioned usage episodes in scenarios (refined iteratively) by maintaining an orientation to the identical key context factors.

With all of the background issues mentioned above, the objective of this paper is to propose a concrete procedure to carry out a human-centred design for a new product by improving the process of the scenario-based design. The proposed design procedure is applied to the interface design of a new autonomous vehicles monitoring system. From the application, we validate the effectiveness of our procedure.

## 2 Improved Scenario-Based Design Using PSFs List

### 2.1 Original Version of Scenario-Based Design for Future System

The scenario-based design was developed by Rosson and Carroll [3, 4]. This approach is recognized as a series of human-centred design techniques that can be applied to devel- opment of a future system/product at an early point in the development process. Various versions of scenarios, in which envisioned usage episodes are described narratively, are used to obtain insights about the specifications via positive/negative consequences experienced by a user in the scenario. Since the scenarios involves vividly de-scribed usage episodes, they enable design teams to focus not on technical aspects but on user experiences. By taking a thinking process where the user's behaviors in the scenarios are deployed to the functionality to be implemented, preliminary users' requirements and specifications can be elicited. Overall image of the design processes is depicted in

Fig. 1. In this paper, our focus is mainly on the creation and interpretation of the initial scenario.

As easily foreseen from the processes, the success of the design is heavily depending on the quality of the scenario. A scenario that can be recognized as a high quality one should have appropriately rough explanation about the users' tasks and contexts. The appropriate level of roughness/ambiguity in scenario's description promotes obtaining creative inspirations. Additionally, such scenario should draw realistic context of use in order to make the system/product fit real users' requirements. The creation of such effective scenarios requires both of rich expertise in theories (e.g., psychological theories relating to interaction designs), the power of creative imagination about the future product/system and its use of context, and good senses in writing. Considering the above-mentioned, some supporting tool to create scenario is strongly required, especially from practical point of view.

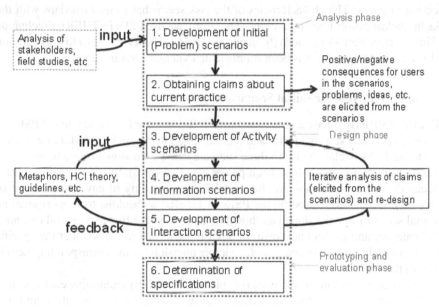

**Fig. 1.** Scenario-based design processes.

## 2.2 Underlying Ideas to Support Creation of Scenario

From Sect. 2.1 discussion, we need to make some supporting tool to create appropriate scenarios. The key idea here is that we provide some cue/guideline not only to create narrative descriptions of usage episodes but also to make scenarios cover critical context factors in use. From practical point of view, additionally, the supports to create effective scenario, especially initial scenario, have to involve the following characteristics: (1) cost effective, meaning that the creation of scenarios can be performed rapidly. (2) systematic procedure, meaning that the creation processes are standardized and can be learnt easily by persons having few skills.

We think that the performance shaping factors (PSFs) used in human reliability analysis (HRA) domain seems promising cues/guidelines for the above-mentioned. The PSFs are referred to as the factors that affect human performances, and key components in HRA (human reliability analysis) (e.g., [5]). For example, PSFs include experience, adequacy of task procedure, task complexity, stress and so forth. There are many types of PSFs depending on HRA methodologies. In most of the HRA methodologies, each PSF is applied by multiplying human error probability for a specified task with the predetermined multiplier. In other word, HRA methodologies equip important PSFs for a specific task. From the PSFs in HRA, it can be expected that the all of the factors can be prepared for a specific task environment. This expectation implies that the what factors have to be considered when creating a scenario can be predetermined by referring PSFs which fits the use of con-text of the product.

In our case study, the product to be designed is HMI of new autonomous vehicles monitoring system. The critical tasks of operators in the system are monitoring and detection of errors. The characteristics of the task seems have many overlaps with the tasks in nuclear power plant operations. Therefore, we use PSFs in THERP (Technique for Human error Rate Prediction) [6] in our discussion. The THERP is a first-generation of HRA methodology, and has been sophisticated via many applications.

### 2.3 Supporting Tool for Initial Scenario Creation

PSFs in THERP have three categories: external PSFs, stressor PSFs and internal PSFs. In each category, some sub-categories and more detailed items are included. For example, the external PSFs is classified into three sub-categories (situational characteristics, job and task instructions, and task and equipment characteristics). Situation characteristics includes items of, for example, architectural features, quality of environment, and so forth (see [6] in detail). Based on the PSFs in THERP, a checklist to support creating an initial scenario was developed as shown in Table 1. In the first and second columns, PSFs' category and its item is shown. In order to make determine whether the specific PSFs item should be considered or not, a simple question for the corresponding item is shown in the third column.

The procedure how the tool is used is depicted in Fig. 2. By examining each question in the table, an answer (yes/no) is filled. If the answer is no, meaning that the item is not related operators' task clearly, we move to the next item. If the answer is yes, on the other hand, we list up use/task characteristics that should be considered. In some cases, it can be expected that the characterizes give inspirations about typical usage episodes. When such inspiration can be obtained, typical usage episode is created. They are filled into the fourth column. In the end of these processes, we can collect PSFs items that should be considered, corresponding characteristics and usage episodes. By summarizing user/task characteristics that should be considered and usage episodes filled in the table, a story describing how the operators' perform tasks which covers important PSFs.

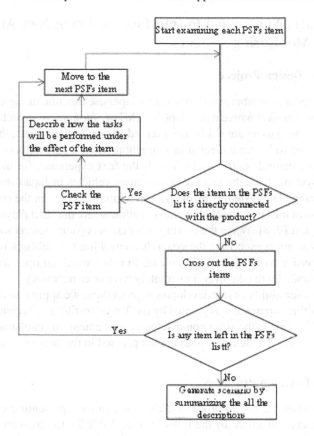

**Fig. 2.** Procedure to us the supporting tool.

**Table 1.** Supporting tool.

| PSF category | Item No. | Item | Question | Check (yes/no) | User/task characteristics that should be considered or typical episodes (if possible) |
|---|---|---|---|---|---|
| Exter nal | 1 | Archit ectural features | Is the architectural features clearly connected with the operators' task performance? | | |
| Exter nal | 2 | Temp erature | Is the temperature clearly connected with the operators' task performance? | | |
| ... | ... | ... | ... | ... | ... |
| (omit) | (omit) | (omit) | (omit) | (omit) | (omit) |
| ... | ... | ... | ... | ... | ... |

## 3   Case Study: Application to Interface Design of New Autonomous Vehicles Monitoring System

### 3.1   Outline of Design Project

The present study is a collaborative work with a Japanese manufacturing company. The company started a project where it developed a HMI of autonomous vehicles monitoring system. The potential users are public bus/taxi industries. In the project, the monitoring system is expected to be implemented in a situation where many autonomous vehicles are managed in a central control room. This is the first experience for the company to develop such system, since the level of autonomous vehicles in Japan is not so high at the time of writing. The system is recognized as a future product in the company.

In the design of the HMI, the challenging situation where the HMI plays a critical role is takeover request [7, 8]. When the driving automation system detects some abnormal events (e.g., some event exceeding the system's control limit), a fallback ready operator has to be responsive to a request to intervene. In other word, an operator in a central control room stands by to take over immediately whenever necessary.

To check the feasibility of our development procedure, we apply it to the early stage of the project. Ethics approval was granted by the Tokyo Institute of Technology Review Board (2022150). Due to the strict non-disclosure agreement, the explanation about the project, interface and detailed processes are suppressed in the pre-sent paper.

### 3.2   Scenario Creation Processes

In the initial scenario creation processes, eight scenarios representing eight different situations were created aid-ed by the PSFs list (see Table 2). In this section, a scenario in which a system requests an intervention since behaviors of a pedestrian near a vehicle seem strange (i.e., parameters representing a pedestrian's behavior exceeds inner limit of a system) is taken as an example.

Following the creation procedure proposed (see Fig. 2), a relevancy of each PSF item to the context of use of the monitoring system is carefully examined by answering each question. When the strong relevancy exits, the attributes that should be considered are listed up, and if possible the typical usage episodes are also created by using the attributes as cues. In this example situation eighteen PSFs items out of seventy six were recognized as those having strong relevancy with the operator's task performance. Table 2 shows a part of the results. (As noted before, not all of the results are shown here due to our non-disclosure agreement.) For example, a PSF categorized in external and work hours/work breaks could be recognized as a very influential one based on the discussion among design team members. By breaking down the PSF item, arousal level mainly caused by fatigue or high/too low workload could be found as key attributes. By using this attribute as a cue to obtain inspiration about an example usage episode, some phrases representing usage contexts relating to arousal levels such as "I work everyday," I frequently experience on intervention to autonomous vehicle for almost all my working time" could be obtained.

By summarizing the all the descriptions in the 5th column in the tool, an initial scenario where a series of human behaviors from the beginning to the end of intervention

**Table 2.** Example of use of supporting tool.

| PSF category | Item No. | Item | Question | Check (yes/no) | User/task characteristics that should be considered or typical episodes (if possible) |
|---|---|---|---|---|---|
| external | 1 | architectural features | Is the architectural features clearly connected with the operators' task performance? | no | N/A |
| external | 2 | temperature | Is the temperature clearly connected with the operators' task performance? | no | N/A |
| (omit) | (omit) | (omit) | (omit) | (omit) | (omit) |
| external | 8 | Work hours/work breaks | Are the work hours/work breaks clearly connected with the operators' task performance? | yes | *Arousal level caused by fatigue and high/low workload.* "I work every day." "I frequently experience an intervention to autonomous vehicle for almost all my working time." |
| external | 9 | Shift rotation | Is the shift rotation clearly connected with the operators' task performance? | yes | *Time when performed tasks, circadian rhythm.* "I work for 12 hours, from noon to midnight." |
| (omit) | (omit) | (omit) | (omit) | (omit) | (omit) |
| external | 16 | Procedure required | Is the procedure required clearly connected with the operators' task performance? | yes | *Quantity/quality of information, contents of information, information format, layout, change of information displayed along with time.* |
| external | 17 | Written or oral communications | Are the written or oral communications clearly connected with the operators' task performance? | no | N/A |
| external | 18 | Cautions and warning | Are the cautions and warning clearly connected with the operators' task performance? | yes | *Warnings styles given to operators.* (Typical screenshot of displays (see Fig. 3)) |
| (omit) | (omit) | (omit) | (omit) | (omit) | (omit) |
| external | 24 | Interpretation | Is the interpretation clearly connected with the operators' task performance? | yes | *Format of information regarding situations.* (Typical screenshot of displays (see Fig. 3)) |
| external | 25 | Decision making | Is the decision making clearly connected with the operators' task performance? | yes | *Format of information regarding situations.* (Typical screenshot of displays (see Fig. 3)) |
| (omit) | (omit) | (omit) | (omit) | (omit) | (omit) |
| internal | 76 | Group identifications | Are the group identifications connected with the operators' task performance? | no | N/A |

are narratively written is created. In the summarizing processes, the first step is to arrange the usage episodes according to the timeline. In most cases, however, many parts may be unclear, out of context, or there may be sudden changes. Thus the second step is to compensating missing behavior, explanations about context, and so forth between any two of the usage episodes. In the last step, the all of written scenario is refined in order to keep consistency of a story. Table 3 (first column) shows a part of the initial

**Table 3.** Example scenario created and implications.

| Scenario created -first version- | Implications for design |
|---|---|
| I frequently experience on intervention to autonomous vehicles every day (*work hours, shift rotation, duration of stress, long, uneventful vigilance periods*). The types of the interventions are very different (*anticipatory requirements, interpretation, complexity*). I feel a kind of pressure since I need to understand the reason why the autonomous system calls me immediately based on very limited information (*long and short-term memory, task speed*). Sometimes, the reason is very severe (*task criticality*). Caused by this, I sometimes feel impatient and irritated during working (*stress*). Honestly speaking, I want a little more information which help me to understand the situation/reason by which the system calls me (*procedure required*)... (omit) | Less workload should be avoided to keep vigilance level. Warning level should be defined appropriately. Knowledge of typical adverse events should be taught in advance. Appropriate wording of adverse events, which is consistent with users' mental model, is necessary... (omit) |
| One day in the afternoon, the system calls me with a warning sound (*perceptual requirements, cautions and warnings, fatigue*). I look at the driving information display immediately, and try to recognize what adverse event occurs (*procedure required*). I can guess that the event is something relating to a pedestrian who can be seen in front of the car (*interpretation, state of current practice or skill*). The only thing I can understand quickly is that the event occurs at an intersection since the monitoring system shows a map around the car (*perceptual requirements, decision making*). I really feel nervous because something happens where a pedestrian is involved (*interpretation, stress, task criticality*). But still what really happens is not clear... (omit) | Present scene, scene when the adverse event occurs, and relating contexts are necessary to understand the situation. Scenes transitions for at least a few seconds seems necessary. Clear mark that highlights the pedestrian is needed. In addition to visual information, auditory information should be perceived by the operator... (omit) |

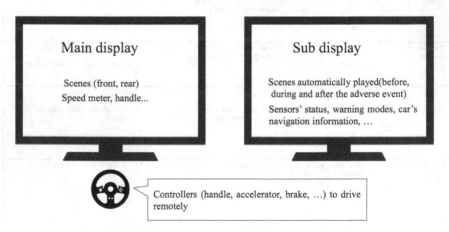

**Fig. 3.** Rough image of HMI prototype.

scenario created. In the scenario created, the corresponding PSFs items are indicated by parentheses.

## 3.3 Example of Specifications Elicitation

The various abstraction levels of design insights (from implications to specifications for the HMI) can be obtained by examining the scenario as shown in the second column.

These were obtained by discussions among the design team. Specification elicitation processes are explained by using the underlined implications below.

Reading the corresponding part of the scenario (i.e., "One day in the afternoon, …what adverse event occurs."), the design team could easily generate the following question: How does the operator identify the current situation? It was obvious that the seeing the present scene was not sufficient because the objects involved in the adverse event (e.g., pedestrian) might have already left from the view sight. This let the team generate a desirable design concept of interface enabling operators to understand the situation immediately by showing both of present status and additional status information for appropriate time interval in which the specific adverse event is valid. By breaking down this design concept, the following basic specifications could be elicited: (1) Information display showing present status constantly, and (2) Additional information display showing warning message of adverse event, and status before, during and after the adverse event whenever necessary. Reflecting the specifications elicited, the first version of the prototype was developed. Figure 3 shows a schematic description of the prototype. Caused by the NDA, only a part of specifications which are directly connected with above-mentioned discussion are roughly described in the figure. One of the notable features equipped in the prototype was an automatically controlled scene playing functionality in the sub display, which are being newly developed by the design team. This functionality will allow an operator to take over from the autonomous vehicles controlling systems smoothly.

## 4 Discussion

### 4.1 Feasibility of the Proposed Approach in Business Context

To check the proposed approach from a practical point of view, we obtained subjective ratings and comments. As for ratings, we asked five project members. One is a project manager and the others are members (one HCD specialist and two programming experts. The ratings are shown in Table 4. The HCD specialist (A) has rich experiences and knowledge of HCD approaches in his work. Programming experts (B and C) have rich technical background of software development, and they are mainly contributing to the design of the interface.

The perceived novelty of the approach was neutral to positive (mean is 3.8). It was notable that the HCD specialist and programming expert felt that our approach was new. Very promising results could be obtained in the question regarding usefulness of our approach. The usefulness perceived was also neutral to positive (mean is 4.0). Both of the programming expert, who directly contributes to development of the interface, showed very positive in terms of usefulness. In addition, the HCD specialist also perceived that our approach is useful. Unfortunately, the degree in which how much easy to learn our approach was slightly negative (mean is 2.3). A typical comment obtained are as follows: "The learning processes needed seems almost the same as difficulty in creating scenario based on PERSONA [9, 10] approach" (obtained from respondent D). The negative feedback may be caused by the fact that procedure that requires human imagination still remains in our approach. Reflecting the negative perceived learnability, it seems that the respondents are neutral to just slightly positive to apply our approach to another future projects.

Table 4. Feedback obtained from design team members.

| | Scales | Respondent | | | |
|---|---|---|---|---|---|
| | | A | B | C | D |
| | | (HCD specialist) | (Programming expert) | (Programming expert) | (Project manager) |
| Perceived novelty | 1: Definitely no~5: Definitely yes. | 4 | 3 | 5 | 3 |
| Usefulness | 1: Definitely not useful~5: Definitely useful. | 4 | 4 | 5 | 3 |
| Perceived learnability | 1: Definitely not easy to learn~5: Definitely easy to learn. | 3 | 2 | 2 | 2 |
| Applicability to future project | 1: Definitely not applicable~5: Definitely applicable. | 3 | 3 | 4 | 3 |

## 4.2 Managerial Implications

Several versions of prototypes of the interface could be developed along with the iterative scenario revisions that were supported by our design approach. The specifications as well as working prototypes are the most important outcomes of the study. Although the explanations about these important outputs have to be suppressed in the paper due to the strict non-disclosure agreement.

Though the technical aspects of the interface were not explained in detail, the interface design processes and its key supporting tool proposed, which are the essence of the approach, was explicitly explained in the paper. As obtained from the members, the usefulness of our approach proposed were recognized as a promising one. In addition to its usefulness, we can expect that the key PSFs items selection processes, which are supported by the tool (see Table 1), seem effective for cultivating of human-centred design mind. The PSFs listed in our tool covers factors affecting generic human monitoring tasks. The processes where the PSFs shown in our tool are examined carefully for the specific product can give a clear knowledge about important factors in generic monitoring tasks, and they kept the attentions to humans needs and behaviors. As supporting evidence, the following comments could be obtained from the respondent C: "In the original version of the scenario-based design, it was terribly difficult because how much we should describe human behavior, especially human cognitive/emotional aspects, especially for a technical person like me. By the list (the supporting tool developed by us) it becomes clear what should be written and what behavior was expected since it (the tool) works as a guideline."

### 4.3 Limitations and Future Work

There were limitations in our research. The primary limitation comes from a poor learnability of the approach observed in feedbacks. We think that this is critical from practical point of view. To compensate the poor learnability, one simple idea may be that we reduce the number of PSFs items, and make representations of questions for each item more understandable ones. This requires us to develop a taxonomy of PSFs which covers a specific task condition (e.g., monitoring task), yet also represents fac-tors in an appropriate level of abstraction. By developing such taxonomy, it can be expected that an improved version of supporting tool showing PSFs items is implemented. This is the future work elicited from the present research.

Another limitation is relating to intrinsical difficulty found in the new product design processes. The processes of design (e.g., creation of design solution) always require human creative thinking processes. Developing concrete design solutions which fits human needs always requires creativity, and this is an intrinsical difficulty. In present paper, we tried to support these creative processes by showing a list of PSFs, which works as cues in creative thinking processes. To tackle with this difficulty, we think that more cases where the approach are applied are essential, because we can expect that iterative applications will provide many hints to improve the way how cues are more inspiring.

## 5 Conclusion

The present paper proposes an improved scenario-based design for a new product design aided by PSFs list. The design approach proposed is focused on the initial scenario creation process, and designed to support creating informative scenarios efficiently. A case study was carried out in which a future HMI was developed for an autonomous vehicle monitoring system. By applying our design approach, the potential for practical use in actual working situations was demonstrated.

As discussed in Sect. 4.2, there are limitations, and we discuss this future work. Based on the discussion, we can say that our approach involves a valuable idea for both HCD researchers and practitioners. For researchers, the approach suggests a necessity of research where new PSFs taxonomy is developed from not HRA but from HCD perspectives. From practitioners point of view, we believe that the iterative applications of our approach contributes to accumulation of knowledges/know-how of HCD or user experiences.

**Acknowledgments.** This research was funded by Mitsubishi Electric Corporation. The authors would like to thank Kohei Tanaka, Yoshiaki Kitamura, Kazuyo Yoshimura, Munetake Nishihira for their great support.

**Disclosure of Interests.**    The authors have received research grants from Mitsubishi Electronic Corporation.

# References

1. International Organization for Standardization: ISO DIS 9241-210 Ergonomics of human system interaction – Part 210: Human-centred design for interactive systems (2010)
2. METI Homepage. https://www.meti.go.jp/shingikai/mono_info_service/jido_soko/pdf/202 20428_1.pdf. Accessed 28 Apr 2022
3. Rosson, M.B., Carroll, J.M.: Usability Engineering: Scenario Based Development of Human Computer Interaction. Morgan Kaufman Publishers, New York (2001)
4. Rosson, M.B., Carroll, J.M.: Scenario based design. In: Jacko, J., Sears, A. (eds.) The Human Computer Interaction Handbook: Fundamentals, Evolving Technologies and Emerging Applications, pp. 1032–1050. Lawrence Erlbaum Associates, Mahwah (2002)
5. Dhillon, B.S.: Human Reliability, Error, and Human Factors in Engineering Maintenance, CRC Press, Boca Raton (2009)
6. Kirwan, B.A.: Guide to Practical Human Reliability Assessment. Taylor and Francis, London (1994)
7. Braunagel, C., Rosentiel, W., Kasneci, E.: Ready for take-over? A new driver assistance system for an automated classification of driver take-over readiness. IEEE Intell. Transp. Syst. Mag. **9**(4), 10–22 (2017)
8. Hergeth, S., Lorenz, L., Krems, J.F.: Prior familiarization with takeover requests affects drivers' takeover performance and automation trust. Hum. Factors **59**(3), 457–470 (2017)
9. Cooper, A., Saffo, P.: The Inmates are Running the Asylum. Macmillan Publishing, New York (1999)
10. Cooper, A., Reimann, R., Cronin, D.: About Face 3: The Essentials of Interaction Design. Willey, New York (2007)

# Iterative Design of an Interactive Augmented Reality Board Game: A Playful Approach to Recruiting Prospective Students

Armi Behzad[1]([✉]) [iD], Disha Sardana[1] [iD], Milomir Vucinic[1,2] [iD],
and Poorvesh Dongre[1] [iD]

[1] Virginia Tech, Blacksburg, VA, USA
abehzad@vt.edu
[2] University of Trento, Trento, Italy

**Abstract.** Virtual and Augmented Reality (VR and AR) technologies have inspired educational institutions to incorporate unique experiences for recruiting prospective students. With the turn to remote engagements and the advancements in AR technology towards immersive and meaningful interactions, we propose a home-based recruitment approach tailored for prospective students, with Virginia Tech as our case study. Through interviews and focus groups with university students, we explore the factors influencing their choice of academic institution. Building on insights from our preliminary study, we introduce an interactive AR board game as a novel recruitment strategy. This novel approach aims to cultivate a playful yet collaborative decision-making experience, facilitating meaningful engagements between prospective students and their families. At the heart of our design lies a commitment to playful information dissemination and the fostering of multi-generational involvement. Our design offers a bespoke experience attuned to the nuances of home-based college recruitment.

**Keywords:** Game design · smart games · augmented reality · campus tour · recruitment · experience design · tangible interaction · human-computer interaction

## 1 Introduction

In recent years, the competitive landscape between public and private institutions has cultivated a demand for a market-driven environment, shaping how educational institutions compete for prospective students [4,5]. This dynamic has prompted a reevaluation of traditional recruitment practices, particularly concerning on-campus tours. While these tours offer invaluable insights, they can also present financial barriers for local applicants and their families, not to mention the logistical challenges faced by international students or those with different mobility.

Conversely, the emergence of augmented technologies has ignited a renaissance in tourism [27], hospitality industries [19], and recruitment landscapes [6], inspiring educational institutions to integrate immersive experiences into their outreach efforts. While there are many examples of on-campus immersive touring experience [15], remote recruitment is less explored. From this juncture emerges a compelling question: What might a home-based campus tour experience entail in the recruitment of prospective students to consider any college or university as their future academic home?

In this research, we engaged this question as a design opportunity and applied Research through Design (RtD) methodology [47] to situate our explorations. We utilized our affiliated institution, Virginia Tech (VT), as our case study through which we aimed to understand students' recruitment and campus life experiences to inform our design directions and alternative modes of recruiting engagements. We employed design research methods, such as focus groups for open discourse [42] and semi-structured interviews [37], to uncover the critical factors that influence students and their families when choosing their future academic destination. We then used these insights to guide our design directions. To achieve this goal, we turned our findings into design considerations, which informed the iterative design and prototyping of a home-based recruitment strategy.

Ultimately, our design manifested as an interactive AR board game featuring virtual and tangible game components. We crafted a prototype tailored to the university's academic ethos while offering insights applicable to any institution's recruitment efforts. Our design suggests a new mode of engagement that not only imparts valuable insights to applicants and their families but also provides a collective virtual campus tour experience from the comfort of their homes. Our work further contributes to design-oriented HCI, tangible interactive systems, and game design research fields, offering an alternative approach for playful interaction and novel experiences.

The following sections present a related body of work, our research approach, design process, prototype development, and evaluation. We conclude with reflections and suggestions for future research in AR tangible game design for recruitment practices.

## 2 Related Work

### 2.1 College Recruitment Strategies

Over the past few years, several universities [8, 11, 13] have incorporated Virtual Reality (VR) experiences as part of their recruitment strategy. From a marketing perspective, VR and AR technologies provide users with an interactive experience as compared to passive tools such as brochures and videos. Thus, elements such as 360-degree videos, interactive online tours, and on-campus AR experiences [15, 16, 20] are becoming part of the recruitment mechanism to invite more students [1]. Other research in marketing suggests that memorable experiences have a significant impact on brand perception and consumer behavior [25]. In line with these studies, in 2015, Savannah College of Art and Design (SCAD) sent Google Cardboard headsets to 30,000 accepted students, allowing them to explore the school's campuses visually. SCAD featured a 26 percent increase in admissions within 12 months of starting the program [10]. In addition, student enrollment at Denver's Regis University grew by more than 3 percent in a year, due in part to the presence of their virtual reality tours [13].

Additionally, factors such as prospective students' financial situation, family time constraints, international students applying abroad, and mobility challenges often limit students from touring university campuses. Therefore, the AR/VR strategy is significantly beneficial for students and parents who find it difficult to attend on-campus tours. These strategies have opened avenues for an inclusive approach, ensuring that university tours are not limited solely to local students.

In this work, we reimagine these efforts and leverage emerging technologies to explore other forms of remote engagements with prospective students that can carry and deliver helpful facts about the institution to invite potential students to consider, apply, and ultimately attend the recruiting academic institution.

### 2.2 AR Tangible Games

In recent years, AR has been explored in the context of tangible games [29], with some researchers focusing on transforming traditional board games into immersive AR experiences [38], while others have studied the educational impact of AR board games compared to non-AR versions [28,35]. AR tangible games blend physical components with digital overlays to provide interactive experiences, often involving players entering a virtual world and manipulating physical objects. Examples include "Art of Defense" [29] and "TanCreator" [30] use physical objects such as tiles and tokens to provide a fun and intuitive experience. Table-top AR games such as Wiimote [34] integrate sensors and AR components for tangible user interactions.

Narratives in AR tangible games have been enriched with innovations like the "Magic Story Cube" [46] and "Jumanji Singapore" [45], enhancing storytelling and promoting tourism. In the edutainment field, AR tangible games have been used to teach subjects such as endangered animal species [31], collaborative play [40], and artistic expression [26]. These games combine traditional board game elements with AR applications, offering immersive experiences and reducing isolation [36], particularly beneficial for audiences with limited AR interaction experience [38].

Research suggests that handheld devices are preferred over Head Mounted Displays (HMDs) for AR board games [29] due to their small viewing area, supporting "seamful design" [18] and keeping players engaged by gradually unfolding information in a timely manner. Inspired by these examples, AR tangible games can be considered as an alternative mode of engagement for recruitment purposes.

## 3 Research Approach

For our research approach, we employed RtD-a well-established methodology in design-oriented HCI that acknowledges the knowledge generated through various processes, techniques, and design artifacts [47]. Our research utilized design research methods such as interviews and focus groups with students and stakeholders. Our learnings unfolded as design considerations, guiding our design direction while supporting our initial research inquiry.

### 3.1 Focus Group and Interviews

For our focus groups and interviews, we recruited a total of 10 undergraduate student participants from diverse origins and educational backgrounds. Participants attended

VT and were in-state and out-of-state residents and international students, making the group culturally diverse. This diversity provided an array of perspectives and experiences in our sessions. We gathered our focus group and interview data through note-taking and audio recordings, which were later transcribed for qualitative analysis, revealing the nuanced insights guiding our exploration. Additionally, we held an informal focus group with the university stakeholders, aiming to better understand their expectations, visions, and goals around the university's remote recruitment experiences. The insights from this session informed the questions we asked in our interviews with students.

In our focus groups with students, we delved into participants' backgrounds, seeking insights into their demographics and prior experience with campus tours. Concurrently, we probed into their encounters at university to better understand how their experiences are woven into their campus journey. In doing so, we were interested in learning about their pre- and post-university immersions. We analyzed the qualitative data from the focus group using thematic analysis [21].

The subsequent interviews were informed by the insights gathered from the focus group discussions. The interview questions aimed to unravel the complexities of the participants' decision-making processes for selecting their future academic institution. Moreover, in our interviews, we ventured into the realm of immersive technologies- informed by stakeholder insights- inquiring about their encounters with VR and AR experiences. By unraveling their past interactions and perspectives on such technologies, we sought to uncover profound insights into their technological experiences, interests, and expectations. Lastly, we analyzed the qualitative data from the interviews using thematic analysis to inform our design directions.

### 3.2 Focus Group and Interview Learnings

We position our learnings from the focus groups and interviews with students into four groups:

*1. Discovery and Touring Experiences:* When asked about discovering academic institutions and campus tour opportunities, participants candidly shared their tendency to dismiss both digital and physical recruitment advertisements, deeming them insufficiently captivating or engaging compared to the experiences during their campus tour at VT. Participants also expressed a profound emotional connection to the unique atmosphere of VT. They articulated how the campus offered a distinctive "special vibe," characterized by an embrace of friendliness, and spatial richness, compared to the experiences encountered at other universities they had toured. Participants also drew particular attention to the unifying influence of "Hokie-Pride" exuded by VT students and alumni, a source of inspiration that notably marked their campus tour experience.[1]

*2. Campus Life While Attending University:* Participants provided additional insights into their ongoing encounters at the university. They expressed the profound influence of seasonal events such as snowball fights and gobbler fests on their overarching journey. Moreover, they found enjoyment in off-campus adventures, embracing the

---

[1] The Hokie Bird is the official mascot of Virginia Tech, and VT students are called Hokies.

serene beauty of local lakes and the adventurous spirit of hiking trails, whether embarking on solitary explorations or bonding in groups. In their reflections, participants also emphasized the enduring significance of shared moments, revolving notably around the vibrant energy of football games and the conviviality of social gatherings, enhancing the collective memories that continue to shape their post-university experiences.

*3. Experiences and Expectations Around AR and VR Technologies:* Another area of significance was the university's research laboratories in shaping participants' experiences. They admired the sophisticated technologies and amenities housed within these spaces, underscoring the pivotal role these resources play in cultivating an environment of innovation and exploration at the school. When discussing their experiences with VR or AR technologies, participants expressed a clear preference for high-quality content and devices, favoring them over more budget-friendly options like the Google Cardboard device. Interestingly, there was minimal engagement regarding specific home-based VR or AR devices among the students.

*4. Decision-Making:* Participants also emphasized the influence of existing university students' and alumni's views about the university on their decision-making processes. Furthermore, they highlighted the significant role of their parents in shaping their choices, prompting us to delve deeper into the dynamics of family interactions. We sought to understand the nature of these relationships and how students engage with their parents during shared activities. Our inquiries revealed that decision-making within families is often a collaborative process involving parents or other family members. Moreover, family time typically revolves around home-based activities such as dining, playing games, and watching television. In seeking to leverage and enrich similar interactions, we learned that playful interactions, such as games, serve as catalysts for bringing together family members of different ages, fostering more engaging and meaningful interactions.

From the focus group with the university stakeholders, we learned that at the heart of their goal is a desire to utilize immersive technologies as a recruitment technique to not only promote the university's technological facilities and programs but to offer prospective students a glimpse into an experiential journey that captures the essence of campus life. By taking these learnings into account, we were able to identify emerging design directions moving forward.

### 3.3 Emerging Design Considerations

Our preliminary study uncovered emerging key factors from students' on-campus tours and their lived experiences while attending the university. Our learnings informed the following design considerations to account for while designing remote experiences for recruitment:

- Sense of community and social collective memories play a role in students' academic life experiences. Thus, we consider incorporating *immersive campus life experiences and information* into a home-based recruitment strategy;
- In support of collective decision-making and family engagement highlighted in our learnings, we consider facilitating *collaborative decision-making through playful family interactions*;

- And in line with students' interest in technology centers and stakeholders' interest in utilizing immersive technologies for recruitment and advocating for its technological facilities and research programs, we consider influencing through *showcasing the institution's commitment to innovation and technology*.

These design considerations presented a chance to reimagine collective decision-making through playful engagement, offering prospective students and families a unique way to explore and understand a potential college experience from the comfort of their homes. Furthermore, examples that support the benefits of gamifying information for a non-gaming context [22, 44], such as providing more engaging and joyful user experience for both parents and their children, motivated us to explore new types of games to engage our intended audience.

## 4    Iterative Design Process

Based on our preliminary research and emerging design considerations, we conceptualized our design around playful information dissemination, collective decision-making, fostering of multigenerational involvement to enhance family engagement, and leveraging immersive technologies.

### 4.1    Initial Design Ideation

We used brainstorming sessions and storyboards to explore initial ideas. Drawing from our interview learnings, we collectively discerned that infusing a gamified approach would serve as an engaging mode for delivering information in a playful manner while bringing students and their families together. Central to our exploration was the notion of leveraging the tangible elements inherent in gaming experiences, recognizing the varying degrees of familiarity across different age demographics in families.

We initially ideated a board game showing a campus map for users to take turns navigating and exploring diverse facts about the institution and facilities within the university landscape. Subsequently, we sought input and critique from a select cohort of our fellow designers and university students. During these invaluable feedback sessions, we learned that students harbored a stronger inclination towards interpersonal engagement and immersive experiences within the campus milieu rather than a mere absorption of factual or historical trivia about the institution. This pivotal insight shifted our approach, emphasizing the promotion of multifaceted experiences over the mere architectural or facility-centric narrative. Furthermore, the insights suggested revisiting the game dynamics, prompting us to consider the overarching objective of the gameplay experience and its role in sustaining player engagement throughout the narrative arc (Fig. 1)

### 4.2    Refining Design Through Iterating Personas

Based on our collected data from the focus groups and interviews and coupled with insights from our feedback session, we redirected our design focus to our intended audience. As such, we crafted four personas to encapsulate the diverse spectrum of prospective university students and users of our design. The personas were constructed based on

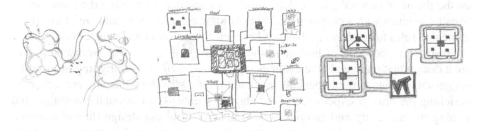

**Fig. 1.** Design iterations: left: organic forms representing the organic form or the campus map; center: including multifaceted experiences; right: ideating visual arrangements

common persona markers, namely gender, origin, age, personality, and major interests. However, we quickly realized the inherent limitations of the conventional persona as the characteristics were not meaningful in our creative process. Reflecting back on our preliminary study, we recalled the subtle yet profound insight shared by participants: the emblematic figure of the university mascot, the Hokie Bird. Participants alluded to the mascot as a symbol of being part of the campus community and feeling a sense of inclusivity. Therefore, we iterated our personas and presented them as different Hokie birds with diverse characteristics and interests. For example, we created Adventurous Hokie, Tech Hokie, and Inclusive Hokie—in support of the university's community-building efforts—, offering the players —prospective students— an initial sense of belonging. We later incorporated the Hokie personas into our game components.

### 4.3 Refining Game Components, Objectives, and Rules

In addition to reimagining personas, we accounted for other game dynamics [43] to inform our iterative design process. We followed these game principles to support our gameplay design:1. Goals: easily defined goals so that the player has a fun and inter-active experience while playing the game. 2. Rules: clear and easy to learn play rules, rather than a complicated gaming experience; 3. Competitiveness: having a challenging aspect of the game, which would make the player immersed; 4. Retention: having the player revisit the game experience.

Building on our learnings from the initial stakeholder and student interviews, in our iterative process, we also took inspiration from classic board games such as Ludo [9] and Guess Who? [7]. Our exploration extended beyond the confines of conventional gameplay when we encountered examples of AR tangible games and applications such as Merge Cube [2], Google Expedition [3], and AR scavenger hunt games [24]. We recognized the unique design space for merging immersive technologies, namely AR, with traditional board games —each common to one generation yet less familiar to another— to design an alternative remote recruitment experience. Following such examples, we iterated and refined the overarching game components, which involved combining tangible components with an AR overlay. We also worked on refining the game narrative, which aimed at promoting the Hokie experience through a scavenger hunt and reflecting on the theme of survival games. Additionally, we focused on refining the game objectives to resonate with a common point-based progression system, and we clarified the gameplay rules to emphasize a balance between collaboration and competition.

Inspired by concepts of built-in reward system [32,41], we were motivated to create a design that transcends the confines of the game itself. This intriguing proposition suggested offering tangible benefits that endure long after the gameplay ends, thereby enriching the broader experience of the player's journey— all through enrollment and joining the university and campus community. As such, our design direction moved towards reimagining existing remote recruitment lifecycles and strategies. We envisioned an interactive AR board game as a novel approach to engage prospective students, thereby reshaping the recruitment landscape with an innovative blend of technology, information dissemination, and multi-generational gameplay.

## 5   Design Prototype

### 5.1   Game Components

Our refined game design brings together a series of tangible and digital components. We embrace the notion of the Internet of Things (IoT) [17] in order to creatively reimagine and conceptually transform traditional game elements such as boards, cards, and tiles into smart game components. Our game design combines multiple smart pieces, including an interactive smart board, smart cards, smart tiles, and a smartphone AR application that accommodates useful information about the institution and campus experience through playful interaction. Inspired by storytelling games that explore medium-as-place narratives [33], our storyline involves players navigating different areas throughout the game while finding artifacts to survive various university experiences and collecting rewards as they progress. While we conceptualized the technical aspects of our

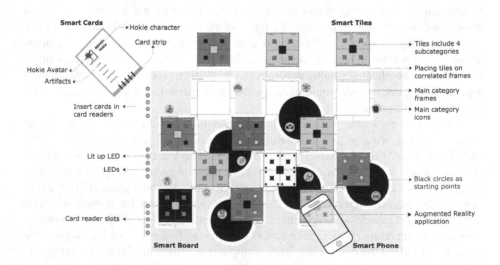

**Fig. 2.** Our AR board game schematic layout

design— which we will explain briefly in the following session— we proceeded with a mid-fidelity working prototype.

The game components include one smart board, 12 smart cards, 11 categorical smart tiles, four pawns, and an AR smartphone application (Fig. 2). Below, we detail each component:

*Smart Board:* The smart board serves as the centerpiece of the interactive experience. It functions as a game board, acting as a hub for smart cards, smart tiles, and the AR application. With limited processing capabilities, it comprises three electronic card readers and three sets of five LED lights, each set connected to a reader. The readers fulfill three main purposes: reading data from inserted cards, illuminating corresponding LED lights, and charging the inserted cards with points. Each LED light is activated through the AR application, serving as a visual cue for the players. Furthermore, the board accommodates a diverse array of categories tailored to suit the purpose of our game, presenting a total of 11 categories.

*Smart Cards:* Smart cards have limited processing capability; each is designed to store and transmit data once inserted into the smart board. They are designed with a curated list of items ranging from artifacts to locations and services. Once inserted into the board, they can store and transmit data regarding the listed items and can be charged up to a completed state of five points during gameplay. Each card showcases five distinctive artifacts, each reflecting a unique facet of a Hokie persona characteristic. The expressive illustrated avatar on each card complements the characteristics and aesthetics of the cards.

*Smart Tiles:* Smart tiles, embedded with sensors and utilizing wireless technology, contain unique markers and identifiers recognized by the AR application. Each tile is intended to correspond with a specific category on the board, requiring placement on the corresponding category. Furthermore, they are visually segmented into four sections (subcategories) to accommodate items listed on the cards.

*Categories:* Informed by the emerging topics from our initial focus groups and feedback sessions, the categories represent the diverse range of experiences and services through which players can immerse themselves and learn about the institution. While many educational resources such as libraries, dining halls, and recreational spaces are common attributes among universities and institutions, certain experiences are distinctly emblematic of particular institutions. To encapsulate such offerings, we carefully selected 11 overarching categories along with four subcategories to showcase shared resources. Each subcategory suggests nuanced experiences that students encounter across campus, which can be found on the tiles. For instance, the Food tile, positioned second on the list below, encompasses subcategories such as cafes, grab-and-go options, vegan and vegetarian choices, and cultural cuisines. Presented below is a comprehensive list of categories and their corresponding subcategories:

1. Healthcare: Health center | Counseling center | Yoga & meditation | Hospitals & clinics
2. Food: Cafe | Vegetarian & vegan | Grab & go | Cultural cuisines
3. Living: Dormitories | Apartments | Fraternity houses | Sorority houses
4. Immigration/ Financial Aid: Immigration services | International center | Bursar office | On-campus jobs

5. Safety: Campus police & safety | Emergency lights | Safe ride | Party positive
6. Facilities: Indoor | Outdoor | Daycare | Art centers
7. Sports: Gym | Swimming pools | Outdoor activities | Footballs & basketball seasons
8. Night Life: Entertainment | Restaurants | Bars | Shops
9. Societies: Religious | LGBTQ | Cultural clubs | Honor societies
10. Study: Library | Studio | Study spaces | Study abroad
11. Accessibility: Parking | Transportation | ADA routes | All gender bathrooms

*AR Application:* The AR experience activates by scanning the tiles using a specially designed AR application installed on a smartphone, which is compatible with both iOS and Android devices. The application can recognize the tile's unique identifiers when a pawn is positioned on one of its quadrants. It prompts the player to the immersive AR experience, offering three distinct scales of visual AR experience: (i) a bird's-eye view of the university campus with a relevant location tag, (ii) 360-degree views of the university's outdoor spaces and buildings, and (iii) 360-degree views from indoor spaces, where an artifact awaits its discovery. Once the artifact is collected, the AR application communicates with the board to charge (with points) the corresponding card that holds the artifact.

*Pawns:* In our design, similar to many traditional board games, pawns serve as essential markers that help players navigate their position on the board. These pawns are 3D-printed replicas of the institution's beloved mascot, available in four vibrant colors.

### 5.2 Gameplay

To begin the game, players shuffle all smart cards, randomly select three, and insert them facing up in the card readers on the smart board. Each player- to themselves- must choose one of the artifacts listed on any of the inserted cards and further guess where it can be found on the tiles. For example, if a player decides to seek the cookies artifact, they would likely guess finding it on the food category tile and in the cafe subcategory. Once players have selected an artifact in confidence, they should place their pawn on the nearest black circle to the targeted subcategory. To determine which player goes first, players can perform a quick rock-paper-scissors. The first player can make between one to five moves to reach their desired subcategory on a tile.

After a player lands their pawn on the subcategory, they then run the smartphone application and scan the tile. In addition to the smart tiles' unique markers, which are recognizable by the AR application, embedded sensors in the tiles identify the placement of a pawn on any particular subcategory and send signals to the smart board. If a match is found with any artifact on the inserted cards, the AR application activates the object for further interaction. This communication employs a system that maps the artifact on the card to its relevant subcategory on the smart tile. Once the tile is scanned, the AR experience would first display the geo-tagged location, for instance, the cafe, shown in a bird's-eye view. The player could navigate to other views by tapping the "next" button on the interface. In the outdoor view, the player could interact with the

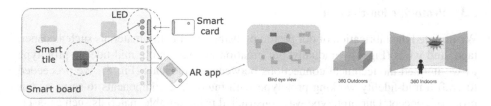

**Fig. 3.** Gameplay schematic: Smart card is inserted in the smart board's charging slot > each LED light on the smart board correlates to an item (orange dot) listed on the smart card > smart tile correlate to category on smart board > an item on the smart card can be found under a category on the smart board and on a subdivision on a smart tile > when pawn (red dot) is placed on the selected smart tile subdivision, scan smart tile (without removing the pawn) using the AR application > AR application will recognize the pattern of scanned smart tile > AR application will show multi-scale views and an AR representations of the item > when item is found in the AR application (orange dot in AR app), the correlating LED light on the smart board lights up (green dot). (Color figure online)

modeled 3D representation of the building. Artifacts are found within the indoor view, where players can collect with a single tap.

To enhance emotional and cognitive feedback, upon the player's tap, the artifact disappears, and an audio cue such as a "Tada" sound effect is played through the AR application. This confirms that the artifact is collected and the event has been recorded by the smart board. The smart board would then translate this event into visual cues by turning on the corresponding LED light. If the collected artifact appears on more than one inserted card, other correlating LED bulbs would simultaneously light up. For an unsuccessful move, the artifact will not appear in the AR indoor view and, thus, will not turn any light on. A player's turn is over whether they collect the artifact in the AR application or simply attempt an unsuccessful move. Figure 3 shows a schematic layout of the gameplay.

Players continue the scavenger hunt to find the artifacts listed on each of the inserted cards. Each time an artifact listed on a card is collected, the smart board increasingly charges the card until all five listed artifacts are found and all five correlating LED bulbs are lit, indicating that the card is fully charged. The player finding the last artifact on a card and lighting up the last correlating bulb would acquire the fully charged smart card, and a new card can then be replaced. The ultimate goal is to fully charge and collect as many smart cards as possible and bring them to the university upon enrollment. Students can then redeem points on their cards by receiving special university merchandise to get them started for their academic experience. The novel gameplay life cycle suggests a breadth of user experience that promotes retention and compliments our concept for playful information decimation. We anticipate 2 to 4 players for the competitive gameplay, and for the non-competitive experience, the student would be the only one with the pawn, and family members would then have a supporting role in guiding and helping discover the survival artifacts.

## 5.3    Prototype Fabrication

We initiated the fabrication of our prototype using low-fidelity materials such as paper, tape, and wires (Fig. 4). Gradually, our creation evolved into a mid-fidelity prototype as we iterated the technical connections between components (Fig. 5). We proceeded to craft a mid-fidelity working prototype with interactive components to serve as our proof of concept. Our prototype was constructed using durable materials such as laser-cut thick cardboard and 3D-printed pawns (see Fig. 6). Although we omitted high-fidelity design and technical implementations from our prototype due to limited time and resources, we did explore alternative technical configurations, as detailed below.

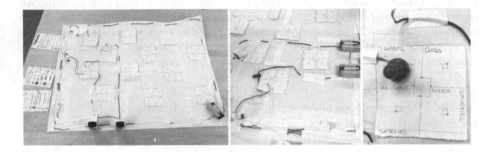

**Fig. 4.** Low-fidelity prototype: left: an overview of the paper prototype; center: close up showing wires, batteries, and mini LED bulbs; right: close up of a paper tile, the pawn and the wire experimenting the interactive aspects

**Fig. 5.** Mid-fidelity prototype: left: applying conductive tape on the backside of board to create the in-built circuit; center: testing and navigating the AR application while scanning a tile; right: demonstrating the connection between a tile, a pawn, and an LED bulb (lit)

In our prototype, we omitted implementing wireless systems as conceptualized due to limited resources and in favor of a tactile approach. We employed physical elements such as wires, conductive tape, mini LED bulbs, and batteries and crafted a basic built-in circuit (see Fig. 5-left). This setup allowed us to connect the tiles, the pawn, and the LEDs, facilitating a clear demonstration of our concept and the interconnections between components. Consequently, we considered making the pawns conductive to facilitate the connection between the tiles and the smart board. We experimented with conductive paint and ultimately decided to apply conductive tape to the base of the pawns. Paired with the conductive materials used on the tiles-connecting subcategories to the LEDs- our design demonstrated the activation of the LED lights when an artifact is successfully collected through the AR application by lightly pressing on the active player's pawn (see (Fig. 5-right). To implement the connection between the tiles and the AR application, we applied color variations and line thicknesses to create a unique yet cohesive pattern. These patterns served as unique markers for the AR application. When iterating the pattern configurations, we also considered the pawn's position on a tile. Ultimately, we crafted 12 unique tiles. We successfully implemented a functioning AR application for our prototype using 3D modeling software, Unity3D [12], and Vuforia [14] that was able to recognize the unique tile markers (see Fig. 5-center). We were unable to find a feasible way to implement the technical aspects of the smart cards.

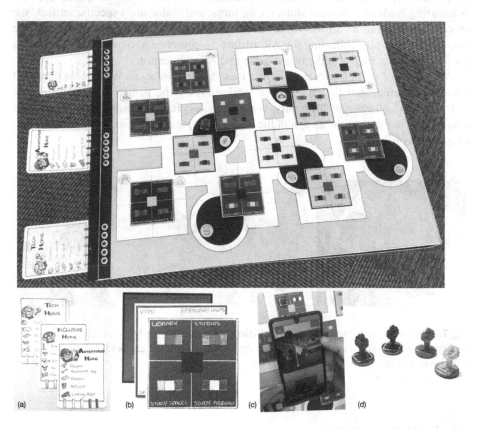

**Fig. 6.** Mid-fidelity prototype: Top: smart board layout with inserted smart cards and placed smart tiles. Bottom: (a) smart cards; (b) smart tiles; (c) AR application showing an artifact in an indoor space; (d) 3D printed pawns replicating the university mascot painted in four vibrant colors

Nevertheless, we incorporated conductive tape into the card design as a tangible manifestation of our concept. We crafted a total of three cards for our prototype.

## 6 Preliminary Evaluation

### 6.1 Evaluation Process

We conducted informal pilot studies and playtesting sessions with five groups of VT student participants to evaluate our prototype design and gameplay rules and flow. First, we provided each participant with an instruction sheet and Dos and Don'ts cards. We then utilized task-based questions to see how well the instructions helped them learn about the game components [33]. We asked questions such as identifying game components, matching artifacts seen on cards with their respective categorical tiles and subcategories, downloading the AR application, and scanning the tiles to activate an AR artifact.

Next, following a think-aloud protocol, we invited the participants to play the game. We provided specific tasks for each participant to accomplish during the gameplay, such as inserting cards into the card slots, taking turns, and collecting a specific artifact- the process of selecting an artifact on a card, finding the relevant category, scanning the tile, and successfully collecting the AR artifact- to complete a round. Figure 7 shows a participant interacting with the board game and AR application.

We observed participant's actions and took descriptive notes. We also documented what they shared verbally as feedback while playing the game, such as their level of frustration and enjoyment. Lastly, we synthesized further design explorations and adjustments to improve the design of the board game, the AR application, and the overall gameplay experience.

**Fig. 7.** Pilot study with participants: left: participants scanning the board; center: viewing and navigating outdoor space on AR application; right: corresponding light bulbs lighting up after a round is completed

### 6.2 Evaluation Learnings

Based on the feedback collected from our playtesting and pilot study sessions, we learned that, like any other game, ours also had a learning curve. We observed that not all participants were patient with reading through the instructions, which contributed to them not fully understanding the game. Therefore, to accommodate such players, we created a short video introducing the game and explaining the gameplay.

While experiencing the AR application, most participants could easily navigate different scenes and collect the artifacts. Some participant's screen interactions varied from our original design intentions. For example, participants tapped on the screen to reach the next view, which was more intuitive for them. Following these insights, we changed the AR application interface and made navigating between three different view scenes easier. Participants also encountered insufficient visual details. For example, on the board design, lines were thinly illustrated, making it difficult for participants to determine clear moves. Taking this shortcoming into consideration, we recreated the board with bolder outlines.

Overall, participants were delighted by the AR experience, even in its mid-fidelity stage. Incorporating a life outside of recruitment and our gameplay, was compelling to stakeholders and students as they complimented the creative choice. Additionally, participants viewed the game design and play experience as "very creative" and "novel", and they found it "a fun way to learn about the school", which gives us the confidence to continue our efforts in this path.

## 7 Reflections and Future Work

Reflecting on our process, this study exemplifies the power of iterative design, rapid prototyping, and continuous feedback loops. Our iterative approach led to a gamified recruitment strategy, combining traditional games with advanced technologies. It further prompted us to think about the technical capabilities and limitations of integrating systems and components and to critically design beyond the customer's lifecycle. Our research was not without its challenges. Balancing competition and collaboration raised concerns among participants, underscoring the need to maintain narrative immersion alongside point collection. Moreover, our university-centric feedback audience may have introduced biases, prompting us to consider broadening our evaluation scope to include diverse voices from outside our case study university. Moving forward, it is beneficial to expand our playtesting by engaging students, designers, and families outside the university.

For future design development, we see several avenues for exploration. Following various quality metrics [23], the AR application can be further improved in visual aesthetics, 360-degree representations, and audio feedback. Opportunities for incorporating collaboration in the AR application can further enhance the collaborative gameplay and overall augmented experience. Lastly, as potential future research, we envision deploying a refined research product [39] to high schools and homes. To that end, technical feasibility, costs, accessibility, and material properties are needed to determine additional technical exploration in developing full-functioning smart components and game pieces.

## 8   Conclusion

Our prototype and pilot study is the beginning of a journey towards reimagining recruitment strategies. Rooted in insights from initial studies with students and stakeholders and informed by feedback sessions with fellow designers and students, we followed the emerging design considerations. Iteratively, we ideated, designed, and refined our prototype. The pilot study provided valuable insight into players' potential experiences with the gameplay. Our prototype introduces a fresh approach to recruitment, offering a home-based platform that nurtures interaction, learning, and shared exploration for parents and children, envisioning their academic future together. It brings together playful information dissemination with multigenerational engagement, showcasing bespoke campus experiences through interactive Augmented Reality gameplay.

Looking beyond recruitment, our design opens avenues for expanding horizons, resonating not only with its intended audience but also sparking interest among younger learners, supported by feedback suggesting it is "very applicable to students as young as nine years old." Furthermore, drawing inspiration from alternative tourism and hospitality endeavors, our design holds potential for travelers seeking novel ways to explore their next destination. Lastly, we extend an invitation to fellow design researchers to embark on alternative trajectories for recruitment and student engagement, building upon our groundwork and exploring further innovation in the field.

**Acknowledgments.** We thank Virginia Tech stakeholder Quentin Baldwin, Dr. Rafael Patrick, Dr. Joe Gabbard, our peers and student volunteers for their support and invaluable feedback.

## References

1. 6 innovative colleges and universities using virtual reality tours to enhance recruitment. https://www.ecityinteractive.com/blog/6-innovative-colleges-universities-using-virtual-reality-tours-enhance-recruitment/. Accessed 15 Feb 2024
2. Ar/vr learning & creation. https://mergevr.com/cube
3. Bring your lessons to life with expeditions | google for education. https://edu.google.com/products/vr-ar/expeditions/
4. Businesses, schools, hospitals test virtual-reality technology. https://www.hartfordbusiness.com/article/businesses-schools-hospitals-test-virtual-reality-technology. Accessed 15 Feb 2024
5. Campus xr. https://www.campusxr.org/. Accessed 15 Feb 2024
6. Ed tech. https://edtechmagazine.com/higher/article/2017/10/college-recruiting-goes-virtual-immersive-technology. Accessed 15 Feb 2024
7. Guess who? https://en.wikipedia.org/wiki/Guess_Who%3F. Accessed 15 Feb 2024
8. Kent state university. https://www.youvisit.com/kent. Accessed 15 Feb 2024
9. Ludo. https://en.wikipedia.org/wiki/Ludo. Accessed 15 Feb 2024
10. Scad extends the campus experience through virtual reality. https://www.scad.edu/about/news-press-and-recognition/2015-02-23-scad-extends-campus-experience-through-virtual-reality. Accessed 15 Feb 2024
11. Texas a&m university interactive map. https://map.concept3d.com/?id=427#!ct/39042. Accessed 15 Feb 2024
12. Unity3d. https://unity3d.com/. Accessed 15 Feb 2024

13. University of denver interactive map. https://map.concept3d.com/?id=64#!ct/4989,4939. Accessed 15 Feb 2024
14. Vuforia. https://www.vuforia.com/. Accessed 15 Feb 2024
15. Andri, C., Alkawaz, M.H., Sallow, A.B.: Adoption of mobile augmented reality as a campus tour application. Int. J. Eng. Technol 7(4.11), 64 (2018)
16. Andri, C., Alkawaz, M.H., Waheed, S.R.: Examining effectiveness and user experiences in 3d mobile based augmented reality for msu virtual tour. In: 2019 IEEE International Conference on Automatic Control and Intelligent Systems (I2CACIS), pp. 161–167. IEEE (2019)
17. Atzori, L., Iera, A., Morabito, G.: The internet of things: a survey. Comput. Networks 10, 1016 (2010)
18. Barkhuus, L., et al.: Picking pockets on the lawn: the development of tactics and strategies in a mobile game. In: Beigl, M., Intille, S., Rekimoto, J., Tokuda, H. (eds.) UbiComp 2005. LNCS, vol. 3660, pp. 358–374. Springer, Heidelberg (2005). https://doi.org/10.1007/11551201_21
19. Prandi, C., Valentina Nisi, C.C., Nunes, N.: Augmenting emerging hospitality services: a playful immersive experience to foster interactions among locals and visitors. Int. J. Hum.-Comput. Interac. 39(2), 363–377 (2023)
20. Chou, T.L., ChanLin, L.J.: Augmented reality smartphone environment orientation application: a case study of the fu-jen university mobile campus touring system. Procedia. Soc. Behav. Sci. 46, 410–416 (2012)
21. Creswell, J.W., Poth, C.N.: Qualitative inquiry and research design: Choosing among five approaches. Sage publications (2016)
22. Deterding, S., Dixon, D., Khaled, R., Nacke, L.: From game design elements to gamefulness: defining "gamification." Association for Computing Machinery, New York, NY, USA (2011)
23. Faqih, K.M.: Factors influencing the behavioral intention to adopt a technological innovation from a developing country context: the case of mobile augmented reality games. Technol. Soc. 69, 101958 (2022). https://www.sciencedirect.com/science/article/pii/S0160791X22000999
24. Gama, K., Wanderley, R., Maranhão, D., Garcia, V.C.: A web-based platform for scavenger hunt games using the internet of things. In: 2015 12th Annual IEEE Consumer Communications and Networking Conference (CCNC), pp. 835–840. IEEE (2015)
25. Gilmore, J.H., B. Joseph Pine, I.: Differentiating hospitality operations via experiences: Why selling services is not enough. Cornell Hotel Restaurant Administration Q. 43(3), 87–96 (2002)
26. Grandhi, U., Chang, I.Y.: Playgami: augmented reality origami creativity platform. In: ACM SIGGRAPH 2019 Appy Hour, pp. 1–2 (2019)
27. Guttentag, D.A.: Virtual reality: applications and implications for tourism. Tour. Manage. 31(5), 637–651 (2010)
28. Huang, C.M., Chang, L.C., Wang, M.C., Sung, C.H., Lin, F.H., Guo, J.L.: Impact of two types of board games on drug-use prevention in adolescents at senior high schools. Games Health J. 11(4), 242–251 (2022)
29. Huynh, D.N.T., Raveendran, K., Xu, Y., Spreen, K., MacIntyre, B.: Art of defense: a collaborative handheld augmented reality board game. In: Proceedings of the 2009 ACM SIGGRAPH Symposium on Video Games, pp. 135–142 (2009)
30. Jin, Q., Wang, D., Sun, F.: Tancreator: A tangible tool for children to create augmented reality games. Association for Computing Machinery, New York, NY, USA (2018). https://doi.org/10.1145/3267305.3267603
31. Juan, C.M., Toffetti, G., Abad, F., Cano, J.: Tangible cubes used as the user interface in an augmented reality game for edutainment. In: 2010 10th IEEE International Conference on Advanced Learning Technologies, pp. 599–603 (2010). https://doi.org/10.1109/ICALT.2010.170

32. Kapp, K.M.: The gamification of learning and instruction: game-based methods and strategies for training and education. John Wiley & Sons (2012)
33. Kim, H., Kim, H., Kwon, Y., Jang, H., Lee, S., Lee, J.: The Implementation of Miro, a Media-as-Place Computer Game. Association for Computing Machinery, New York (2019)
34. Liarokapis, F., Macan, L., Malone, G., Rebolledo-Mendez, G., De Freitas, S.: Multimodal augmented reality tangible gaming. Vis. Comput. **25**, 1109–1120 (2009)
35. Lin, H.C.K., Lin, Y.H., Wang, T.H., Su, L.K., Huang, Y.M.: Effects of incorporating ar into a board game on learning outcomes and emotions in health education. Electronics **9**(11), 1752 (2020)
36. Mandryk, R.L., Maranan, D.S.: False prophets: exploring hybrid board/video games. In: CHI'02 Extended Abstracts on Human Factors in Computing Systems, pp. 640–641 (2002)
37. Maxwell, J.A.: Qualitative Research Design: An Interactive Approach. Sage publications (2012)
38. Molla, E., Lepetit, V.: Augmented reality for board games. In: 2010 IEEE International Symposium on Mixed and Augmented Reality, pp. 253–254. IEEE (2010)
39. Odom, W., Wakkary, R., Lim, Y.k., Desjardins, A., Hengeveld, B., Banks, R.: From research prototype to research product. In: Proceedings of the 2016 CHI Conference on Human Factors in Computing Systems, pp. 2549–2561 (2016)
40. Peitz, J., Eriksson, D., Björk, S.: Augmented board games - using electronics to enhance gameplay in board games, January 2005
41. Schell, J.: The Art of Game Design: A Book of Lenses. CRC press (2008)
42. Smithson, J.: Using and analysing focus groups: limitations and possibilities. Int. J. Soc. Res. Methodol. **3**(2), 103–119 (2000)
43. Tekinbas, K.S., Zimmerman, E.: Rules of Play: Game Design Fundamentals. MIT Press (2003)
44. Zeybek, N., Saygı, E.: Gamification in education: why, where, when, and how?-a systematic review. Games Culture **19**(2), 237–264 (2024)
45. Zhou, Z., Cheok, A.D., Chan, T., Li, Y.: Jumanji singapore: an interactive 3d board game turning hollywood fantasy into reality. In: Proceedings of the 2004 ACM SIGCHI International Conference on Advances in Computer Entertainment Technology, pp. 362–363 (2004)
46. Zhou, Z., Cheok, A.D., Pan, J., Li, Y.: Magic story cube: an interactive tangible interface for storytelling. In: Proceedings of the 2004 ACM SIGCHI International Conference on Advances in Computer Entertainment Technology, pp. 364–365 (2004)
47. Zimmerman, J., Forlizzi, J., Evenson, S.: Research through design as a method for interaction design research in HCI. In: Proceedings of the SIGCHI Conference on Human Factors in Computing Systems, pp. 493–502 (2007)

# Mobile Application for Identifying Anomalous Behavior and Conducting Time Series Analysis Using Heterogeneous Data

Maruthi Prasanna Chellatore[1] and Sharad Sharma[2(✉)] 🔟

[1] Department of Computer Science, University of North Texas, Denton, TX, USA
maruthiprasannachellatore@my.unt.edu
[2] Department of Information Science, University of North Texas, Denton, TX, USA
sharad.sharma@unt.edu

**Abstract.** Understanding anomalous behavior and spatial changes in an urban parking area can enhance decision-making and situational awareness insights for sustainable urban parking management. Decision-making relies on data that comes in overwhelming velocity and volume, that one cannot comprehend without some layer of analysis and visualization. This work presents a mobile application that performs time series analysis and anomaly detection on parking lot data for decision-making. The mobile application allows users to add pins in the parking lot and analyze the pin data over a period of time. Our approach uses parking pins to identify each vehicle and then collect specific data, such as temporal variables like latitude, longitude, time, date, and text (information from the license plate), as well as images and videos shot at the location. Users have the option of placing pins at the location where their car is parked, and the information collected can be used for time series analysis. By examining the data pattern, we may quickly identify vehicles parked in restricted spaces but without authorization and vehicles parked in disabled spaces but owned by regular users. This time series analysis enables the extraction of meaningful insights, making it useful in the identification of recurring patterns in parking lot occupancy over time. This information aids in predicting future demands, enabling parking administrators to allocate resources efficiently during peak hours and optimize space usage. It can be used in detecting irregularities in parking patterns, aiding in the prompt identification of unauthorized or abnormal parking and parking violations which includes parking of the wrong type of vehicle, and parking at restricted or reserved areas.

**Keywords:** Heterogeneous Data · Time Series Analysis · Anomalous Behavior · Object Detection · Data Visualization

## 1  Introduction

Efficient urban parking management is a crucial component of urban planning and transportation management, particularly in densely populated urban areas as it directly impacts traffic flow, congestion, and environmental sustainability. With the continuous growth of vehicle numbers and limited parking spaces, optimizing the utilization of

J. Wei and G. Margetis (Eds.): HCII 2024, LNCS 14737, pp. 167–182, 2024.
https://doi.org/10.1007/978-3-031-60458-4_12

available parking resources has become imperative. To effectively manage parking areas, decision-makers require accurate and timely insights into parking behavior and patterns. However, this objective is often challenged by anomalous behaviors that occur in parking lots, such as unauthorized parking, violations of parking regulations, and irregular occupancy patterns. To address this issue, this paper introduces a mobile application that leverages time series analysis and anomaly detection techniques to identify anomalous behavior and conduct comprehensive analysis using heterogeneous data collected from parking lots.

The mobile app harnesses the power of time series analysis to analyze diverse data sources, including location information, timestamps, and license plate details. By collecting and analyzing this data, the app provides parking administrators with valuable insights into parking patterns and enables real-time detection of anomalies. It consists of two modules: The Information Gathering Module and the Time Series Analysis Module. The Information Gathering Module allows users to conveniently add pins to mark specific parking areas of interest as shown in Fig. 1. These pins capture diverse data, including temporal variables such as latitude, longitude, time, date, and textual information derived from license plates. Additionally, users can capture images and videos at the parking location, providing additional context for analysis as shown in Fig. 2. The Time Series Analysis Module is a powerful tool that enables users to analyze the accumulated pins over a defined period. By applying time series analysis techniques to the collected data, meaningful patterns and trends in parking behavior can be extracted. This analysis facilitates the identification of recurring patterns in parking lot occupancy over time, aiding in predicting future demands and optimizing resource allocation during peak hours. It also enables parking administrators to optimize space usage and enhance overall management efficiency. The mobile application's capabilities extend beyond identifying recurring patterns. It also plays a crucial role in detecting anomalous parking behaviors and violations. By examining the data patterns, the application can quickly identify vehicles parked in restricted spaces without authorization and those occupying disabled spaces despite belonging to regular users. This functionality helps maintain parking regulations, prevent unauthorized parking, and ensure fair and efficient utilization of parking spaces.

The real-time anomaly detection capability of the mobile app is of great significance as it allows for prompt action and response. Instances of unauthorized parking can be rapidly detected, enabling parking administrators to take appropriate measures such as issuing warnings or imposing penalties. Similarly, violations of parking regulations, such as parking in restricted areas or exceeding time limits, can be promptly identified, ensuring compliance, and maintaining order within parking lots. The benefits of the mobile application extend to decision-makers in urban parking management. By providing comprehensive insights into parking behavior and facilitating data-driven decision-making, the application enhances situational awareness and enables proactive resource allocation. Decision-makers can make informed choices regarding parking regulations, optimize parking space usage, and effectively address parking violations, ultimately contributing to more sustainable and efficient urban parking management. The utilization of time series analysis techniques in the mobile app offers several advantages. Trend identification facilitates the prediction of future parking demands, enabling parking administrators to allocate resources effectively. Occupancy pattern detection helps identify irregular parking behaviors, such as vehicles exceeding designated time limits or displaying inconsistent parking patterns. These insights contribute to proactive decision-making and more efficient resource allocation, ultimately leading to improved space utilization and reduced congestion in parking lots.

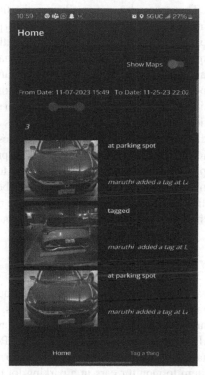

**Fig. 1.** Time series analysis showing pins captured over parking lot.

**Fig. 2.** Parked vehicle at parking lot

The mobile application can provide real-time information on available parking spaces. By integrating with parking infrastructure such as sensors or surveillance systems, the app can collect data on occupancy levels in parking lots in real-time. This data is then processed and made available to users through the app. Users can access the app to check the availability of parking spaces in specific areas or parking lots. The app can display the number of available spaces, indicate whether a parking lot is full or nearing capacity, and provide real-time updates as spaces become available or occupied. The real-time information on available parking spaces helps drivers plan their parking more efficiently, saving time and reducing frustration. It also contributes to better space utilization by directing drivers to parking lots with available spaces, minimizing the search for parking, and reducing traffic congestion in urban areas. Additionally, parking administrators can use the real-time occupancy data to monitor and manage parking lots more effectively. The effectiveness and accuracy of the proposed mobile application and time series analysis techniques have been validated through real-world experiments conducted on diverse parking lot datasets. The results demonstrate the app's ability to detect anomalous behavior with high precision, providing parking administrators with reliable information to make informed decisions and take appropriate actions. Time series analysis using heterogeneous data is needed in many applications such as smart homes, autonomous cars, and aviation. Data analysis of a time series data set is challenging due to data mining complexity. Gers [1] et al. have explored heterogeneous time series, using neural networks.

This research aims to advance the field of parking lot management by offering a comprehensive solution to the challenges posed by anomalous behavior. The data-driven approach of the mobile app, combined with its real-time analysis capabilities, contributes to more efficient and proactive parking management strategies. By optimizing space utilization, improving traffic flow, and enhancing the overall urban experience, the mobile app has the potential to revolutionize parking management in urban areas, benefiting both residents and visitors by improving urban mobility. This paper introduces a mobile application that leverages time series analysis and anomaly detection techniques to enhance decision-making and situational awareness in urban parking management. By utilizing heterogeneous data and providing comprehensive insights into parking behavior, the application empowers decision-makers to optimize resource allocation, predict future demands, and detect anomalous parking behaviors. The subsequent sections of this paper will delve into the technical details of the mobile application's architecture, data analysis techniques, and the results obtained through its implementation.

## 2  Related Work

Gwo-Jiun et. al. [2] have used cellular automata as a recommendation mechanism for smart parking in vehicular environments. They have developed SPARK: Smart Parking Management System that incorporates remote parking monitoring, automated guidance, and parking reservation mechanism. SPARK provided real-time parking navigation, smart theft protection, and parking information. O'Donovan et al. [3] have proposed a system to monitor cars in a parking lot to inform the user of free parking spaces and their location. They have used wireless sensor network system in parking areas to gather this information. Whereas, Jin et al. [4] have focused on security issues in a parking lot for identifying the user's car. On the other hand, Hanzl [5] has proposed a parking information guidance systems application used in urban areas and multistory car parks. Shin et.al [6] have introduced a smart parking guidance system by developing intelligent parking guidance algorithm. Geng et al. [7] have developed and conducted pilot studies for smart parking guidance system.

Sharma et al. [8–10] have developed a mobile augmented reality (AR) system for emergency response, which provided real-time information and instructions during emergencies. These studies highlight the use of mobile applications for data collection, analysis, and enhancing emergency response in various contexts. Augmented reality (AR) applications have been developed for object detection, safety using parking data [11]. Caliskan et al. [12] have built a parking guide system based on vehicular ad hoc networks (VANETs) that uses a continuous-time homogeneous Markov model for parking availability prediction. Prediction of parking space availability in real time is challenging problem that has been presented by Caicedo et al. [13]. They have introduced an intelligent parking reservation (IPR) system, which lets users provide real-time parking information using their parking preferences.

Smart phones have been used to detect empty parking spaces. Lan et al. [14] have proposed an intelligent driver location system for smart parking using smart phones where the relevant parking space can be detected when the driver parks or leaves the parking space. Performance analysis of proximity and light sensors for smart parking has also been examined [15]. Atif et al. [16] have used a cloud-based architecture and internet of things (IoT) approach to bring together parking space service providers and drivers. The use of IoT devices in car parking has also brought security issues. Chatzigiannakis et al. [17] have emphasized a privacy-preserving smart parking system using an IoT elliptic curve based security platform. They have demonstrated elliptical encryption methods to be more efficient as compared to other encryption methods. Smart services of parking structures have been also examined for smart parking solutions in urban areas [18].

## 3 Heterogeneous Data and System Architecture

The mobile application for identifying anomalous behavior and conducting time series analysis relies on the utilization of heterogeneous data from various sources. This diverse dataset provides a comprehensive understanding of parking behavior and facilitates accurate anomaly detection. The application collects and integrates the following types of data:

1. Temporal Data:
   Temporal data plays a crucial role in analyzing parking behavior over time. By examining temporal patterns, the application can identify recurring behaviors, such as daily or weekly parking routines, and detect deviations from the norm. This information is valuable for understanding parking demand patterns, identifying irregularities or anomalies in behavior, and predicting future parking trends. It can also help optimize resource allocation by aligning parking supply with demand during specific time periods. In the application, a feature that tracks and analyzes parking behavior over time is implemented. The pins which user has marked in home section helps in identifying recurring patterns and anomalies in parking routines and provide predictive analytics to forecast future parking trends based on temporal data. This ultimately optimizes resource allocation by aligning parking supply with demand during specific time periods.
2. Geographical Data:
   Geographical data provides spatial context to the analysis of parking behavior. By integrating geographical information, such as the location of parking areas and the surrounding environment, the application can identify spatial patterns, parking hotspots, and areas with high parking demand. This enables urban planners and parking administrators to make informed decisions about parking infrastructure development, pricing strategies, and enforcement efforts. Geographical data also supports the identification of parking patterns based on proximity to popular destinations, transportation hubs, or events. The geographical data displays parking locations on a map within the application. It also provides information about the parking spots within 100 meters'

range, and it enables users to search for parking based on location and proximity to their destination.

3. Sensor Data:

Sensor data, such as information from parking occupancy sensors or smart meters, offers real-time insights into parking availability and utilization. By integrating sensor data into the application, it can provide up-to-date information on parking occupancy levels, detect anomalies or unusual parking events in real-time, and optimize parking operations. This data allows for efficient management of parking resources, improved enforcement actions, and enhanced user experience by providing accurate information on available parking spaces. Application integrates real-time sensor data from parking using the camera of the device and GPS location. This sensor data helps to display current parking availability and occupancy levels in real-time. In future it can send notifications or alerts to users when parking spaces become available or when anomalies are detected. Hence sensor data is used to optimize parking operations and resource management.

4. Textual Data:

Textual data derived from license plates or other sources can provide additional context and insights into parking behavior. By analyzing textual data, the application can identify specific vehicles, track repeat offenders, and detect parking violations. This information is valuable for enforcement purposes, enabling targeted actions against violators and improved compliance with parking regulations. Textual data also facilitates the identification of abnormal or unauthorized parking instances and supports evidence-based decision-making. In the Time Series analysis and Anomalies detection application, a system is implemented to analyze and process textual data that user has implemented. In future it can detect parking violations and track repeat offenders. The textual data provides evidence-based decision-making for enforcement actions. This application enables users to save the information which includes user details, car information which they have entered and helps to report parking issues by submitting textual information.

5. Multimedia Data:

The application's ability to capture images and videos at parking locations allows for visual documentation and verification of parking behavior. Multimedia data can be used to verify parking violations, assess parking space occupancy visually, and gather evidence for enforcement actions. This visual context enhances the accuracy of anomaly detection and provides transparency in the enforcement process. It also supports user engagement by allowing users to report parking issues through visual evidence. The application allows users to capture and upload images or videos of car when parked. The multimedia data helps to visually verify parking behavior and occupancy. This enhances anomaly detection and provide transparency in the enforcement process and supports user engagement by enabling visual evidence submission for parking-related concerns with the data in database.

6. External Data Sources:

Integration with external data sources, such as weather conditions, events, or public transportation schedules, further enhances the analysis of parking behavior. For example, considering weather data helps identify weather-induced changes in parking demand, such as increased parking activity during pleasant weather. Incorporating event data allows the application to detect anomalies associated with large gatherings or special occasions, enabling proactive management strategies to address heightened parking demand during such events. Integration with public transportation schedules can provide insights into parking patterns influenced by transit usage and help optimize multimodal transportation planning. The application incorporates event data to detect anomalies associated with large gatherings or special occasions and it can use public transportation schedules to understand parking patterns influenced by transit usage and optimize transportation planning.

By leveraging the diverse nature of heterogeneous data, the mobile application can provide a comprehensive understanding of parking behavior, detect anomalies, and facilitate evidence-based decision-making. The combination of various data types allows for a more nuanced analysis, leading to improved parking management, enhanced user experience, and sustainable urban development.

**Fig. 3.** Time series analysis showing pins captured over parking lot.

**Fig. 4.** Tag section where information of the image is captured.

The mobile application for identifying anomalous behavior and conducting time series analysis using heterogeneous data utilizes a robust and scalable system architecture. The architecture is designed to handle the collection, integration, processing, and analysis of diverse data types from heterogeneous sources. The key components of the system architecture:

- Data Collection Layer:
    The data collection layer is responsible for gathering data from various sources. It includes modules or components that interact with different data providers, such as

parking occupancy sensors, smart meters, external APIs (Application Programming Interfaces), user input, and multimedia capture functionalities as shown in Fig 3. The data collection layer ensures the acquisition of different types of heterogeneous data needed for the analysis.

- Data Integration Layer:

    The data integration layer is responsible for consolidating and harmonizing the heterogeneous data collected from different sources. It includes data pre-processing modules that transform and standardize the data to ensure compatibility and consistency. This layer may also involve data cleansing and data quality verification processes to address any inconsistencies, errors, or missing values in the data.

- Data Storage Layer:

    The data storage layer is responsible for storing the integrated and processed data captured in Fig 4. It may employ a combination of databases, data lakes, or data warehouses to accommodate the diverse data types and support efficient data retrieval and querying. The storage layer ensures the availability and scalability of the data for analysis and future reference.

- Analytics and Processing Layer:

    The analytics and processing layer encompasses the core functionalities of the mobile application. It includes modules for conducting time series analysis, anomaly detection, and predictive modeling. This layer applies advanced algorithms and techniques to the heterogeneous data to uncover patterns, detect anomalies, and generate actionable insights. It may involve statistical analysis, machine learning, or data mining techniques tailored to the specific requirements of the application.

- Visualization and User Interface Layer:

    The visualization and user interface layer focus on presenting the analysis results and providing an intuitive user experience. It includes components for generating interactive visualizations, charts, and reports to communicate the findings effectively. The user interface layer enables users to interact with the application, input data, configure analysis parameters, and access the results. It may also provide real-time notifications, alerts, or recommendations based on the analysis outcomes.

- Integration with External Systems:

    The mobile application may require integration with external systems or APIs to access additional data sources or services. For example, it may integrate with weather APIs to retrieve real-time weather data or with event management systems to obtain information on scheduled events. These integrations enhance the contextual analysis and provide a more comprehensive understanding of parking behavior.

- Security and Privacy:

    The system architecture incorporates robust security measures to protect the privacy and integrity of the data. It includes authentication mechanisms, secure data transmission protocols, and access control mechanisms to ensure that only authorized individuals can access sensitive information. Privacy considerations are considered during data collection, storage, and handling to comply with applicable privacy regulations and protect user data.

- Scalability and Performance:

    The system architecture is designed to handle large volumes of data and support scalability. It leverages technologies such as distributed processing frameworks, parallel computing, or cloud-based infrastructure to efficiently process and analyze the heterogeneous data. This ensures that the application can handle increasing data loads and accommodate future growth in user base and data sources without compromising performance.

- Real-time Processing:

  To provide timely insights and enable real-time anomaly detection, the system architecture incorporates real-time data processing capabilities. It includes components that can ingest and process streaming data from sensors or other real-time sources. Real-time processing allows for immediate detection and response to anomalous behavior, enabling proactive management strategies and timely notifications to users.

- Data Governance and Metadata Management:

  The system architecture incorporates data governance principles and metadata management practices. It includes mechanisms for data cataloging, data lineage tracking, and data lifecycle management. This ensures that data can be traced back to its source, and metadata about the data, such as its origin, quality, and transformations applied, is captured, and maintained. Data governance and metadata management support data integrity, compliance, and facilitate reproducibility of analysis results.

- Model Training and Re-training:

  If the mobile application utilizes machine learning or predictive modeling techniques, the system architecture includes components for model training and re-training. It may involve a separate module for model development and training using historical data. Periodic re-training of models allows them to adapt to changing patterns and behaviors, ensuring the application's accuracy and effectiveness over time.

- API Management:

  The system architecture includes an API management layer to expose functionalities and data to external systems or third-party developers. It provides secure and controlled access to the application's capabilities through well-defined APIs. API management enables integration with external systems, data exchange with partners, or the development of third-party applications that can leverage the mobile application's functionalities.

- Data Privacy and Compliance:

  The system architecture incorporates privacy and compliance measures to safeguard user data and ensure compliance with relevant regulations, such as data protection laws. It includes mechanisms for data anonymization, encryption, and access control to protect sensitive information. The architecture also supports audit trails and logging to track data access and usage for compliance and security purposes.

- Continuous Monitoring and Alerting:

  To ensure the reliability and availability of the application, the system architecture includes components for continuous monitoring and alerting. It may involve monitoring the performance of the application, data quality, and system health. Real-time alerts and notifications are generated when anomalies or issues are detected, allowing for prompt resolution, and minimizing downtime.

- Integration with External Tools and Services:

  The system architecture allows for seamless integration with external tools and services that complement the mobile application's functionalities. For example, it may integrate with data visualization tools, statistical analysis software, or cloud-based storage services. These integrations enhance the application's capabilities, expand its functionality, and leverage existing tools and services in the ecosystem.

## 4    Time Series Analysis Implementation

This mobile application leverages a multi-layered architecture to provide a seamless experience for exploring locations and capturing associated images as shown in Fig. 5. The Key components includes user interface, google maps api, camera, file storage.

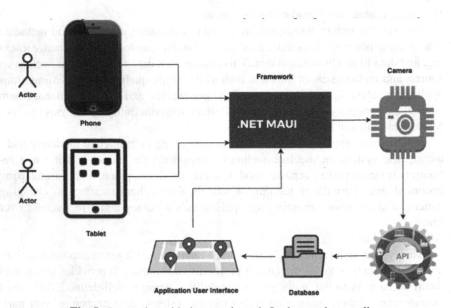

**Fig. 5.**  Interacting with the map through Oculus touch controllers.

User interacts with the application's UI on a phone or tablet. The application is built with.NET MAUI for cross-platform development using C# and XAML. It handles UI interactions, location services, and data management. Google Maps API provides map data, geocoding, and location functionalities. Local database store's location pins, associated information, and user-captured images securely and the device camera is used for capturing images at specific locations..NET MAUI enables efficient cross-platform development with a single codebase for Android, iOS, and other platforms and C# facilitates development and XAML allows for visually appealing UI design. The application provides a user-friendly interface with essential elements like a map displaying location pins, buttons for interaction, and image displays. The application utilizes a dedicated data access layer (e.g., Entity Framework Core) to interact with the local database, providing abstraction and data management logic. Offline functionality is also achieved by caching map data and pins locally. When online, synchronization with cloud storage or other data sources ensures consistency. Images are stored as references to external files or embedded within the database, considering storage efficiency and performance trade-offs. Compression techniques might be used to optimize image size. The application caches map data and relevant location pins while online, allowing basic functionality even without internet connectivity. Updates can be downloaded and applied when online. Real-time Updates (if applicable): Integration with real-time data sources like traffic APIs could enable dynamic updates on the map, enhancing user experience. The architecture is modular and adaptable to accommodate future growth, new features, or changing requirements. Offline data management, image storage limitations, and security concerns can also be addressed with appropriate techniques and architectural decisions implemented in the application.

**Table 1.** Framework Characteristics Summary

| Characteristics | Framework |
|---|---|
| Engine | .NET MAUI |
| Programming Language | C# |
| Decision-Making System | ✓ |
| Dynamic agents | ✓ |
| Intension support | ✓ |

As mentioned previously the application was implemented in .NET MAUI. It is integrated with location services API which helps to get the google coordinates of the location. Table 1 summarizes the characteristics of our framework.

## 5 Anomaly Detection and Time Series Analysis

### 5.1 Anomaly Detection

The anomaly detection functionality of the application plays a crucial role in identifying irregularities and abnormal parking behavior. It utilizes advanced anomaly detection algorithms to analyze the collected time series data and detect deviations from expected patterns. These algorithms can identify outliers, anomalies, and unusual trends in the parking data. By leveraging anomaly detection, the application can promptly flag instances of unauthorized or abnormal parking. For example, it can detect vehicles parked in restricted areas without proper authorization, vehicles occupying disabled parking spaces without the necessary permits, or vehicles parked for extended periods in time-limited zones. This helps parking administrators to take immediate action and enforce parking regulations effectively. The anomaly detection algorithm in the mobile application is designed to handle different types of parking violations by leveraging various techniques and data features. Here's how it can address different parking violations:

1. Unauthorized Parking in Restricted Areas:

The algorithm utilizes location data, such as latitude and longitude, to determine if a vehicle is parked in a restricted area. It compares the parked vehicle's location with predefined boundaries or zones that indicate restricted areas. If the vehicle is detected within a restricted zone without proper authorization, the algorithm flags it as an anomaly.

2. Occupying Disabled Parking Spaces without Authorization:

To identify vehicles occupying disabled parking spaces without the necessary permits, the algorithm incorporates additional data such as information from the license plate. It compares the license plate information with a database of authorized permits and disabled parking registrations. If a vehicle is found to be parked in a disabled space without valid authorization, it is flagged as an anomaly.

3. Time-Limited Parking Violations:

The algorithm considers time-related variables, such as date and time of parking, to detect violations related to time-limited parking zones. It compares the duration of parking against the specified time limits for a particular area. If a vehicle exceeds the allowed time limit, it is identified as an anomaly, indicating a time-limited parking violation.

4. Parking in Reserved or Designated Areas:

The algorithm utilizes predefined data or user-inputted information regarding reserved or designated parking areas. It checks if a vehicle is parked in an area that is designated for specific users, such as employees, residents, or permit holders. If a vehicle is found in a reserved area without the appropriate authorization, it is flagged as an anomaly.

5. Wrong Vehicle Type Parking:

The algorithm can consider additional data sources, such as vehicle registration information and user-provided details, to identify parking violations related to the wrong type of vehicle. For example, it can detect if a motorcycle is parked in a space designated for cars or if a commercial vehicle is parked in a residential area where it is prohibited. If a vehicle is parked in a space that is incompatible with its type, it is marked as an anomaly.

## 5.2 Time Series Analysis

The time series analysis module of the application is designed to extract meaningful insights from the collected parking data over a specific period. It enables administrators to understand the occupancy patterns and trends in the parking lot over time. Through time series analysis, the application can identify recurring patterns in parking lot occupancy, such as peak hours or days with high parking demand. This information is vital for predicting future parking demands and optimizing the allocation of parking resources. By accurately forecasting parking needs, administrators can ensure that sufficient parking spaces are available during peak periods, reducing congestion and improving overall parking efficiency. Additionally, time series analysis allows administrators to track changes in parking behavior and identify long-term trends. For example, it can reveal shifts in parking preferences or changes in the utilization of specific parking areas. This insight enables administrators to make informed decisions regarding the allocation of parking spaces, adjustments to parking regulations, or the implementation of new parking strategies. The time series analysis module can indeed help in evaluating the impact of policy changes in parking management. By analyzing the historical parking data before and after the implementation of policy changes, administrators can assess the effectiveness and consequences of those changes. Here's how the time series analysis module can assist in evaluating policy impact:

1. Comparative Analysis: The module allows administrators to compare the parking occupancy patterns and trends before and after the policy changes. By examining the time series data, they can identify any significant shifts in parking behavior, such as changes in occupancy rates, parking durations, or utilization of specific parking areas. This comparative analysis helps assess the direct impact of the policy changes on parking dynamics.

2. Identification of Changes in Demand: Time series analysis can reveal changes in parking demand resulting from policy changes. For example, if a new parking regulation is implemented that restricts parking in a particular area, the module can track the occupancy levels in that area over time. By comparing the occupancy patterns pre- and post-policy change, administrators can determine whether the policy has effectively influenced the parking behavior and demand in the intended manner.

3. Forecasting Accuracy: The time series analysis module can evaluate the accuracy of forecasting models in predicting parking demand after policy changes. By comparing the predicted demand based on historical data with the actual observed demand after policy implementation, administrators can assess the effectiveness of their forecasting methods. This evaluation provides insights into the reliability of the forecasts and helps refine the forecasting models for future policy evaluations.

4. Impact on Congestion and Efficiency: Policy changes often aim to reduce parking congestion and improve overall parking efficiency. The time series analysis module can assess whether the implemented policies have achieved these goals. By analyzing occupancy patterns and trends, administrators can measure the changes in parking availability, utilization rates, or the average time taken to find parking spaces. This evaluation helps determine whether the policy changes have resulted in reduced congestion and improved parking efficiency.

5. Iterative Policy Refinement: The insights derived from the time series analysis can guide administrators in refining and fine-tuning parking policies. By understanding the impact of previous policy changes, administrators can make informed decisions about further adjustments or modifications to better align with the desired outcomes. The module provides a feedback loop that supports an iterative approach to policy refinement based on data-driven insights.

By combining anomaly detection with time series analysis, the application offers a comprehensive approach to parking management. Anomaly detection helps identify and address parking violations and irregularities, while time series analysis provides insights into occupancy patterns, trends, and forecasting. These functionalities assist administrators in effectively managing parking resources, enforcing regulations, and enhancing the overall parking experience for users.

# 6   Conclusions

The development of a mobile application incorporating time series analysis and anomaly detection for urban parking management offers significant benefits for decision-making and situational awareness. The application addresses the challenges posed by the over-whelming velocity and volume of parking data by providing analysis and visualization capabilities. By utilizing the information gathering module, users can add pins to parking lots, capturing essential data such as location, time, date, license plate information, images, and videos. The time series analysis module then analyzes the collected data, enabling the identification of recurring patterns in parking lot occupancy and the detection of anomalies or irregularities. The application's ability to identify unauthorized parking in restricted spaces or violations such as parking in disabled areas without authorization enhances decision-making and supports prompt action by parking administrators. Furthermore, the analysis of parking patterns aids in predicting future demands and optimizing resource allocation during peak hours, contributing to efficient space utilization, and improved operational efficiency.

The application's ability to perform time series analysis on parking data provides parking managers with valuable insights for informed decision-making. By analyzing historical occupancy patterns, administrators can make data-driven decisions regarding pricing strategies, resource allocation, and infrastructure planning. This promotes more efficient and effective parking management practices. Understanding parking occupancy patterns through time series analysis enables parking managers to allocate resources more efficiently. By identifying peak hours and high-demand areas, administrators can adjust staffing levels, implement dynamic pricing schemes, or even introduce shuttle services to optimize resource utilization and improve customer satisfaction. The application's analysis of parking patterns helps identify underutilized or over utilized parking spaces. This knowledge allows parking administrators to optimize space utilization by reallocating resources or implementing strategies such as shared parking arrangements or dynamic space allocation systems. Maximizing space utilization can alleviate parking congestion and reduce the need for additional parking infrastructure. Anomaly detection capabilities enable the application to identify unauthorized parking, parking violations, and abnormal occupancy patterns in real-time. Prompt identification of such issues allows for proactive interventions, such as issuing fines, sending alerts to parking enforcement personnel, or implementing automated enforcement systems. This promotes compliance with parking regulations and contributes to improved safety and security in parking areas.

The insights gained from time series analysis can inform long-term planning and expansion efforts. By understanding parking demand trends, administrators can plan for future infrastructure development, identify areas for potential expansion, or implement new parking facilities in locations with high projected demand. This data-driven approach ensures that parking systems are designed to meet the needs of growing urban areas. By leveraging time series analysis insights, parking managers can enhance the overall user experience for parkers. This can include providing real-time parking availability information through mobile apps or digital signage, offering personalized parking recommendations based on historical data, or implementing seamless payment systems to streamline the parking experience. Effective parking management contributes to environmental sustainability by reducing traffic congestion and associated emissions. By optimizing parking resource allocation and providing real-time information on parking availability, the application helps minimize unnecessary circling and search for parking, leading to reduced traffic congestion and lower carbon emissions. Overall, the mobile application's integration of time series analysis and anomaly detection empowers parking managers with valuable insights for sustainable urban parking management. By leveraging data-driven decision-making, administrators can enhance situational awareness, optimize resource allocation, and improve the overall effectiveness and efficiency of urban parking systems.

**Acknowledgments.** This work is funded in part by the NSF award 2321539 and Sub Award No. NSF00123-08 for NSF Award 2118285. The authors would also like to acknowledge the support of NSF Award 2319752, and NSF Award 2321574.

# References

1. Gers, F.A., Schmidhuber, J., Cummins, F.: Learning to forget: continual prediction with LSTM. Neural Comput. **12**, 2451–2471 (2000)
2. Horng, G.-J., Wang, C.-H., Cheng, S.-T.: Using cellular automata on recommendation mechanism for smart parking in vehicular environments. In: 2012 2nd International Conference on Consumer Electronics, Communications and Networks (CECNet), pp. 3683–3686 (2012)
3. O'Donovan, T., Benson, J., Roedig, U., Sreenan, C.J.: Priority interrupts of Duty Cycled communications in wireless sensor networks. In: 33rd IEEE Conference on Local Computer Networks, LCN 2008, pp. 732–739 (2008)
4. Gu, J., Zhang, Z., Yu, F., Liu, Q.: Design and implementation of a street parking system using wireless sensor networks. In: 10th IEEE International Conference on Industrial Informatics (INDIN), pp. 1212–2217 (2012)
5. Hanzl, J.: Parking information guidance systems and smart technologies application used in urban areas and multi-story car parks. Transp. Res. Procedia **44**, 361–368 (2020)
6. Shin, J.-H., Jun, H.-B.: A study on smart parking guidance algorithm. Transp. Res. C, Emerg. Technol. **44**, 299–317 (2014)
7. Geng, Y., Cassandras, C.G.: A new 'smart parking' system infrastructure and implementation. Procedia Soc. Behav. Sci. **54**, 1278–1287 (2012)
8. Sharma, S.: Mobile augmented reality system for emergency response. In: Proceedings of the 21st IEEE/ACIS International Conference on Software Engineering, Management and Applications (SERA 2023), Orlando, USA, 23–25 May (2023)
9. Sharma, S., Stigall, J., Bodempudi, S.T.: Situational awareness-based Augmented Reality Instructional (ARI) module for building evacuation. In: Proceedings of the 27th IEEE Conference on Virtual Reality and 3D User Interfaces, Training XR Workshop, Atlanta, GA, USA, pp. 70–78, March 22–26 (2020). https://doi.org/10.1109/VRW50115.2020.00020
10. Sharma, S., Jerripothula, S.: An indoor augmented reality mobile application for simulation of building evacuation. In: Proc. SPIE Conf. Eng. Reality of Virtual Reality, San Francisco, CA, 9–10 February (2015)

11. Sharma, S., Engel, D.: Mobile augmented reality system for object detection, alert, and safety. In: Proceedings of the IS&T International Symposium on Electronic Imaging (EI 2023) in the Engineering Reality of Virtual Reality Conference, 15–19 January (2023)
12. Caliskan, M., Barthels, A., Scheuermann, B., Mauve, M.: Predicting parking lot occupancy in vehicular ad hoc networks. In: IEEE VTC (2007)
13. Caicedo, F., Blazquez, C., Miranda, P.: Prediction of parking space availability in real time. Expert Syst. Apps. **39**(8), 7281–7290 (2012)
14. Lan, K.-C., Shih, W.-Y.: An intelligent driver location system for smart parking. Expert Syst. Appl. **41**(5), 2443–2456 (2014)
15. Bachani, M., Qureshi, U.M., Shaikh, F.K.: Performance analysis of proximity and light sensors for smart parking. Procedia Comput. Sci. **83**, 385–392 (2016)
16. Atif, Y., Ding, J., Jeusfeld, M.A.: Internet of Things approach to cloud based smart car parking. Procedia Comput. Sci. **98**, 193–198 (2016)
17. Chatzigiannakis, I., Vitaletti, A., Pyrgelis, A.: A privacy-preserving smart parking system using an IoT elliptic curve based security platform. Comput. Commun. **89**(90), 165–177 (2016)
18. Polycarpou, E., Lambrinos, L., Protopapadakis, E.: Smart parking solutions for urban areas. In: Proc. IEEE 14th Int. Symp. World Wireless, Mobile Multimedia Netw. (WoWMoM), Jun., pp. 1–6 (2013)

# Exploring Player Experience in Mobile Learning Through Location-Based Games

Zi-Ru Chen[✉] and Chiu-Chun Lam

Southern Taiwan University of Science and Technology, No. 1, Nan-Tai Street, Yungkang District, Tainan City 710, Taiwan R.O.C.
zrchen@stust.edu.tw

**Abstract.** Modern society's challenges in science and technology underscore the importance of science education. Effective science education, however, often necessitates outdoor learning and observation, addressing the limitations of traditional classrooms. These limitations, such as a lack of diverse teaching methods, lead to fewer opportunities for hands-on activities, diminishing student interest in learning. To address this, scholars integrate games and outdoor teaching methods, including location-based games that adapt to players' geographical locations, fostering a connection between the virtual and physical worlds. Playability and player experience, linked to intrinsic motivation, are critical in game-based learning. This study investigates whether incorporating location-based elements into educational games with high playability results in positive player experiences. Focused on plant ecology education, the research develops location-based and non-location-based game versions for experimentation. The quasi-experimental approach involves participants playing both versions and completing a player experience questionnaire. Statistical analysis reveals the location-based game provides a superior player experience, boosting satisfaction and confidence. These findings offer valuable insights for developers of future educational location-based games.

**Keywords:** Location-based Game · Playability · Player Experience

## 1 Introduction

Modern citizens frequently encounter issues related to science and technology, highlighting the imperative of advancing science education. However, effective science education cannot achieve optimal outcomes without incorporating outdoor learning and observation. Traditional science classrooms often rely on limited teaching methods and overly prioritize academic performance. Consequently, students have fewer opportunities for hands-on activities and observations, resulting in a diminishing interest and enthusiasm for learning (Lin, 2018). Therefore, previous studies have integrated games into teaching and combined mobile learning with outdoor teaching methods to bolster students' motivation to learn (Priyaadharshini et al., 2020; Kiili, 2005).

Games are activities in which individuals actively engage driven by intrinsic motivations, such as interest and curiosity (Chang, 2004). Previous studies have suggested

J. Wei and G. Margetis (Eds.): HCII 2024, LNCS 14737, pp. 183–195, 2024.
https://doi.org/10.1007/978-3-031-60458-4_13

that games contribute significantly to the learning process. In comparison to traditional learning methods, digital game-based learning is more accessible and has the potential to boost students' motivation to learn. The knowledge acquired through games tends to be retained for a longer duration. Additionally, games stimulate students to conduct explorations and experiments (Prensky, 2003; Paraskeva et al., 2010; Priyaadharshini et al., 2020).

Location-based games represent a form that modifies the player's gaming experience based on their geographical location (Lehmann, 2012). Therefore, these games can be integrated with outdoor teaching methods to establish a connection between the virtual and real world, ultimately enhancing the effectiveness of science education (Avouris & Yiannoutsou, 2012).

Playability is generally regarded as a concept that reflects the overall quality of a game. It serves to enhance the allure and enjoyment of a game, providing game developers and designers with valuable insights into the factors that attract players (Paavilainen, 2020; Li et al., 2021). Player experience serves as a means of comprehending how individuals choose to interact with electronic entertainment products and the reasons behind their choices. It encompasses players' perceptions during the interaction (Nacke et al., 2009; Gerling et al., 2011). When an educational game achieves high playability and seamlessly integrates virtual and real elements, it can create a positive player experience. Consequently, this enhances the game's appeal and enjoyment, sparking students' intrinsic motivation. In essence, this approach encourages students to participate in learning activities with a more proactive and positive attitude. Therefore, both playability and player experience are pivotal factors for assessing the effectiveness of game-based learning.

## 2  Problem and Objective

In the field of science education, optimal learning outcomes are achieved when learners have the opportunity to practice and apply their knowledge in real-world settings. Outdoor teaching not only exposes students to experiential learning activities but also fosters a connection between students and nature, nurturing various forms of intelligence. Consequently, providing students with real-world learning scenarios and effective learning strategies is essential (Huang et al., 2010).

Previous studies have emphasized the positive impact of activities that integrate mobile learning systems with outdoor teaching (Huang et al., 2010; Chang, 2015). The incorporation of games into teaching has the potential to enhance students' learning motivation. Moreover, the concepts of playability and player experience are closely intertwined with intrinsic motivation, elevating the attractiveness and enjoyment of games and thereby stimulating learners' intrinsic motivation.

Researchers have noted that many previous studies and evaluation methods on playability have overlooked the role of mobility, specifically whether a game can adapt to diverse environments and respond to disruptions. This underscores the need for playability evaluations tailored to mobile games (Korhonen & Koivisto, 2006). In the era of burgeoning mobile technology, mobility has become a focal point in playability studies. Location-based games, which adjust the player's gaming experience based on their geographical location, exemplify mobility. Thus, this study aims to explore whether learning through mobile games, combined with location-based elements, can yield a positive player experience. The objective is to develop an educational location-based game with high playability, utilizing the university campus in Taiwan as the teaching materials. Furthermore, employing a quasi-experimental approach, this study seeks to investigate the effects of location-based factors on player experience and observe relevant phenomena.

# 3 Literature Reviews

## 3.1 Location-Based Game

The current surge in smartphone technology has led to the enhancement of smartphones' features, making it feasible to leverage the unique capabilities of smartphones, such as the Global Positioning System (GPS), in gaming. The GPS system, capable of pin-pointing a mobile phone's location, enhances the player's gaming experience based on their geographical coordinates, giving rise to a new category of games known as location-based games. In mobile education, location emerges as a crucial contextual factor (Brown, 2010). Location-based games seamlessly integrate the real-world environment into gameplay, blurring the boundaries between reality and the game itself (Lehmann, 2012; Avouris & Yiannoutsou, 2012).

These games not only encourage players to explore the city but also effectively heighten their interest (Ebling & Caceres, 2010). Lehmann (2012) suggests that integrating location-based games into education establishes a connection between a location and a narrative, rendering the story more authentic. This approach imparts knowledge about the location in a compelling manner, ultimately leading to enhanced educational outcomes. Avouris and Yiannoutsou (2012) underscore the use of location-based games to leverage the physical environment in the real world, connecting the real and virtual worlds through activities and events. Additionally, these games employ a narrative structure in the virtual world to facilitate player learning.

## 3.2 Playability

Playability is rooted in the necessity to design captivating applications and user interfaces, serving as an indicator of players' satisfaction with the game (Li et al., 2021). Consequently, researchers have proposed various design principles and factors related to playability. Initially, Clanton (1998) delved into human-computer interaction in games, presenting foundational principles for game design that constitute an early framework for playability. These principles are categorized into three levels: game interface, game mechanics, and gameplay. Firstly, the game interface encompasses physical devices enabling player-game interaction, such as a mouse or joystick, as well as the information displayed on the game screen. Secondly, game mechanics involve the "physics" governing the game world, including the player-controlled character's movement and the flight dynamics of an aircraft. Thirdly, gameplay incorporates the diverse quests and challenges players encounter in the game. Järvinen et al. (2002) explored the definitions of playability and gameplay, perceiving them as the interaction between players and games. Korhonen and Koivisto (2006) expanded playability to the design of mobile devices, introducing mobility as an additional factor alongside existing concepts of game usability and gameplay.

Järvinen et al. (2002) explored the definitions of playability and gameplay, perceiving them as the interaction between players and games. Korhonen and Koivisto (2006) expanded playability to the design of mobile devices, introducing mobility as an additional factor alongside existing concepts of game usability and gameplay. According to Korhonen and Koivisto, mobility addresses how easily players can enter the game world and how the game functions in various environments or scenarios. Paavilainen (2020) argued that playability should focus solely on aspects incorporable by the game designer, emphasizing the need to distinguish playability from player experience. He maintained that the playability of a game system should cover, at a minimum, functionality, usability, and gameplay.

This study aims to explore the player experience delivered by educational location-based games. Therefore, the game design is grounded in the playability criteria proposed by Paavilainen (2020), integrating mobility suggested by Korhonen and Koivisto (2006), and learnability presented by Atmaja (2021) as the foundation for designing educational location-based games.

### 3.3   Player Experience and Its Evaluation Methods

The concept of player experience emerged as scholars sought to apply insights from user experience to digital games. However, they quickly recognized that player experience fundamentally differs from user experience, requiring distinct analytical approaches (Tsai and Wang, 2018). Nacke et al. (2009) asserted that playability is a byproduct of game design, while player experience results from the interaction between players and games. Player experience is constructed upon playability, and there is a widely accepted belief that good playability leads to a positive player experience. Sánchez and Vela (2014) introduced a playability model to assess player experience. They gathered player experience data through various methods, including observations, heart rate measurements, interviews, and surveys. Their objective was to identify playability attributes that would have a more significant impact on the interactive experience, ultimately achieving the best possible player experience in the game. The findings indicated that high-quality game screens and effects contribute to increased player satisfaction, motivation, and emotional engagement, sparking enthusiasm for continued gameplay. Furthermore, the results highlighted a strong correlation between player experience and playability.

Methods for assessing player experience include the Player Experience of Need Satisfaction (PENS) (Ryan et al., 2006) and the Game Experience Questionnaire (GEQ) (IJsselsteijn et al., 2008). The PENS is grounded in established motivation theories, suggesting that an experience satisfying needs is more likely to intrinsically motivate people to engage in the activity. The GEQ is based on the conceptual description of player experience and insights from focus group interviews with digital game players. Additionally, there are models specifically crafted for evaluating player experience in educational games, such as the Model for the Evaluation of Educational Games (MEEGA model) (Savi et al., 2011) and the refined MEEGA + model introduced by Petri et al. (2016).

The MEEGA + model is a scale designed to assess the quality of educational games from the students' perspective. Introduced by Petri et al. (2016) following a comprehensive literature review on educational game evaluations, this model enhances the MEEGA model developed by Savi et al. (2011). It addresses issues with the previous version, such as overlapping dimensions of quality factors and a lack of reliability and validity. Utilizing a 5-point Likert scale as the response format, the MEEGA + model evaluates two quality factors: Player experience and perceived learning. The former includes eight dimensions: Focused attention, fun, challenge, social interaction, confidence, relevance, satisfaction, and usability. The latter consists of two dimensions: Short-term learning and learning goal.

## 4 Methodology and Steps

This study aims to create an educational location-based game with enhanced playability and investigate the influence of location-based factors on player experience. Initially, a systematic implementation approach was employed to develop both location-based and non-location-based versions of the educational game. Following this, a quasi-experiment, coupled with a survey, was conducted to collect data on player experience. By analyzing and comparing the gathered data, the study identified the impact of location-based factors on player experience, drawing insights from the observed phenomena.

### 4.1 System Implementation Method

**Learning Material Preparation.** Initially, this study involved planning of the teaching materials for the educational games, with a subsequent analysis of playability factors. The design of the game interface and flow followed, adhering to established playability design principles. Subsequently, the study progressed to the practical development of the game systems, encompassing both location-based and non-location-based versions, using the Construct 3 game editor.

For this study, the teaching materials centered around "plant ecology," an integral component of science education commonly integrated into educational games (Huang et al., 2010). The learning goal was to deepen students' understanding of common plants. Given the easy accessibility of campus plants, they were chosen as the primary teaching materials. Additionally, experts were consulted to provide comprehensive information on various plant parts, including stems, leaves, flowers, and fruits.

Each participant was then invited to interact with both game versions, featuring information on four distinct plants each, totaling eight different plants across the two versions to minimize potential learning bias. In the location-based version, players were assigned the task of locating physical target plants and observing them. The chosen experimental site was a university in southern Taiwan, where four campus trees—royal palm, orchid tree, banyan tree, and bodhi tree—were selected as learning materials based on their geographical locations. Figure 1 depicts the appearances and locations of these trees. When playing the non-location-based version, students were not required to observe real plants, and the activity took place in a classroom. Consequently, the teaching materials for this version comprised four common plants found on Taiwanese campuses, namely the madras thorn, royal poinciana, Araucaria cunninghamii, and frangipani.

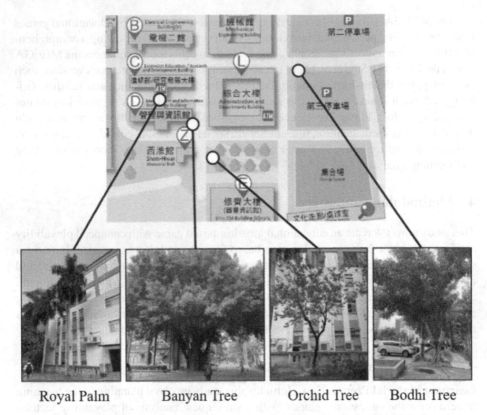

Royal Palm        Banyan Tree        Orchid Tree        Bodhi Tree

**Fig. 1.** The location and appearance of the four guided plants in the location-based version.

**Playability Factor Analysis.** The educational game in this study is anchored in the playability principle proposed by Paavilainen (2020), encompassing functionality, usability, and gameplay. Given the focus on mobile educational games, two additional factors were integrated: mobility, as proposed by Korhonen and Koivisto (2006), and learnability, as suggested by Atmaja (2021). These two factors serve as the foundational principles for designing the educational location-based game in this study. The playability factors and design principles for this game are summarized in Table 1.

The design of playability for the educational game in this study is grounded in the design principles outlined in Table 1. The specifics of the game design are elaborated below, considering the five playability factors, and the design outcomes of the game interface are illustrated in Fig. 2:

- **Functionality:** To ensure system stability and smooth operation, the game was developed using the Android system. Being the most widely used smartphone operating system, Android provides significant stability and an immediately responsive touch interface, contributing to excellent functionality.
- **Usability:** Prioritizing visual clarity, user-friendly interface, and clear information presentation, the game features a high brightness and color saturation interface. Simple colors, text, and images enhance visual clarity. The interface is easily controlled

**Table 1.** Arrangement of play factors and design principle.

| References | Playability Factors | Factor Definitions | Design Principles |
|---|---|---|---|
| Paavilainen (2020) | **Functionality** | Technical factors that affect whether the game operates smoothly | stability, consistent performance, smooth frame rates, short loading times, and error-free operation |
| | **Usability** | Refers to the user interface of the game and its ease of use | visual clarity, interface layout, controls, indicators, feedback, terminology, information, and assistance |
| | **Gameplay** | Distinguishes between games and utility programs, providing rules for game dynamics | goals, progress, challenges, and rewards |
| Korhonen & Koivisto (2006) | **Mobility** | The functions of the game and gameplay can be quickly initiated The game can adapt to the surrounding environment | Adapting to environmental disruptions such as lighting, weather, noisc, and the influence of other people within the vicinity affecting the gaming experience |
| | | Appropriately addressing issues of interference and interruptions Players need to move during the game | The game can pause when interrupted by external events |
| | | Missions should require players to connect areas, locations, physical objects, concepts, themes, etc | |
| Atmaja (2021) | **Learnability** | The gameplay is easy to learn | Teach players how to play the game with short tutorials |

through tapping, and critical information is highlighted in bright colors for clear visibility.

- **Gameplay**: To increase playability, the game should incorpo-rate such elements as goals, challenges, and rewards. This game requires the sub-jects to answer all questions correctly and clear all quiz stages. The challenge mainly lies in the observation of the details of the plants to find the correct an-swers. The rewards for correct answers include plant illustrations and detailed knowledge.
- **Mobility:** Player movement is integral to the gaming process, and the game's theme is linked to the player's location. Responding to interruptions and disturbances during gameplay is required. Thus, players are prompted to move, locate specific places, and observe real plants to find answers, connecting the game with the real world.
- **Learnability:** The gameplay should be easy to learn. This underscores the necessity of tutorials for players before they begin to play this game. In other words, a brief description of the gameplay should be presented through text boxes and dialogue boxes in order that players can review the tutorials at any time.

### 4.2   Quasi-Experimental Design

This study aims to investigate the impact of educational games that combine playability with location-based factors on player experience. To achieve this, a quasi-experimental design approach was adopted, allowing participants to engage with both versions of the educational game – one with location-based elements and the other without. Furthermore, a

.+n MEEGA + survey was conducted to discern differences in player experience between the two game versions. In this experiment, the location-based version was designated as the experimental group, while the non-location-based version served as the control group.

**Experiment Procedure.**  The experimental procedure is outlined in Fig. 3. To compare player experience differences between the experimental and control groups, each participant played both the location-based and non-location-based versions of the educational game. A convenience sampling method was utilized, recruiting 30 subjects. To minimize the potential impact of the sequence of playing the two game versions on the experimental outcomes, 15 subjects played the location-based version followed by the non-location-based version (referred to as Group A), while the other 15 subjects experienced the non-location-based version first, followed by the location-based version (referred to as Group B). The educational location-based game incorporated plant learning materials and maps based on those found on the campus of a university in southern Taiwan. Since the experiment was conducted on a university campus, the subjects mainly consisted of university students.

The experiment began with a 5-min explanation. In Group A, participants started by playing the location-based version of the educational game and then completed the initial MEEGA + questionnaire. Subsequently, they engaged with the non-location-based version and filled out the second MEEGA + questionnaire. The content of both questionnaires remained consistent. Since the plant-based educational game in this study

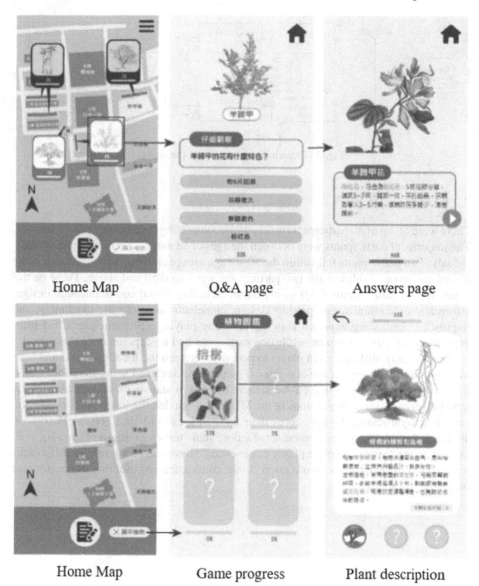

Home Map                    Q&A page                    Answers page

Home Map                    Game progress               Plant description

**Fig. 2.** The design outcomes of the game interface.

is designed for individual players, each experiment involved a single subject. Consequently, the social interaction dimension of the MEEGA + model of player experience was not included in the questionnaire. The location-based version experiment lasted approximately 30 min, while the non-location-based version experiment took around 25 min. Therefore, the entire experiment lasted about one hour.

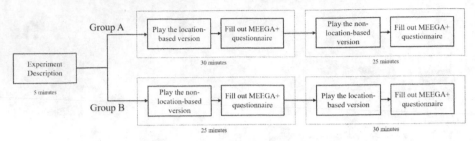

**Fig. 3.** Experiment procedure of the study.

## 5   Research Results

There were a total of 30 participants in this study, comprising seven males and 23 females. The majority of participants were between the ages of 18 and 29, accounting for 25 individuals. Two participants fell within the 30–39 age group, and one participant was in the 40–49 age group. Additionally, two participants were aged 50 and above. These participants represented various fields of expertise, including visual communication design, information communication, product design, optoelectronics, electric machinery, and linguistics. Regarding experience in digital game playing, 29 participants had prior experience with digital games, while one participant had no experience in this regard.

In this study, differences in player experience between the location-based and non-location-based versions of the educational game were analyzed using the SPSS statistical software, employing the paired sample t-test as a statistical method. Across the nine player experience dimensions of the MEEGA + model, the location-based version exhibited significantly higher scores than the non-location-based version in focused attention, fun, challenge, relevance, satisfaction, short-term learning, and learning goal, as well as the "overall average player experience." However, no significant differences were observed between the two versions in the confidence and usability dimensions, as indicated in Table 2.

**Table 2.** The results of Location-based version and Non-location-based version in eight dimensions of player experience

| Dimension | Location-based version | | Non-location-based version | | Significance |
|---|---|---|---|---|---|
| | Mean | SD | Mean | SD | |
| Focused attention | 3.58 | 0.68 | 3.14 | 0.74 | Significantly |
| Fun | 4.20 | 0.68 | 3.57 | 0.89 | Significantly |
| Challenge | 3.93 | 0.64 | 3.33 | 0.71 | Significantly |
| Confidence | 4.20 | 0.50 | 4.12 | 0.54 | Not significant |
| Relevance | 4.15 | 0.43 | 3.83 | 0.44 | Significantly |
| Satisfaction | 4.19 | 0.52 | 3.80 | 0.65 | Significantly |
| Usability | 4.00 | 0.35 | 4.01 | 0.41 | Not significant |
| Short-term learning | 4.50 | 0.39 | 4.20 | 0.57 | Significantly |
| Learning goal | 4.67 | 0.48 | 4.20 | 0.55 | Significantly |
| **Overall average** | **4.07** | **0.36** | **3.82** | **0.40** | **Significantly** |

## 6  Conclusion

This study aims to develop an educational location-based game with playability, investigate the impact of location-based factors on player experience, and report the observed phenomena. Following the experiment and statistical analyses, the study identified two phenomena:

1. **Incorporating location-based characteristics into educational games enhances player experience.**

   The findings reveal a substantial enhancement in subjects' experience across dimensions like focused attention, fun, challenge, relevance, satisfaction, short-term learning, and learning goal after incorporating location-based factors into the educational game. This suggests that educational games with location-based features not only effectively capture learners' attention but also immerse them, making them lose track of time and surroundings. These games provide a sense of joy and relaxation and maintain learners' interest through sufficient challenges. Additionally, they establish a profound connection between games and learning content, allowing learners to feel the results of their efforts and learn more effectively.

2. **Location-based factors have no significant effect on confidence and usability.**

   The results indicate that location-based factors do not significantly affect overall confidence. This implies that subjects can make progress in learning the teaching materials through hard work and abilities when playing both versions of the game. However, statistical differences between items of the MEEGA + model suggest that subjects believe the content and structure of the location-based game are more conducive to boosting their confidence in learning through gaming. For instance, some subjects mentioned that "Direct interaction with real plants can deepen their memory" and "made the acquired knowledge more enduring." In contrast, a higher number of subjects forget the information acquired during the non-location-based version, as expressed by a subject, "The non-location-based version game makes it difficult for me to quickly remember the knowledge acquired while playing." The lack of significant differences in the usability dimension between the two game versions may be attributed to the minimal distinctions in their game interfaces. Additionally, both versions were developed following the same usability design principles, contributing to a consistently high level of usability across both versions.

The integration of games into education has emerged as a significant educational approach in recent years, demonstrating its potential to significantly enhance students' learning outcomes and motivation. The incorporation of location-based features further amplifies the effectiveness of educational games. While this study suggests that introducing location-based factors may not necessarily boost students' confidence in learning teaching materials, it does enhance engagement and a sense of fulfillment, ultimately contributing to an overall improved player experience. In the current era of widespread smartphone use, the popularity and applications of location-based games are expected to grow, expanding their domain accordingly. As this study focuses solely on plant ecology for teaching materials, future research could explore other subject areas. To conduct more robust studies, games could be developed with increased complexity, diversifying gameplay, storylines, and the number of teaching materials. Additionally, it is recommended to broaden the sampling scope, increase the sample size, and investigate the varying experiences of players in different age groups and backgrounds.

**Acknowledgments.** The funding for this research was provided through a grant from the National Science Council of Taiwan, with the project number NSTC 112–2221-E-218–018 -. The plant illustration materials utilized in this study were graciously provided with permission by the 'Tainan Park & Plants' design team of STUST. We express our gratitude to the 30 subjects for their voluntary assistance, crucial for data collection in this research. Special thanks to Teacher Chen Tzuyin from Taoyuan Municipal Wu-Ling Senior High School in Taiwan for her valuable support in developing the educational content for the game.

# References

Atmaja, P.W.: The relationships between aspects of playability and learning content in educational games. In: 2021 IEEE 7th Information Technology International Seminar (ITIS), pp. 1–6 (2021)

Avouris, N.M., Yiannoutsou, N.: A review of mobile location-based games for learning across physical and virtual spaces. J. Univers. Comput. Sci. **18**(15), 2120–2142 (2012)

Brown, E.: Introduction to location-based mobile learning. In: Education in the Wild: Contextual and Location-Based Mobile Learning in Action: A Report from the STELLAR Alpine Rendez-Vous Workshop Series, E. Brown (Ed.). University of Nottingham, UK, pp. 7–9 (2010)

Chang, T.J.: The educational significance of game aesthetics in the digital era. Research in Arts Education, 5 (2004)

Clanton, C.: An interpreted demonstration of computer game design. In: CHI 98 conference summary on Human factors in computing systems, pp. 1–2 (1998)

Ebling, M.R., Cáceres, R.: Gaming and augmented reality come to location-based services. IEEE Pervasive Comput. **9**(01), 5–6 (2010)

Gerling, K.M., Klauser, M., Niesenhaus, J.: Measuring the impact of game controllers on player experience in FPS games. In: Proceedings of the 15th International Academic MindTrek Conference: Envisioning Future Media Environments, pp. 83–86 (2011)

Hwang, G.H., Lee, L.M., Wang, H.Y., Hong, P.J., Wu, J.R., Lai, X.L.: Development and effectiveness analysis of ubiquitous learning systems - a case study for elementary school children to recognize campus plants. Int. J. Digital Learn. Technol. **2**(3), 19–41 (2010)

IJsselsteijn, W.A., de Kort, Y.A.W., Poels, K.: The Game Experience Questionnaire. Technische Universiteit Eindhoven (2013)

Järvinen, A., Heliö, S., Mäyrä, F.: Communication and community in digital entertainment services. Prestudy Research Report (2002)

Killi, K.: Digital game-based learning- Towards an experiential gaming model. Internet High. Educ. **8**, 13–24 (2005)

Korhonen, H., Koivisto, E.M.: Playability heuristics for mobile games. In: Proceedings of the 8th Conference on Human-Computer Interaction with Mobile Devices and Services, pp. 9–16 (2006)

Lehmann, L.A.: Location-Based Mobile Games. GRIN Verlag, Munich, Germany (2012)

Li, X., Zhang, Z., Stefanidis, K.: A data-driven approach for video game playability analysis based on players' reviews. Information **12**(3), 129 (2021)

Lin, K.Y.: Reflection on the current situation of STEM education in Taiwan. J. Youth Stud. **21**(1), 41 (2018)

Nacke, L., Drachen, A.: Towards a framework of player experience research. In: Proceedings of the Second International Workshop on Evaluating Player Experience in Games at FDG, vol. 11 (2011)

Paavilainen, J.: Defining playability of games: functionality, usability, and gameplay. In: Proceedings of the 23rd International Conference on Academic Mindtrek, pp. 55–64 (2020)

Paraskeva, F., Mysirlaki, S., Papagianni, A.: Multiplayer online games as educational tools- facing new challenges in learning. Comput. Educ. **54**(2), 498–505 (2010)

Petri, G., von Wangenheim, C.G., Borgatto, A.F.: MEEGA+: an evolution of a model for the evaluation of educational games. INCoD/GQS **3**, 1–40 (2016)

Prensky, M.: Digital game-based learning. Comput. Entertainment (CIE) **1**(1), 21 (2003)

Priyaadharshini, M., Dakshina, R., Sandhya, S.: Learning analytics: game-based learning for programming course in higher education. Procedia Comput. Sci. **172**, 468–472 (2020)

Sánchez, J.L.G., Vela, F.L.G.: Assessing the player interaction experiences based on playability. Entertainment Comput. **5**(4), 259–267 (2014)

Savi, R., von Wangenheim, C.G., Borgatto, A.F.: A model for the evaluation of educational games for teaching software engineering. In: 2011 25th Brazilian Symposium on Software Engineering, pp. 194–203 (2011)

Tsai, W.D., Wang, C.Y.: Pokémon go player's experiences as an entrepreneuring process: a hermeneutic phenomenology approach. Sun Yat-Sen Manag. Rev. **26**(1), 85–111 (2018)

Zhang, Y.K.: Integrating action learning into the teaching evaluation of natural science in elementary schools - taking the moon phase observation unit as an example. Unpublished master's thesis in Xingwu University of Science and Technology Information Technology Application Research Institute (2015)

# "Furnish Your Reality" - Intelligent Mobile AR Application for Personalized Furniture

Minh Dung Do[✉], Nanna Dahlem, Moritz Paulus, Mathias Krick, Laura Steffny, and Dirk Werth

August-Wilhelm Scheer Institut für Digitale Produkte und Prozesse gGmbH, Uni Campus Nord D 5 1, 66123 Saarbrücken, Germany
minhdung.do@aws-institut.de

**Abstract.** Today's online retailers are faced with the challenge of providing a convenient solution for their customers to browse through a wide range of products. Simultaneously, they must meet individual customer needs by creating unique, personalized, one-of-a-kind items. Technological advances in areas such as Augmented Reality (AR), Artificial Intelligence (AI) or sensors (e.g. LiDAR), have the potential to address these challenges by enhancing the customer experience in new ways. One option is to implement "phygital" commerce solutions, which combines the benefits of physical and digital environments to improve the customer journey.

This work presents a concept for a mobile AR application that integrates LiDAR and an AI-powered recommender system to create a unique phygital customer journey in the context of furniture shopping. The combination of AR, LiDAR and AI enables an accurate immersive experience along with personalized product designs. This concept aims to deliver benefits in terms of usability, convenience, time savings and user experience, while bridging the gap between mass-produced and personalized products. The new possibilities for merging virtual with physical environments hold immense potential, but this work also highlights challenges for customers as well as for online platform providers and future researchers.

**Keywords:** Mobile Human Computer Interfaces · Augmented Reality · Artificial Intelligence · Recommender system · Phygital customer journey · Personalized product design · Generative AI · LiDAR · User-centered design

## 1 Introduction

According to estimates, the global m-commerce will generate sales of approximately 1,901 billion USD by 2028 [1]. This could be due to, the tremendous technological advances which have led to significant changes in m-commerce [2, 3]. Hence, technologies and sensors built into modern smart devices, such as LiDAR and Augmented Reality (AR) [4, 5] are changing the customer experience in many ways, for example by delivering a "try before you buy" experience [6–8]. In that regard, it has been demonstrated that enriching the user experience with AR can lead to higher user satisfaction and higher purchase intentions [9]. Conclusively, merging digital artefacts with the real world holds the potential to enable new and unique product experiences [7]. By allowing a user to manipulate virtual objects, AR creates a kind of realistic impression of the virtual object [10] finally potentially facilitating a consumers' decision making process towards product choice. Hence, when consumers consider purchasing a product online, many might find it difficult to visualize this product, such as a piece of furniture, within their own homes, affecting their ability to make informed purchasing decisions [11]. In this context, mobile AR can be used to support users' ability to envision a product within a specific environment, one of the shortcoming consumers encounter when online-shopping, especially in the field of furniture [12].

Moreover, with the emergence of technologies such as artificial intelligence (AI), it is possible to leverage AI for personalized product design by incorporating user needs and preferences in the design process [13], or to provide users with automated and more personalized recommendations [14]. This holds the potential to increase the hedonic value of consumer products, considered as "an overall assessment (i.e., judgment) of experimental benefits and sacrifices, such as entertainment and escapism" [15]. This increasingly manifests in "adventure shopping", and "idea shopping" [16]. Hence, in today's B2C market, customers expect more than conventional attributes like fair pricing, high quality or speed of service [17]. In contrast, they want to engage in value creating activities, desiring new experiences and pleasure-oriented attributes like aesthetic and security as well as flow, arousal, and recognition [17]. Nowadays, especially online retailers in the field of furniture are increasingly faced with the challenge of providing customers with a comfortable digital solution offering a broad variety of options while addressing individual customer needs by producing personalized one-of a-kind pieces [11]. Although furniture still only accounts for a comparatively small proportion of the global e-commerce sales [18], sales in online furniture retail are expected to expand to around 332.5 million USD by 2028 [18].

The steady increase in growth of interest in the field of m- and e-commerce can be similarly observed in scientific research, especially with respect to the development of (technological) applications [19]. Meanwhile, there is an increasing usage of the term "Phygital"(commerce), composed of the words "physical" and "digital" and refers to combining the advantages of both environments to improve the customer experience [20, 21]. However, research in the field of phygital technologies is still fragmented but constantly evolving [20, 21] and thus, can be advanced in various areas such as m-commerce and in specific fields such as online furniture shopping. In that regard, del Vecchio et al. [20] recently presented a research framework "for moving ahead the research on phygital technologies" [20] which includes omni-channel integration technology and AR.

This paper contributes to the evolving landscape of online furniture shopping and phygital commerce, by describing the development and architecture of a holistic, user-centric mobile application that combines the potential of generative AI, sensor technology (i.e., LiDAR) and AR. Thereby, this work aims to demonstrate a new way of experiencing convenience, personalization, and precise information generation when shopping online. Through the unique combination of the digital components, the conceptualized and developed mobile AR application allows for customizable, generatively produced furniture while reducing the complexity for measurement, configuration, selection, and product purchase. The application provides valuable insights into how the infusion of different technologies can be exploited in the context of online furniture shopping. Additionally, the impact of these technologies on the (phygital) customer journey can be analyzed. In this context, phygital customer journey refers to "the path in which technological solutions eliminate the boundaries between reality and virtuality, allowing customers to immerse themselves and take advantage of their desired level of connectivity wherever they are. It takes place within a synergistic online and offline context enabled by smart technologies" [21]. Furthermore, this work aims to highlight which user- and provider- (e.g., online furniture retailer) specific advantages can be associated with the interplay of the applied technology-types, thereby addressing the gap between mass-produced and personalized products.

This paper proceeds as follows. First the general concept and the interplay between the technological components is explained. Subsequently, the individual components are described in more detail, including important insights into their general functionality as well as specific explanations of their technical conception. Followed by this, the advantages and limitations of the overarching mobile application are discussed in the context of user acceptance and experience. The contribution of this paper to the evolving landscape of online furniture shopping and phygital commerce is outlined afterwards. Finally, this work concludes with an outlook for future research.

## 2 General Concept

To address the aforementioned challenges for m-commerce with current technologies, a concept for an AR application was developed (see Fig. 1). The aim is to combine the potential of *AR, LiDAR,* and *generative AI* to create a holistic, user-centric mobile application for furniture shopping. This serves as basis for the development of a working prototype which offers personalized creation of freely formable shelves. The prototype will be used to evaluate the concept in terms of usability, convenience, time consumption, and user experience.

The *UI* of the AR application was designed to realize an interactive part of the phygital customer journey. An intuitive and user-centered interface is essential to ensure a straightforward and user-friendly application. Especially when introducing an unconventional measurement method, it is necessary to provide the user with an engaging interface to mitigate potential challenges. It is also particularly important to minimize the duration of a time-consuming process, as prolonged processes significantly increase the likelihood of a drop-off point for the user [22]. Accordingly, the general concept of the application can be illustrated using the following user process along with the user's interaction with the AR application. The user is guided through the entire process in five steps.

### 2.1 Start

The mobile application starts with a compelling call to action: "Discover your new favorite piece of furniture now." This emotionally engaging phrase, coupled with the notion of uncovering something novel, fosters curiosity. Furthermore, it's directly evident

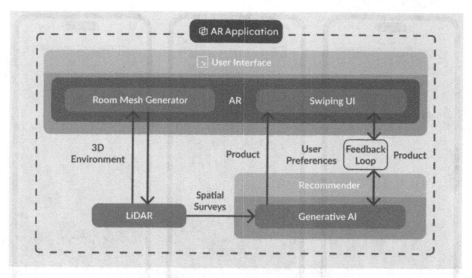

**Fig. 1.** Diagram illustrating the general concept of the AR application.

that this app delivers a highly personalized experience. The term "favorite piece of furniture" adds a personal touch, enhancing relatability. By selecting "Start now" users initiate the AR measurement process.

## 2.2 Spatial Surveys via LiDAR

Users are guided through the measurement process utilizing intuitive dialog boxes and visual cues in *AR*. The *Room Mesh Generator* swiftly generates a 3D mesh of the scanned environment. The wall-floor edge is highlighted with a yellow guideline. The 3D cursor automatically aligns to this edge for width, height, and depth measurement. Thereby, users achieve precise placement for the furniture while parallax errors are reduced (see Fig. 2).

This process ensures that the furniture is aligned with the environment. The measurement is supported with visual cues to help the users moving the mobile phone correctly. Users control the cursor by moving their smartphone and confirming points by tapping the screen. The distance between two selected points is automatically measured and displayed to the user (see Fig. 3). To enhance dimensional clarity in AR, a transparent box is displayed as the cursor is moved during height setting. Once the measurements are complete, the user can review and confirm them.

In order to improve the accuracy of AR and spatial measurement, the power of *LiDAR sensors* is harnessed within different measurement processes. This saves users a significant amount of time and effort when measuring the room in which the furniture has to be placed and improves the AR experience within phygital customer journey.

**Fig. 2.** View within the AR application when measuring a room using the Room Mesh Generator.

**Fig. 3.** View within the AR application during single line measurement process.

## 2.3 Generation of Product Suggestions via Generative AI

The measured spatial values are used as input variables for the *generative AI* that creates product designs for suitable shelves. The AI utilizes data from spatial surveys, as well as old product variants from an online shop's database for personalized shelves. The AI is embedded in an intelligent *Recommender System* that evaluates the generated shelves according to the user's preferences.

## 2.4 Selection of Suitable Product Suggestions

To facilitate personalized evaluation a *Swiping UI* is implemented, which presents an AI-generated shelf as a virtual furniture model in the real-world environment within the application (see Fig. 4). The highly accurate immersive experience allows users to make a more profound assessment of the furniture in terms of matching their preferences (e.g., design and size of the furniture).

In the *Swiping UI,* a consistent button layout is observed at the bottom of the AR space, with four distinct buttons. The primary button, for approving displayed furniture, is accompanied by a secondary button for disapproval. Both buttons are equally sized to avoid bias, which is crucial for the recommender system. Liked furniture is stored in the favorites view, with additional feedback provided through micro-interactions in the navigation bar. Another button allows users to undo the last decision, while another one allows to display the furniture's actual size. Users can also swipe left to disapprove or right to approve and move on to the next design. This provides them with a fast and enjoyable way [23] to browse through a variety of potential matching furniture models. The different user actions are integrated into a continuous *feedback loop*, which constantly feeds the *Recommender System* with user preferences. This iterative process improves the evaluation of generated shelves, thereby refining the selection of suitable products presented to the user. Throughout the entire process, the user has the option to undo a step.

During the interactive measurement and selection process, users experience a sense of participation, which fosters a stronger emotional connection to the product compared to a simple numerical input [24]. Thereby, the presented concept demonstrates a new way of experiencing convenience, personalization, and precise information generation in online furniture shopping through the unique combination of the digital components within an AR application.

## 2.5 Triggering Ordering Process

Once a suitable piece of furniture has been created, users can order the product directly from the AR application. The order details, including precise size specifications, appearance, color, and material preferences, are then send to the online furniture provider. This streamlined and efficient process minimizes time consumption for users, the online retailer and furniture producer, ensuring a smooth and dynamic workflow.

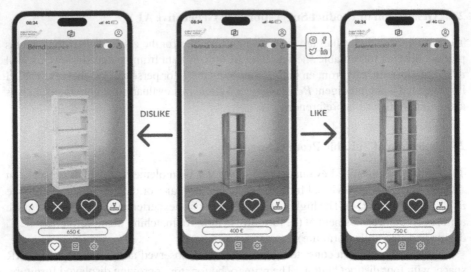

**Fig. 4.** Swiping UI view within the AR application to evaluate and select different products.

## 3   Integrated Technologies

In order to provide a deeper understanding of the interplay between the different components, the technologies used and their integration into the AR application are described in more detail below.

### 3.1   LiDAR Based AR

The conceptualized and developed AR application aims to assist users create personalized furniture according to their preferences. For this purpose, AR requires "the integration of virtual objects (of any type) into a real environment in real time" [25]. However, the degree of precision of such applications in terms of the relative dimensions of virtual and real objects varies depending on the specific application (e.g. hardware components). In order to provide an authentic AR experience, accurate measurement of dimensions is critical. This ensures that the application processes information accurately to generate furniture that smoothly fits into the selected space.

However, AR applications often face challenges in spatial measurement due to the lack of depth information [26]. Consequently, the data generated by the LiDAR sensor, such as in the iPhone 13 Pro, combined with AR features holds potential to improve these measurements. By using the LiDAR sensor to scan the environment and accessing this information through ARKit [27], 3D-generated meshes containing the environment's depth information can be acquired [28]. In the AR application presented here, these meshes serve as an accurate virtual representation of the real world. They can be continuously updated and recomputed when the user moves the mobile device around scanning the surrounding environment. This element allows the user to be immersed in the realistic experience, as they can see the actual real-world objects that appear in the virtual environment.

Once the surrounding environment and objects are displayed through generated meshes, another essential aspect is accurately placing reference digital points. The application uses these points to calculate the distances that users want to measure. Employing the Raycasting technique [29] from AR Foundation, a ray is projected from the middle of the camera in a forward direction, allowing users to accurately place reference points by adjusting their device's position and orientation.

Despite the enhanced depth information provided by LiDAR-generated data, human and technical errors during point placement can still introduce inaccuracies. To address this, the application integrates the OpenCV library. This involves capturing the device camera's image texture and applying the Canny edge detection algorithm [30] as well as Hough Line Transform (HoughLinesP) [31]. By detecting potential edges or lines in the real-world environment, the application provides users with reliable reference points to initiate accurate measurements. This enhances the immersive shopping experience while the innovative measurement reduces the necessary time required, improving the perceived usefulness of the application.

## 3.2 Generative AI

To further enrich the shopping experience and make it unique in terms of generating a one-of-a-kind product, it is necessary to implement a flexible but automated solution to keep this level of personalization feasible for e- and m-commerce providers. Currently, rule-based systems dominate the e-commerce landscape for creating personalized products. These systems facilitate adaptive customization while ensuring product manufacturability [32]. However, product creation relies heavily on the users' design expertise and requires a significant time investment. To address these challenges, AI algorithms are increasingly being applied to creative domains [33–36]. Methods within generative AI, such as Variational Autoencoders (VAEs) and Generative Adversarial Networks (GANs) are particularly promising for this purpose. GANs [37] are deep learning models that consist of two neural networks. The generator network is responsible to create synthetic data, while the discriminator tries to distinguish real data samples from the generated ones. Both are trained simultaneously in a competitive manner to generate data that closely resembles real data distributions. VAEs [38] also allow the generation of new data samples, but in contrast they encode the input data into a latent space and then decode it back into the original data space.

Within the AR application, GANs are used in conjunction with VAEs. This combination is achieved by integrating an encoder into the generator of a GAN to map the high-dimensional geometric representation of the shelves to a low-dimensional latent vector representation. The generator, the encoder and the discriminator are trained simultaneously during the training process. To create new product variants, the low-dimensional vector is manipulated to generate new designs through the generator network. This approach is expected to improve the control over the manipulation of the latent vector with respect to features of the underlying data model of the shelves.

### 3.3 Intelligent Recommender System

To increase the diversity within the generated designs, it is advantageous to embed the AI in a distinct recommender system. This reduces the risk of AI-generated suggestions towards converging towards similarity, while allowing more control over the evaluation process. By providing the ability to deploy and evaluate different recommender systems independently of the underlying AI framework, the approach yields higher flexibility and more adaptability with respect to available user data. Most known types of recommender systems - content-based and collaborative filtering methods - exhibit inherent limitations [39–41]. While hybrid filtering techniques serve to enrich diversity, especially in creative domains, the use of bandit algorithms or ensemble methods emerges as the predominant choice for increased recommendation diversity. Ensemble methods combine different filtering techniques while bandit algorithms use decision-making strategies that balance exploration and exploitation to adapt actions over time and changing conditions.

However, for applications that require real-time responsiveness, such as the swiping functionality in the presented AR application an ensemble approach is less suitable due the increased computational costs. Bandit algorithms in contrast are computational efficient while improving recommender systems by increasing their ability to dynamically adapt [42] and avoiding cold start problems [41]. One way to make bandit recommenders even more dynamic, is to integrate Reinforcement Learning (RL) [41]. RL can be applied to improve personalization, especially in systems with changing environments [43], contextual information, interactive, explicit and implicit user feedback [44], and sequential decision-making [41]. To accurately model the sequential decision-making process via the swiping UI, the designed recommender system incorporates reinforcement learning within a bandit algorithm. This allows the recommender system to continuously learn to make personalized and adaptive recommendations, which is expected to increase user satisfaction and engagement.

## 4 Discussion

The presented concept for a mobile AR application, including its implementation for online furniture retail, shows new ways in which the (phygital) consumer journey can be shaped through the combination of innovative technologies. The new possibilities for merging the virtual with the real world hold significant potential. But also challenges are emerging for customers (users), online platform providers, and producers [21] in terms of time and cost management, as well as usage and acceptance behavior [25]. In line with this, a significant numbers of studies have shown that factors such as perceived usefulness, ease of use and time savings, in particular can have a positive impact on the consumers' intention to use digital services, such as mobile applications [45]. Accordingly, practitioners could benefit from the concept described in this paper or the implementation of such an application, as they can introduce new products to the market, especially products that are traditionally bought in stationary retail stores, such as furniture. Furthermore, increasing the usefulness of the AR application through the accuracy of LiDAR technology for spatial measurement could lead consumers to better evaluate the application, or rather this type of AR, compared to existing solutions. Thus, in their study on the acceptance behavior of AR applications Rese et al. [25] examined four different applications. Thereby, the authors distinguished between marker-based (hard-coded objects) and applications with a higher augmentation level in which the real environment is captured to make virtual objects appear [25]. In this context, Rese et al. [25] were not only able to show that the overall opinion is more positive for applications with a high level of augmentation than for those with markers. The authors also showed that applications that provide a high degree of augmentation providing a personalized, spatially dynamic AR experience, are better evaluated in terms of recommendation and use intentions [25]. Consequently, the LiDAR-enabled, more accurate AR experience could have a positive effect on the evaluation of the application, which may be associated with a more positive evaluation of the provider and the product, potentially resulting increased sales. Thus, researchers found that using (branded) AR apps can have a positive impact on customers' attitude towards the brand [46]. Therefore, the presented AR application can have a significant practical impact for furniture sellers by helping them to strengthen their brand image and thereby increase customer acquisition and loyalty.

From the manufacturer's point of view, there is another decisive advantage, namely the conservation of resources. Accordingly, the AR application supports on-demand, manufacturing. Therefore, it can help to minimize customer returns, as customers can visualize and preview the pieces in their living environment and furniture pieces can be tailored to individual customer needs. In addition, individually designed pieces of furniture might be used for longer and replaced less quickly, as people might attach a more personal value to them. In terms of sustainability, this can be referred to as emotionally durable design [47]. Thus, $CO_2$ emissions can be saved, and production cost can be minimized by facilitating a customized and responsible product design.

Regarding the focus of this work, however, it is worth noting that there are limitations with regard to the explanatory power concerning user behavior as well as the ecological and economic potential of the mobile AR application. On the one hand, this work addresses the conceptualization and technical realization of an AR application for m-commerce, which is realized for furniture shopping. It also aims to illustrate how the components and technologies used might influence the phygital customer journey [21] and what user- and provider-specific benefits could be implied. On the other hand, the effects outlined in this paper on the perception and user behavior on the part of the users as well as the possible economic advantages on the part of suppliers are based on theoretical assumptions and expectations. Thus, the findings of this work could serve future researchers as a basis for further qualitative and quantitative empirical studies that theoretically and empirically underline the concept and implications drawn in this work.

## 5 Conclusion and Future Research Perspectives

Incorporating new, emerging technologies into business practice allows for new ways to create value for customers and retailers alike. This work presents a novel phygital commerce application that combines generative AI, LiDAR and AR to offer customers the opportunity to virtually display and customize their furniture directly in the living environment.

Regarding the novelty of the integrated solution, future evaluation of the system should consider the user experience. Appropriate techniques and methods should be used to test users' cognitive and emotional responses to the system. For instance, neurophysiological tools allow the measurement of human responses to stimuli, which is also possible for IT interfaces [48], and can therefore be used to evaluate IT artefacts [49]. This enables a more objective measurement of effects on users, for example by analyzing brain activity or other neurophysiological parameters like heart rate or skin response [49]. Future research should apply these tools to investigate differences in the neurophysiological reaction of consumers. Especially the combination of generative AI and mobile AR should be examined to determine how they impact the online shopping experience by generating product recommendations that can be virtually placed within a real environment.

Moreover, future research should investigate the transferability of the developed AR application to further phygital commerce application contexts and areas, such as urban development [20] or products whose spatial placement can be planned more easily and realistically with the help of the technologies presented, such as consumer electronics or decorative items. In this context, user-centric studies can be carried out to identify new areas of application for the system, based on which the feasibility of the technical implementation can then be assessed.

When it comes to decision making and purchase intention in the context of mobile or phygital commerce, there are two influencing factors, which could be addressed in the context of the AI enabled AR mobile applications: "the feeling of psychological ownership" and "decision comfort" [50, 51]. Psychological ownership refers to a feeling of ownership for objects as long as they allow to operate and satisfy specific ground principles [52]. The feeling is associated with three central experiences (1) controlling the ownership target, (2) intimately knowing the target and (3) investing the self into the target [52]. It can be assumed that these experiences come to bear in the design process, as the user controls the product through the customization process (1), knows it well over the design process (2) and invests his or her own time and taste in the product as well as customizes it to his or her individual spatial conditions (3). Correspondingly, prior research argues that these experiences might influence the purchase intention of customers, especially in the context of AR applications [51, 53]. Therefore, it would be interesting to include the effect of user-centered customization (with the assistance of AI and AR) on the sense of psychological ownership in future research.

Conversely, "decision comfort" describes the satisfaction and feeling at ease with a decision and has been incorporated as a relevant component of customers decision-making experience [54, 55]. AR-based services are accompanied by increased spatial presence, which provides customers with substantial decision comfort [54]. In the presented application, users not only aim for a finished product, as has been investigated in previous work [54, 56]. The users require a product with a personalized visual and spatial design. The product design process involves users directly and includes simulated physical control and environmental embedding through AR, which is expected to increase decision comfort [54]. Therefore, user-centered applications for product design should be directly addressed in future research, given the importance of decision comfort on decision-making processes and the simultaneous development of new technologies in mobile and phygital commerce.

The technologies integrated in the presented application do not only offer new possibilities to enhance the experience of mobile or phygital commerce, but also have combined potential yet unexplored effects on the factors discussed. Therefore, these could be addressed in future research on the emotional, psychological, and cognitive effects of applications similar to the one discussed in this paper in order to gain broader and deeper insights. For instance, the willingness of sellers to integrate the app into their e-commerce offering is a possible avenue for future research. Furthermore, future research should quantify the impact of the AR application concept on sustainability by examining the process from user-centric furniture design to disposal as well as on further marked relevant variables such as willingness to pay and sales growth.

**Acknowledgments.** This work is part of the research project iperMö funded by the german Federal Ministry of Education and Research (BMBF, funding label: 01IS22039B).

**Disclosure of Interests.**    The authors declare that they have no known competing financial interests or personal relationships that could have appeared to influence the work reported in this article.

# References

1. Polaris Market Research: ennzahlen zum Mobile Commerce weltweit im Jahr 2021 sowie eine Prognose für das Jahr 2030 [Graph], https://de.statista.com/statistik/daten/studie/139 1473/umfrage/kennzahlen-mobile-commerce-weltweit/. Accessed 15 Jan 2024
2. AlmeidaLucas, G., Lunardi, G.L., BittencourtDolci, D.: From e-commerce to m-commerce: an analysis of the user's experience with different access platforms. Electron. Commer. Res. Appl. **58**, 101240 (2023). https://doi.org/10.1016/j.elerap.2023.101240
3. Idrees, S., Vignali, G., Gill, S.: Interactive marketing with virtual commerce tools: purchasing right size and fitted garment in fashion metaverse. In: Wang, C.L. (ed.) The Palgrave Handbook of Interactive Marketing, pp. 329–351. Springer International Publishing, Cham (2023). https://doi.org/10.1007/978-3-031-14961-0_15
4. Aemmer, D., Bigler, J., Birkhofer, M., Pešková, M.B., Harder, D.: Augmented reality als entscheidungshilfe beim Möbelkauf. In: Schellinger, J., Tokarski, K.O., Kissling-Näf, I. (eds.) Digitale Transformation und Unternehmensführung: Trends und Perspektiven für die Praxis, pp. 355–381. Springer Fachmedien Wiesbaden, Wiesbaden (2020). https://doi.org/10.1007/978-3-658-26960-9_13
5. Azuma, R.T.: A survey of augmented reality. Presence Teleoper. Virtual Environ. **6**(4), 355–385 (1997). https://doi.org/10.1162/pres.1997.6.4.355
6. Afrin, S., Zaman, S.R., Sadekeen, D., Islam, Z., Tabassum, N., Islam, M.N.: How usability and user experience vary among the basic m-commerce, AR and VR based user interfaces of mobile application for online shopping. In: Martins, N., Brandão, D. (eds.) Advances in Design and Digital Communication II: Proceedings of the 5th International Conference on Design and Digital Communication, Digicom 2021, November 4–6, 2021, Barcelos, Portugal, pp. 44–53. Springer International Publishing, Cham (2022). https://doi.org/10.1007/978-3-030-89735-2_4
7. Hoffmann, S., Mai, R.: Consumer behavior in augmented shopping reality. a review, synthesis, and research agenda. Front. Virtual Real. **3**, 961236 (2022). https://doi.org/10.3389/frvir.2022.961236

8. Smink, A.R., Van Reijmersdal, E.A., Van Noort, G., Neijens, P.C.: Shopping in augmented reality: the effects of spatial presence, personalization and intrusiveness on app and brand responses. J. Bus. Res. **118**, 474–485 (2020). https://doi.org/10.1016/j.jbusres.2020.07.018

9. Poushneh, A., Vasquez-Parraga, A.Z.: Discernible impact of augmented reality on retail customer's experience, satisfaction and willingness to buy. J. Retail. Consum. Serv. **34**, 229–234 (2017). https://doi.org/10.1016/j.jretconser.2016.10.005

10. Adhani, N.I., Rambli, D.R.A.: A Survey of Mobile Augmented Reality Applications (2012)

11. Oh, H., Yoon, S.-Y., Shyu, C.-R.: How can virtual reality reshape furniture retailing? Cloth. Text. Res. J. **26**, 143–163 (2008). https://doi.org/10.1177/0887302X08314789

12. PWC: Die deutsche Möbelbranche. Struktur, Trends und Herausforderungen. https://store.pwc.de/de/publications/die-deutsche-moebelbranche-struktur-trends-und-herausforderungen. Accessed 27 Oct 2023

13. Wang, L., Liu, Z., Liu, A., Tao, F.: Artificial intelligence in product lifecycle management. Int. J. Adv. Manuf. Technol. **114**, 771–796 (2021). https://doi.org/10.1007/s00170-021-06882-1

14. Chinchanachokchai, S., Thontirawong, P., Chinchanachokchai, P.: A tale of two recommender systems: the moderating role of consumer expertise on artificial intelligence based product recommendations. J. Retail. Consum. Serv. **61**, 102528 (2021). https://doi.org/10.1016/j.jretconser.2021.102528

15. Overby, J.W., Lee, E.-J.: The effects of utilitarian and hedonic online shopping value on consumer preference and intentions. J. Bus. Res. **59**, 1160–1166 (2006). https://doi.org/10.1016/j.jbusres.2006.03.008

16. Arnold, M.J., Reynolds, K.E.: Hedonic shopping motivations. J. Retail. **79**, 77–95 (2003). https://doi.org/10.1016/S0022-4359(03)00007-1

17. Lee, S.M., Lee, D.: "Untact": a new customer service strategy in the digital age. Serv. Bus. **14**(1), 1–22 (2019). https://doi.org/10.1007/s11628-019-00408-2

18. Statista: Umsätze im E-Commerce nach Segmenten in der Welt im Jahr 2028 sowie eine Prognose bis 2028 (in Millionen Euro) [Graph]. https://de.statista.com/prognosen/484965/prognose-der-umsaetze-im-e-commerce-nach-segmenten-in-der-welt. Accessed 15 Jan 2024

19. Ngai, E.W.T., Gunasekaran, A.: A review for mobile commerce research and applications. Decis. Support Syst. **43**, 3–15 (2007). https://doi.org/10.1016/j.dss.2005.05.003

20. Del Vecchio, P., Secundo, G., Garzoni, A.: Phygital technologies and environments for breakthrough innovation in customers' and citizens' journey. a critical literature review and future agenda review for mobile commerce research and applications. Technol. Forecast. Soc. Change **189**, 122342 (2023). https://doi.org/10.1016/j.techfore.2023.122342

21. Mele, C., Spena, T.R., Marzullo, M., Di Bernardo, I.: The phygital transformation: a systematic review and a research agenda. Ital. J. Mark. **2023**, 323–349 (2023). https://doi.org/10.1007/s43039-023-00070-7

22. Lo, L.Y.-S., Lin, S.-W., Hsu, L.-Y.: Motivation for online impulse buying: a two-factor theory perspective. Int. J. Inf. Manage. **36**, 759–772 (2016). https://doi.org/10.1016/j.ijinfomgt.2016.04.012

23. Abolfathi, N., Santamaria, S.: Dating disruption: How Tinder gamified an industry. Sloan Manage. Rev. **61**, 7–11 (2020)

24. Mochon, D., Norton, M.I., Ariely, D.: Bolstering and restoring feelings of competence via the IKEA effect. Int. J. Res. Mark. **29**, 363–369 (2012). https://doi.org/10.1016/j.ijresmar.2012.05.001

25. Rese, A., Baier, D., Geyer-Schulz, A., Schreiber, S.: How augmented reality apps are accepted by consumers: a comparative analysis using scales and opinions. Technol. Forecast. Soc. Chang. **124**, 306–319 (2017). https://doi.org/10.1016/j.techfore.2016.10.010

26. Xi, N., Chen, J., Gama, F., Riar, M., Hamari, J.: The challenges of entering the metaverse: an experiment on the effect of extended reality on workload. Inf. Syst. Front. (2022). https://doi.org/10.1007/s10796-022-10244-x
27. Unity Meshing: ARKit XR Plugin | 4.0.12, https://docs.unity3d.com/Packages/com.unity.xr.arkit@4.0/manual/arkit-meshing.html. Accessed 22 Jan 2024
28. Rutkowski, W., Lipecki, T.: Use of the iPhone 13 Pro LiDAR scanner for inspection and measurement in the mineshaft sinking process. Rem. Sens. 15, 5089 (2023). https://doi.org/10.3390/rs15215089
29. Unity Physics: Physics.Raycast. https://docs.unity3d.com/ScriptReference/Physics.Raycast.html. Accessed 22 Jan 2024
30. Kuzmic, J., Rudolph, G.: Comparison between filtered canny edge detector and convolutional neural network for real time lane detection in a unity 3D simulator: In: Proceedings of the 6th International Conference on Internet of Things, Big Data and Security, pp. 148–155. SCITEPRESS - Science and Technology Publications, Online Streaming, --- Select a Country --- (2021). https://doi.org/10.5220/0010383701480155
31. Rahmdel, P., Comley, R., Shi, D., McElduff, S.: A review of Hough transform and line segment detection approaches: In: Proceedings of the 10th International Conference on Computer Vision Theory and Applications, pp. 411–418. SCITEPRESS - Science and and Technology Publications, Berlin, Germany (2015). https://doi.org/10.5220/0005268904110418
32. Gembarski, P., Lachmayer, R.: How rule-based systems impact product complexity. Ann. Faculty Eng. Hunedoara Int. J. Eng. 15, 17–24 (2017)
33. Cao, Y., Qian, X., Wang, T., Lee, R., Huo, K., Ramani, K.: An exploratory study of augmented reality presence for tutoring machine tasks. In: Proceedings of the 2020 CHI Conference on Human Factors in Computing Systems. pp. 1–13. ACM, Honolulu, HI, USA (2020). https://doi.org/10.1145/3313831.3376688
34. Chen, Y., Tu, S., Yi, Y., Xu, L.: Sketch-pix2seq: a Model to Generate Sketches of Multiple Categories (2017)
35. Oh, S., Jung, Y., Lee, I., Kang, N.: Design automation by integrating generative adversarial networks and topology optimization. In: ASME 2018 International Design Engineering Technical Conferences and Computers and Information in Engineering Conference November, vol. 2 (2018). https://doi.org/10.1115/DETC2018-85506
36. Wu, J., Zhang, C., Xue, T., Freeman, W.T., Tenenbaum, J.B.: Learning a probabilistic latent space of object shapes via 3D generative-adversarial modeling http://arxiv.org/abs/1610.07584 (2017). https://doi.org/10.48550/arXiv.1610.07584
37. Goodfellow, I.J., et al.: Generative Adversarial Networks. http://arxiv.org/abs/1406.2661 (2014). https://doi.org/10.48550/arXiv.1406.2661
38. Kingma, D.P., Welling, M.: Auto-Encoding Variational Bayes. http://arxiv.org/abs/1312.6114 (2022). https://doi.org/10.48550/arXiv.1312.6114
39. da Costa, A.F., Manzato, M.G., Campello, R.J.G.B.: Boosting collaborative filtering with an ensemble of co-trained recommenders. Expert Syst. Appl. 115, 427–441 (2019). https://doi.org/10.1016/j.eswa.2018.08.020
40. Da'u, A., Salim, N.: Recommendation system based on deep learning methods: a systematic review and new directions. Artif Intell Rev. 53, 2709–2748 (2020). https://doi.org/10.1007/s10462-019-09744-1
41. Gangan, E., Kudus, M., Ilyushin, E.: Survey of multiarmed bandit algorithms applied to recommendation systems. Int. J. Open Inf. Technol. 9, 12–27 (2021)
42. Huang, W., Labille, K., Wu, X., Lee, D., Heffernan, N.: Fairness-aware Bandit-based recommendation. In: 2021 IEEE International Conference on Big Data (Big Data), pp. 1273–1278 (2021). https://doi.org/10.1109/BigData52589.2021.9671959

43. Padakandla, S.: A survey of reinforcement learning algorithms for dynamically varying environments. ACM Comput. Surv. **54**, 127:1–127:25 (2021). https://doi.org/10.1145/345 9991

44. Xin, X., Karatzoglou, A., Arapakis, I., Jose, J.M.: Self-supervised reinforcement learning for recommender systems. In: Proceedings of the 43rd International ACM SIGIR Conference on Research and Development in Information Retrieval, pp. 931–940. Association for Computing Machinery, New York, NY, USA (2020). https://doi.org/10.1145/3397271.3401147

45. Paulus, M., Jordanow, S., Millemann, J.A.: Adoption factors of digital services—a systematic literature review. Serv. Sci. **14**, 318–350 (2022). https://doi.org/10.1287/serv.2022.0305

46. Rauschnabel, P.A., Felix, R., Hinsch, C.: Augmented reality marketing: how mobile AR-apps can improve brands through inspiration. J. Retail. Consum. Serv. **49**, 43–53 (2019). https://doi.org/10.1016/j.jretconser.2019.03.004

47. Ceschin, F., Gaziulusoy, I.: Evolution of design for sustainability: from product design to design for system innovations and transitions. Des. Stud. **47**, 118–163 (2016). https://doi.org/10.1016/j.destud.2016.09.002

48. Dimoka, A., et al.: On the use of neurophysiological tools in IS research: developing a research agenda for NeuroIS. MIS Q. **36**, 679–702 (2012)

49. vom Brocke, J., Riedl, R., Léger, P.-M.: Application strategies for neuroscience in information systems design science research. J. Comput. Inf. Syst. **53**, 1–13 (2013)

50. Johnson, M., Barlow, R.: Defining the Phygital marketing advantage. JTAER **16**, 2365–2385 (2021). https://doi.org/10.3390/jtaer16060130

51. Song, H.K., Baek, E., Choo, H.J.: Try-on experience with augmented reality comforts your decision: focusing on the roles of immersion and psychological ownership. ITP. **33**, 1214–1234 (2019). https://doi.org/10.1108/ITP-02-2019-0092

52. Pierce, J.L., Kostova, T., Dirks, K.T.: The state of psychological ownership: integrating and extending a century of research. Rev. Gen. Psychol. **7**, 84–107 (2003)

53. Brengman, M., Willems, K., Van Kerrebroeck, H.: Can't touch this: the impact of augmented reality versus touch and non-touch interfaces on perceived ownership. Virtual Reality **23**, 269–280 (2019). https://doi.org/10.1007/s10055-018-0335-6

54. Hilken, T., De Ruyter, K., Chylinski, M., Mahr, D., Keeling, D.I.: Augmenting the eye of the beholder: exploring the strategic potential of augmented reality to enhance online service experiences. J. Acad. Mark. Sci. **45**, 884–905 (2017). https://doi.org/10.1007/s11747-017-0541-x

55. Parker, J.R., Lehmann, D.R., Xie, Y.: Decision comfort. J. Consum. Res. **43**, 113–133 (2016). https://doi.org/10.1093/jcr/ucw010

56. Beck, M., Crié, D.: I virtually try it … I want it ! Virtual fitting room: a tool to increase on-line and off-line exploratory behavior, patronage and purchase intentions. J. Retail. Consum. Serv. **40**, 279–286 (2018). https://doi.org/10.1016/j.jretconser.2016.08.006

# UXAR-CT – An Approach for Measuring UX for Mobile Augmented Reality Applications in Corporate Training

Stefan Graser[1]([✉]) [iD], Martin Schrepp[2] [iD], and Stephan Böhm[1] [iD]

[1] RheinMain University of Applied Sciences, Wiesbaden, Germany
{stefan.graser,stephan.boehm}@hs-rm.de
[2] SAP SE, Walldorf, Germany
martin.schrepp@sap.com

**Abstract.** Applying Mobile Augmented Reality (MAR) in a Corporate Training (CT) environment can improve the learning effectiveness of trainees. Therefore, a positive User Experience (UX) concerning the MAR application is crucial. To ensure this, the UX of MAR must be measured. However, hardly any standardized UX questionnaire for MAR can be found in the literature. This research is a two-study approach. The first quantitative study was conducted to evaluate the importance of UX quality aspects concerning MAR in CT. Based on this, a standardized UX questionnaire for MAR in CT (UXAR-CT) was developed. Therefore, suitable UX measurement items were selected by the researchers from a pool of 1500 measurement items referring to 60 UX questionnaires. Preliminary evaluation was conducted in a second quantitative study referring to MAR learning scenarios. Results show, that the UX quality aspects Dependability, Perspicuity, Usefulness, Efficiency, Clarity, and Value are important concerning the UX of MAR in CT. Based on these quality aspects, the UXAR-CT questionnaire was developed. Preliminary results concerning the item selection and validation are described.

**Keywords:** User Experience (UX) · UX Quality Aspects · (Mobile) Augmented Reality (MAR) · Corporate Training (CT)

## 1 Introduction

The technology Augmented Reality (AR) features three characteristics: (1) combining real and virtual, (2) being interactive in real-time, and (3) being registered in three dimensions. It is further defined as the enhancement of the real environment with digital, computer-generated content [3]. Due to technical progress in the last decades, mobile devices have developed further in terms of their performance [9]. Thus, modern AR applications are supported by the current generation of mobile devices, which is defined as Mobile Augmented Reality (MAR) [19]. This results in the widespread of AR technology in different application fields in daily life, such as education and training [14].

© The Author(s), under exclusive license to Springer Nature Switzerland AG 2024
J. Wei and G. Margetis (Eds.): HCII 2024, LNCS 14737, pp. 211–234, 2024.
https://doi.org/10.1007/978-3-031-60458-4_15

Among other application scenarios, the field of education and training in particular shows a high potential for improvement by MAR applications. This field can further be broken down into academic teaching and corporate training, where the latter refers to education and training within a corporate environment. Only a little research can be identified in the field of MAR in corporate training [14].

MAR can enhance both teaching and learning by creating an educational benefit. In particular, it is a new way to experience educational content. The technology helps students and trainees to capture content in a new way. Multimodality and interactivity improve learning activities by engaging and immersing students actively [4]. Moreover, the learning effectiveness and motivation can be enhanced by MAR [6,8].

However, innovations such as MAR create new interaction paradigms. Thus, the user experience (UX) differs in relation to the specific product or activity [33]. UX is defined as the person's subjective perception of a product, system, or service [38]. A positive UX is a critical success factor for developing, designing, and applying information and communication technology (ICT) applications [26]. Moreover, a good UX is related to improving the learning effectiveness using MAR [39]. To create a positive UX, it is thus important to understand the subjective impression of people using and interacting with MAR applications in a corporate training environment.

This paper is a two-study approach. We (1) determined the importance of UX quality aspects concerning MAR in Corporate Training (CT). For this, we have conducted a quantitative study evaluating the importance of existing UX quality aspects [35]. Based on this, we (2) developed a standardized UX questionnaire for MAR in CT (UXAR-CT). In a second study, the draft of the UXAR-CT questionnaire was applied to MAR-based learning scenarios in CT. The first results of this study are reported in this paper.

This article is structured as follows: Sect. 2 describes the theoretical foundation and related work concerning the concept of UX, UX Measurement, and UX questionnaires in relation to MAR. Section 3 shows the first quantitative study referring to the importance of UX quality aspects. Section 4 illustrates the first steps of the development and evaluation of the UXAR-CT questionnaire. A conclusion and outlook is given in Sect. 5.

## 2   Theoretical Foundation and Related Work

### 2.1   Concept of User Experience

UX is declared as a multidimensional construct consisting of different dimensions and aspects. The most commonly used definition of the term user experience (UX) is given by ISO 9241-210 (International Organization for Standardization, 2019) [38]. This norm defines UX as a "person's perceptions and responses that result from the use or anticipated use of a product, system or service". Thus, UX is in this understanding a purely subjective perception concerning certain qualities of a product (in the following, we also use the term product to refer to systems or services). This directly implies that there are no objective criteria to measure UX, users need to be asked about their experiences and different users may have different opinions about the UX of the same product. In addition, the UX of the product may be perceived as poor for one usage scenario, but good for another. This directly implies that UX is always relative to the target group and context of use.

But according to the definition above, UX covers not only the actual usage experience of a product but also the anticipated use [20,41], which refers to expectations towards a product that a person wants to use in the future but has not yet actually used. This is a point that differentiates UX from the concept of usability. Some studies show that expectations concerning future usage may even influence the subjective perception of the actual experience when users later actively start working with the product [25].

The ISO definition of UX cited above is quite abstract. It does not help much if the goal is to design a product that shows a good UX or to question how to measure the UX of a product. Therefore, several approaches were conducted to break down and define the construct of UX. In addition, some research work has aimed to consolidate quality aspects by analyzing their empirical as well as semantic similarity [13,15,16,18,35,46].

A common perspective is the distinction of UX into specific UX quality aspects [27,34,35]. This approach is also followed in many UX questionnaires that measure UX on distinct scales (for example, [7,21,23,24,36,44]). Such a UX quality aspect or scale of a UX questionnaire describes the subjective impression of users towards a semantically clearly described aspect of the interaction with a product, for example, efficiency, aesthetic appeal, ease of learning, or fun of use [35]. For this paper, we follow this approach of breaking UX down into a set of semantically clearly described quality aspects based on [35].

## 2.2   Importance of UX Quality Aspects

New products create new interaction paradigms. Hence, not all UX quality aspects are equally important for all products. Consider, for example, an application that is used once a year to do the tax declaration. We cannot expect a user to remember details from last year's usage. Thus, intuitive use is extremely important for such an application. Efficient data entry is less important since the application is used only once a year for a short period of time. For a business application that is used many hours during a workday (for example an ERP sales order application), things are different. Inefficient design, for example, the need to perform duplicate data entry or unnecessary clicks, really hurts in such scenarios and, thus, efficiency is extremely important. On the other hand, such applications are not expected to be used purely intuitively. Some sort of learning is usually required and accepted, thus intuitive use is nice but not mandatory.

Two studies on which we base our work, investigated the importance of 16 clearly described UX aspects (for example, efficiency, intuitive use, controllability, visual aesthetics, stimulation, or trust) for 15 common product categories (for example, webshops, new portals, social networks, messengers, word processing, spreadsheets, video conferencing) [35,45]. All quality aspects and their definitions are shown in the following Table 1.

**Table 1.** Consolidated UX Quality Aspects based on [35]

|      | UX Quality Aspect | Definition |
|------|-------------------|------------|
| (1)  | Perspicuity       | Is it easy to get familiar with the product and to learn how to use it? |
| (2)  | Efficiency        | Can users solve their tasks without unnecessary effort? Does the product react fast? |
| (3)  | Dependability     | Does the user feel in control of the interaction? Does the product react predictably and consistently to user commands? |
| (4)  | Usefulness        | Does using the product bring advantages to the user? Does using the product save time and effort? |
| (5)  | Intuitive Use     | Can the product be used immediately without any training or help? |
| (6)  | Adaptability      | Can the product be adapted to personal preferences or personal working styles? |
| (7)  | Novelty           | Is the design of the product creative? Does it catch the interest of users? |
| (8)  | Stimulation       | Is it exciting and motivating to use the product? Is it fun to use? |
| (9)  | Clarity           | Does the user interface of the product look ordered, tidy, and clear? |
| (10) | Quality of Content | Is the information provided by the product always actual and of good quality? |
| (11) | Immersion         | Does the user forget time and sink completely into the interaction with the product? |
| (12) | Aesthetics        | Does the product look beautiful and appealing? |
| (13) | Identity          | Does the product help the user to socialize and to present themselves positively to other people? |
| (14) | Loyalty           | Do people stick with the product even if there are alternative products for the same task? |
| (15) | Trust             | Do users think that their data is in safe hands and not misused to harm them? |
| (16) | Value             | Does the product design look professional and of high quality? |

Results showed clear differences in the collected importance ratings between different product categories. In a replication with Indonesian participants [31] the influence of the cultural background of the participants on the importance of UX quality aspects was investigated. Results showed that the importance ratings of the German and Indonesian participants were quite similar. Compared to interindividual preferences and the product categories the influence of the cultural background was rather small.

To sum up, the importance of UX quality aspects depends mainly on the product category and the main use cases of a product. Concerning the design of such products it is of course central to know which aspects of the interaction between product and user are the most important ones for the overall judgement of the UX quality. It makes sense to focus on these aspects during the design phase. In addition, this knowledge is a prerequisite for the development of questionnaires measuring the UX of users with a minimal number of items. In this context, our study tries to clarify the importance of common UX quality aspects for the relatively new field of mobile augmented reality applications.

### 2.3 Measuring User Experience via Standardized Questionnaires

To gather insights into the subjective impression of users, UX must be measured. Various methods to measure the UX can be found in scientific literature [1]. Not all measurement methods fit well to a given evaluation scenario [28]. In general, the evaluation goal of every method is to gather qualitative empirical data on the user's perception. It can be differentiated between objective and subjective methods. Objective evaluations gather analytical data, e.g., log files. In contrast, subjective methods collect self-reported data relying on the direct and independent feedback of the user. Self-reported data is one of the most important data sources as it gathers users' subjective impressions of the evaluation object. Thus, self-reported metrics are a popular method in Human-Computer Interaction. The most common way to collect self-reported data is through the application of standardized questionnaires that can be applied quickly, simply, and cost-effectively in almost every evaluation scenario [1,2].

In scientific literature, 40 established UX questionnaires can be found [33]. Typically, these questionnaires are based on a set of factors or quality aspects (as described in Sect. 2.2) breaking down the construct of UX. Often, these factors are measured by different items and scales. Moreover, the structure and qualities within the different questionnaires vary [13,15,16,18,33].

The most established and widely applied questionnaire is the User Experience Questionnaire (UEQ) [10] developed by [23]. The questionnaire consists of six UX quality aspects differentiated into pragmatic and hedonic properties based on the UX framework by [17,23]:

- **Attractiveness**: Overall impression of the product. Do users like or dislike it?
- **Perspicuity**: Is it easy to get familiar with the product and to learn how to use it?
- **Efficiency**: Can users solve their tasks without unnecessary effort? Does it react fast?
- **Dependability**: Does the user feel in control of the interaction? Is it secure and predictable?
- **Stimulation**: Is it exciting and motivating to use the product? Is it fun to use?

– **Novelty**: Is the design of the product creative? Does it catch the interest of users?

The different quality aspects are based on a 7-point Likert Scale using a semantic differential scale, i.e., pairs of terms with opposite meanings (e.g., good/bad). Further details on the UEQ can be found online (https://www.ueq-online.org/) [43]. The questionnaire aims to gather comprehensive insights into the subjective impression in relation to the interaction products.

Other UX questionnaires contain different quality aspects and, thus, pursue a different focus concerning the construct of UX. This is indicated by different scales, measurement items, or/and quality aspects. In fact, no questionnaire can cover all UX quality aspects as different products refer to different interaction paradigms. In research, it is a common way to combine different metrics to cover all relevant research objectives. However, this can lead to difficulties for the participants during the evaluation process due to the heterogeneity of the questionnaires. Against this background, [36] developed the User Experience Questionnaire Plus (UEQ+) as an extension of the UEQ. The UEQ+ is a measurement framework containing 16 UX aspects and their respective semantic differential scales. Each scale consists of four item pairs based on a 7-point Likert scale. The main goal of this approach is to provide an adjustable UX framework that can be applied to various products and application scenarios [36]. Detailed information on the UEQ+ can be found online (https://ueqplus.ueq-research.org/) [32].

Nevertheless, these metrics are holistic questionnaires without a specific focus. Thus, they can be applied to different products and application scenarios. However, the general applicability also means that particular quality aspects of specific application contexts are not captured. In the following, specific UX questionnaires referring to MAR are introduced.

## 2.4    Augmented Reality UX Questionnaires

Only a limited number of UX questionnaires specialized in immersive technology exist. Due to the focus of this study, UX questionnaires on Virtual Reality (VR) were not considered [37,40]. Based on our literature research, only the following three questionnaires related to MAR UX were found:

– (1) **Handheld Augmented Reality Usability Scale (HARUS)** [29,30]
– (2) **Augmented Reality Immersion (ARI) Questionnaire** [12]
– (3) **Customizable Interactions Questionnaire (CIQ)** [11]

These three questionnaires differ in their structures, characteristics, and focus. The questionnaires will be discussed in the following.

**Handheld Augmented Reality Usability Scale:** The Handheld Augmented Reality Usability Scale (HARUS) by [29,30] was developed in a five-step approach focusing on the usability of handheld AR devices. In particular, the

HARUS refers to ergonomic and perceptual handheld AR issues. The question-naire consists of the factors *Manipulability* referring to the ease of handling of the device and *Comprehensibility* concerning the ease of understanding the presented information. A mixture of eight positively and negatively formulated statements was assigned to each of the two factors based on a seven-point Likert scale (1 is "strongly disagree" and 7 is "strongly agree"). The evaluation procedure is similar to that of the SUS [5] computing a usability score from 0 to 100 [29,30].

**Augmented Reality Immersion Questionnaire:** The Augmented Reality Immersion Questionnaire (ARI) focuses on immersion in location-aware AR set-tings and was developed by [12]. Immersion refers to cognitive and emotional absorption while using interactive media such as AR. The questionnaire was developed and validated in a multi-step process resulting in the three factors *Engagement, Engrossment,* and *Total Immersion.* These factors were further divided into the six sub-factors *Interest, Usability, Emotional Attachment, Focus of Attention, Presence,* and *Flow.* A total of 21 items were based on a seven-point Likert scale [12].

**Customizable Interactions Questionnaire:** The Customizable Interactions Questionnaire (CIQ) developed by [11] measures the subjective UX with a focus on the quality of interaction with objects in AR scenarios. The questionnaire con-sists of the five factors *Quality of Interactions, Comfort, Assessment of Task Per-formance, Consistency with Expectation,* and *Quality of the Sensory Enhance-ments* referring to the user satisfaction. The metrics contain 17 items based on a five-point Likert scale [11].

## 2.5   Research Objective and Methodological Approach

Sects. 2.3 and 2.4 introduced generic as well as AR-specific UX questionnaires. Concerning the AR-specific UX questionnaires, the different focuses must be stated. Specifically, the factors of usability, immersion, and quality of interaction are evaluated. However, it is not clear whether and which factors are actually relevant for MAR UX. Moreover, there is only a small overlap with the UX quality aspects regarding a general perspective on UX (See Sect. 2.1 and 2.2, [35]). Thus, a lack of applicability for MAR in CT can be stated.

To sum up, on the one side, existing UX questionnaires refer to a general view without regard to a specific technology. For this, it remains unclear which UX quality aspects are relevant for MAR. On the other side, existing AR-specific questionnaires only cover certain subsets of the construct UX or technology-specific attributes of the technology AR, but not all relevant aspects. Moreover, no questionnaire refers to (M)AR in the application field of CT. Besides this, there is still a lack of common ground and understanding concerning the con-struct of UX among the existing questionnaires [13,16].

Against this background, we address the following research questions:

*RQ1: How important are the different UX quality aspects for MAR in corporate training?*

*RQ2: How can a standardized UX questionnaire be designed to evaluate the UX of MAR applications in corporate training?*

The methodological approach consists of two quantitative studies. The first study aimed to answer the first research question by evaluating the importance of the UX quality aspects for MAR in CT. Based on these results, we developed the User Experience Augmented Reality Corporate Training (UXAR-CT) questionnaire. In the second survey, we applied the developed UXAR-CT questionnaire to evaluate AR application scenarios in the field of corporate training addressing the second research question. The methodological approach is shown in the following Fig. 1:

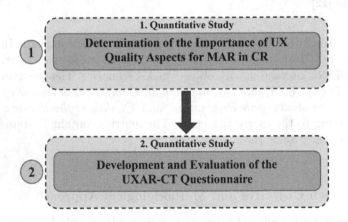

**Fig. 1.** Methodological Approach

Both studies are described in the following Sects. 3 and 4.

## 3    Quantitative Study 1: Determination of Important UX Quality Aspects

The main goal of the first study was to determine the importance of UX quality aspects concerning MAR in the field of CT. Therefore, a quantitative survey was conducted. Study participants were acquired by a paid online panel. Results were analyzed and the significance was evaluated by applying pairwise t-tests. In the following, the detailed approach and its results are shown.

## 3.1  Study Approach

**Data Collection and Sample.** The study was conducted in the German language. Data was collected by applying a quantitative online survey via an online panel. The sample includes people who can be assigned to the field of corporate training. The participants were asked to rate the importance of UX quality aspects referring to MAR in CT. The detailed structure of the survey is described in the following.

**Survey Structure.** The sample's participants were filtered by two aspects. Firstly, we screened potential participants based on their experience in industrial or handicraft environments. In particular, participants were asked if they have specific experience in (1) manual work in a craft company, (2) production and manufacturing in an industrial company, or (3) maintenance and repair in an industrial company. Secondly, we filtered based on their experience with CT. Only people who have completed or are currently completing training or advanced professional training, or who are instructors/trainers in a related activity, were permitted to participate.

The first part of the quantitative survey contains general questions referring to the work and knowledge about MAR. The technology MAR was explained in detail. Based on this, a video showing the CT scenario applying MAR was displayed to the participants. This ensures that all participants understand the application of MAR in a respective CP scenario. Afterward, a general explanation of UX quality aspects was given. We rely on the theoretical consolidation of UX quality aspects by [35]. UX quality aspects based on [35] were introduced with a general description as well as an explanatory example. We did not include all UX quality aspects but removed those considered irrelevant for MAR. More precisely, the aspects *(13) Identity*, *(14) Loyalty*, and *(15) Trust* (see Table 1) were excluded. The step was performed by the researchers. This results in a list of 13 UX quality aspects as shown in the following. The comprehensive list with its descriptive statements in relation to MAR in CT is illustrated in Appendix B.

- *(1) Efficiency - **EF***
- *(2) Perspicuity - **PE***
- *(3) Dependability - **DE***
- *(4) Usefulness - **US***
- *(5) Intuitive Use - **IU***
- *(6) Adaptability - **AD***
- *(7) Novelty - **NO***
- *(8) Stimulation - **ST***
- *(9) Clarity - **CL***
- *(10) Quality of Content - **QC***
- *(11) Immersion - **IM***
- *(12) Aesthetics - **AE***
- *(13) Value - **VA***

Based on this, participants had to rate the importance of each UX quality aspect in relation to the shown CT scenario. For the rating, we applied a five-point Likert scale (from *"not important at all"* to *"very important"*). An example of a described UX quality aspects *Efficiency* is shown in Appendix A. As the study was conducted in the German language, Appendix A shows a translated example.

Moreover, all participants had to choose the six most important as well as the six most unimportant UX quality aspects. Lastly, demographic data was asked. In the following, the results are shown.

## 3.2  Results

In this section, the results of the first quantitative study are discussed. Firstly, the demographic data in relation to the study participants is presented. Secondly, the evaluation results concerning the importance ratings of the UX quality aspects are shown. Thirdly, the significance testing based on pairwise t-tests is described. For significance testing, pairwise t-tests with a significance level of 5 percent ($\alpha = 0.05$) were performed.

**Demographics and Descriptive Results:** In the following, we present the demographic data of the study. As already described, data was collected via an online panel. The survey was started 242 times. With dropouts and screenouts, 121 participants completed the survey. Thus, a completion rate of 50 percent was reached. About three-quarters (75.20%) of the participants were male, whereas 23.96% were female. One participant declared to be diverse. Seven participants were younger than 25. In comparison, one participant was older than 64. The other age ranges in between were almost equally distributed. 21 participants were between 25 and 34 whereas 24 people were in the range between 45 and 54. Both ranges 35–44 and 55–64 have 34 participants.

Besides these aspects, we also queried some descriptive data. We first examined the position of the participants. Most participants (81) are employees without management responsibility, followed by 28 with status as heads of department. Two study participants were managing directors whereas seven people were instructors in their function. Secondly, the work experience was asked. 56 participants have experience in the craft sector. In comparison, 90 people declared to be experienced in the production of industry. Only 29 participants are working in the field of maintenance referring to the industry.

We thirdly conducted the experience concerning CT. Almost all study participants completed professional qualifications (114), whereas almost half (60) took part in further training. 13 people have already planned and performed further training courses. However, only four participants are instructors/trainers in their function.

Finally, we examined the knowledge and perception towards MAR. Thirty-eight participants already knew the technology MAR. Sixty-eight people had not heard about it whereas 15 were unsure. Additionally, most of the participants

(47) have no knowledge of MAR. In summary, 50 people knew little about MAR. 22 study participants stated that they had average knowledge. Only four people declared to have comprehensive knowledge.

Most companies (84) the participants work for have not applied MAR in any processes yet. Eighteen participants knew about its application in their company. Therefore, 21 companies have applied the technology in working processes and 17 companies use MAR for Corporate Training scenarios. Concerning the future potential, more than half of the participants (63) consider a potential for the application of MAR. In each case, 29 people declared that there is no potential or they are not sure about it.

Qualitative information from the survey shows that company size and processes are the key factors for MAR deployment. For small companies and work processes that are too specific, the implementation of MAR is perceived as not useful. The implementation costs exceed the actual benefit. To sum up, this clearly shows that the use of MAR is not yet widespread. Furthermore, the working environment and processes are crucial factors influencing the deployment status of MAR in CT.

**Overall Importance Ratings:** In Fig. 2, the overall importance ratings are illustrated. The Y-axis presents the gradation of the applied five-point Likert scale (from *"not important at all"–1* to *"very important"–5*). The X-axis shows the mean values for the evaluated UX quality aspects. The highest rated and thus most important aspect for MAR in CT is *Perspicuity* with an average score of 4.69 whereas the lowest rated one is *Aesthetics* with an average score of 3.17. Nevertheless, none of the quality aspects were rated as being not important (or < 3) on average. It can be shown that the quality aspects *Efficiency, Perspicuity, Dependability, Usefulness, Intuitive use, Adaptability, Stimulation, Clarity, Quality of Content*, and *Value* were rated as rather important to important. *Novelty, Immersion*, and *Aesthetics* were evaluated as neutral to rather important. The standard deviation ranges from 0.73 to 1.07 (see Fig. 2).

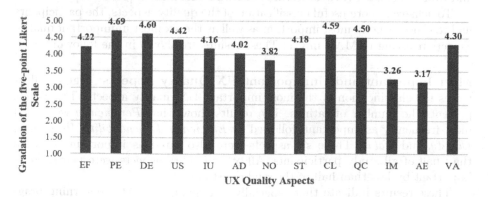

**Fig. 2.** Importance Rating of UX Quality Aspects Concerning MAR in CT

Furthermore, significance testing using pairwise t-tests was performed to determine statistically significant differences in the importance evaluation between the UX quality aspects. The different significance values are shown in Table 2.

**Table 2.** Significance Testing of Overall Ratings Using T-tests

|     | EF | PE | DE | US | IU | AD | NO | ST | CL | QC | IM | AE |
|-----|----|----|----|----|----|----|----|----|----|----|----|----|
| EF | – | | | | | | | | | | | |
| PE | 0.000 | – | | | | | | | | | | |
| DE | 0.000 | *0.102* | – | | | | | | | | | |
| US | 0.043 | 0.000 | 0.038 | – | | | | | | | | |
| IU | *0.309* | 0.000 | 0.000 | 0.003 | – | | | | | | | |
| AD | 0.019 | 0.000 | 0.000 | 0.000 | *0.128* | – | | | | | | |
| NO | 0.000 | 0.000 | 0.000 | 0.000 | 0.007 | *0.141* | – | | | | | |
| ST | *0.736* | 0.000 | 0.000 | 0.025 | *0.534* | 0.025 | 0.000 | – | | | | |
| CL | 0.000 | *0.149* | *0.889* | *0.066* | 0.000 | 0.000 | 0.000 | 0.000 | – | | | |
| QC | 0.004 | 0.013 | *0.166* | *0.304* | 0.000 | 0.000 | 0.000 | 0.000 | 0.217 | – | | |
| IM | 0.000 | 0.000 | 0.000 | 0.000 | 0.000 | 0.000 | 0.000 | 0.000 | 0.000 | 0.000 | – | |
| AE | 0.000 | 0.000 | 0.000 | 0.000 | 0.000 | 0.000 | 0.000 | 0.000 | 0.000 | 0.000 | *0.559* | – |
| VA | *0.474* | 0.000 | 0.000 | *0.183* | *0.091* | 0.00 | 0.00 | *0.245* | 0.000 | 0.010 | 0.000 | 0.000 |

In general, a significant difference can be indicated between most of the quality aspects. However, some values are above the significance threshold marked in bold and italic (see Table 2) indicating non-significant differences between quality aspects. These values range between 0.066 and 0.889. For the quality aspects in concern, it can be stated that mostly two pragmatic or two hedonic aspects are not significantly different, e.g., *Dependability* and *Perspicuity*. This indicates, that the UX quality aspects and their items as well as descriptions share some common characteristics. These are not always clearly distinctive from each other and overlaps exist. Previous research confirms this finding [18, 35, 45].

To achieve a more useful classification of the quality aspects, the participants had to choose the six most important as well as the six most unimportant quality aspects referring to MAR in CT. These results are shown in the following.

**Most Important and Unimportant UX Quality Aspects:** Figure 3 illustrates the classification of the most important UX quality aspects. The Y-axis presents the number of ratings. The results show, that *Perspicuity* was rated most frequently as important, followed by *Efficiency, Dependability, Usefulness, Clarity,* and *Value*. These six aspects were also rated as important by more than half of all study participants. All other quality aspects were perceived as important by less than half of the study participants.

These results indicate that especially UX quality aspects concerning pragmatic properties were perceived as important. This can be confirmed by considering the least important rated quality aspects as shown in Fig. 4. The least selected

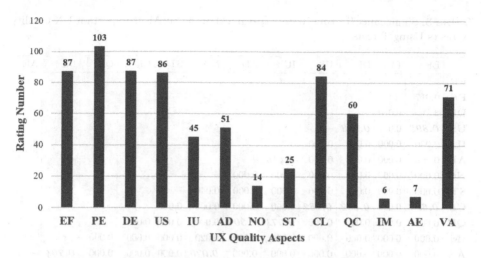

**Fig. 3.** Most Important UX Quality Aspects in relation to MAR in CT

quality aspects in relation to Fig. 3 were most frequently evaluated as unimportant (see Fig. 4). *Aesthetics* was rated least important followed by *Immersion*, *Novelty*, and *Stimulation*. All four quality aspects are of a hedonic quality. Lastly, *Intuitive Use* and *Adaptability* were considered as not important. Both aspects concerning a more pragmatic view show a gap between the four least important aspects. *Quality of Content* represents the middle in both Figures.

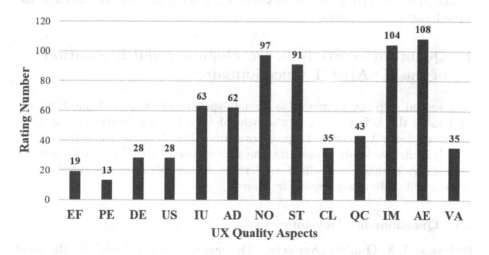

**Fig. 4.** Most Unimportant UX Quality Aspects in relation to MAR in CT

Lastly, we again performed pairwise t-tests conducting the significance of the six most important rated quality aspects. Table 3 illustrates the testing results.

**Table 3.** Significance Testing Results (p-values) of the Six Most Important UX Quality Aspects Using T-tests

|     | EF | PE | DE | US | IU | AD | NO | ST | CL | QC | IM | AE |
|-----|-----|-----|-----|-----|-----|-----|-----|-----|-----|-----|-----|-----|
| EF | – | | | | | | | | | | | |
| PE | 0.017 | – | | | | | | | | | | |
| DE | *1* | 0.010 | – | | | | | | | | | |
| US | *0.893* | 0.007 | *0.893* | – | | | | | | | | |
| IU | 0.000 | 0.000 | 0.000 | 0.000 | – | | | | | | | |
| AD | 0.000 | 0.000 | 0.000 | 0.000 | *0.416* | – | | | | | | |
| NO | 0.000 | 0.000 | 0.000 | 0.000 | 0.000 | 0.000 | – | | | | | |
| ST | 0.000 | 0.000 | 0.000 | 0.000 | 0.000 | 0.000 | 0.040 | – | | | | |
| CL | *0.687* | 0.003 | *0.682* | *0.782* | 0.000 | 0.000 | 0.000 | 0.000 | – | | | |
| QC | 0.000 | 0.000 | 0.000 | 0.000 | *0.074* | *0.307* | 0.000 | 0.000 | 0.004 | – | | |
| IM | 0.000 | 0.000 | 0.000 | 0.000 | 0.000 | 0.000 | 0.020 | 0.000 | 0.000 | 0.000 | – | |
| AE | 0.000 | 0.000 | 0.000 | 0.000 | 0.000 | 0.000 | *0.070* | 0.000 | 0.000 | 0.000 | *0.764* | – |
| VA | 0.041 | 0.000 | 0.035 | *0.054* | 0.001 | 0.019 | 0.000 | 0.000 | *0.079* | *0.180* | 0.000 | 0.000 |

To sum up, the importance rating is consistent. Results indicate that pragmatic qualities are more important than hedonic qualities concerning MAR in the field of CT. The six most important UX quality aspects are *Efficiency*, *Perspicuity*, *Dependability*, *Usefulness*, *Clarity*, and *Value*. Concerning results, it is important that the application of MAR in CT should be a simple, easy-to-understand, and value-adding experience for task completion.

Based on the first quantitative study, a further study was conducted as the second part of this approach.

## 4  Quantitative Study 2: Development and Evaluation of the UXAR-CT Questionnaire

In a second step, we developed a domain-specific, standardized questionnaire addressing the UX of MAR in the field of CT. The questionnaire was given the short name **UXAR-CT questionnaire**. The development relies on the first quantitative study concerning the importance of the UX quality aspects. Preliminary evaluation results were derived. In the following, the development process and preliminary results are shown.

### 4.1  Questionnaire Development

**Relevant UX Quality Aspects:** The questionnaire is based on the most important UX quality aspects. The researchers selected the most important UX quality aspects identified in the first study (see Fig. 3). In particular, the UX quality aspects *Efficiency*, *Perspicuity*, *Dependability*, *Usefulness*, and *Clarity* were selected. We only selected the first five UX quality aspects to keep the questionnaire as short and simple as possible.

**Item Pool Generation:** In the second step, measurement items for the selected UX quality aspects were identified. For this, the researchers analyzed an item pool with about 1500 measurement items referring to 60 UX questionnaires. Ten suitable items for each UX quality aspect were extracted. In the next step, the three authors of the study independently selected the five most representative items based on their expertise. Afterward, this item selection was merged and evaluated. Relevant items were identified based on the overlapping ratings of the researchers. Thus, the five relevant items for each factor of the questionnaire were derived. Finally, the formulation of the identified measurement items was adjusted referring to the object of investigation to create consistency among the questionnaire.

**Questionnaire Design:** In the third step, the questionnaire was set up. An introductory statement regarding MAR in CT was added and the aim of the questionnaire was described. In addition, an example of the applied scale was provided as an aid to completing the questionnaire. In the first section, participants have to fill in demographic information concerning age and gender. Moreover, the training occupation as well as the specific learning process on which MAR was applied was questioned. In the second section, the identified items were integrated in random order. The evaluation was based on a 7-point Likert scale. Moreover, a question regarding the overall satisfaction was applied. In the third section, two open questions were inserted. For this, participants were able to indicate what they liked the most and what should be improved. The measurement items are shown in Table 4 (items are ordered by their corresponding UX quality aspect).

## 4.2   Data Collection

**Augmented Reality Corporate Training Scenario:** For data collection, we collaborated with the Chamber of Crafts for Lower Franconia in Schweinfurt, Bavaria (Germany). This institution worked on the project *Augmented Reality in corporate training (ARihA)* (https://www.projekt-ariha.de/) funded by the German Federal Ministry of Education and Research (BMBF). The basic idea of the project was to integrate immersive learning and action-oriented teaching into the training of different handicraft trades at the Chamber of Crafts through the use of AR. Therefore, they aimed to enhance learning effectiveness and learning motivation by implementing innovative AR-based learning and teaching applications. In this context, five MAR CT applications were developed as part of the project. The respective CT scenarios of the developed AR applications are listed in the following:

- (1) Testing of electronic devices
- (2) Processing of high-grade steel and aluminum
- (3) Installation of locking and security systems
- (4) Troubleshooting and use of measurement devices on a car lighting wall
- (5) Changing the timing belt on a car engine

The presented scenarios are part of the apprenticeship in the electrical engineering, metal construction, and automotive engineering sectors. For the applications, head-mounted displays (Holo-Lens 2) and handheld devices (tablets and smartphones) were applied. The developed MAR applications of the different CT scenarios are regularly used in daily teaching activities. Figure 5 and 6 show selected examples of the developed applications. Comprehensive project descriptions can be found online (https://www.projekt-ariha.de/ergebnisse).

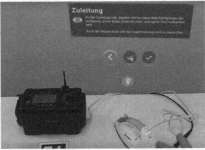

**Fig. 5.** Developed MAR Application for CT Scenario (1) at the Chamber of Crafts for Lower Franconia in Schweinfurt, Bavaria (Germany)

**Fig. 6.** Developed MAR Application for CT Scenario (4) at the Chamber of Crafts for Lower Franconia in Schweinfurt, Bavaria (Germany)

We applied the UXAR-CT questionnaire to evaluate the different scenarios.

**Preliminary Evaluation Results:** As part of the second study, we want to present preliminary evaluation results. We applied the UXAR-CT questionnaire among the five AR-based CT scenarios in the Chamber of Crafts. In particular, the survey was conducted in the respective scenarios in the period from December 2023 to January 2024. Data collection for the final selection of the best-fitting items is still running. We want to collect data from trainees using several MAR applications in real learning contexts. Thus, we rely on the course structure of our partner Chamber of Crafts for Lower Franconia. Since their MAR-based courses do only run in certain periods with a limited number of learners data collection will require a longer time. Thus, the amount of data collected so far is still small. However, we can present preliminary results based on the data of 20 trainees.

We aimed to analyze the correlation between the different measurement items of the respective UX quality aspects and the overall satisfaction item. In the context of questionnaire development, it is common to perform a principal component analysis (PCA) to check whether the selected items represent the respective construct. This means that all items essentially measure the same underlying construct or dimension [23].

Per scale, we did a PCA to check if the scales are uni-dimensional. Within a uni-dimensional scale, all items are closely related measuring the same. Responses to all items of one scale should normally correlate strongly with each other as the same construct is represented. In particular, the Kaiser-Guttmann criterion was applied. This provides an initial indication of the relationship between the overall satisfaction and the different UX quality aspects.

The following Table 4 shows the correlation of the constructed items with the overall satisfaction of the application (the corresponding question in the survey is "I am completely satisfied with the use of the application for learning and teaching processes."). Of course, the number of responses is not sufficient and thus the result must be interpreted with care. However, according to the Kaiser-Guttmann criterion (select the components with an eigenvalue $> 1$) four of our five scales could be best represented by a single component. The only exception was the scale *Perspicuity* where a second component was minimally above 1, but this may be caused by the small number of responses.

**Table 4.** Preliminary Results of the Correlation Analysis between the Overall Satisfaction and the Remaining Items

| UX Quality Aspects | Measurement Items | Correlation to Overall Satisfaction |
|---|---|---|
| **Efficiency** | | |
| **EF1** | Using the application for learning is practical | 0.70 |
| **EF2** | The application reduces the learning effort | 0.44 |
| **EF3** | The application helps me to learn faster | 0.78 |
| **EF4** | The application saves me time while learning | 0.59 |
| **EF5** | The application improves my learning and work performance | 0.49 |
| **Perspicuity** | | |
| **PE1** | It was clear from the start how I had to use the application for learning | −0.10 |
| **PE2** | It is easy/simple to learn how to use the application | 0.27 |

continued

**Table 4.** continued

| UX Quality Aspects | Measurement Items | Correlation to Overall Satisfaction |
|---|---|---|
| **PE3** | The information in the application is easy to understand | 0.11 |
| **PE4** | The operation of the application is logical | 0.16 |
| **PE5** | It is easy to navigate between individual parts of the application | 0.21 |
| **Dependability** | | |
| **DE1** | The behavior of the application always meets my expectations | 0.70 |
| **DE2** | I am confident in using the application at all times | 0.34 |
| **DE3** | The application is easy to control | 0.20 |
| **DE4** | I always have control over the application at every step | 0.63 |
| **DE5** | It is easy to find your way around the application | 0.49 |
| **DE6** | The application always responds comprehensible | 0.12 |
| **Usefulness** | | |
| **US1** | The application helps me to learn | 0.76 |
| **US2** | It is a great advantage to use the application when learning | 0.69 |
| **US3** | The application is useful for learning | 0.74 |
| **US4** | I find the application useful for learning | 0.81 |
| **US5** | The application fully meets my expectations | 0.48 |
| **Clarity** | | |
| **CL1** | The information on the display is clearly laid out | 0.46 |
| **CL2** | The information on the display is clear | 0.17 |
| **CL3** | The display of the application looks tidy | 0.37 |
| **CL4** | It's easy to find the information I need | 0.33 |

Data collection will continue for several months and a final result for the item selection based on a PCA will then be done if sufficient data are available.

## 5    Conclusion

In this article, we present a two-study approach referring to the UX of MAR in CT environment. We aimed to investigate the importance of UX quality aspects for MAR in CT and develop a domain-specific standardized UX questionnaire. Therefore, a quantitative survey based on a panel was conducted to evaluate the importance of UX quality aspects. Based on the evaluation results, the UXAR-CT questionnaire was developed. Preliminary results of the evaluation of the UXAR-CT questionnaire were presented.

## 5.1 Implications

To conclude, this article presents the most important UX quality aspects for MAR in CT. For this evaluation, this study relies on the common perspective introduced by [35] breaking down the UX into different quality aspects. This enables us to semantically clearly describe and distinguish the construct of UX. Considering results, the six quality aspects *Efficiency, Perspicuity, Dependability, Usefulness, Clarity,* and *Value* were evaluated as most important. Thus, pragmatic qualities clearly dominate.

Additionally, a domain-specific standardized UX questionnaire called **UXAR-CT** was developed. The development was based on the first study referring to the most important UX quality aspects. Thus, the UXAR-CT questionnaire relies on (1) an established theoretical foundation concerning UX and (2) covers the relevant UX concepts of MAR in CT. For item selection, the most common UX questionnaires and their measurement items were examined. Thus, this study provides a domain-specific UX MAR questionnaire based on common UX quality aspects identified as important. Preliminary evaluation results were conducted. However, the questionnaire further data is necessary to validate the respective scales of the questionnaire. Both research questions could be answered. In the following, a discussion and paper limitations are declared. Finally, an outlook for future research is discussed.

## 5.2 Discussion and Limitations

Referring to this research, some limitations must be drawn. Concerning the first study, it should be pointed out that this is a panel study. Secondly, we used a video for the presentation of the CT scenario. This means that the study participants did not encounter the real experience. Furthermore, the participants had only little knowledge about MAR.

In relation to the second study, the research context concerning MAR in CT must be mentioned. Up to now, the application of MAR in CT is not yet widespread. Gathering data is thus currently very difficult. As a consequence, only preliminary results can be presented in this study. For further evaluation and validation, more data will be gathered to confirm the uni-dimensionality of the scales. It is essential to ensure that each item measures the same within a construct.

Nevertheless, it can be stated that the questionnaire development was done by UX experts. Moreover, the construction relies on a comprehensive collection of UX questionnaires and items.

## 5.3    Outlook and Future Research

For future research, we plan to conduct a longitudinal study for the validation of the UXAR-CT questionnaire. Therefore, the questionnaire is regularly applied in the respective AR-based CT scenarios at the Chamber of Crafts to gather sufficient data for validation. The main objective is to validate the questionnaire in order to present a reliable and valid UX metric referring to MAR in CT. This further contributes to the existing lack of research in this field as we will provide a standardized UX questionnaire for MAR in CT based on a common theoretical foundation.

Furthermore, an extension of the developed UXAR-CT questionnaire should be considered. Firstly, the inclusion of further pragmatic UX quality aspects rated as imported but not being included, e.g., **Value**, should be discussed. Secondly, the extent to which UX quality aspects concerning hedonic properties must also be addressed. Even though hedonic aspects were considered rather unimportant, previous research confirms a relationship between hedonic and pragmatic qualities [22,42]. Thus, the expansion and inclusion of hedonic components should be investigated. Thirdly, the consideration of (M)AR-specific qualities regarding the UX should be discussed. Lastly, the topic of GenAI should be taken into account as it shows high potential for further UX research [13,16]. For this, GenAI could be integrated into the UX evaluation process to enhance assessment and results. The integration of GenAI could therefore be useful for the development and application of UX questionnaires.

However, as UX is a multidimensional construct, there is still a lack of common understanding among UX measurements. No questionnaire exists that refers to MAR considering the most important UX quality aspects based on a common systematization. Thus, this research is the first to introduce a UX metric based on the most important quality aspects of MAR in CT. In this article, we present the *UXAR-CT questionnaire* as a domain-specific quantitative UX metric for MAR in CT.

**Acknowledgement.** We would like to express special thanks to our partner the Chamber of Crafts for Lower Franconia in Schweinfurt, Bavaria (Germany) supporting our research.

## A    Exemplarily description of the UX quality aspect Efficiency translated in English

### Efficiency

Description of the UX Quality Aspects:
**Subjective impression of the user who can complete the task without unnecessary effort.**

**How important is it to be able to carry out work and learning processes with mobile augmented reality and not have any unnecessary effort?**

Assess the importance.

| very unimportant | rather unimportant | neither | rather important | very important | No estimation possible |

# B    Statements of the UX Quality Aspects from the Quantitative Study

| UX Quality Aspect | Statement in relation to MAR in CT |
|---|---|
| Efficiency | How important is it to be able to carry out work and learning processes with Mobile Augmented Reality and not have any unnecessary effort? |
| Perspicuity | How important is it that the Mobile Augmented Reality application is easy to learn how to use? |
| Dependability | How important is it that the interaction and commands are consistent and controllable while using the Mobile Augmented Reality application? |
| Usefulness | How important is it that you save time and are more productive in work and learning processes by using Mobile Augmented Reality? |
| Intuitive use | How important is it that you can use the Mobile Augmented Reality application immediately without training or help? |
| Adaptability | How important is it that you can customize and individualize the mobile augmented reality application to your personal preferences? |
| Novelty | How important is it that the innovative Mobile Augmented Reality application is creative and arouses my interest in using it? |
| Stimulation | How important is it that the use of the Mobile Augmented Reality application is motivating, exciting, and fun? |
| Clarity | How important is it that the user interface of the Mobile Augmented Reality application is orderly, tidy, and clear? |
| Quality of Content | How important is it that the information visualized and shown by the Mobile Augmented Reality application about the working and learning process is up-to-date, well presented, and interesting? |
| Immersion | How important is it that while using the Mobile Augmented Reality application you forget about the time while performing the work or learning process and get completely absorbed in the interaction? |
| Aesthetics | How important is it that the Mobile Augmented Reality application looks beautiful and appealing? |
| Value | How important is it that the Mobile Augmented Reality application is professionally designed and of high quality? |

# References

1. Albert, W.B., Tullis, T.T.: Measuring the User Experience. Collecting, Analyzing, and Presenting UX Metrics. Morgan Kaufmann (2022)
2. Assila, A., de Oliveira, K.M., Ezzedine, H.: Standardized usability questionnaires: features and quality focus. Comput. Sci. Inf. Technol. **6** (2016). https://api.semanticscholar.org/CorpusID:54726201
3. Azuma, R.T.: A survey of augmented reality. Presence Teleoperators Virtual Environ. **6**, 355–385 (1997)
4. Billinghurst, M., Duenser, A.: Augmented reality in the classroom. Computer **45**(7), 56–63 (2012). https://doi.org/10.1109/MC.2012.111
5. Brooke, J.: SUS: a quick and dirty usability scale. Usability Eval. Ind. **189**(194), 4–7 (1995)
6. Chang, Y.S., Hu, K.J., Chiang, C.W., Lugmayr, A.: Applying mobile augmented reality (AR) to teach interior design students in layout plans: evaluation of learning effectiveness based on the arcs model of learning motivation theory. Sensors **20**(1), 105 (2020) https://doi.org/10.3390/s20010105, https://www.mdpi.com/1424-8220/20/1/105
7. Chin, J.P., Diehl, V.A., Norman, K.L.: Development of an instrument measuring user satisfaction of the human-computer interface. In: Proceedings of the SIGCHI Conference on Human Factors in Computing Systems, pp. 213–218 (1988)
8. Criollo-C, S., Abad-Vásquez, D., Martic-Nieto, M., Velásquez-G, F.A., Pérez-Medina, J.L., Luján-Mora, S.: Towards a new learning experience through a mobile application with augmented reality in engineering education. Appl. Sci. **11**(11), 4921 (2021). https://www.mdpi.com/2076-3417/11/11/4921
9. Dirin, A., Laine, T.: User experience in mobile augmented reality: emotions, challenges, opportunities and best practices. Computers **7**, 33 (2018). https://doi.org/10.3390/computers7020033
10. Díaz-Oreiro, I., López, G., Quesada, L., Guerrero, L.A.: Standardized questionnaires for user experience evaluation: a systematic literature review. Proceedings **31**, 14 (2019).https://doi.org/10.3390/proceedings2019031014
11. Gao, M., Boehm-Davis, D.: Development of a customizable interactions questionnaire (CIQ) for evaluating interactions with objects in augmented/virtual reality. Virtual Reality **27**, 1–18 (2022).https://doi.org/10.1007/s10055-022-00678-8
12. Georgiou, Y., Kyza, E.A.: The development and validation of the ARI questionnaire: an instrument for measuring immersion in location-based augmented reality settings. Int. J. Hum Comput. Stud. **98**, 24–37 (2017). https://doi.org/10.1016/j.ijhcs.2016.09.014
13. Graser, S., Böhm, S.: Quantifying user experience through self-reporting questionnaires: a systematic analysis of the sentence similarity between the items of the measurement approaches. In: Stephanidis, C., Antona, M., Ntoa, S., Salvendy, G. (eds.) HCI International 2023 - Late Breaking Posters, pp. 138–145. Springer Nature Switzerland, Cham (2024). https://doi.org/10.1007/978-3-031-49212-9_19
14. Graser, S., Böhm, S.: A systematic literature review on technology acceptance research on augmented reality in the field of training and education. In: CENTRIC 2022, The Fifteenth International Conference on Advances in Human-oriented and Personalized Mechanisms, Technologies, and Services, pp. 20–22 (2022)
15. Graser, S., Böhm, S.: Applying augmented SBERT and BERTopic in UX research: a sentence similarity and topic modeling approach to analyzing items from multiple questionnaires. In: Proceedings of the IWEMB 2023, Seventh International Workshop on Entrepreneurship, Electronic, and Mobile Business (2023)

16. Graser, S., Böhm, S., Schrepp, M.: Using chatGPT-4 for the identification of common UX factors within a pool of measurement items from established UX questionnaires. In: CENTRIC 2023, The Sixteenth International Conference on Advances in Human-oriented and Personalized Mechanisms, Technologies, and Services (2023)

17. Hassenzahl, M.: The Thing and I: Understanding the Relationship Between User and Product, pp. 31–42. Springer Netherlands, Dordrecht (2004).https://doi.org/10.1007/1-4020-2967-5_4

18. Hinderks, A., Winter, D., Schrepp, M., Thomaschewski, J.: Applicability of user experience and usability questionnaires. J. Univers. Comput. Sci. **25**, 1717–1735 (2019). https://api.semanticscholar.org/CorpusID:210937088

19. Irshad, S., Rambli, D.R.A.: Advances in mobile augmented reality from user experience perspective: a review of studies. In: International Visual Informatics Conference (2017)

20. Karapanos, E., Zimmerman, J., Forlizzi, J., Martens, J.B.: User experience over time: an initial framework. In: Proceedings of the SIGCHI Conference on Human Factors in Computing Systems, pp. 729–738 (2009)

21. Kirakowski, J., Corbett, M., Sumi, M.: The software usability measurement inventory. Br. J. Educ. Technol. **24**(3), 210–2 (1993)

22. Kuroso, M., Kashimura, K.: Apparent usability vs. inherent usability, chi'95 conference companion. In: Conference on Human Factors in Computing Systems, Denver, Colorado, pp. 292–293 (1995)

23. Laugwitz, B., Held, T., Schrepp, M.: Construction and evaluation of a user experience questionnaire. In: Holzinger, A. (ed.) HCI and Usability for Education and Work, pp. 63–76. Springer, Berlin Heidelberg, Berlin, Heidelberg (2008)

24. Lin, H.X., Choong, Y.Y., Salvendy, G.: A proposed index of usability: a method for comparing the relative usability of different software systems. Behav. Inf. Technol. **16**(4–5), 267–277 (1997)

25. Raita, E., Oulasvirta, A.: Too good to be bad: favorable product expectations boost subjective usability ratings. Interact. Comput. **23**(4), 363–371 (2011)

26. Rauschenberger, M., Schrepp, M., Cota, M.P., Olschner, S., Thomaschewski, J.: Efficient measurement of the user experience of interactive products. How to use the user experience questionnaire (UEQ).example: Spanish language version. Int. J. Interact. Multim. Artif. Intell. **2**, 39–45 (2013)

27. Rogers, Y., Sharp, H., Preece, J.: Interaction Design-Beyond Human-Computer Interaction Wiley, 2002. Google Scholar Google Scholar Digital Library Digital Library (2002)

28. Rohrer, C.: When to use which user-experience research methods (2022). https://www.nngroup.com/articles/which-ux-research-methods/. retrieved: 10/2023

29. Santos, M.E.C., Polvi, J., Taketomi, T., Yamamoto, G., Sandor, C., Kato, H.: Toward standard usability questionnaires for handheld augmented reality. IEEE Comput. Graphics Appl. **35**(5), 66–75 (2015). https://doi.org/10.1109/MCG.2015.94

30. Santos, M.E.C., Taketomi, T., Sandor, C., Polvi, J., Yamamoto, G., Kato, H.: A usability scale for handheld augmented reality. In: VRST '14, Association for Computing Machinery, New York, NY, USA (2014). https://doi.org/10.1145/2671015.2671019

31. Santoso, H.B., Schrepp, M.: The impact of culture and product on the subjective importance of user experience aspects. Heliyon **5**, e02434 (2019). https://api.semanticscholar.org/CorpusID:202579259

32. Schrepp, M.: UEQ+ a modular extension of the user experience questionnaire (2019). http://www.ueqplus.ueq-research.org/. retrieved: 10/2023

33. Schrepp, M.: A comparison of UX questionnaires - what is their underlying concept of user experience? In: Hansen, C., Nürnberger, A., Preim, B. (eds.) Mensch und Computer 2020 - Workshopband. Gesellschaft für Informatik e.V., Bonn (2020). https://doi.org/10.18420/muc2020-ws105-236 Titel anhand dieser DOI in Citavi-Projekt übernehmen
34. Schrepp, M.: User Experience Questionnaires: How to use questionnaires to measure the user experience of your products? KDP, ISBN-13: 979-8736459766 Titel anhand dieser ISBN in Citavi-Projekt übernehmen (2021)
35. Schrepp, M., et al.: On the importance of UX quality aspects for different product categories. Int. J. Interact. Multimedia Artif. Intell. **8**, 1 (2023). https://doi.org/10.9781/ijimai.2023.03.001
36. Schrepp, M., Thomaschewski, J.: Design and validation of a framework for the creation of user experience questionnaires. Int. J. Interact. Multimedia Artif. Intell. **InPress**, 1 (2019). https://doi.org/10.9781/ijimai.2019.06.006
37. Somrak, A., Pogačnik, M., Guna, J.: Suitability and comparison of questionnaires assessing virtual reality-induced symptoms and effects and user experience in virtual environments. Sensors **21**(4), 1185 (2021).https://doi.org/10.3390/s21041185
38. for Standardization 9241-210:2019, I.O.: Ergonomics of human-system interaction - Part 210: Human-centred design for interactive systems. ISO - International Organization for Standardization (2019)
39. Subandi, Joniriadi, Syahidi, A.A., Mohamed, A.: Mobile augmented reality application with multi-interaction for learning solutions on the topic of computer network devices (effectiveness, interface, and experience design). In: 2020 Third International Conference on Vocational Education and Electrical Engineering (ICVEE), pp. 1–6 (2020).https://doi.org/10.1109/ICVEE50212.2020.9243292
40. Tcha-Tokey, K., Loup-Escande, E., Christmann, O., Richir, S.: A questionnaire to measure the user experience in immersive virtual environments (2016). https://doi.org/10.1145/2927929.2927955
41. Thüring, M., Mahlke, S.: Usability, aesthetics and emotions in human-technology interaction. Int. J. Psychol. **42**(4), 253–264 (2007)
42. Tractinsky, N.: Aesthetics and apparent usability: empirically assessing cultural and methodological issues. In: Proceedings of the ACM SIGCHI Conference on Human Factors in Computing Systems, pp. 115–122 (1997)
43. UEQ, T.: UEQ user experience questionnaire (2018). https://www.ueq-online.org/. retrieved: 10/2023
44. Willumeit, H., Gediga, G., Hamborg, K.C.: IsometricsI: Ein verfahren zur formativen evaluation von software nach iso 9241/10. Ergonomie und Informatik **27**, 5–12 (1996)
45. Winter, D., Hinderks, A., Schrepp, M., Thomaschewski, J.: Welche ux faktoren sind für mein produkt wichtig? Mensch und Computer 2017-Usability Professionals (2017)
46. Winter, D., Schrepp, M., Thomaschewski, J.: Faktoren der User Experience: Systematische Übersicht über produktrelevante UX-Qualitätsaspekte, pp. 33–41. De Gruyter, Berlin, München, Boston (2015).https://doi.org/10.1515/9783110443882-005

# Augmented Astronomy for Science Teaching and Learning

Leonor Huerta-Cancino[1] and Jhon Alé-Silva[2]

[1] University of Santiago, Santiago, Chile
leonor.huerta@usach.cl
[2] University of Chile, Santiago, Chile
jhon.ale@ug.uchile.cl

**Abstract.** Often, students' 'prior ideas' and 'alternative conceptions' about natural phenomena do not align with established scientific models in science education. In the field of astronomy, some of these ideas and conceptions are ingrained from an early age and persist over the years even after receiving formal instruction, highlighting the urgent need to design resources and activities to enhance scientific literacy. In this regard, Extended Reality (XR) emerges as an easily accessible technology with broad applications for astronomy education, making it a useful tool with the potential to address this issue. From this perspective, this study aims to present the design and preliminary evaluation of eight Augmented Reality (AR) educational resources focused on addressing reported alternative conceptions during the learning and teaching of astronomy. Through a methodology based on Educational Design Research, we developed and preliminarily evaluated these astronomy AR resources through simple activities with primary and secondary school students. The evaluation results contributed to improving the software, providing students with access to rigorous scientific content focused on overcoming alternative conceptions in astronomy and tailored to their needs.

**Keywords:** Extended Reality · Earth and Universe Sciences · Alternative Conceptions

## 1 Introduction

In its current sense, a student is said to be scientifically literate when "willing to engage in discourse about science and technology." This willingness implies a critical commitment to the ideas and concepts of science and technology based on science [1, 2]. When students enter the classroom, they bring their own experiences and conceptions about natural phenomena, which do not always align with established scientific models. These pre-existing conceptions, known in the literature as "preconceptions" or "alternative conceptions," tend to persist even after formal instruction [3].

In the field of astronomy, various alternative conceptions have been identified: for example, that the Earth is closer to the Sun in summer and farther in winter, the scales of distances and relative sizes of planets and the Sun, the orbits of planets and comets in the Solar System, that the Moon emits its own light, and the temperatures of stars based on their color, etc. [3]. Since these conceptions take root from an early age and tend to endure, it is imperative to create educational resources that contribute to scientific literacy [3]. The curricular integration of technology [4, 5], particularly Extended Reality (XR), plays a crucial role in improving instruction, motivation, and academic performance of students [6, 7]. Experiences in science education have also reported these benefits for students [8, 9].

Despite its benefits, there are still ongoing challenges in balancing the visual richness of XR's 3D models with the precision of scientific models [10–12]. Additionally, evidence indicates that natural science teachers seldom incorporate these technologies into their classrooms, and when they do, they often employ less effective strategies for teaching and learning [13, 14].

Furthermore, in the specific context of astronomy education with XR, a trend has been observed in most studies not to address alternative conceptions in their designs and developments. Additionally, these studies tend to focus exclusively on phenomena related to planetary movements and eclipse formation, as evidenced in previous research [11, 15–21].

Considering these backgrounds, the study aimed to design and evaluate Augmented Reality educational resources while safeguarding their scientific accuracy, starting from students' astronomical alternative conceptions.

## 2 Related Work

### 2.1 Alternative Conceptions in Astronomy Education

Since 1970s, a significant number of research have been carried out on students' ideas or knowledge about various natural phenomena, calling them prior ideas, misconceptions, preconceptions, pre-instructional ideas, alternative conceptions, among others [22, 23]. In this context, it will be understood that alternative conceptions correspond to student's mental representations of the natural world that differ from current scientific knowledge (hence the name "alternatives"), whether or not they were prior to specific school action [3].

According to [24], to improve students learning, it is necessary to identify student's alternative conceptions about some content (for example, astronomical concepts and topics), analyze how these alternative conceptions influence learning process, facilitating or limiting it, and with this information design a learning strategy that considers these alternative conceptions and facilitates a conceptual change. This is important because several studies have shown that a strong feature of alternative conceptions is their persistence [25–28]. Students maintain certain alternative conceptions even after years of schooling: "they are persistent, that is, they are not easily modified by traditional science teaching, even when the instruction is repeated" [29]. In other words, students do not totally get rid of their alternative conceptions, but rather add (or discriminate) meanings to them [30].

Regarding primary and high school student's alternative conceptions on astronomy, research has mostly reported results for topics such as seasons, Moon phases, eclipses, and day and night. A fairly well-known result corresponds to the majority alternative conception among students that seasons are caused by Earth's distance from the Sun: in summer Earth is closer to the Sun, and in winter it is farthest [31–36].

To [37], students must be able to visualize the movement of Earth around the Sun and the Moon around Earth in order to form a coherent scientific explanation of lunar phases. To achieve this, students must understand the relative sizes of Earth, Sun, and Moon and the distances between these bodies. However, even when students learn accurate knowledge about astronomical phenomena, "spatial thinking skills are needed for the student to create accurate mental models of complex phenomena that are too vast to see" [37].

Spatial thinking skills in astronomy education helps to understand locations, distances and sizes of different astronomical objects. "Challenging science topics, such as the cause of moon phases, need special emphasis on spatial relationships, perspectives, and pathways for students to truly visualize, grasp, and understand" [38, 39].

Using low cost materials, students learn to make their own scale models of the solar system in schools: scale models of the size of the planets and the Sun, and scale models of the distances between them. At school, both 2D and 3D scale models can be created with some ease: 2D scale models are drawings made by students representing the distances or relative sizes of the planets and the sun. The relative sizes of the planets and the sun are not well represented in 2D, and to create 3D scale models, students generally use plasticine or various spherical objects (such as balls, fruits, seeds, etc.). Nevertheless, student-made scale models have the disadvantage of being static. Only in the case of 3D models, students would have the opportunity to explore movements and relative positions, but with the difficulties presented by manipulating objects made with low-cost materials. In this context, the development of spatial thinking skills is hindered as it requires students to manipulate objects built to scale with low-cost materials.

On the other hand, with the development of digital technologies, the availability of digital objects for education (such as images, videos, interactive simulations, applets, educational software, among others) diversified. Digital technologies facilitate access to 3D models and Extended Realities (XR) objects.

## 2.2 Extended Reality for Teaching and Learning

Extended Realities (XR) encompass a broad and complex set of technologies that give rise to Augmented Reality (AR), Virtual Reality (VR), and, more recently, Mixed Realities (MR), each with varying levels of immersion in real and virtual environments [40]. In general terms, several studies have emphasized that XR can significantly contribute to improving students' interest and motivation in their learning process, enhancing their imagination, improving the visualization of abstract concepts and models, fostering problem-solving skills, and improving academic success [41–44].

Specifically, AR focuses on visualizing three-dimensional objects through the camera of mobile devices such as smartphones, tablets, iPhones & iPads, to blend them with the physical environment. Various studies indicate that AR, when applied from a socio constructivist perspective, contributes to a better understanding of abstract concepts and models [44–47], promotes collaboration, innovation, and creativity [48], optimizes teachers' performance [49, 50], facilitates the construction of safe learning environments [51], and increases attention, combining motivational and positive attitudinal aspects

[44, 52]. Additionally, when combined with strategies like gaming, it proves effective in enhancing learning processes [51].

On the other hand, VR focuses on presenting immersive and entirely virtual scenarios through the use of headsets. Studies indicate that VR provides students with the opportunity to learn meaningfully, explore solutions, actively participate in the process, develop empathy, improve creativity, and collaborate with peers through solving authentic problems [53]. It can also enhance learning outcomes, increase engagement, and generate positive emotions [54].

MR environments integrate elements of AR with VR to generate a combined digital and physical environment. MR technologies are less explored and offer promising opportunities for interactivity [55]. Their effectiveness has been analyzed in terms of rapid reading [56], medical education [57], biology [58], and mathematics education [59].

As explained, the combination of XR technologies with innovative approaches has the potential to transform the way teaching and learning are conducted, stimulating students' curiosity and participation in various disciplines and knowledge areas, highlighting their importance for current and future research.

## 2.3   Extended Reality for Astronomy Education

In the field of astronomical education, Extended Reality (XR) technologies have emerged as exceptional tools to enrich the teaching and learning process, providing diverse pedagogical opportunities.

Augmented Reality (AR) has been the subject of research highlighting its multiple potentialities to support and enhance educational processes in astronomy. Studies indicate that AR can help eradicate misconceptions and increase interest in specific topics, such as eclipses and characteristics of the solar system [11]. Moreover, its effectiveness has been demonstrated in detailed observation of planets, satellites, and stars, using the senses [60], improving astronomical observation through representations on the armillary sphere [61], and facilitating the understanding of phenomena such as planetary movements and eclipses [15–21]. Additionally, AR has proven to be an effective tool for recording the apparent path of the Sun, allowing the combination of situated learning with spatial cognition [62]. Its application promotes collaboration and communication during the resolution of astronomical problems [63], and enhances students' astronomical performance and interest compared to traditional strategies [64, 65]. Direct interaction with celestial objects through AR turns learning into an exploration and knowledge-building process highly accepted by students, positively influencing their cognitive process [66, 67].

Virtual Reality (VR) also stands out as a valuable pedagogical tool for the teaching and learning of astronomy. Through the use of virtual laboratories, VR allows students to observe in detail the features of geographical objects [68], as well as artificial satellites and their assemblies, launches, and movements in orbit [69]. Its capacity to enhance the understanding of various scientific concepts, such as thermal radiation balance, seismic waves, the Earth's internal layers, ocean movements, and specific features of the planets in the solar system, has been evidenced [70]. Research also indicates that VR significantly contributes to improving argumentation quality and critical thinking skills in astronomical education [71]. Its facilitating role for collaborative work during problem-solving, enhancing interaction and collaboration among students, has been highlighted [63]. Furthermore, VR-centered games on astronomical themes have been shown to motivate students to explore historical aspects of astronomy, such as space missions to the Moon [72].

Although Mixed Reality (MR) is a technology in an earlier stage of exploration, pioneering research suggests that it can have a positive impact on fostering collaborative learning in astronomical education [73]. MR, by providing immersive and collaborative experiences, opens intriguing perspectives to enrich astronomy teaching.

The three emerging XR technologies offer a range of opportunities to support astronomical education, providing more immersive, interactive, and collaborative experiences that can significantly enhance students' learning processes.

The novelty and significant contributions of the following study lie in the design and evaluation of educational resources that leverage the learning opportunities of XR for astronomy education while safeguarding scientific accuracy through a design process that starts from less explored astronomical alternative conceptions in current scientific research. In focusing on alternative conceptions, our work contributes to advancing the field by proposing a pedagogical model more aligned with educational needs.

## 3   Method

### 3.1   Design-Based Educational Research

This study adopts a Design-Based Educational Research approach [74–77]. A methodological approach is employed based on cycles of design, implementation, analysis, and redesign. This highly flexible approach does not adhere to a specific educational theory or tool during any phase of implementation [77–79].

- In our work, we have established four strategic phases:

  1 Initial Phase: We laid the foundations and conceptual bases supporting the design of three-dimensional (3D) representations of scientific models for astronomy education. This step is essential to ground subsequent decisions in terms of designing and developing Extended Reality (XR) educational resources, specifically Augmented Reality (AR) educational resources.

  2 Design Phase: Once the foundations were set, we delved into the design phase of AR educational resources, initially constructing paper prototypes. This stage involved materializing identified preliminary ideas as a starting point for the development of each design.

  3 Implementation Phase: The third phase encompassed the development and implementation of simple educational activities integrating the use of previously designed AR educational resources. This stage allowed us to evaluate the feasibility of the prototypes in a real educational environment, contributing to the iteration of the design.

  4 Evaluation Phase: Subsequently, during the evaluation phase, analyses of the results obtained during implementation were conducted. Based on these evaluations, the AR educational resources underwent redesign, refining their structure and content to enhance their educational purpose.

Together, this design approach not only provides a robust methodological framework but also underscores the importance of flexibility and adaptability in design-based educational research, allowing continuous adjustments in response to changing dynamics in the educational environment.

Considering the described stages, we developed 8 open and accessible AR educational resources that are not only free but also address alternative conceptions about astronomy that have received limited attention in the specialized scientific literature.

The creation of 3D models was carried out using the specialized software Blender 4.0.1, leveraging graphic textures of planets and dwarf planets available on NASA's 3D websites. Our project is hosted on Git and GitHub, facilitating not only development management but also promoting transparency and collaboration. In the field of AR, we utilized engines that leverage ARCore's "ground recognition" and HTML5 components of Model-Viewer, both developed by Google.

The implementation of AR was done using the technology called "AR-web" This technology does not require downloading and installing mobile applications (apps). It works by opening a website in the mobile device's browser, such as smartphones or tablets, facilitating access and use. Upon accessing the website, users simply need to tap the "View in Augmented Reality" button, activating the device's camera, enabling "ground recognition," and displaying the 3D object in the user's environment, allowing them to adjust it as needed.

## 4 Results

### 4.1 Augmented Reality Astronomy Resources

We have taken into account various alternative conceptions about astronomy for the designs of Augmented Reality (AR) resources. Below, we will describe the resources in their final version after the evaluations carried out.

In Fig. 1, a 3D model presents the scaled sizes of the sun and planets. The representation is rigorous in depicting the diameters and the textures used for each of the surfaces. The planets are ordered from the smallest (Mercury) to the largest (Jupiter). Additionally, the textures allow observation of some surface features of each planet (e.g., Olympus Mons and the ice caps of Mars), prompting geological questions about their structure and exterior composition.

In Fig. 2, a 3D model displays the scale distances of the planets in the Solar System on the same plane (aligned), with the Sun as a reference. The representation is rigorous in depicting each planet's average distance from the Sun. Planets are ordered from the nearest to the Sun (Mercury) to the farthest from the Sun (Neptune). Furthermore, all planets have a size with an equal diameter, while the Sun is slightly larger to distinguish it from the rest. None of the sizes are to scale. The models' textures are simple representations of the colors of their surfaces and do not allow observation of specific geological features.

Figure 3 presents a 3D model of the Solar System, depicting the movements of the planets, the asteroid belt, and the Kuiper belt on the same plane. The representation does not consider the size scales of planets and the Sun, nor the distance scales between

**Fig. 1.** Image depicting planets and the Sun in Augmented Reality, with scaled sizes according to diameters and textures. https://universopantagina.cl/escaladiametros.html

**Fig. 2.** Image illustrating planets and the Sun in Augmented Reality, respecting the scale of distances from the Sun. https://universopantagina.cl/distancias.html

objects. The features of the Oort cloud have not been incorporated due to their excessively large, scaled size. This model highlights the characteristics of the asteroid belt and the Kuiper belt, both elements of the Solar System often omitted in 3D models. Like the previous model, the models' textures are simple representations of the colors of their surfaces and do not allow observation of geological features.

In Fig. 4, various 3D models present the shapes and scaled sizes of the main "dwarf planets" in the Solar System. The representation is rigorous in depicting sizes, shapes, and some characteristics of their textures. This allows observation of specific features, such as the bowling pin shape of the dwarf planet "Haumea".

Figure 5 showcases three 3D models with features of the Sun. The first model allows observation of the solar photosphere. The second model details its anatomy (core, radiative zone, convective zone, photosphere, chromosphere, sunspots, flares, among others). The third model enables observation of specific features of the differential rotation of sunspots, a phenomenon observable with a telescope and filter, occurring in the solar photosphere.

In Fig. 6, two 3D models present the constellations "Gemini" and "Orion." Both constellation models were designed as if being viewed through a telescope or monocular,

**Fig. 3.** The image displays Solar System objects, respecting the location of the ring belt and Kuiper belt in Augmented Reality. https://universopantagina.cl/sistema_solar.html

**Fig. 4.** The image shows dwarf planets in Augmented Reality, respecting their proportional sizes, shapes, textures, and colors. https://universopantagina.cl/enanos.html

hence appearing within circular discs. Both constellations are accurate in representing the main stars with their colors (cool reddish stars like Pollux and hot bluish stars like Castor). The Orion constellation also indicates the location of other celestial bodies, such as the Orion Nebula or the Open Cluster. Less relevant stars have been represented in white.

Figure 7 presents a very simple 3D model to represent the Milky Way, ensuring the curvature of its disk ("wrap" of the Milky Way) is visible. This resource also rigorously models the characteristics of our galaxy, including its core, bulge, spiral arms, and galactic disk. Each star in the Milky Way has been represented with a point to optimize graphic resources and necessary data for observation.

**Fig. 5.** The image presents some external and internal features of the Sun in Augmented Reality, preserving colors, shapes, and sizes. https://universopantagina.cl/sun.html and https://universop antagina.cl/sunanatomy.html

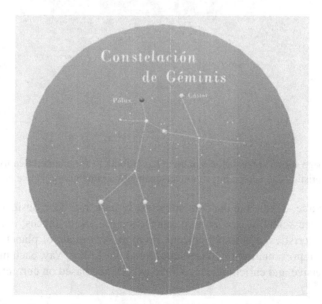

**Fig. 6.** The image displays the constellations of Gemini and Orion in Augmented Reality, safeguarding the colors of their main stars. https://universopantagina.cl/constelaciones.html

In Fig. 8, a 3D model represents the characteristics of the Helix Nebula. The representation displays gas and dust of the planetary nebulae with different colors (according to temperature), and in the center, a white dwarf can be observed.

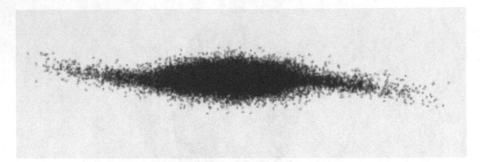

**Fig. 7.** The image shows some characteristics of the Milky Way in Augmented Reality, preserving the curvature in the shape of the galactic disk. https://universopantagina.cl/via_lactea.html

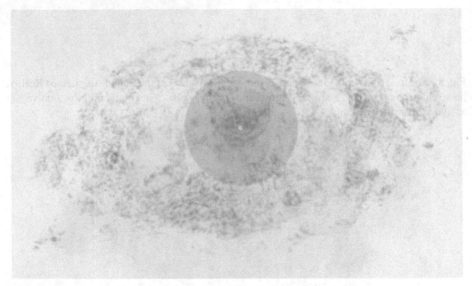

**Fig. 8.** The image shows some features of the Helix Nebula in Augmented Reality, safeguarding typical characteristics and colors. https://universopantagina.cl/nebulosa_helice.html

Each resource, detailed in the corresponding figures, has been designed with precision to guarantee scientific accuracy in representing sizes, distances, movements, and specific characteristics of celestial objects. From the size scale of planets compared to the Sun to the representation of constellations and the Milky Way, each model seeks to offer an immersive and enriching educational experience based on current astronomical knowledge.

## 4.2 Activities for Educational Environments

In conjunction with the Augmented Reality (AR) resources, we have developed two educational activities that offer simple dynamics to facilitate the learning of astronomical concepts. Both activities allow for result evaluation through a pre-post approach, providing preliminary insights into the impact of using the developed AR astronomy resources.

## Sorting Planet Sizes

**Step 1**: Write in order the name of each planet, from the smallest to the largest:

Planets: *Mercury – Venus – Earth – Mars – Jupiter – Saturn – Uranus – Neptune*

| Order | Planet name |
|---|---|
| + Small | |
| | |
| | |
| | |
| | |
| | |
| | |
| + Large | |

**Step 2**: Scan the QR codes and observe the characteristics of the planets in Augmented Reality. After finishing, rewrite in order the name of each planet, from the smallest to the largest:

Terrestrial Planets            Jovian Planets            All Planets Together

| Order | Planet name |
|---|---|
| + Small | |
| | |
| | |
| | |
| | |
| | |
| | |
| + Large | |

**Fig. 9.** The image illustrates educational activities integrating Augmented Reality (https://universopantagina.cl/escaladiametros.html) to observe and compare the sizes of each planet in the Solar System.

**Sorting Planet Sizes.** The first activity focuses on sorting the sizes of the planets in the Solar System. In this dynamic, students initially arrange the sizes of the planets based on their prior beliefs, from smallest to largest, as presented in Fig. 9. Subsequently, they explore the 3D model shown in Fig. 1, identifying sizes and then comparing them with their initial record in the pre-activity phase.

After implementing the activity with school students, preliminary results have been obtained (see example in Fig. 10). The responses suggest that students not only successfully identified the order of planetary diameters through the observation of three-dimensional Augmented Reality (AR) models but also demonstrated an effective ability to compare these observations with their initial conceptions. The comparative analysis provides valuable input on the conceptual change process that may be taking place in the context of teaching astronomy, enabling students to build a deeper and more meaningful understanding of astronomical phenomena. The students' ability to evaluate their own preconceived ideas is a testimony with transformative potential, suggesting that AR can be integrated with activities that not only enhance comprehension but also foster reflective and metacognitive thinking.

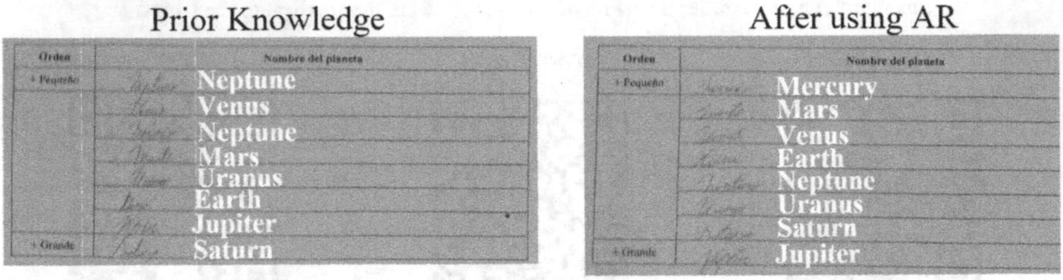

Fig. 10. The photograph provides an example of responses from the "Ordering the Size of Planets" activity, before and after using Augmented Reality.

**Recognizing the Anatomy of the Sun.** The second activity focuses on recognizing some internal and external features of the Sun. In this context, students begin by observing an image of the Sun and, based on their prior knowledge, identify the names of different parts, as shown in Fig. 11. Subsequently, by scanning a QR code, they access the Augmented Reality representation of solar anatomy, exploring the 3D models from Fig. 5 and proceeding to identify these features, which are then compared with their initial records.

Preliminary results obtained from implementing the activity with school students reveal preliminary success in identifying solar features through the observation of 3D AR models (see Fig. 12). Students were able to distinguish surface elements such as the photosphere, sunspots, the corona, and solar flares, as well as more complex aspects of the Sun's interior, such as the core, radiative zones, and convective zones. This result underscores the ability of AR to offer a detailed and three-dimensional representation of abstract astronomical phenomena, allowing students to explore the solar anatomy in depth.

## Recognizing Parts of the Sun

Step 1: Observe the image and based on your previous ideas, write the name of each part of the Sun
*(Note: no problem if you make a mistake or don't know all the parts).*

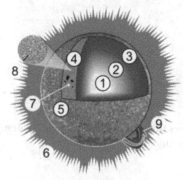

Names of the Parts of the Sun: Sunspot – Photosphere – Core – Chromosphere – Radiative Zone – Granule – Eruption – Corona – Convective Zone.

| Nº | Name of the part of the Sun: |
|----|------------------------------|
| 1 | |
| 2 | |
| 3 | |
| 4 | |
| 5 | |
| 6 | |
| 7 | |
| 8 | |
| 9 | |

Step 2: Scan the QR code to see the features and names of the Sun's parts in Augmented Reality.
Afterward, rewrite the name of each part of the Sun.

VIEW THE SUN IN
AUGMENTED REALITY

| Nº | Name of the part of the Sun: |
|----|------------------------------|
| 1 | |
| 2 | |
| 3 | |
| 4 | |
| 5 | |
| 6 | |
| 7 | |
| 8 | |
| 9 | |

**Fig. 11.** The image showcases educational activities integrating Augmented Reality (https://universopantagina.cl/sunanatomy.html and https://universopantagina.cl/sun.html) to observe and compare the characteristics of the Sun.

On the other hand, similar to the previous activity, students' ability to compare their observations in AR with their pre-existing conceptions also helps monitor and unveil possible conceptual changes experienced by students during these educational activities.

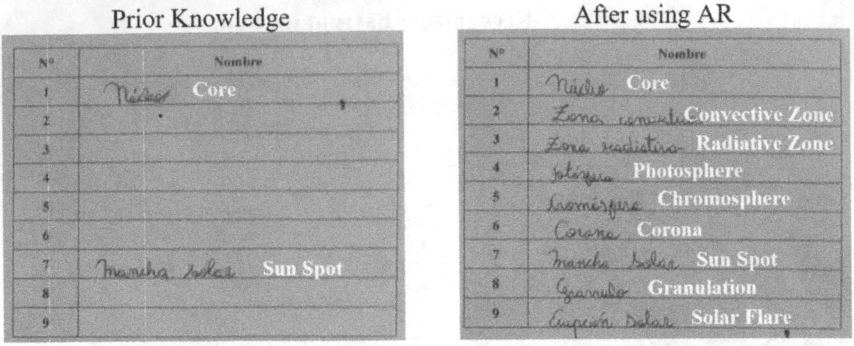

Prior Knowledge                              After using AR

**Fig. 12.** The photograph illustrates an example of responses from the "Recognizing the Anatomy of the Sun" activity, before and after using Augmented Reality.

## 5 Conclusions

In this Design-Based Educational study, we have developed and evaluated Augmented Reality (AR) educational resources in the field of astronomy. Adopting a flexible methodological approach, we followed a structured process of design, implementation, analysis, and redesign. The utilization of this approach has enabled the creation of eight accessible and free AR educational resources, focusing on addressing alternative conceptions in astronomy.

The three-dimensional representation of scientific models, supported by solid conceptual foundations, has been essential in designing these resources. Each resource, from the scale of planetary sizes to the detailed representation of the Sun, constellations, and galaxies, has been meticulously designed to offer an immersive and rigorous educational experience.

In the first evaluated activity challenging students to order planetary sizes, preliminary results revealed initial success. Students not only accurately identified the order of planetary diameters through the observation of 3D AR models but also demonstrated an effective ability to compare these observations with their initial conceptions. This comparative analysis provides valuable insights into the process of conceptual change in teaching astronomy.

In the second activity, focusing on recognizing solar anatomy, students showed notable progress in identifying both surface and internal features of the Sun. From the photosphere and sunspots to more complex aspects such as radiative and convective zones, students successfully used AR to explore the solar anatomy in depth. This capacity not only underscores the effectiveness of AR in offering detailed representations of astronomical phenomena but also highlights students' ability to compare their observations in AR with their pre-existing conceptions.

Both activities, supported by the use of AR, not only improved students' conceptual understanding of astronomy but also fostered reflective and metacognitive thinking.

## 5.1 Limitations

While this study has made strides in integrating AR resources into astronomical education, it presents limitations that should be considered.

The first limitation lies in the preliminary evaluation conducted with school students, which could benefit from a more extensive and diverse sampling to validate the generalization of results. Additionally, the creation and evaluation of resources have focused on specific astronomical knowledge, leaving room for expansion to other areas of astronomical misconceptions in future research.

The dynamic nature of educational technology suggests the need for periodic updates to maintain the relevance and effectiveness of resources. In this study, we used web-based AR technology through "ground recognition"; however, other types of AR technologies could also contribute to learning.

## 5.2 Future Work

Considering the limitations, several directions for future research are identified. Firstly, there is a proposal to broaden the evaluation to different educational levels and contexts, allowing a more comprehensive understanding of the link between AR resources. Strategies will be explored to incorporate continuous feedback from educators and students in the design and improvement process. Additionally, efforts will be made to expand the set of educational resources to address other alternative conceptions of astronomy and explore the possibility of interdisciplinary collaborations to further enrich the educational experience.

Future research will also focus on the precise measurement of long-term conceptual change, delving into the mechanisms underlying the improvement of astronomical understanding through the use of AR. This will require the technology to be curricularly integrated into programs and curricula in different territories.

**Disclosure of Interests.** The authors have no competing interests to declare that are relevant to the content of this article.

## References

1. OECD: PISA 2015 Assessment and Analytical Framework: Science, Reading, Mathematic, Financial Literacy and Collaborative Problem Solving. OECD Publishing (2017)
2. OECD: PISA 2018 Assessment and Analytical Framework.: OECD Publishing (2019)
3. Huerta-Cancino, L.: Concepciones alternativas mayoritarias sobre Universo en profesores de Física en formación. Estudios Pedagógicos 43(2), 147–162 (2017)
4. Sánchez, J.: Integración Curricular de TICS Conceptos y Modelos. Revista Enfoques Educacionales 5(1), 51–65 (2017)
5. Sánchez, J.: Bases constructivistas para la integración de TICs. Revista Enfoques Educacionales 6(1), 75–89 (2018)
6. Zhang, J., Li, G., Huang, Q., Feng, Q., Luo, H.: Augmented reality in K–12 education: a systematic review and meta-analysis of the literature from 2000 to 2020. Sustainability 14(15), 9725 (2022)

7. Chang, H., et al.: Years of augmented reality in education: a meta-analysis of (quasi-) experimental studies to investigate the impact. Comput. Educ. **191**, 104641 (2022)
8. Kalemkuş, J., Kalemkuş, F.: Effect of the use of augmented reality applications on academic achievement of student in science education: meta analysis review. Interact. Learn. Environ. **31**(9), 6017–6034 (2022)
9. Hidayat, R., Wardat, Y.: A systematic review of augmented reality in science, technology, engineering and mathematics education. Educ. Inf. Technol. 1–26 (2023)
10. Kersting M., Bondell J., Steier R., Myers, M.: Virtual reality in astronomy education: reflecting on design principles through a dialogue between researchers and practitioners. Int. J. Sci. Edu. **Part B**, 1–20 (2023)
11. Durukan, U., Güntepe, E., Usta, N.: Evaluation of the effectiveness of augmented reality-based teaching material: the solar system. Int. J. Hum. Comput. Interact. **39**(12), 2542–2556 (2023)
12. Bakas, C., Mikropoulos, T.: Design of virtual environments for the comprehension of planetary phenomena based on students' ideas. Int. J. Sci. Educ. **25**(8), 949–967 (2003)
13. Timur, B., Ozdemir, M.: Fen egitiminde artirilmis gerceklik ortamlarinin kullanimina iliskin ogretmen gorusleri [Teachers' views on the use of augmented reality environments in science education]. Int. J. Turk. Educ. Sci. **6**(10), 62–75 (2018)
14. Seckin, M., Yurtseven, Z., Sural, I.: Innovative approaches in development of educational materials: a case study of science teachers. Turk. Online J. Distance Educ. **22**(4), 58–81 (2021)
15. Chen, C., Chen, H., Wang, T.: Creative situated augmented reality learning for astronomy curricula. Educ. Technol. Soc. **25**(2), 148–162 (2022)
16. Liou, H., Yang, S.H., Chen, S., Tarng, W.: The influences of the 2D image-based augmented reality and virtual reality on student learning. Educ. Technol. Soc. **20**(3), 110–121 (2017)
17. Fleck, S., Simon, G.: An augmented reality environment for astronomy learning in elementary grades: an exploratory study. In: Proceedings of the 25th Conference on l'Interaction Homme-Machine ACM, pp. 14–22 (2013)
18. Kerawalla, L., Luckin, R., Seljeflot, S., Woolard, A.: Making it real: exploring the potential of augmented reality for teaching primary school science. Virtual Reality **10**, 163–174 (2006)
19. Shelton, B., Hedley, N.: Using augmented reality for teaching earth-sun relationships to undergraduate geography students. In: The 1st IEEE International Augmented Reality Toolkit Workshop. Darmstadt, vol. 29, no. 8 (2002)
20. Sin, A., Zaman, H.: Live solar system (LSS): Evaluation of an augmented reality book-based educational tool. In: Proceedings of 2010 International Symposium on Information Technology, vol. 1, pp. 1–6 (2010)
21. Yen, J., Tsai, C., Wu, M.: Augmented reality in the higher education: Students' science concept learning and academic achievement in astronomy. Procedia Soc. Behav. Sci. **103**, 165–173 (2013)
22. Cubero, R.: Concepciones alternativas, preconceptos, errores conceptuales... ¿distinta terminología y un mismo significado? Investigación en la Escuela **23**, 33–42 (1994)
23. Driver, R.: Students' conceptions and the learning of science. Int. J. Sci. Educ. **11**, 481–490 (1989)
24. Cuellar, Z.: Las concepciones alternativas de los estudiantes sobre la naturaleza de la materia. Revista Iberoamericana de Educación **50**, 1–10 (2009)
25. Gil, D.: Los errores conceptuales como origen de un nuevo modelo didactico: de la búsqueda a la investigación. Investigación en la Escuela **1**, 35–41 (1987)
26. Bello, S.: Ideas previas y cambio conceptual. Educación Química **15**(3), 210–217 (2004)
27. García, A., Bolívar, J.: Efecto de las simulaciones interactivas sobre las concepciones de los alumnos en relación con el movimiento armónico simple. Revista Electrónica de Enseñanza de las Ciencias **7**(3), 681–703 (2008)

28. Varela, M., Pérez, U., Serrallé, J., Arias, A.: Evolución de las concepciones sobre Astronomía de profesorado en formación tras una intervención educativa con actividades de simulación. Enseñanza de las Ciencias **31**, 3612–3617 (2013)
29. Mora, C., Herrera, D.: Una revisión sobre ideas previas del concepto de fuerza. Revista Latinoamericana de Física Educativa **3**(1), 72–86 (2009)
30. Moreira, M., Greca, I.: Cambio conceptual: análisis crítico y propuestas a la luz de la teoríadel aprendizaje significativo. Ciência e Educação **9**(2), 301–315 (2003)
31. Camino, N.: Ideas previas y cambio conceptual en Astronomía. Un estudio con maestros de primaria sobre el día y la noche, las estaciones y las fases de la luna. Enseñanza de las ciencias **13**(1), 81–96 (1995)
32. De Manuel, J.: ¿Por qué hay veranos e inviernos? Representaciones de estudiantes (12–18) y de futuros maestros sobre algunos aspectos del modelo Sol-Tierra. Enseñanza de las ciencias **13**(2), 227–236 (1995)
33. Vega, A.: Tenerife tiene seguro de Sol (y de Luna): Representaciones del profesorado de primaria acerca del día y la noche. Enseñanza de las Ciencias **19**, 31–44 (2001)
34. Gil, J., Martinez, B.: El modelo sol-tierra-luna en el lenguaje iconográfico de estudiantes de magisterio. Enseñanza de las Ciencias **23**(2), 153–166 (2005)
35. Delgado, R., Cubilla, K.: La necesidad de investigar la comprensión de conceptos básicos de astronomía y ciencias en general, en pre-media y media. 10° Latin American and Caribbean conference for engineering and technology, pp. 1–10 (2012)
36. Vilches, J., Ramos, C.: La enseñanza-aprendizaje de fenómenos astronómicos cotidianos en la educación primaria española. Revista Eureka sobre enseñanza y divulgación de las ciencias **12**(1), 2–21 (2015)
37. Cole, M., Cohen, C., Wilhelm, J., Lindell, R.: Spatial thinking in astronomy education research. Phys. Rev. Phys. Educ. Res. **14**(1), 010139 (2018)
38. Wilhelm, J., Cole, M., Cohen, C., Lindell, R.: How middle level science teachers visualize and translate motion, scale, and geometric space of the Earth-Mon-Sun system with their students. Phys. Rev. Phys. Educ. Res. **14**, 010150 (2018)
39. Wilhelm, J., et al.: Grade level influence in middle school students' spatial-scientific understandings of lunar phases. School Sci. Math **122**, 128–141 (2022)
40. Milgram, P., Kishino, F.: A taxonomy of mixed reality visual displays. IEICE. Trans. Inf. Syst. **E77-D**(12), 1321–1329 (1994)
41. Kirikkaya, E., Sentürk, M.: The impact of using augmented reality technology in the solar system and beyond unit on the academic achievement of the students. Kastamonu Eğitim Dergisi **26**(1), 181–189 (2018)
42. Yilmaz, R.: Augmented Reality Trends in Education between 2016 and 2017 Years. In: Tech (2018)
43. Huang, K., Ball, C., Francis, J., Ratan, R., Boumis, J., Fordham, J.: Augmented versus virtual reality in education: an exploratory study examining science knowledge retention when using augmented reality/virtual reality mobile applications. Cyberpsychol. Behav. Soc. Netw. **22**(2), 105–110 (2019)
44. Saidin, N., Abd Halim, N., Yahaya, N.: A review of research on augmented reality in education: advantages and applications. Int. Educ. Stud. **8**(13), 1–8 (2015)
45. Bos, A., et al.: Educational technology and its contributions in students' focus and attention regarding augmented reality environments and the use of sensors. J. Educ. Comput. Res. **57**(7), 1832–1848 (2019)
46. Baran, B., Yecan, E., Kaptan, B., Pasayigit, O.: Using augmented reality to teach fifth grade students about electrical circuits. Educ. Inf. Technol. **25**, 1371–1385 (2020)
47. Ozdemir, M., Sahin, C., Arcagok, S., y Demir, M.: The effect of augmented reality applications in the learning process: A meta-analysis study. Eurasian J. Educ. Res. **74**(2018), 165–186 (2018)

48. Coimbra, M., Cardoso, T., Mateus, A.: Augmented reality: an enhancer for higher education students in math's learning? Procedia Comput. Sci. **67**, 332–339 (2015)
49. Korenova, L., Guncaga, J.: Augmented reality in mathematics education for pre-service teachers in primary level. In: APLIMAT: 17th Conference on Applied Mathematics. Bratislava: STU, pp. 597–605 (2018)
50. Guncaga, J., Janiga, R.: Virtual labs and educational software as a tool for more effective teaching STEM subjects. In: The Third International Conference on Computer Science, Computer Engineering, and Education Technologies. Łodz: Łodz University of Technology, pp. 1–12 (2016)
51. Laine, T.: Mobile educational augmented reality games: a systematic literature review and two case studies. Computers **7**(1), 19 (2018)
52. Ewais, A., Troyer, O.: A usability and acceptance evaluation of the use of augmented reality for learning atoms and molecules reaction by primary school female students in Palestine. J. Educ. Comput. Res. **57**(7), 1643–1670 (2019)
53. Hu-Au, E., Lee, J.: Virtual reality in education: a tool for learning in the experience age by Elliot. Int. J. Innovation Educ. (IJIIE). **4**(4), 215 (2017)
54. Allcoat, D., Von Mühlenen, A.: Learning in virtual reality: Effects on performance, emotion and engagement. Res. Learn. Technol. **26**, 2140 (2018)
55. Steffen, J., Gaskin, J., Meservy, T., Jenkins, J., Wolman, I.: Framework of affordances for virtual reality and augmented reality. J. Manag. Inf. Syst. **36**(3), 683–729 (2019)
56. Rau, P., Zheng, J., Guo, Z., Li, J.: Speed reading on virtual reality and augmented reality. Comput. Educ. **125**, 240–245 (2018)
57. Bin, S., Masood, S., Jung, Y.: Virtual and Augmented Reality in Medicine. Biomedical Information Technology (Second Edition), pp. 673–686 (2020)
58. Garcia-Bonete, M., Jensen, M., Katona, G.: A practical guide to developing virtual and augmented reality exercises for teaching structural biology. Biochem. Mol. Biol. Educ. **47**(1), 16–24 (2018)
59. Voronina, M., Tretyakova, Z., Krivonozhkina, E., Buslaev, S., Sidorenko, G.: Augmented reality in teaching descriptive geometry, engineering and computer graphics – systematic review and results ofthe russian teachers' experience'. EURASIA J. Math. Sci. Technol. Educ. **15**(12), 1–17 (2019)
60. Pérez-Lisboa, S., Ríos-Binimelis, C., Castillo-Allaria, J.: Realidad Aumentada y Stellarium: astronomía para niños y niñas de cinco años. Alteridad **15**(1), 25–35 (2020)
61. Zhang, J., Sung, Y., Hou, H., Chang, K.: The development and evaluation of an augmented reality-based armillary sphere for astronomical observation instruction. Comput. Educ. **73**, 178–188 (2014)
62. Tarng, W., Ou, K., Lu, Y., Shih, Y., Liou, H.: A sun path observation systema based on augment reality and mobile learning. Mob. Inf. Syst. **5950732**, 1–10 (2018)
63. Planey, J., Rajarathinam, R., Mercier, E., Lindgren, R.: Gesture-mediated collaboration with augmented reality headsets in a problem-based astronomy task. Int. J. Comput.-Support. Collab. Learn. **18**, 259–289 (2023)
64. Önal, N., Önal, N.: El efecto de la realidad aumentada en el rendimiento en astronomía y el nivel de interés de los estudiantes superdotados. Educ. Inf. Technol. **26**, 4573–4599 (2021)
65. Stoyanova, D., Kafadarova, N., Stoyanova-Petrova, S.: Enhancing elementary student learning in natural sciences through mobile augmented reality technology. Bul. Chem. Commun. **47**(B), 532–536 (2015)
66. Papakostas, C., Troussas, C., Krouska, A., Sgouropoulou, C.: Exploring users' behavioral intention to adopt mobile augmented reality in education through an extended technology acceptance model. Int. J. Hum. Comput. Interaction **39**(6), 1294–1302 (2023)
67. Guimarães, M., Gnecco, B.: Teaching astronomy and celestial mechanics through virtual reality. Comput. Appl. Eng. Educ. **17**(2), 196–205 (2009)

68. Ramasundarm, V., Grunwald, S., Mangeot, A., Comerford, N., Bliss, C.: Development of an environmental virtual field laboratory. Comput. **45**, 21–34 (2005)
69. Atta, G., Abdelsattar, A., Elfiky, D., Zahran, M., Farag, M., Slim, S.: Virtual reality in space technology education. Educ. Sci. **12**(12), 890 (2022)
70. Shin, Y.: Virtual reality simulations in Web-based science education. Comput. Appl. Eng. Educ. **10**(1), 18–25 (2002)
71. Demircioglu, T., Karakus, M., Ucar, S.: Developing students' critical thinking skills and argumentation abilities through augmented reality-based argumentation activities in science classes. Sci. Educ. **32**, 1165–1195 (2023)
72. Cao, L., Peng, C., Hansberger, J.: Usability and engagement study for a serious virtual reality game of lunar exploration missions. Informatics **6**(4), 44 (2019)
73. Birchfield, D., Megowan-Romanowicz, C.: Earth science learning in SMALLab: a design experiment for mixed reality. Comput. Support. Learn. **4**, 403–421 (2009)
74. Juuti, K., Lavonen, J.: Design-based research in science education: one step towards methodology. NorDiNa **4**, 54–68 (2006)
75. Plomp, T., Nieveen, N.: Educational Design Research. SLO-Netherlands Institute for Curriculum Development (2010)
76. Sandoval, W.: Conjecture mapping: an approach to systematic educational design research. J. Learn. Sci. **23**(1), 18–36 (2014)
77. Guisasola, J., Ametller, J., Zuza, K.: Investigación basada en el diseño de Secuencias de Enseñanza-Aprendizaje: una línea de investigación emergente en Enseñanza de las Ciencias. Revista Eureka sobre Enseñanza y Divulgación de las Ciencias **18**(1), 1801 (2021)
78. Easterday, M., Rees-Lewis, D., Gerbe, E.: Design-based research process: problems, phases, and applications. In: Proceedings of International Conference of Learning Sciences, (eds.) Polman, J. L.: International Society of the Learning Sciences, Boulder, CO, pp. 317–324 (2014)
79. Alghamdi, A., Li, L.: Adapting design-based research as a research methodology in educational settings. Int. J. Educ. Res. **1**(10), 1–12 (2013)

# Self-location and Reorientation of Individuals Without Reading Maps: Increased Spatial Memory During GPS Navigation Using AR City Walls

Xiaoyu Zhang[1,2] and Sunao Iwaki[1,2(✉)]

[1] University of Tsukuba, 1-1-1 Tennodai, Tsukuba, Ibaraki, Japan
[2] National Institute of Advanced Industrial Science and Technology (AIST),
AIST Tsukuba Central, 1-1-1 Higashi, Tsukuba, Ibaraki, Japan
s.iwaki@aist.go.jp

**Abstract.** Consulting a map on navigation assistance systems while navigating the real-world environment can reduce spatial memory. The current augmented reality (AR) view, which merges physical and virtual information spaces, facilitates wayfinding by overlaying route indications in the real-world environment. Traditionally, switching from the AR to the map view has been considered essential for encoding spatial representations in the brain constructing the cognitive map. However, we propose that the need for maps can be reduced by utilizing AR objects that simulate the environmental boundary surrounding the navigation area. Based on this concept, we designed a prototype, AR City Walls, and conducted an experiment to evaluate spatial memory and workload during Global Positioning System (GPS)-aided navigation without map exposure. Compared to the AR view displaying route indications only, the AR City Walls combining route indications significantly improved cognitive map construction and wayfinding while maintaining a low workload. Simulating real environmental cues crucial for spatial cognition during navigation embodies the simplicity, naturalness, and immediacy of virtual information displays.

**Keywords:** Spatial Memory · Navigation · Augmented Reality · Cognitive Map · Wayfinding

## 1 Introduction

The spatial ability to navigate their environment plays a crucial role in interactions with the physical world. The widespread use of navigation assistance systems, such as Google Maps, has diminished the frequency of self-guided navigation. Global Positioning System (GPS) navigation refers to users navigating from their start point to their intended destination following the guidance provided by a navigation assistance system. Currently, the primary guidance method for GPS navigation systems is turn-by-turn direction indications for a given path displayed in the map view. Studies have reported reduced spatial memory as the

J. Wei and G. Margetis (Eds.): HCII 2024, LNCS 14737, pp. 254–267, 2024.
https://doi.org/10.1007/978-3-031-60458-4_17

consequence of utilizing GPS navigation systems [9,13], with habitual GPS users exhibiting poor spatial memory in self-guided navigation [5].

Spatial information is embedded in the physical world as environmental cues in the physical world and the virtual contexts provided by map view on mobile GPS devices. While users of GPS navigation system obtain spatial information from a map on a digital screen, their attention diverges from the real environment, resulting in spatial memory impairment and safety risks [9,14]. The development of AR view in navigation assistance enables the overlaying of digital content and information onto the physical world, showing the potential for acquire spatial knowledge from the environment without relying on a map view. Compared with traditional navigation guidance offered by digital maps, AR view enhances wayfinding by providing route indication marks in the physical environment around users [18,28,29].

However, users may still lose track of their locations and orientations, with long travel distances and frequent turns potentially leading to disorientation during path-following. To reorient themselves and construct the cognitive map reflecting the location relationship in the physical world, users should switch to a North-up map that includes the whole navigation area, which anchors them in a stable allocentric reference frame. Such a global map can be deficient in details regarding the road conditions around users, leading to poor wayfinding performance. Switching between the track-up and north-up view in current GPS navigation seems inevitable due to the trade-off between wayfinding and cognitive map construction [26,27]. Additionally, view-switching operations such as map rotation and perspective zooming during GPS navigation required additional workload.

Moreover, previous research indicated that cognitive map construction is significantly influenced by maps almost immediately upon reading them. In contrast, real-environment navigation can hardly benefit the cognitive map without extended experience of landmarks and paths [10,20,21,32]. For example, the individual needs to learn a path repetitively to comprehend the relative relationships between different locations. In environments lacking prominent landmarks, such as deserts and forests, reorientation becomes nearly impossible. Previous studies in AR attempted to visualize global landmarks to enhance cognitive map construction during aided navigation [4,31]. However, these efforts have not managed to decrease the necessity for extended experience. In summary, AR navigators might not be efficient enough to immediately support our self-location and reorientation when we find ourselves disorientated.

Fortunately, numerous cross-species studies on the neuroscience of navigation [2,3,8] have proven that a specific visual cue can efficiently facilitate cognitive map construction in the real environment. This cue, referred to as a boundary, represents a continuous surface enclosing the navigation area [19,25,34] and inherently carries geometric information crucial for direction and distance measurements (e.g., walls of room and borders of street blocks). This concept finds support in neurobiological evidence reflected in the firing patterns of various types of cognitive-map-related brain cells. For instance, grid cells in the entorhinal cortex integrate locations through metrical distance coding, binding a hexagonal lattice pattern like a paving tile, according to the shape of the boundary [11]. Boundary vector cells fire whenever an environmental boundary intersects a receptive field positioned at a specific distance from an individual in an allocentric direction [22]. Daily experiences can explain this boundary effect intuitively. Upon entering a square room, individuals can swiftly determine their location in relation to the surrounding walls at a glance, simplifying indoor reorientation compared to outdoor scenarios. However, the effects of boundaries on cognitive map construction reported by these neurobiological studies are typically confined to indoor settings. Furthermore, high-visibility boundaries outdoors in large-scale environments are uncommon. Therefore, it is unclear whether an AR boundary can support efficient cognitive map construction and wayfinding during large-scale GPS navigation.

In this study, we propose a prototype named AR City Walls. We assume that incorporating AR City Walls into outdoor navigation can enhance self-location and reorientation based on the cognitive map. It can facilitate the development of navigation assistance to improve spatial memory during GPS navigation. By extending theoretical achievement in neuroscience from the laboratory to real-world GPS navigation scenarios, we bring integrate virtual information into meaningful real-world contexts, ensuring that user interactions with the physical world are more natural, simple, and direct.

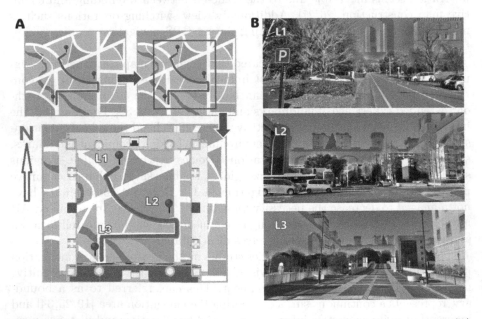

**Fig. 1.** The AR City Walls. (A) An aerial view illustrates its generation steps. (B) First-person views of AR navigator users when they move to three locations and face north.

## 2  Design Prototyping

The AR City Walls is a virtual boundary, resembling a distal castle with four
city walls positioned to the north, south, east, and west. These walls enclose a
square navigation area (see Figs. 1 and 2(B)).

### 2.1  Generation Logic

In the GPS navigation systems, users are guided along specific paths to reach
their desired destinations. The navigation area in the map view is a square that
encompasses all potential locations users may pass through from their starting
point to the destination. The size of this navigation area is calculated based on
the maximum horizontal (north-south) and vertical (east-west) distance between
these locations. The virtual castle is located on the four sides of the square (see
Fig. 1(A)). Users of the AR navigator perceive this virtual castle overlaying onto
the street while maintaining a clear view of the real environment and route
indications within their field of view. This creates the illusion that the castle
is situated at a distance (see Fig. 1(B)). It is essential to emphasize occlusion
culling of the city walls covered by street scenery based on perspective principles
in AR interactions [24]. Attributes such as the location and height of the virtual
city castle remain constant once the navigation area is determined, ensuring the
visibility of the distal city walls throughout the navigation. This approach allows
users, during GPS navigation, to orient themselves and determine their positions
relative to the city walls. For example, when users stand at the center of the
navigation area facing north, the midline blue-spire building of the northern city
wall is in front of them. As users move northward, the north city wall becomes
more prominent and appears larger (see Fig. 1(B)).

### 2.2  Design Elements

The diverse appearance of virtual city walls is acceptable, with the exception
of shape and context. These two design elements, rooted in previous research
on the neuroscience of navigation, are crucial for the construction of cognitive
maps.

**Square Shape.** The effect of shape on cognitive map construction was more
pronounced in the case of the polygon, especially the square. Previous research
indicated that trapezoids and rectangles tend to introduce greater errors in
assessing spatial relationships and result in more distorted cognitive map representations compared to squares [1,17]. Maintaining the square shape is also
motivated by the fact that a similar-shaped environment is more likely to be
recognized as familiar, leading to a consistent cognitive map representation [23].
Displaying the same distal city walls can expedite spatial processing when navigating unfamiliar places. In essence, diverse environments can be coded within
the same allocentric reference frame embodied by the square.

**Distinguishable Contexts.** The ability to reorientate oneself was tested in a cylinder featuring distinct contexts (e.g., stripe texture on the side of the wall). Typically, the firing direction of head direction cells aligns consistently with the context [19,34]. In a rectangular chamber, place cells and head direction cells tend to exhibit two preferred firing locations and directions. These preferred firing patterns rotate 180° from each other due to the symmetry of the boundary shape [15,16,35], can be influenced by the context on each side of the boundary. Using a context that differs from the opposite side can make the preferred firing pattern of cells more exclusive in a symmetrical shape. Therefore, each side of a square boundary should feature a distinct context to differentiate cardinal directions (North, South, East, and West).

In our study, the four city walls had different contexts. The north wall was blue with a spire building in the middle, the south wall was gray, and the east and west walls were white with red and blue towers in the middle (see Fig. 2(B)).

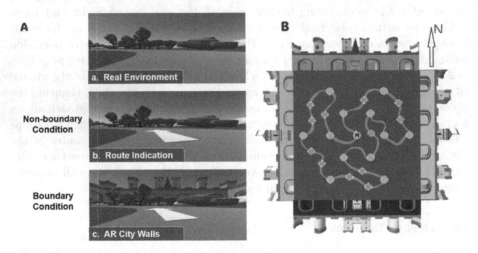

**Fig. 2.** (A) Views of experimental conditions. (B) One of the three map layouts surrounded by the AR City Walls elevations. (Color figure online)

## 3   Experiment

We assumed that incorporating the boundary in the AR view can enhance spatial memory processing during GPS navigation, thereby removing the need for a map view on navigational devices. To verify this assumption, we compared two AR views (i.e., boundary and non-boundary conditions) during GPS navigation in the absence of assistance from a map view.

The effects of these AR views on spatial memory, including cognitive map construction and wayfinding, were assessed in terms of their performances in two spatial tasks (i.e., homing and wayfinding) in the virtual reality experiment. The workload for GPS navigation was measured using the NASA-TLX [12].

## 3.1 Participants

Thirty normal vision (or corrected to normal vision) participants were recruited on the local online bulletin board (14 females, age 25.4 ± 2.4, ranging from 21 to 30). All of them were right-handed and gave written informed consent to this research. The local ethics committee approved the current research (internal review board, IRB, National Institute of Advanced Industrial Science and Technology, AIST). Four participants (all females) quit the experiment due to the simulator sickness and were excluded from the analysis. All participants were asked to conduct the same procedure in the within-subjects experiment.

## 3.2 Navigation Environment

The experimental environment was built by the Unity3D game engine (Unity Technologies, San Francisco, California, USA) and rendered using an HTC Vive Pro head-mounted display (HTC Corporation, Taoyuan, Taïwan).

**VR Operations.** Participants moved in the VR environment using the combination of head rotation recorded by the VR movement tracker and trackpad on the left-hand controller. The positive and negative y-axes of the trackpad were moved forward and backward, respectively. Movement speed (1.2 ± 1.2 m/s) was accelerated from the middle to both ends of this axis. The moving direction was congruent with the heading in the 2-dimension plane parallel to the transverse section of the individual head. The dolly movement controlled by the left trackpad multiplies the head rotation, resulting in smooth and ergonomic movement in the VR environment. This movement avoided simulation sickness induced by bouncing up and down in actual walking and maintained the subjective head direction important for spatial processing during navigation [6,15,19]. The trigger of the right-hand controller was used to confirm answers to spatial tasks.

**Map Layouts.** The navigation area of each map is 500 × 500 m. A winding, closed-loop road through the forest formed the main course on each map. Each road passed through 25 locations, including the home, which served as both the start and the end point of the journey. Thirteen of these locations were configured as nested hexagons on each map. The vertices of the two hexagons shared the same center (i.e., home). The side length (240 m) of the first hexagon was twice that of the second. In each map, the sequence of main roads passing through the 13 locations varied in the map layout. The other 12 locations were set after the fixed locations had been connected by the circular road, with the following prerequisite: there should be one or two turns between the two points that had been successively passed on the main road. The turns on the circle were generally curved and lacked clear angular information. When participants were at a specific location, they could not see the other locations because their view was obstructed by the forest, thereby avoiding the beacon effect. The layouts of the maps were arranged in this manner to disorientate participants and determine whether our AR navigation assistance system could enhance the spatial cognition of individuals in such difficult situations.

### 3.3 Conditions

All the participants were subjected to two AR viewing conditions (non-boundary and boundary); route indication was the baseline included in all the conditions (see Fig. 2(A)). In our experiment, arrows were arranged at 25 locations on each map. If there were multiple directions, and participants did not know the correct direction during wayfinding, the arrows served as route indications to the right direction. These arrows did not appear until the participants were close to the location. Overall, the participants completed their journey with the aid of the arrows. In the boundary condition, the participants could also acquire spatial knowledge from the AR City Walls.

### 3.4 Procedure

The experiment followed a within-subjects design and included three runs: one for practice and two for the formal experiment.

After the practice run, participants became familiar with the different AR views without knowing the three map layouts. In the formal experiment, a condition matched a map layout to ensure participants evaluated each AR view condition in an unfamiliar environment. Counterbalancing was performed between participants for the randomized matching of the conditions and map layouts. During the experiment, no participant had been exposed to the global map layout from the aerial view. Participants took 10 to 20 min to conduct a run. After each run for the formal experiment, the VR head-mounted display was removed, questions on the NASA-TLX questionnaire were answered on a laptop by mouseclick, and a break proceeded.

Once a run began, participants were settled at home (the center of the navigation area), where they looked around to encode their location with the help of the AR view. Once the home location was memorized, participants were asked to follow a path given by the navigation assistance system. Each time participants moved from the current location to the next (i.e., a road section), they were asked to complete four stages. A trial involved a four-stage road section, and each run comprised 24 trials. These stages were self-navigation, GPS navigation, homing, and wayfinding. The stages flows are described below:

**Self-navigation.** After passing the route indication pointing forward, participants had to cover a distance of one-third to half of the road section without any navigation assistance.

**GPS Navigation.** The distal boundary in the AR view was automatically ON to help the rest of the road section in the boundary condition. No AR view was presented in the non-boundary condition, and the self-navigation continued.

**Homing Task.** The AR view was automatically off when participants had reached the next location. Participants were asked to face the direction of the home and pull the right trigger to confirm their answer. At this stage, participants were unmoveable and had to rely on the spatial knowledge acquired from the prior navigation experience to recall the home location relative to their current location. The angle difference between the answer and the actual relative direction measured the cognitive map representation accuracy.

**Wayfinding Task.** After completing the cognitive-map-based homing task, the route indication showed immediately to tell the next turning direction. Participants faced the arrow and triggered the right controller to show they had found their way. After the wayfinding confirmation, participants could move to the next location and repeat the flow until they returned home. Participants were warned if they took any wrong directions and walked for a distance. Participants could go back to the right way following the indication after the warning.

## 4  Results and Discussion

Homing and wayfinding task performance were recorded during GPS navigation to evaluate the effect of different AR views (non-boundary and boundary conditions) on spatial memory (cognitive map construction and wayfinding), and NASA-TLX was used to assess the workload under these conditions after each run. We used paired samples t-tests in SPSS 23 to conduct statistical analysis.

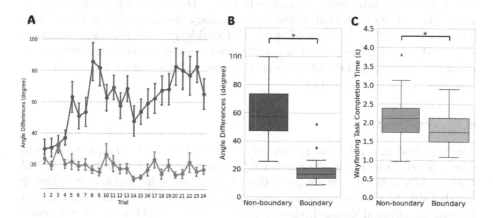

**Fig. 3.** Results of spatial memory. (A) Angle differences of trials. (B) The average angle differences in the homing task indicate cognitive map recall accuracy. (C) Wayfinding task completion time.

## 4.1  Spatial Memory

**Cognitive Map Construction.** In the homing task, the angle differences between the direction that the participant faced and the actual home direction for each trial were calculated for each participant.

*Angle Difference of Trials.* The change of mean values and standard errors of angle difference of all participants on each trial were calculated (see Fig. 3(A)). The angle differences increased with trials in the non-boundary condition but maintained a low level in the boundary condition. It means that when there was no boundary, the cognitive map describing the relative location between the home and the participant was distorted with longer navigation distance and time because they were disorientated during the self-navigation stage. When the participants perceived the boundary, they efficiently and successfully conducted self-location and reorientation after disorientation in the self-navigation stage.

*Cognitive Map Recall Accuracy.* Cognitive map recall accuracy was represented by average angle differences between the actual home direction and answers for each condition and participant.

Comparing with the non-boundary condition ($M = 61.27$, $SD = 18.43$), the boundary condition ($M = 16.57$, $SD = 4.63$, $t(25) = 12.36$, $p < 0.01$) significantly decreased the average angle differences of homing task(see Fig. 3(B)). Since the AR view was off during the homing task, the AR City Walls improved cognitive map recall accuracy during GPS navigation.

**Wayfinding.** Since no participants turned in the wrong direction during GPS navigation in all conditions, the AR view effectively supported wayfinding. The boundary could optimize wayfinding processing, as evidenced by the wayfinding task completion time being significantly less in the boundary condition ($M = 1.81$, $SD = 0.48$) than that in the non-boundary condition ($M = 2.18$, $SD = 0.61$, $t(25) = 4.79$, $p < 0.01$, see Fig. 3(C)). Considering that the distal boundary improved the cognitive map, it is possible that bearing the cognitive map in the brain can strengthen the confidence of GPS users in following the route indication provided by external guidance.

## 4.2  Workload

The workload in the boundary condition ($M = 52.92$, $SD = 13.23$) was significantly lower than that in the non-boundary conditions ($M = 76.32$, $SD = 9.47$, $t(25) = 8.04$, $p < 0.01$). We suggest that this difference in workload is primarily attributable to cognitive map construction processing during GPS navigation. Except for physical demand, there was an increased workload in all subdimensions of the non-boundary condition compared with that in the boundary condition because it had been difficult to acquire direction and distance information from the route indications and real environment. More details for subdimensions are present in Table 1.

**Table 1.** Statistical analysis results of the subdimensions of NASA-TLX. Statistically significant entries are marked with a star*.

| Scale | Condition | M | SD | t | df | p |
|-------|-----------|-----|-----|-----|-----|-----|
| Mental Demand | Non Boundary | 83.65 | 17.75 | 4.85 | 25 | <0.01* |
|  |  | 67.69 | 21.78 |  |  |  |
| Physical Demand | Non Boundary | 51.92 | 23.24 | 1.98 | 25 | 0.06 |
|  |  | 43.65 | 22.25 |  |  |  |
| Temporal Demand | Non Boundary | 49.04 | 17.72 | 2.99 | 25 | 0.01* |
|  |  | 37.12 | 18.18 |  |  |  |
| Performance | Non Boundary | 73.46 | 21.48 | 5.56 | 25 | <0.01* |
|  |  | 40.00 | 20.74 |  |  |  |
| Effort | Non Boundary | 77.31 | 12.98 | 4.62 | 25 | <0.01* |
|  |  | 61.15 | 19.51 |  |  |  |
| Frustration | Non Boundary | 66.54 | 24.44 | 6.71 | 25 | <0.01* |
|  |  | 33.85 | 19.56 |  |  |  |

## 4.3 Limitations and Future Work

This research provides valuable design insights for reducing the necessity of map view switching and improving the AR view to benefit the spatial memory of GPS users in both wayfinding and cognitive map construction. At the same time, the limitations to these approaches and ways to deal with these limitations should be analyzed from both practical and social liability perspectives.

**Relations Between Spatial Information Acquired from the AR View and the Physical World.** To evaluate spatial knowledge acquired from GPS navigation assistance independent of that in the real environment, we asked participants to follow a winding circular road in a forest, which greatly reduced the accessible spatial information from the actual surroundings. In the physical world, especially in urban areas, spatial information can be acquired from landmarks and the regular shapes of road traffic systems. The interaction between route indications and city walls in the AR view with landmarks in the real environment and their effect on spatial memory requires further investigation.

**Objective Workload and Long-Term Spatial Memory Measurement.** The NASA-TLX is a self-reporting subjective workload evaluation method. The task completion time may partly reflect the workload for spatial information processing during spatial tasks but not the navigation period. To avoid motion sickness triggered by violent head rotation and the misalignment of the head and body, we set forward movements dependent on the heading direction and did not stress that participants should respond as quickly as possible in the spatial tasks. Thus, navigation time in our research could not assess workload during the AR view activation period. Objective workload criteria for navigation, such as eye-tracking data, should be analyzed in the future. Furthermore, we only evaluated spatial memory during GPS navigation, not after it. The ability to maintain spatial knowledge acquired during GPS navigation and use it in a novel navigation environment is vital for user cognition development and requires further study.

**Practical Applications.** Regarding the technical bottleneck in AR technology and user safety considerations, the practical application of the AR City Walls is challenging. In our experiment, the navigation environment was a park for pedestrians. Our original AR City Walls prototype design should be verified in other application scenarios, such as urban navigation and driving, which have complex traffic conditions. Navigational devices that display the AR view should be further studied. For example, the excellent spatial task performances of participants in our AR view using a head-mounted display may decrease in an AR view shot by the smartphone camera. In addition to the accuracy of AR object location, another technical problem is occlusion [24, 29], which can ensure AR City Walls at a distance in users' field of view without covering the street view around GPS users. The visibility of the distal boundary decreases in the dense clusters of tall buildings, resulting in discontinuous spatial information acquisition. Fortunately, in our research, the discontinuous display of the AR view led to good spatial task performance. Other studies [7, 30, 33] were consistent with our results have reported that environmental cues function when an individual encounters them rather than during continuous contact. Due to its outstanding ability to locate and reorient users, we suggested that tourism is the preferred application scenario for the AR City Walls. Instead of following the tour set by a tour guide or the shortest path offered by navigation assistance, AR City Walls surrounding the scenic area can encourage tourists to explore freely without worrying about disorientation and provide an immersive landscape experience uninterrupted by regular map consultation.

## 5   Conclusions

We propose that displaying a global view map for navigation assistance is not necessary for self-location or reorientation. Displaying specific environmental cues generalized from the neuroscience of navigation in an AR view, the AR City Walls benefits spatial memory during GPS navigation. Route indications in the current AR view can only support wayfinding, whereas the AR City Walls contribute to cognitive map construction and accelerate wayfinding processing during GPS navigation with a low workload.

Based on the findings from the neuroscience of navigation, we propose a design prototype with the potential to improve next-generation GPS navigation assistance systems based on the AR view. It overlays route indications on the streets around users and displays distal city walls in the background; thus, it can simultaneously enhance wayfinding and cognitive map construction. To the best of our knowledge, this is the first study to demonstrate that the distal boundary, which had been limited by indoor experiments in the neuroscience of navigation, contributes to outdoor GPS navigation. Our work expands the application field of the neuroscience of navigation, helps us better understand spatial cognition in GPS navigation, and supports GPS user interaction between the virtual context and the physical world in a simple, natural, and direct manner.

**Acknowledgments.** This study was supported by JST SPRING (grant number JPMJSP2124) and JSPS Kakenhi (grant number 21H03787).

# References

1. Bellmund, J.L.S., de Cothi, W., Ruiter, T.A., Nau, M., Barry, C., Doeller, C.F.: Deforming the metric of cognitive maps distorts memory. Nat. Hum. Behav. **4**(2), 177–188 (2020). https://doi.org/10.1038/s41562-019-0767-3
2. Cheng, K.: A purely geometric module in the rat's spatial representation. Cognition **23**(2), 149–178 (1986). https://doi.org/10.1016/0010-0277(86)90041-7
3. Cheng, K., Newcombe, N.S.: Is there a geometric module for spatial orientation? Squaring theory and evidence. Psychon. Bull. Rev. **12**(1), 1–23 (2005). https://doi.org/10.3758/BF03196346
4. Clemenson, G.D., Maselli, A., Fiannaca, A.J., Miller, A., Gonzalez-Franco, M.: Rethinking GPS navigation: creating cognitive maps through auditory clues. Sci. Rep. **11**(1), 7764 (2021). https://doi.org/10.1038/s41598-021-87148-4
5. Dahmani, L., Bohbot, V.D.: Habitual use of GPS negatively impacts spatial memory during self-guided navigation. Sci. Rep. **10**(1), 6310 (2020). https://doi.org/10.1038/s41598-020-62877-0
6. Epstein, R.A., Patai, E.Z., Julian, J.B., Spiers, H.J.: The cognitive map in humans: spatial navigation and beyond. Nat. Neurosci. **20**(11), 1504–1513 (2017). https://doi.org/10.1038/nn.4656
7. Epstein, R.A., Vass, L.K.: Neural systems for landmark-based wayfinding in humans. Philos. Trans. R. Soc. B Biol. Sci. **369**(1635), 20120533 (2014). https://doi.org/10.1098/rstb.2012.0533
8. Gallistel, C.: Representations in animal cognition: an introduction. Cognition **37**(1), 1–22 (1990). Special Issue Animal Cognition. https://doi.org/10.1016/0010-0277(90)90016-D
9. Gardony, A.L., Brunyé, T.T., Mahoney, C.R., Taylor, H.A.: How navigational aids impair spatial memory: evidence for divided attention. Spat. Cogn. Comput. **13**(4), 319–350 (2013). https://doi.org/10.1080/13875868.2013.792821
10. Golledge, R.G., Spector, A.N.: Comprehending the urban environment: theory and practice. Geogr. Anal. **10**(4), 403–426 (1978). https://doi.org/10.1111/j.1538-4632.1978.tb00667.x
11. Hafting, T., Fyhn, M., Molden, S., Moser, M.B., Moser, E.I.: Microstructure of a spatial map in the entorhinal cortex. Nature **436**(7052), 801–806 (2005). https://doi.org/10.1038/nature03721
12. Hart, S.G., Staveland, L.E.: Development of NASA-TLX (task load index): results of empirical and theoretical research. In: Hancock, P.A., Meshkati, N. (eds.) Human Mental Workload, Advances in Psychology, North-Holland, vol. 52, pp. 139–183 (1988). https://doi.org/10.1016/S0166-4115(08)62386-9

13. Hejtmánek, L., Oravcová, I., Motýl, J., Horáček, J., Fajnerová, I.: Spatial knowledge impairment after GPS guided navigation: eye-tracking study in a virtual town. Int. J. Hum. Comput. Stud. **116**, 15–24 (2018). https://doi.org/10.1016/j.ijhcs.2018.04.006

14. Ishikawa, T., Fujiwara, H., Imai, O., Okabe, A.: Wayfinding with a GPS-based mobile navigation system: a comparison with maps and direct experience. J. Environ. Psychol. **28**(1), 74–82 (2008). https://doi.org/10.1016/j.jenvp.2007.09.002

15. Julian, J.B., Keinath, A.T., Marchette, S.A., Epstein, R.A.: The neurocognitive basis of spatial reorientation. Curr. Biol. **28**(17), R1059–R1073 (2018). https://doi.org/10.1016/j.cub.2018.04.057

16. Keinath, A.T., Julian, J.B., Epstein, R.A., Muzzio, I.A.: Environmental geometry aligns the hippocampal map during spatial reorientation. Curr. Biol. **27**(3), 309–317 (2017). https://doi.org/10.1016/j.cub.2016.11.046

17. Keinath, A.T., Rechnitz, O., Balasubramanian, V., Epstein, R.A.: Environmental deformations dynamically shift human spatial memory. Hippocampus **31**(1), 89–101 (2021). https://doi.org/10.1002/hipo.23265

18. Kim, S., Dey, A.K.: Simulated augmented reality windshield display as a cognitive mapping aid for elder driver navigation. In: Proceedings of the SIGCHI Conference on Human Factors in Computing Systems, CHI 2009, pp. 133–142. Association for Computing Machinery, New York (2009). https://doi.org/10.1145/1518701.1518724

19. Knierim, J.J., Hamilton, D.A.: Framing spatial cognition: neural representations of proximal and distal frames of reference and their roles in navigation. Physiol. Rev. **91**(4), 1245–1279 (2011). pMID: 22013211. https://doi.org/10.1152/physrev.00021.2010

20. Kuipers, B., Tecuci, D.G., Stankiewicz, B.J.: The skeleton in the cognitive map: a computational and empirical exploration. Environ. Behav. **35**(1), 81–106 (2003). https://doi.org/10.1177/0013916502238866

21. Lee, P.U., Tversky, B.: Interplay between visual and spatial: the effect of landmark descriptions on comprehension of route/survey spatial descriptions. Spat. Cogn. Comput. **5**(2–3), 163–185 (2005). https://doi.org/10.1080/13875868.2005.9683802

22. Lever, C., Burton, S., Jeewajee, A., O'Keefe, J., Burgess, N.: Boundary vector cells in the subiculum of the hippocampal formation. J. Neurosci. **29**(31), 9771–9777 (2009). https://doi.org/10.1523/JNEUROSCI.1319-09.2009

23. Lever, C., Wills, T., Cacucci, F., Burgess, N., O'Keefe, J.: Long-term plasticity in hippocampal place-cell representation of environmental geometry. Nature **416**(6876), 90–94 (2002). https://doi.org/10.1038/416090a

24. Macedo, M.C.F., Apolinário, A.L.: Occlusion handling in augmented reality: past, present and future. IEEE Trans. Vis. Comput. Graph. **29**(2), 1590–1609 (2023). https://doi.org/10.1109/TVCG.2021.3117866

25. Morris, R.: Developments of a water-maze procedure for studying spatial learning in the rat. J. Neurosci. Meth. **11**(1), 47–60 (1984). https://doi.org/10.1016/0165-0270(84)90007-4

26. Münzer, S., Lörch, L., Frankenstein, J.: Wayfinding and acquisition of spatial knowledge with navigation assistance. J. Exp. Psychol. Appl. **26**(1), 73–88 (2020). https://doi.org/10.1037/xap0000237

27. Münzer, S., Zimmer, H.D., Baus, J.: Navigation assistance: a trade-off between wayfinding support and configural learning support. J. Exp. Psychol. Appl. **18**(1), 18–37 (2012). https://doi.org/10.1037/a0026553

28. Narzt, P., Ferscha, K., Muller, W., Hortner, L.: Pervasive information acquisition for mobile AR-navigation systems. In: 2003 Proceedings Fifth IEEE Workshop on Mobile Computing Systems and Applications, pp. 13–20 (2003). https://doi.org/10.1109/MCSA.2003.1240763
29. Narzt, W., et al.: Augmented reality navigation systems. Univ. Access Inf. Soc. 4(3), 177–187 (2006). https://doi.org/10.1007/s10209-005-0017-5
30. O'Keefe, J., Nadel, L.: The Hippocampus as a Cognitive Map. Clarendon Press, Oxford (1978). http://hdl.handle.net/10150/620894
31. Singh, A.K., Liu, J., Tirado Cortes, C.A., Lin, C.T.: Virtual global landmark: an augmented reality technique to improve spatial navigation learning. In: Extended Abstracts of the 2021 CHI Conference on Human Factors in Computing Systems, CHI EA '21, p. 6. Association for Computing Machinery, New York, NY, USA (2021). https://doi.org/10.1145/3411763.3451634
32. Thorndyke, P.W., Hayes-Roth, B.: Differences in spatial knowledge acquired from maps and navigation. Cogn. Psychol. 14(4), 560–589 (1982). https://doi.org/10.1016/0010-0285(82)90019-6
33. Vass, L.K., Epstein, R.A.: Common neural representations for visually guided reorientation and spatial imagery. Cereb. Cortex 27(2), 1457–1471 (2016). https://doi.org/10.1093/cercor/bhv343
34. Vorhees, C.V., Williams, M.T.: Morris water maze: procedures for assessing spatial and related forms of learning and memory. Nat. Protoc. 1(2), 848–858 (2006). https://doi.org/10.1038/nprot.2006.116
35. Weiss, S., Talhami, G., Gofman-Regev, X., Rapoport, S., Eilam, D., Derdikman, D.: Consistency of spatial representations in rat entorhinal cortex predicts performance in a reorientation task. Curr. Biol. 27(23), 3658–3665 (2017). https://doi.org/10.1016/j.cub.2017.10.015

# Research on the Impact of Mobile Terminal Information Layout on Visual Search-Taking Bookkeeping Application as an Example

Xiaowei Zhao$^{(\boxtimes)}$ (iD) and Zhixin Wu

Nanjing University of Science and Technology, Nanjing 210094, China
zhaoxiaowei@njust.edu.cn

**Abstract.** In mobile application interface design, choosing an appropriate infor-mation layout has a greater impact on users' perception and access to interface in-formation, which largely affects the experience of using mobile applications. However, the current design decisions are usually based on subjective experi-ence and lack of scientific basis. In this article, we experimentally compare the effects of four types of information layout on users' visual search in financial bookkeeping apps, and explore the appropriate information layout in this kind of application scenario based on the "Shark Bookkeeping" app as a design exam-ple. Firstly, we analyze the existing common mobile interface information layout methods through literature and current research, and search for suitable experi-mental objects. Then, through a series of experiments, we asked the participants to perform specific tasks under different layout styles, and recorded their search time and subjective evaluation of satisfaction, and the experimental data were processed by SPSS software. The results of the study show that the card layout approach is more conducive for users to find the required information quickly compared to other approaches, while the subjective satisfaction ratings support the objective experimental measurements. This finding has practical implications for the design of mobile applications related to bookkeeping software, which can improve user efficiency and satisfaction.

**Keywords:** User Interface Design · Information Layout · Visual Search

## 1 Introduction

With the popularity of mobile devices, users are increasingly dependent on mobile appli-cations, and the importance of mobile interface design in terms of user experience and usage efficiency has gradually become more prominent. Interface layout refers to a method of reasonably arranging interface elements within a limited range, summarizing messy interfaces and messy content, organizing and arranging them in an interrelated manner, clarifying the relationship between interface elements and space, and provid-ing users with smooth User experience [1]. In the interface layout, information content should be the core to ensure the space utilization of the interface [2]. At the same time, the cleanliness of the interface and the accessibility of information are very important.

J. Wei and G. Margetis (Eds.): HCII 2024, LNCS 14737, pp. 268–281, 2024.
https://doi.org/10.1007/978-3-031-60458-4_18

When users use the interface, disorganized information will cause problems such as long search time, delayed decision-making, inability to focus on the main task, and excessive cognitive load [3]. Visual search is the process in which users find targets or information on the screen. It involves the user's attention allocation, target positioning, information recognition and other cognitive processes. An important aspect to emphasize in visual search interfaces is the possibility of increasing user retention through the use of design aspects such as color, size, shape, orientation, position, organization and content relationships [4]. Therefore, the information arrangement on the mobile interface has an important impact on the user's visual search efficiency.

Usually designers' considerations for information layout when designing mobile pages often come from subjective experience or existing layout forms. How to choose the commonly used information layout forms on mobile terminals in specific scenarios is usually left to the designer's own judgment or based on some Basic design knowledge. Considering layout aesthetics through professional aesthetic literacy will indeed have an impact on visual perception and search [5]. However, as mobile applications continue to be subdivided, it is difficult for this design method to meet the design requirements of all software interfaces. There have been some studies focusing on the impact of information layout on mobile interfaces on users' visual search, and found that information layout affects the efficiency of information recognition [6, 6]. However, there are still some problems to be solved. For example, most current research focuses on the impact of specific arrangement methods or text, spacing, color, etc. [8], which may be different for different types of applications. The degree of digital intelligence is accelerating, and mobile applications accompany everything people do, such as communication, shopping, payment, etc. Different types of mobile applications often need to explore more suitable information layout methods to provide them with Better user experience.

In order to explore the impact of interface information layout on users' visual search in more refined application scenarios, we selected a scenario in a financial bookkeeping application. A reasonable information layout can directly affect the user's search efficiency. Financial bookkeeping involves a large amount of data and transaction records, and users need to quickly locate and find specific financial information, such as bills, transaction details, or balances. In addition, the design of information layout can help users quickly identify and understand financial data. Reasonably arranging and highlighting key information, such as account balances or overdue reminders, can help users access important information in a split second without having to browse through the entire interface, and this kind of quick identification of information is crucial for financial decision-making and management.

Based on the selected application scenario, we choose a representative application "Shark Bookkeeping" as a practical example. First of all, we collected all the commonly used mobile information layout methods in the market through desktop research, which represent the layout forms that designers will consider when designing the current mobile interface. In order to ensure the unity of information presentation and consistency of the interaction level, after screening, we finally chose the list type, card type, palace format, waterfall flow type four types of information layout as the experimental object. The specific experiment includes two parts: completing the search task and completing the subjective satisfaction evaluation. A series of search tasks were constructed in the experiment, and the experimental data were collected and imported into SPSS software and analyzed to find out the differences in visual search efficiency of several information layout methods.

## 2 Related Work

Currently, there have been many studies at home and abroad on the information layout of interactive interfaces. Raeisi et al. [9] used the chain value analysis method to calculate the importance and frequency comprehensive weight of the links between panel elements to design the information layout of the interactive interface. The research results of Li Jing et al. [10] show that the information layout design in the interactive interface that conforms to cognitive characteristics can improve the work efficiency of operators. The mapping between the interface layout spatial structure and the information organization structure not only enables users to easily grasp the relationship between the position and function of element information, but also helps to grasp the overall interface information. Niemelä et al. [11] pointed out that the search efficiency of grouped icons is significantly higher than that of ungrouped icons. The interface space structure reflects the organizational relationship within the interface information and determines the difficulty of obtaining information. Zhou Lei et al. [12] further improved the interface layout beauty evaluation index, used the gray correlation method to comprehensively evaluate the interface beauty, and simulated the design fine-tuning process of "small sample, high correlation". Li et al. [13] proposed an interface design aesthetic evaluation method for interface layout design, and analyzed the perceptual image structure of interface aesthetics from the perspective of aesthetic cognition. Six aesthetic image factors that affect interface aesthetics were extracted through factor analysis, including proportion, simplicity, order, rhythm, density and balance, and the variance contribution rate of each factor was used as the weight. Mendel et al. [14] pointed out that consistent layout design can better guide users to obtain information. Another study shows that mobile application interfaces using grid layout can provide better predictability and information organization, helping users find target information faster. Information density also has a significant impact on users' visual search efficiency. Information density refers to the amount of information presented in a given space. Some studies have found that moderate information density can improve users' search efficiency, but too high or too low information density can interfere with users' search process. Holsanova et al. [15] pointed out that different spatial layouts have a significant impact on human eye movements, and the layout design should fully consider the spatial proximity of the area. Gen has developed a mobile hybrid segmentation method for adaptive layout when browsing web pages on mobile phones. This method segments web pages more accurately and largely retains the problem of incomplete information being segmented due to non-PC terminals [16]. Through an experiment on the perception of interface design layout between designers and users in mobile shopping programs, Yu found that there are differences in the perceived preferences of UI distribution between the two in different layout modes [17].

In terms of research methodology, eye tracking techniques are widely used in mobile interface research to record the user's gaze point and gaze order on the interface. Jose et al. proposed a new automated procedure for obtaining the optimal layout of a software interface, which is based on collecting eye tracking and mouse tracking data while using the interface, which is automatically generated according to an algorithm based on a genetic algorithm generated [18]. Eye movements can detect unconscious cognitive mental processes that cannot be revealed by subjective reports [19], and by analyzing eye movement data, researchers can gain a more accurate understanding of the user's visual search paths and attention distribution, and thus assess the impact of different layout methods on the user.

## 3 Research Questions

### 3.1 Research Focus

In order to provide a real case study and to specify the research object, "Shark Bookkeeping" app is chosen as a research case. Due to the short development time, there are still a lot of negative comments about the use and experience of the prod-uct. Specifically, it is manifested in the single language of illustration, low differentia-tion of information, unreasonable classification, etc., which has a greater impact on users' ability to view income and expenditure, and to determine different categories of income and expenditure and income and expenditure data more easily. As the detail page of the application is an important interface for users to record and man-age their personal finances, design optimization is very important to enhance user experience and improve the efficiency of bookkeeping.

In this context, this study focuses on investigating the impact of different information layout styles on users' visual search on the detail page of the Shark Bookkeeping app. Specifically, the following research questions will be addressed:

1. What is the impact of different information layout styles on users' visual search efficiency in the detail page of Shark Bookkeeping app. By comparing different information layout styles, such as linear, grid, and card layout, we will determine which layout style is more effective in helping users to quickly navigate and locate specific bookkeeping details.
2. What are users' preferences and satisfaction with the different ways of organiz-ing information. User questionnaires, feedback, and subjective ratings are used to under-stand users' subjective feelings and satisfaction with different layout methods. This will help to understand users' acceptance and personal preference for different information layout methods, and provide valuable guidance and suggestions for the inter-face design of bookkeeping software.

In summary, this study aims to explore the advantages and disadvantages of different information layout methods in the detail page of bookkeeping software, so as to provide empirical evidence and reference for mobile application interface design. Meanwhile, by choosing the "Shark Bookkeeping" app as a case study, we can more accurately evaluate the impact of different information layout styles on users' visual search under the application category. The results of the study are expected to pro-vide insights for developers and designers to help them better optimize the interface layout, and improve the visual search efficiency and overall user experience.

## 3.2 Research Material

In order to complete the comparative experiment, we collected information display layout forms commonly used in current mobile application interface design to collect original experimental materials. Usually there is no particularly standardized style for the form of information layout, but most of them are designed according to the following eight forms, including list layout, palace layout, instrument layout, card layout, waterfall flow layout, Gallery layout, accordion layout, and multi-panel layout. Due to differences in interaction levels and information display, eight layout forms were screened to ensure the unity of experimental variables, and four information layout forms, including list layout, palace layout, card layout, and waterfall flow layout, were finally retained as independent variables. The details are shown in Fig. 1.

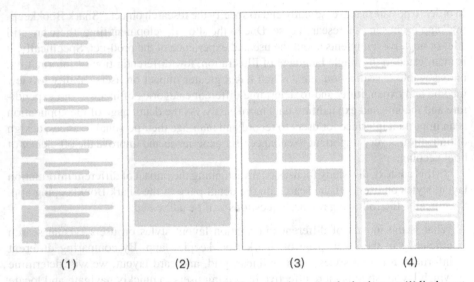

**Fig. 1.** The figure shows four mobile terminal information layout methods, they are (1) list layout, (2) card layout, (3) palace format layout, and (4) waterfall flow layout.

List layout presents information in a vertical linear arrangement. Each item usually occupies one row, and users can scroll through the page to view them one by one. The layout is clean and concise and suitable for longer lists of information. Card layout presents information in the form of cards. Each card usually contains a complete unit of information. There are obvious boundaries and spacing between cards, making the overall structure of the information clearer. The palace layout arranges information in regular rectangular areas, similar to the nine-square grid layout. Each area usually contains an icon or thumbnail that provides certain information. The waterfall flow layout presents information in an irregular manner, and the size and height of each block element may be different, making the interface more interesting and dynamic, and users can view more content by sliding or clicking.

## 4  Study on the Influence of Mobile Information Layout on Users' Visual Search in Financial Bookkeeping Apps

### 4.1  Experiment Preparation

Twenty-five current graduate students were selected to participate in this experiment, including 15 male students and 10 female students, the age of the subjects was from 19 to 25 years old, all the subjects had normal naked eye vision or corrected vision, were skilled in using smartphones, and all of them had more than half a year's experience in using bookkeeping software.

The experimental materials were derived from four common information layout methods in the current mobile terminal, including list layout, card layout, palace format layout and waterfall flow layout, and the information layout of the bookkeeping detail page of Shark Bookkeeping APP was redesigned according to the four layout methods. According to the existing research, for the page displaying rich information, the information layout usually needs to consider a more reasonable modularization and unitization design, which can improve the accessibility of page information through reasonable spatial structure and consistency design. In the above four ways, there is a big difference in the way of information layout, and the way of information collection is also different. Therefore, the following hypotheses are proposed: (1) The four different information layout methods under the same page have a significant effect on the time required for users to complete the search task. (2) The card layout with better information aggregation and reasonable spacing has the highest user satisfaction.

### 4.2  Experiment Preparation

In the experiments of this paper, the information layout of the Shark Bookkeeping income and expenditure detail page is divided into four kinds, as shown in Fig. 2, and the information display mainly includes three categories, icon information, income and expenditure category information, and income and expenditure amount information. Two groups of experimental tasks are set up in the experiment, the first group of experiments to test the time consumed by the subjects to complete the search task under different information layout methods, the subjects in this group of experiments need to complete different search tasks under the level of the four independent variables, in order to ensure that the search task has the same level of difficulty, all of which are the categories of daily life expenses and the amount of money, and at the same time, in order to increase the time of the task to ensure that it is measurable, the experiment adds more interfering items, i.e., the same as the other options similar to the experimental task, utilizing the time taken to complete the same level of information search task as a basis for visual search efficiency. The second set of experiments tested the effect of different information layout styles on user satisfaction. This set of experiments required subjects to score their satisfaction with each information layout style after completing the two experiments mentioned above, in the form of a 5-point Likert questionnaire, with 1 being strongly disagree and 5 being strongly agree, with higher scores indicating that subjects were more satisfied with that type of page.

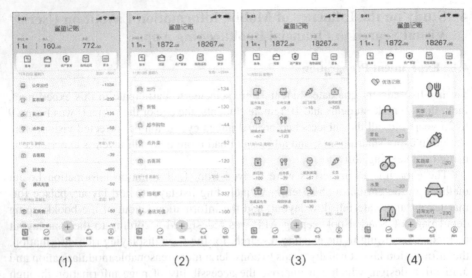

**Fig. 2.** Experimental materials for four information layout forms.

The four groups of search information involved in the experiment are shown in Table 1, which randomly correspond to the interface settings of the four types of information layouts, the content of the four groups of search information is different, but the level of difficulty is the same, and the key pages involved in the experiment are shown in Fig. 3.

**Table 1.** Four sets of search task information.

| Experimental tasks | Example |
|---|---|
| Task 1 | ①Buying fruit costs 50;②Travel costs 50 |
| Task 2 | ①Eating costs 120;②Bus trip costs 44 |
| Task 3 | ①Buying clothes costs 5079;②Ordering takeout costs 39 |
| Task 4 | ①Buying fruit costs 23;②Bus trip costs 18 |

This experiment is controlled by a smart phone and an ipad, the phone model is iphoneXR, the resolution of the screen is 375 × 812 pixels, the subject operates the task by using figma high fidelity simulation shark bookkeeping app prototype, and records the behavioral data of the subject by recording the screen, the ipad model is air3, which is used to display the information of the task during the experiment for the subject to view.

### 4.3 Experimental Procedures

This experiment was conducted as an individually administered test, and subjects were provided with detailed instructions on the experimental tasks and operations before the

**Fig. 3.** Partial simulation interface of the experimental process.

formal experiment began. An opportunity for practice was also provided to familiarize subjects with the experimental task and procedure. After the completion of the practice experiment, the subjects took a 1-min break before conducting the formal experiment. At the beginning of the experiment, the screen will display the welcome page of Shark Bookkeeping, after clicking on any position, it will be switched to the task information page, the center of the screen will display the two bookkeeping income and expenditure information that need to be searched for by the subjects, after presenting 10s, the page is automatically switched to the task page (at this time, the auxiliary ipad displays the task information for the subjects to view, to prevent forgetting the task information), the screen will appear in a kind of test conditions of information Arrangement, the subjects need to search in the page before the presentation of the task information, if you find the target information, then click, the screen will appear to complete the prompt, continue the next search, until the completion of all the search tasks. Experiment 2: After completing the above experiments, the subjects scored their satisfaction with each information layout method, and the scores were tallied.

# 5   Results and Analysis

According to the design of the experimental procedure, the time spent by the subjects to complete the search task was recorded, obtained by screen recording and accurately intercepted with video editing software to ensure the science and accuracy of the experiment, the data were processed by SPSS software, and the experimental data were analyzed using the One-way Repeated Measures ANOVA test method.

## 5.1   Visual Search Time Analysis of Different Visual Search Strategies

The results of normal distribution test on the subjects' time data for completing the task in four cases of layout1 (list-based information layout), layout2 (card-based information layout), layout3 (palace-format information layout), and layout4 (waterfall information layout) showed that the differences in the time data for completing the task in the four layouts were not significant, $p > 0.05$, the one-way repeated measures condition was satisfied. The Mauchly test of sphericity showed that the four information layout sample groups met the requirement of sphericity, $p > 0.05$. A One-way Repeated Measures ANOVA test revealed that there was a significant difference in the visual search time between the four experimental conditions, $p < 0.05$, $\eta_p^2 = 0.19$. Estimating the mean values according to Table 2 It can be seen that the shortest search time ($10.1 \pm 0.27$) was found in the layout2 condition, and based on within-group pairwise comparisons, it was found that not all of the experimental data from the four experimental conditions differed significantly from each other, as shown in Table 3. The search time in the layout2 condition ($10.1 \pm 0.27$) was significantly shorter than that in layout3 ($11.82 \pm 0.39$), $p < 0.05$, and the search time in the layout2 condition ($10.1 \pm 0.27$) was significantly shorter than that in layout4 ($12.27 \pm 0.47$), $p < 0.05$, while no significant differences were presented between the other groups.

**Table 2.** Mean estimates of search time for four sets of experimental data under visual task search experiments with different levels of independent variables.

| Estimated Value | | | | |
|---|---|---|---|---|
| measured value:time 95% confidence interval | | | | |
| Layout | average value | standard error | lower limit | limit |
| 1 | 11.484 | 0.601 | 10.244 | 12.724 |
| 2 | 10.101 | 0.271 | 9.543 | 10.660 |
| 3 | 11.829 | 0.398 | 11.008 | 12.650 |
| 4 | 12.274 | 0.473 | 11.298 | 13.250 |

The visual search efficiency of card layout is higher than that of other information layout forms. To a certain extent, the information layout of the mobile interface will affect the user's visual search efficiency, because the card layout is to display the information in the form of cards, and each card usually contains a complete information unit. With the existence of boundaries and spacing between cards, users can scan and recognize the content of interest faster, thus improving search efficiency. This hierarchy of contrast and content differentiation better improves readability for quick viewing [20]. Waterfall layout requires users to constantly swipe the page and adjust their attention to find the content of interest due to the irregular arrangement of block elements, which may lead to an increase in the time-consuming search task. There were not all significant differences between the four groups of experimental data in the experiment, and in addition to the fact that the way the information was laid out in itself may not satisfy the significant differences between all the groups, there are some limitations due to the fact that the sample of experimental data is a small sample.

**Table 3.** Pairwise comparisons of within-group variability of four sets of experimental data under the visual task search experiment with different levels of independent variables. The significance level for the difference in means is 0.05. b. Multiple comparison adjustment: The Bonferroni method.

| Within-group Variation | | | | | | |
|---|---|---|---|---|---|---|
| measured value:time 95% confidence interval for the difference[b] | | | | | | |
| (I)layout | (J)layout | standard deviation(I-J) | standard error | significance level[b] | lower limit | limit |
| 1 | 2 | 1.383 | 0.593 | 0.170 | -0.322 | 3.087 |
|   | 3 | -0.345 | 0.631 | 1.000 | -2.158 | 1.468 |
|   | 4 | -0.790 | 0.571 | 1.000 | -2.431 | 0.851 |
| 2 | 1 | -1.383 | 0.593 | 0.170 | -3.087 | 0.322 |
|   | 3 | -1.728 | 0.487 | 0.010 | -3.127 | -0.329 |
|   | 4 | -2.173 | 0.461 | < 0.001 | -3.498 | -0.848 |
| 3 | 1 | 0.345 | 0.631 | 1.000 | -1.468 | 2.158 |
|   | 2 | 1.728 | 0.487 | 0.010 | 0.329 | 3.127 |
|   | 4 | -0.445 | 0.593 | 1.000 | -2.151 | 1.260 |
| 4 | 1 | 0.790 | 0.571 | 1.000 | -0.851 | 2.431 |
|   | 2 | 2.173 | 0.461 | < 0.001 | 0.848 | 3.498 |
|   | 3 | 0.445 | 0.593 | 1.000 | -1.260 | 2.151 |

## 5.2 User Satisfaction Analysis of Different Visual Search Strategies

The results of the normal distribution test of the subjects' satisfaction score data for four scenarios, Layout 1 (List Information Layout), Layout 2 (Card Information Layout), Layout 3 (Palace Information Layout), and Layout 4 (Waterfall Stream Information Layout), showed that there was a significant difference between the user satisfaction score data of the four layouts with $P < 0.05$, which rejected the original hypothesis, that is, it did not conform to normality. Analysis of variance (ANOVA) was performed using Friedman's test. Friedman's test showed that there was a significant difference between the satisfaction scores of the four information layouts, $P < 0.001$, $W_{Kendall} = 0.43$. After Bonferroni adjusted test, as shown in Table 4, the subjects' satisfaction scores of Layout 2 ($3.88 \pm 1.13$) were significantly higher than the satisfaction scores of Layout 1 ($2.64 \pm 0.86$), $P = 0.022$. Satisfaction ratings for Layout 2 ($3.88 \pm 1.13$) were significantly higher than satisfaction ratings for Layout 4 ($1.72 \pm 0.93$), $p < 0.001$. Satisfaction ratings for Layout 3 ($2.96 \pm 0.88$) were significantly higher than satisfaction ratings for Layout 4 ($1.72 \pm 0.93$), $p < 0.001$.

Carded information layouts have the highest average score in user satisfaction ratings. From a visibility perspective, card-based layouts provide distinct boundaries and spacing, making each information unit more prominent and recognizable so that users

**Table 4.** Pairwise comparisons of within-group variability of four sets of experimental data with different levels of independent variables under the satisfaction evaluation experiment. The level of significance is 0.050. a. Significance has been adjusted for multiple tests by Bonferroni correction method

Within-group Variation

| Samole1-sample2 | inspection statistics | standard error | Standardized test statistics | significance level | Adj.significance level[a] |
|---|---|---|---|---|---|
| layout4-1ayout1 | 0.960 | 0.365 | 2.629 | 0.009 | 0.051 |
| layout4-1ayout3 | 1.340 | 0.365 | 3.670 | < 0.001 | 0.001 |
| layout4-1ayout2 | 2.020 | 0.365 | 5.532 | < 0.001 | 0.000 |
| layout1-1ayout3 | -0.380 | 0.365 | -1.041 | 0.298 | 1.000 |
| layout1-1ayout2 | -1.060 | 0.365 | -2.903 | 0.004 | 0.022 |
| layout3-1ayout2 | 0.680 | 0.365 | 1.862 | 0.063 | 0.375 |

can quickly navigate and select content of interest. This clear structure and visual hierarchy increases user satisfaction. Card Layout presents each information unit as a separate card, making it easier for users to distinguish and understand the relationship between items. Waterfall Layout scores low in user satisfaction evaluation, probably due to its irregular arrangement that causes users to constantly slide the page and adjust their attention when searching for the content of interest, which increases the cognitive load and search time consuming for users. And the waterfall layout is not obvious enough to present the overall structure and relationship of the information, which also reduces user satisfaction.

## 6  Discussion

The experimental results of this article show that the mobile terminal information layout has a significant impact on information visual search efficiency and user satisfaction. Although it is found that the card-style information layout application has better performance in visual search efficiency and user satisfaction on the financial accounting details page, there are still some limitations and areas for improvement.

### 6.1  Add Control Independent Variable

In this study, we focus on the effects of different mobile interface information layout approaches on users' visual search efficiency. However, in order to explore the impact of information layout more comprehensively, other independent variables related to information layout can be introduced. Specifically, the density of different information layout styles, the internal arrangement pattern of unit modules, and the size of unit module styles of different information layout styles can be taken into consideration for the study.

Different information layout styles may lead to different levels of information density. A high information density layout may trigger more visual interference and make users need more time to sift through the information. Therefore, future research can introduce information density as a dependent variable to gain insight into the impact of different information layout styles on search efficiency. In addition, the internal arrangement pattern of unit modules may also have an important impact on search. Different layout styles may lead to the presentation of information within the unit module in different arrangement patterns, such as linear arrangement, grid arrangement, etc. This may affect users' attention allocation and search strategies. Therefore, future research could consider the information arrangement pattern of smaller units as the independent variable to analyze the effect of different layout styles in more detail.

### 6.2 Improving Visual Search Experiments

The visual search experiment of this study only recorded the search time, but did not further analyze the user's visual search path. Eye trackers are powerful tools that can be used to capture a user's eye movement data to gain a more detailed understanding of their visual behavior. Future research can use eye trackers to analyze information such as users' fixation points, fixation durations, and scan paths under different information layouts.

Through analysis of eye tracker data, we can better understand why certain ways of laying out information lead to greater search efficiency. For example, we could study whether users are more likely to focus on important information first in a card layout, or if they are more likely to get lost in a large amount of information in a palace layout. These in-depth visual analyzes can provide more specific suggestions and guidance for interface design.

## 7  Conclusion

In this paper, in order to explore the influence of mobile interface information layout on visual search, we take financial bookkeeping apps as the research scenario, and take "Shark Bookkeeping" app as the design example to conduct comparative experiments. In order to better achieve the research purpose, we measured the differences between the independent variables with task search time and subjective satisfaction as dependent variables. The results of the study show that (1) the information layout of the detail page of the mobile interface bookkeeping software affects the visual search efficiency, and the search efficiency is significantly higher in the card-type information layout than in the list-type layout and the waterfall layout, but there is no significant difference in the information search efficiency between the other groups, but from the point of view of the average value of the time spent on the search, the waterfall information layout takes the most time to complete the task of searching for information. (2) From the satisfaction evaluation of the bookkeeping detail page under the four forms of information layout, the card-type information layout has the highest user satisfaction evaluation score, which is significantly higher than the other three forms of information layout. Therefore, it can be found that in mobile financial bookkeeping applications, because the detail page needs to display a large amount of income and expenditure information, a reasonable information layout is particularly important, and the card layout has a greater advantage in visual search efficiency and user satisfaction, and the results of this paper provide a certain reference for the interface design and user experience of the mobile terminal. Due to the small experimental sample data and experimental research to consider fewer variables, so there are some limitations, the future will be combined with eye-tracking technology, as well as further analysis of the interface information layout related elements to carry out in-depth research.

# References

1. Shao, J., Xue, C., Wang, F., Wang, H.: Research of digital interface layout design based on eye-tracking. In: MATEC Web of Conferences, vol. 22, p. 01018. EDP Sciences (2015)
2. Wang, P., Wang, J.: Research on the application of data visualization in the UI interface Design of Health Apps. In: 2021 International Wireless Communications and Mobile Computing (IWCMC), pp. 2013–2019. IEEE (2021)
3. Yang, Z., Yin, Z., Wang, H.: Combining user interaction behavior and resource content for resource recommendation. J. Comput.-Aided Design Graph. 26(5), 747–754 (2014)
4. Gaona-Garcia, P.A., Martin-Moncunill, D., Montenegro-Marin, C.E.: Trends and challenges of visual search interfaces in digital libraries and repositories. Electron. Libr. 35(1), 69–98 (2017)
5. Salimun, C., Purchase, H. C., Simmons, D. R., Brewster, S.: The effect of aesthetically pleasing composition on visual search performance. In: Proceedings of the 6th Nordic Conference on Human-Computer Interaction: Extending Boundaries, pp. 422–431(2010)
6. Van Schaik, P., Ling, J.: The effects of frame layout and differential background contrast on visual search performance in web pages. Interact. Comput. 13(5), 513–525 (2001)
7. Simonin, J., Kieffer, S., Carbonell, N.: Effects of display layout on gaze activity during visual search. In: Costabile, M.F., Paternò, F. (eds.) INTERACT 2005. LNCS, vol. 3585, pp. 1054–1057. Springer, Heidelberg (2005). https://doi.org/10.1007/11555261_103
8. Tang, X.T., Yao, J., Hu, H.F.: Visual search experiment on text characteristics of vital signs monitor interface. Displays 62, 101944 (2020)
9. Raeisi, S., Osqueizadeh, R.E.Z.A., Maghsoudipour, M., Jafarpisheh, A.S.: Ergonomic redesign of an industrial control panel. Int. J. Occup. Environ. Med. 7(3), 186 (2016)
10. Li, J., Yu, S., Liu, W.: Evaluation of cognitive properties of CNC interface layout based on eye tracking. J. Comput. Aided Design Graph. 29(7), 1334–1342 (2017)
11. Niemelä, M., Saarinen, J.: Visual search for grouped versus ungrouped icons in a computer interface. Hum. Factors 42(4), 630–635 (2000)
12. Lei, z., Xue, C., Tang, W., Li, J., Niu, Y.: An aesthetic evaluation method for interface element layout design. J. Comput. Aided Design Graph. (05), 758–766 (2013)
13. Deng, Li., Wang, G.: Quantitative evaluation of visual aesthetics of human-machine interaction interface layout. Comput. Intell. Neurosci. 2020, 1–14 (2020). https://doi.org/10.1155/2020/9815937
14. Mendel, J., Pak, R.: The effect of interface consistency and cognitive load on user performance in an information search task. In: Proceedings of the Human Factors and Ergonomics Society Annual Meeting, Vol. 53, No. 22, pp. 1684–1688(2009)
15. Holsanova, J., Holmberg, N., Holmqvist, K.: Reading information graphics: The role of spatial contiguity and dual attentional guidance. Applied Cognitive Psychology Official Journal of the Society for Applied Research in Memory Cognition 23(9), 1215–1226 (2009)

16. Hattori, G., Hoashi, K., Matsumoto, K., Sugaya, F.: Robust web page segmentation for mobile terminal using content-distances and page layout information. In: Proceedings of the 16th International Conference on World Wide Web, pp. 361–370(2007)
17. Fu, Y., Jiang, H., Zhang, D., Zhang, X.: Comparison of perceptual differences between users and designers in mobile shopping app interface design: implications for evaluation practice. IEEE Access **7**, 23459–23470 (2019)
18. Diego-Mas, J.A., Garzon-Leal, D., Poveda-Bautista, R., Alcaide-Marzal, J.: User-interfaces layout optimization using eye-tracking, mouse movements and genetic algorithms. Appl. Ergon. **78**, 197–209 (2019)
19. Xie, W., Xin, X.Y., Ding, J.W.: Interaction design of product HMI based on eye tracking testing. J Mach Des **32**(12), 110–115 (2015)
20. Kamaruddin, N., Sulaiman, S.: Understanding interface design principles and elements guidelines: A content analysis of established scholars. In: Anwar, R., Mahamood, M., Md. Zain, D.H., Abd Aziz, M.K., Hassan, O.H., Abidin, S.Z. (eds.) Proceedings of the Art and Design International Conference (AnDIC 2016), pp. 89–100. Springer, Singapore (2018). https://doi.org/10.1007/978-981-13-0487-3_11

# Author Index

Printed in the United States
by Baker & Taylor Publisher Services